CONTEMPORARY ARCHAEOLOGY AND THE CITY

Contemporary Archaeology and the City

Creativity, Ruination, and Political Action

Edited by
LAURA McATACKNEY AND KRYSTA RYZEWSKI

OXFORD
UNIVERSITY PRESS

OXFORD
UNIVERSITY PRESS

Great Clarendon Street, Oxford, OX2 6DP,
United Kingdom

Oxford University Press is a department of the University of Oxford.
It furthers the University's objective of excellence in research, scholarship,
and education by publishing worldwide. Oxford is a registered trade mark of
Oxford University Press in the UK and in certain other countries

© Oxford University Press 2017

The moral rights of the authors have been asserted

First Edition published in 2017

Impression: 1

Published in the United States of America by Oxford University Press
198 Madison Avenue, New York, NY 10016, United States of America

British Library Cataloguing in Publication Data
Data available

Library of Congress Control Number: 2017931025

ISBN 978-0-19-880360-7

Printed and bound by
CPI Group (UK) Ltd, Croydon, CR0 4YY

To
our inspirational Bs!

Acknowledgements

First, we would like to thank the Wenner-Gren Foundation for Anthropological Research for providing us with the generous funding to support the international *Archaeologies of the Present: Critical Engagements with Post-industrial Transformations* workshop, held in August of 2014 at Wayne State University in Detroit. It was the motivation for this volume. The papers that the participants prepared in advance for the workshop, the multiple days spent touring contemporary archaeological landscapes around Detroit, and the emergent discussions inspired the vision for and organization of this book. We are particularly thankful for the enthusiasm of our workshop grant administrator Laurie Obbink at the Wenner-Gren Foundation.

Our motivation to pursue the workshop funding was inspired by the tenth anniversary of the UK-based Contemporary and Historical Archaeology in Theory group (CHAT). Both of us served on the CHAT Standing Committee at the time of the funding proposal and have attended the majority of annual CHAT conferences since the first meeting in Bristol, 2003. We are especially thankful to our colleagues on the CHAT Standing Committees, past and present, for their encouragement of our ideas for this workshop and book, and more so for establishing the momentum for the approaches to contemporary archaeology that appears in the following contributions. Our thoughts about the intersections between anthropology, archaeology, and post-industrial cities were enriched during the workshop by extended conversations between the contributors and our urban anthropology colleagues in Detroit, including Andrew Newman, Julia Yezbick, and John Chenoweth. We also thank the anonymous reviewers, who provided excellent feedback on earlier versions of the chapters, and our editors at Oxford University Press Charlotte Loveridge and Tom Perridge for their support, advice, and encouragement. We are indebted to the Wayne State University Department of Anthropology, the School of Social Justice at University College Dublin, and Archaeology and Heritage Studies at Aarhus Universitet, as well as our graduate students, for their assistance during the workshop and publication processes. Krysta would also like to thank Kaitlin for her continued support, and Kazimir, for enlivening the publication process with his arrival in 2015. Laura would like to thank her family—especially her much-missed father, Alex—for their unwavering (if reassuringly disinterested) support and Jon for being a willing (and much appreciated) trailing spouse.

We are most grateful to all of our contributing authors for their inspiring contributions, collegial dialogue, and enthusiastic willingness to participate in the process of asserting innovative and daring new directions for urban contemporary archaeology, from the inception of the workshop through to the final publication of the volume.

Krysta Ryzewski
Laura McAtackney

Detroit, Sept 2016
Aarhus, Sept 2016

Table of Contents

SECTION III POLITICAL ACTION

List of Figures and Table

Figures

Table

List of Colour Plates

1. Wolfgang Ganter's studio 'outside space', Berlin. Top: Ladder to storage area, plastic sheeting curtain that divides the space, table-saw used for framemaking, and dust. Bottom: Supplies used for framing and cleaning. Photos by Steven Seidenberg.

2. Wolfgang Ganter's studio 'inside space' showing light table used for injecting slides with bacteria, Berlin. Photo by Steven Seidenberg.

3. Top: Elmgreen & Dragset studio, Berlin, a renovated water pumping station in Neukölln. Photo by Steven Seidenberg. Bottom: Interior of Elmgreen & Dragset studio. View of main floor and mezzanine with staging area for exhibition below. The summer working space for staff is visible on the left side. Photo by Steven Seidenberg.

4. Top: Installation view of *An Innocent City*, Istanbul. July 2014. Photo by Ian Alden Russell. Bottom: Installation view of objects borrowed from the local community from *An Innocent City*. July 2014. Photo by Ian Alden Russell.

5. Top: Postcards with stories written on them left by visitors to *An Innocent City*, Istanbul. July 2014. Photo by Ian Alden Russell. Bottom: Interior of the former Michigan Theatre, Detroit, built on the site of Henry Ford's first garage, and current home to a car park. Wikicommons, 2011.

6. Top: The remains of the Grande Ballroom, Detroit. The Ballroom is currently slated for demolition. Wikicommons, 2012. Bottom: Cooks' Cottage, the Fitzroy Gardens, Melbourne, Australia. Photo by Brian Shanahan.

7. Ruins associated with the Boyds Corners Reservoir (New York) include a mill adjacent to a now dry waterway (top left), and a cemetery located in secondary growth forest (bottom left) and cut off from all roadways by the destruction of a bridge (bottom middle). Ruins associated with the Ashokan Reservoir include very large stone walls constructed to clear the landscape for livestock (top right) and house foundations (bottom right). Photos by A. M. Beisaw and students.

8. Top: Abandoned nineteenth-century houses in the historic centre of Belém do Pará, Brazil. Photo by Alfredo González-Ruibal, 2008. Bottom: An illegal settlement of landless peasants inside an Awá reservation, Maranhão. Photo by Alfredo González-Ruibal, 2006.

9. Top: A street with ruins of early twentieth-century buildings in Rio Grande, Brazil. Bottom: A decaying art nouveau house in Rio Grande, partly occupied by a shop. Photos by Alfredo González-Ruibal, 2013.

Notes on Contributors

April M. Beisaw, Assistant Professor of Anthropology, Vassar College. Beisaw is a North American archaeologist who researches culture change and resilience in the relatively recent past (1300 AD to yesterday). She is particularly interested in the ethics of Native American repatriation, the untold stories of existing archaeological collections, the non-subsistence applications of faunal analysis, and the allure of a well-told ghost story.

Christian Ernsten, PhD, University of Cape Town, African Studies, South Africa; lecturer, Reinwardt Academy, Amsterdam University of Applied Arts, the Netherlands. Ernsten has a fascination for heritage as traces of a deep past and as result of identity politics and struggles for social and environmental justice.

Alfredo González-Ruibal is an archaeologist with the Institute of Heritage Sciences of the Spanish National Research Council (Incipit-CSIC). His research focuses on the archaeology of the contemporary past, particularly on the dark side of modernity, and social resistance in the past and present. He has conducted fieldwork in different countries, including Spain, Brazil, Equatorial Guinea, and Ethiopia.

Rebecca S. Graff, Assistant Professor of Anthropology, Department of Sociology and Anthropology, Lake Forest College. Graff is a historical archaeologist with research interests in the relationship between temporality, modernity, memory, material culture, tourism, and nostalgic consumption in late nineteenth- and early twentieth-century Chicago. Her archival and archaeological work includes research on the 1893 World's Columbian Exposition and the Louis Sullivan and Frank Lloyd Wright-designed Charnley-Persky House.

Laura McAtackney, Associate Professor of Sustainable Heritage Management, Aarhus University, Denmark. Laura has been researching in the areas of dark heritage and contemporary and historical archaeology for over ten years. Focuses include the material culture of political imprisonment, institutional graffiti, and the uses/impacts of barriers and walls in urban segregation.

Paul R. Mullins, Professor, Indiana University–Purdue University, Indianapolis. Mullins is a historical archaeologist who studies consumer culture and the intersection of material consumption and the colour line. He is the Charles R. Bantz Chancellor's Community Fellow (2016–17) at Indiana University–Purdue University, Indianapolis (IUPUI); Docent in Historical Archaeology at the University of Oulu (Finland); Past-President of the Society for Historical Archaeology (2012–13); and a former Fulbright Scholar in Fall 2012 at the University of Oulu (Finland). He is the author of *Race and Affluence: An Archaeology of African America and Consumer Culture* (1999) and *The Archaeology of Consumer Culture* (2011).

Sefryn Penrose, Senior Heritage Consultant, Atkins. Penrose is a heritage specialist, with considerable experience across the UK sector, particularly in policy and planning. Her diverse clients include Historic England and the Nuclear Decommissioning Authority. Her research work is focused on the recent past, and with UCL Institute of Archaeology, on diversity across biological and cultural heritage, and particularly their overlap. She is the chair of the Contemporary and Historical Archaeology in Theory (CHAT) conference committee.

Ian Alden Russell is an international curator based in Providence, Rhode Island. Currently the Curator of Brown University's David Winton Bell Gallery, his curatorial work has been hosted by Artpace (San Antonio), Chinese University of Hong Kong, Fire Station Artists' Studios (Dublin), Koç University (Istanbul), Ormston House (Limerick, Ireland), Irish Museum of Modern Art, Jockey Club Creative Arts Centre (Hong Kong), the Museum of Innocence (Istanbul), and the National College of Art & Design (Dublin). His writings on contemporary art and cultural heritage have been published by Cambridge University Press, Cittadellarte, deCordova Museum & Sculpture Park, Lars Muller Publishers, Museum of Contemporary Art, Chicago, Oxford University Press, Springer-Kluwer, and Yapı Kredi Publishers.

Krysta Ryzewski is a historical archaeologist and an Associate Professor of Anthropology at Wayne State University in Detroit, where she co-leads the Anthropology of the City initiative. Her research explores the consequences of disruptive social and environmental pressures on past landscapes, communities, and material culture production. She conducts projects that focus on these relationships in the Caribbean (Montserrat) and urban North America (Detroit). In Detroit she is currently leading the Unearthing Detroit project, a multisited, collections-based and public archaeology initiative that involves work on a nineteenth-century working-class neighbourhood (Roosevelt Park), and the remains of of popular music venues (including the Grande Ballroom), among other sites.

Brian Shanahan, Doctoral Candidate at the National University of Ireland, Galway. Shanahan has over twenty years' experience as a research and consultant archaeologist in Ireland and Australia. He specializes in medieval and historical archaeology, landscape and settlement studies, and the application of spatial and digital technologies.

Madeline Shanahan, Honorary Associate at La Trobe University and Archaeology Manager at GML Heritage. Shanahan has practised as a consultant archaeologist in Ireland and Australia for over ten years. She holds a PhD in archaeology from University College Dublin and specializes in the archaeological analysis of textual objects. Her research interests relate to food and cookery, Australian historical archaeology, and archaeological theory.

Steven Seidenberg is a San Francisco-based artist and writer.

Courtney Singleton, Doctoral Candidate, Columbia University Department of Anthropology. Singleton has worked for eight years as a contemporary and historic archaeologist in the United States, focusing on issues of class and race in urban environments. She has been interested in examining issues surrounding social justice, poverty, and race through a semiotics of home.

Carolyn L. White, Associate Professor and Mamie Kleberg Chair in Historic Preservation, Department of Anthropology, University of Nevada, Reno. White's archaeological work spans four centuries, focusing on eighteenth-century personal adornment, mining communities in the American West, the built environment of Black Rock City, and the relationship between art and archaeology. Her book, *The Archaeology of Burning Man*, is forthcoming from University of New Mexico Press.

Introduction

Contemporary Archaeology and the City: Creativity, Ruination, and Political Action

Laura McAtackney and Krysta Ryzewski

Changes in Detroit's motor vehicle industries affect counterparts in Tokyo, struggling financial sectors in Athens rattle the economy of Dublin, construction booms in Vancouver stimulate investments by Hong Kong speculators, uprisings by Berlin artists against 'creative' redevelopment projects inspire protests by graffiti artists in Mexico City, and inadequate water supplies in greater Los Angeles limit the availability of imported foodstuffs for consumers in Delhi. The contemporary city is essentially an (post-)industrial, modern, and interconnected place where capitalist accumulation, growth, and decline often operate simultaneously, are experienced locally, and resonate globally leaving material traces on urban and associated hinterland landscapes. With the majority of the world's population now dwelling in cities, historical and future-oriented urban identities face global challenges associated with the logistics and inequalities of deindustrialization. The fast pace of change in cities, as well as the tremendous scale of urban landscapes and the complexities of personal interactions with them, poses an unrivalled challenge to archaeologists whose work begins with contemporary remains. *Contemporary Archaeology and the City* foregrounds the archaeological study of (post-)industrial and other urban transformations through a diverse, international collection of case studies on present-day cities.

The deep historical roots of citizenship in contemporary cities directly affect how communities craft notions of belonging within urban ecologies in the present. For example, the former industrial stronghold of East Belfast has experienced decades-long post-industrial economic decline alongside longstanding sectarian tensions. However, the arrival of new immigrant populations have shifted loyalist narratives in working class neighbourhoods from an identity defined by a self-conceived progressive ethos to one that asserts exclusionary material boundaries around an increasingly inward-looking, defensive community (McAtackney, Chapter 9). Meanwhile, Detroit's built environment and cultural heritage suffer at the hands of an ongoing, decades-long social disaster perpetuated by a constellation of political corruption, economic mismanagement, and legacies of racial conflicts. While the media perpetuates inaccurate portrayals of Detroit and other comparable cities as landscapes of abandonment, where people and built environments are increasingly absent, the contributors to this volume adopt a more nuanced approach. They envisage post-industrial cities as variably inhabited places and emergent ecologies—hybrid metropolises that expand and contract over the course of multi-generational life cycles—places that are complicated by conceptual divisions between city and nature, industry and creativity, sustainability and profitability (Millington 2013: 279; Ryzewski 2016; see Ryzewski, Chapter 3).

I.1 VOLUME SCOPE

This volume aims to position the city as one of the most important and dynamic arenas for archaeological studies of the contemporary. The contributors present case studies that demonstrate how the shape, function, and continuous material (re)creation of the city, in its myriad forms, is central to the experience of modernity. The importance of the contemporary city in the arts, humanities, and social sciences has ensured that, as an entity, it has been central to many recent studies in anthropology (Pardo and Prato 2012), sustainability (Dawson et al. 2014), and literature (McNamara 2014). The very complexity of working in such environments means that the overwhelming material realities of cities is a topic about which contemporary archaeology is uniquely placed to provide thought-provoking and empowering insights. However, despite numerous archaeological studies conducted within present-day urban centres, the concept and scale of the city has not been positioned as central to the imaginary of contemporary archaeology. This compilation takes an important, initial step in redressing this disparity by presenting a range of theoretically engaged case studies that highlight some of the major issues that the study of contemporary cities pose for archaeologists.

In the shadows of modern and industrial aftermaths, the cities in this volume struggle to resurrect themselves from the over-determined planning initiatives, civic programmes, socio-political conflicts, and industrial monopolies of the late nineteenth and twentieth centuries, all of which implanted prescribed visual forms, social orders, and labour structures in urban centres (Sennett 2006: 1; Ryzewski 2015). Currently, many contemporary cities are attempting to assert their distinctiveness within an interconnected world by (re)branding themselves as 'creative cities'—places where creativity and difference are marketed to highlight the unique, local materialities that define particular urban identities (UNESCO 2013, 2015). Such efforts are challenged and in some cases contradicted by gentrification, increasing disparities in wealth, and neoliberal policies of privatization; processes that threaten to undermine the sustainability of contemporary cities as places of inclusivity (see Harvey 2012: 15; Herzfeld 2015).

Following Henri Lefebvre (1996, 2003), the contemporary city as conceptualized in this volume is defined as 'a distinctive place of belonging within a perpetually shifting spatio-temporal order' (Harvey 2012: xvii). An object of 'utopian desire', the materiality of the city and the relationships between the city and citizenship combine with the dynamic but identifiable dimensions of place to 'give [the city] a political meaning that mobilizes a crucial political imaginary' (Harvey 2012: xvii). Though perhaps idealized by expectations of what the contemporary city should be, inclusive notions of citizenship and belonging are particularly important for contemporary archaeologists to consider because they foster localized identities that are intimately connected to narratives of history, archaeology, and cultural heritage—the very elements that many present-day civic and economic initiatives seek to assert, preserve, and in some cases exploit (on heritage and identity in globalized settings, see Biehl et al. 2014; Russell, Chapter 2; Shanahan and Shanahan, Chapter 5). In the wake of the Faro Convention (Council of Europe 2005) the role of cultural heritage is increasingly being articulated in Europe as an invaluable resource in underpinning not only identity but also quality of life and sustainable development in the contemporary world. In this regard, acknowledging the cultural heritage potential of the city and the constituent parts of it ensures the cities in this volume are conceived as retaining their latent potential for positive and transformative possibilities. This perspective stands alongside recent academic works on the crisis of cities, including that of Richard Sennett, who considers how the materialities of twentieth-century 'Brittle Cities'—characterized by public housing, factories, infrastructure, neighbourhood subdivisions—are artefacts of relict twentieth-century zoning regulations, urban planning initiatives, and government policies that 'decay much more quickly than urban fabric inherited from the past' (2006: 1). The fabric of present-day cities, an uneasy co-existence of modern decay with remnants inherited from the more distant past that have survived processes of urban renewal, deindustrialization, and adaptive reuse, is a major theme throughout the volume.

The following case studies offer a comparative spatio-temporal perspective on the manifestation of transformative global urban processes in local contexts. They include research involving the struggling, post-industrial cities of Detroit, Belfast, Indianapolis, Berlin, Liverpool, Belém, and post-apartheid Cape Town, as well as the thriving urban centres of Melbourne, New York City, London, Chicago, and Istanbul. Together, the contributions demonstrate how the contemporary city is an urban palimpsest comprised by archaeological assemblages—of the built environment, the surface, and buried subsurface—that are traces of the various pasts entangled with one another in the present. As assemblages, contemporary cities are impermanent, disorderly, and incoherent spaces. Like archaeological deposits cities are unsettled, shifting compositions where destruction, adaptation, and innovation are enlisted at differing paces and scales to suit the constantly changing demands of local environments.

I.2 CONTEMPORARY ARCHAEOLOGY

Influenced by earlier modern material culture studies (Gould and Schiffer 1981; Rathje 1979; Graves-Brown 2000; Buchli and Lucas 2001), contemporary archaeology engages critically with the material remnants and social phenomena of late modern societies (González-Ruibal et al. 2014; Harrison 2011; Harrison and Schofield 2010; Graves-Brown et al. 2013). Spatially, it recognizes the transitory and fluid state of landscapes, things, and memories (Hicks et al. 2007; Olsen et al. 2012; Pearson and Shanks 2001). Temporally, its focus is continuously shifting; examining a moving moment that is not fixed to a particular, bounded period (Witmore 2012). Materially, the physical traces of the past in the present are viewed diachronically as palimpsests—assemblages of layered, overlapping histories (Harrison 2011). As illustrated by the following case studies, contemporary archaeology is a burgeoning, emergent specialization within archaeology and anthropology that also incorporates perspectives from history, ethnography, urban geography, art, and urban studies to interpret the social, and often political, implications of contemporary life by engaging with their spatial and temporal dimensions as well as their material realities. By explicitly materializing unconsidered, forgotten, or hidden aspects of the city, contemporary archaeology allows us to view global processes through the lens of local expressions.

The term contemporary archaeology is often used interchangeably with the 'archaeology of the recent past', 'archaeology of the present', 'archaeology of the contemporary past', or even as a broadening temporal extension of 'later historical archaeology' (Buchli and Lucas 2001; McAtackney et al. 2007; McAtackney and Penrose 2016; Olivier 2001; Harrison and Schofield 2009, 2010). Recognizing that each of these titles pose subtle but potentially significant contrasts in the scope and definition of the emergent specialization, for the purposes of the volume we adopt the use of 'contemporary archaeology'. We conceive it as a deliberately broad, framing term that is consistent with the breadth of practice and theoretical frameworks found within this volume (on further defining the scope of contemporary archaeology, see González-Ruibal et al. 2014).

We view contemporary archaeology as a politically engaged cultural critique and practice that can be unsettling in its recognition of the extreme contrasts and consequences of past decisions on present-day experiences and inequality. It is also a creative practice that challenges practitioners to articulate responses that are bound up in the uncontrollable: raw emotion, nostalgia, personal memories, and imagination. The constructive tensions inherent in contemporary archaeology ensure that it retains the potential to break down traditional subject/object divisions that have marked traditional archaeological thought. Contemporary archaeological projects often consider marginalized groups and the effects of modernity on people, material culture, and place (Shanks et al. 2004; González-Ruibal 2006). These projects include critical engagements with homelessness (Zimmerman et al. 2010), imprisonment (McAtackney 2014), mass disaster (Gould 2007; Crossland 2002), urban renewal (Mullins 2006), ruins (Pétursdóttir and Olsen 2014) and deindustrialization (Symonds 2004; Orange 2014). They also offer canny and insightful critiques on the misleadingly mundane world of popular culture and the everyday (Holtorf 2007). The intersection of contemporary archaeology with public memory, heritage, activism, and recently lived experiences inherently prevents detachments between researchers, their subject matter, and associated political, social, or ecological issues (González-Ruibal 2008; Harrison 2015). Often the outcomes of contemporary archaeological studies serve as epistemological critiques of the ways in which archaeological knowledge is produced; in some cases its practice has contributed to transformative processes, both within and beyond the discipline (Edgeworth 2012; Witmore 2012).

A nascent area of study, contemporary archaeology challenges conventional anthropological and archaeological conceptions of the past by pushing temporal boundaries closer to, if not into, the present. As a global phenomenon, it has developed unevenly, emerging strongest where it engages with the parallel development of critical heritage studies (see Harrison 2012; Smith 2006). Contemporary archaeology's academic presence exists primarily in Europe and North America, and to lesser degrees in South Africa and Australia. It has only achieved a distinct identity as a subfield of archaeology in British and Northern European academia. The backbone of this momentum has been the UK-based Contemporary and Historical Archaeology in Theory group (CHAT), which has held annual conferences since 2003 and from which various influential publications have resulted (e.g. Beaudry and Parno 2013; Fortenberry and McAtackney 2012; May et al. 2012; Fortenberry and Myers 2010; McAtackney et al. 2007). Scholars from North America have made substantial contributions to the emergent specialization over the past decade, especially through CHAT, but contemporary archaeology has not developed into a cohesive, recognizable subfield within North American academia, where archaeologists are commonly housed within university departments of anthropology (including Clark 2010; Wilkie 2014; Fortenberry and Myers 2010; and contributions in Graves-Brown et al. 2013). The launch of the *Journal of Contemporary Archaeology* in 2014, the first digitally accessible international venue for the specialization's dialogue and dissemination, marked an important turning point in scholarly visibility.

Despite ongoing debate about its identity, purpose and the defining features of its practice, over the past decade contemporary archaeology has emerged as a dynamic force for dissecting and contextualizing the material complexities of present-day societies. Contemporary archaeologists, individually or in small collectives, have examined materialized tensions that evoke, provoke, and rebuke the realities of urban spaces (Dawdy 2010, 2015). They have employed a variety of interventions, including conventional archaeological methods (Cherry et al. 2013) and multi-scalar approaches (McAtackney 2014). They have creatively engaged with art (Dixon 2007; Russell and Cochrane 2014) and digital media (Perry and Beale 2015; González-Ruibal 2013); and explored urban transitions through the medium of post-industrial landscapes (Penrose 2007), abandonment (Olsen and Pétursdóttir 2014), decay (DeSilvey 2006), modern material culture (Graves-Brown 2009), ephemera (White 2013), socio-political movements (Dawdy 2010; Dixon 2013), and mobility (Beaudry and Parno 2013). Poignantly, although much of this work has taken place in urban settings, contemporary cities have not yet emerged as a cohesive or explicit focus among practitioners.

This volume is a timely opportunity for a significant group of international scholars to convene and explicitly reflect upon the extent to which contemporary archaeology is developing shared interests about cities on a global scale. Most of the contributions that follow were the products of a five-day intensive workshop, *Archaeologies of the Present: Critical Engagements with Post-industrial Urban Transformations,* sponsored by the Wenner-Gren Foundation for Anthropological Research, co-organized by Krysta Ryzewski and Laura McAtackney and hosted by Wayne State University in Detroit, Michigan, during August 2014. *Contemporary Archaeology and the City* reflects the experiences of the workshop in that it reveals strong synergies in ethos, as well as marked differences in expression, amongst the disparate group of archaeologists brought together in Detroit. Commonalities may be located in terms of accepting an enduring, if evolving, relationship between the contemporary and the historical city and identifying multiple, contradictory meanings inherent in the ever-changing urban environment. Divergences exist among contributors' methodological approaches and theoretical standpoints. We argue these differences are positive indicators of a confident, robust subfield of enquiry that allows for a variety of approaches, conceptions, and focuses to co-exist. Such variations in perspective emerge from divergent geographical, socio-political, cultural, and economic areas of study and the many different urban contexts of growth, decline and/or renewal that they are experiencing today.

The definition and identity of contemporary archaeology was a significant subject of discussion and debate. During the *Archaeologies of the Present* workshop participants ultimately conceded that at this moment in the specialization's development it seemed a term and practice best left loosely defined. Contributors did not unanimously agree with each another about the need to identify contemporary archaeology as a paradigmatic shift or as a temporally bounded type of archaeology. Differences in perspective highlight the diverse academic cultures, disciplinary configurations, and societal contexts present among those from distinct institutional and intellectual backgrounds. They also signal potentially lengthier forms of debate that may soon emerge as contemporary archaeology continues to expand internationally (see Lucas in González-Ruibal et al. 2014: 278). Rather than making any grand claims about contemporary archaeology the following contributions promote the two primary objectives of the workshop: strengthening the existing international community of contemporary archaeologists by facilitating new discussions and collaborations, and developing specific theoretical and methodological positions that emphasize the importance of material approaches to contemporary urbanism.

I.3 CONTEMPORARY CITIES: AN ARCHAEOLOGICAL PERSPECTIVE

Archaeological studies of cities and the processes of urbanization have been central to the discipline from its inception. The proto-cities of ancient civilizations have always been considered appropriate places for the archaeologist to explore. Later forms of urbanization have been included, but usually only after they enter a state of abandonment, such as with the study of ghost towns in the American West or Famine villages in Ireland, or when they are considered in terminal decline, as with particular manufacturing spaces or workers' housing in early industrial cities in the UK. Retrieving 'lost cities' by focusing on the past glories of once venerable centres or the downturn of now-abandoned settlements has long been a common focus in archaeological practice; however, there has been little interest shown in the vast array of present-day cities and how they continue to evolve and emerge (even if simultaneously considered 'in decline').

Within the subfield of historical archaeology urban archaeological research emerged as a prolific focus in the 1960s. Nicknamed 'skyscraper archaeology' by its earliest practitioners in North America, particularly in Detroit (Pilling 1967), the increasing popularity of urban historical archaeology developed alongside broader historical archaeological interests in academia, as well as in tandem with the implementation of contract archaeology and cultural resource management legislation in both the US and UK. Urban archaeology's popularity rapidly expanded to the point where, by the early 1980s, it was being touted as not only 'the trendiest new specialty within historical archaeology', but also potentially one of the most important, due to the position of cities as the 'loci of much more human activity' (Dickens 1982: xiii). Today urban historical archaeology remains a robust area of research; in this generation a number of influential publications by historical archaeologists have significantly broadened the scope of theoretical and methodological approaches to understanding urban settings in the past (including Green and Leech 2006; Dawdy 2008; Leone 2006; Mayne and Murray 2001; Mrozowski 2006; Rothschild and Wall 2014; Wall 1994; Yamin 2001). Given the lineage in the practice of urban historical archaeology, it is perhaps a natural progression in the field's evolution that individual and global comparative studies in urban contemporary archaeology, as evidenced by the work in this volume, are now developing and gaining traction.

Archaeologists conducting excavations in cities are not in short supply, but engagements with the scale of the city through projects that include contemporary and comparative dimensions are notably few. Two factors might explain this apparent lack of engagement. Firstly, the undeniable fracture between work undertaken, and knowledge created, by archaeologists working in contract units (CRM in the US) and academic, university-based practitioners has resulted in the city being increasingly subsumed under the former. In effect, the archaeology in and of cities has been largely considered the realm of archaeology undertaken during the course of urban (re)development. This is problematic because such archaeologies can only partially engage with the scale of the city due to the fact that contract work is economically driven and results in research concentrated solely on areas where development is being undertaken. Mainly, the projects are either excavation-based or focused on specific standing structures. Furthermore, the knowledge these archaeologies create about the city is frequently relegated to the grey literature of site reports, unless subvented for publication by the developer (see *Post Medieval Archaeology* for evidence of significant publications, especially from the Museum of London Archaeology Service). There exist notable exceptions to this state of affairs—such as the development of contract excavation at York in the North of England into a long-term, community archaeology project with major academic and public outputs (see http://www.yorkarchaeology.co.uk), the impressive projects conducted in New York City, Boston, and Sacramento involving collaborations between CRM, museum, and academic institutions (Cantwell and Wall 2001; Lewis 2001; Praetzellis and Praetzellis 2004), and community-engaged collections-based research involving contract archaeology collections housed in university museums or other government repositories (Voss 2012; Unearthing Detroit 2015). However, it is important to note that these examples remain largely focused on connecting present-day communities with the distant pasts of major cities. The ability and desire for archaeologists to be able to view the city in totality and as a contemporary organism is limited in practice.

Another factor complicating the archaeology of contemporary cities is that the scale of the present-day city ensures that the examination of it as an entity is a daunting prospect for researchers (on issues of scale in modern cities, see Murray and Crook 2005). The sheer range of materials and relationships that archaeologists encounter in multi-scalar research requires operating with ambitious aims. Archaeologists who choose to study the contemporary city cannot only be confined to the typical archaeological scales of analysis—concentrating on, or moving between, excavated artefacts, standing structures and bounded landscapes. Rather it is necessary to engage with a messy and ill-defined range of ephemeral, mutable, and contested material traces that are at once embedded, evolving, and even in the process of being actively extracted from the moving moment of the lived city. The contemporary city is not a collection of discrete structures or artefactual scatters, but instead might be considered as a complex, multi-scalar entity. Contemporary archaeologists have the potential to broaden the view of what and how the materials constitute the city in, with, and separate to its human and non-human actors. Although excavation and site-based research is still relevant in contemporary archaeology, the study of the contemporary city cannot be limited to extracting excavated remains; our aim is not to *dig through* the present to reveal the static city of the past.

Archaeologies of contemporary cities include the vast, largely unconsidered, material infrastructure that directs the flow of the city and reflects the visions of urban planners that essentially aim to control (and often curtail) movement and access. From this perspective artefacts, standing structures, and landscapes should be viewed collectively to allow the city to be examined as an evolving entity that responds to different imaginaries, concepts, and plans. Contemporary cities do not act as a surface cover; they are at once undefinable and moving assemblages of materials and relationships that are still 'out there'. Constantly in flux, the contemporary city is a materially defined, designed, and governed entity that retains the ability to be immaterial, unconstituted, and uncontrollable. The contemporary city can be examined as a single entity, through small-scale studies as a microcosm of its whole, or it can be reconceived as a boundless collection of comparative characteristics. Ultimately the material worlds of cities are the logical conclusion of Harrison's articulation of archaeology 'of and in the present'; they are essentially 'palimpsests, the assemblages at the surface of which are mixed and contain traces from a number of different occupations which are jumbled together' (2011: 155).

Contemporary archaeologies of cities, as conceived in this volume, make no attempt to define and delineate the city. Some case studies explore the city through focused engagements with specific remnants and structures (see Graff, Shanahan and Shanahan), and others concentrate on particular political landscapes (see Singleton, Mullins, Ernsten). A number of multisited case studies move around the city exploring creative themes pertinent to its self-identity (Ryzewski, White, and Seidenberg) or its everyday experiences (Russell). Other contributors examine the city as a global entity through situated responses to neoliberal reformulation (Penrose, McAtackney) and non-Western materializations of industrial failure and subsequent ruination (González-Ruibal). In one case, the city is extended beyond its own geographical and cultural boundaries, the unruly wildness of nature and rurality also having a prominent place in facilitating urban realities (Beisaw).

Contemporary Archaeology and the City presents twelve case studies that reveal the potentialities of the city as a subject and scale of analysis and examine the interplay of global processes at the local level in ways that allow an interrogating of 'us'. The place of people is central to the contributors' conceptualizations of conducting contemporary archaeologies of cities. However important materials and methods are in archaeological approaches to cities, it is critical that studies do not bypass how human inhabitants contribute to and are impacted by the transformations of urban spaces that archaeologists document. While it may be necessary to forefront material expressions of the city to allow the recovery of what Buchli has called 'the unspoken, the unconstituted, the non-discursive, the non-textual voices which cannot be articulated and which cannot be presenced in any other way except by the techniques archaeology affords' (quoted in González-Ruibal et al. 2014: 267), human voices should not be excluded where they exist. Rather, there is an opportunity to synthesize reflexively the voices, memories, and opinions of people who live within cities alongside the material and to inject the perspectives of those who effectively constitute the city. In other words, to be conscious of the role we give to human experiences and voices; to empower but avoid reifying as fact; to resist presenting testimonies that are solely designed to support our interpretations (see Orange 2014: Introduction).

This volume argues for the inclusion of human voices while maintaining an appreciation of Orange's warning against the reification and homogenizing of social memory as a purported communal, subaltern, recovery (2014: 16). Following Hewitson (2012: 47) we contend that 'the use of multiple strands of evidence may create the truest picture of past events' and thereby they require a variety of interpretations. The following contributions include human voices, where present and appropriate, and recognize the ways in which they play complex roles in constructing the city and our understandings of it.

I.4 CONTEMPORARY URBAN SETTINGS

Within this volume two particular conceptions of contemporary urban settings resonate as overriding visions: post-industrial cities and conflicting cities.

I.4.1 Post-industrial Cities

Studying the industrial and post-industrial is not new to archaeology (see Casella and Symonds 2005; Casella and Croucher 2010; Orange 2014), nor is their circumstance, and frequent decline, an inevitable result of moving economic markets (see Penrose, Chapter 8). Nevertheless, existing studies have a tendency to view industry as both spatially situated and as a materialization of past or obsolescent processes. In those cases, the (post-)industrial materializes as static forms that we, the archaeologists, are able to retrieve, record, and interpret for posterity. They are infrequently situated in and of the contemporary, as part of ongoing, and larger, negotiations. One of the discussions that arose during the Detroit workshop involved critiques of postmodern, capitalist ruins (see Olsen and Pétursdóttir 2014; González-Ruibal 2013) not always engaging with the reality that not all high modern cities can be defined as post-industrial. The post-industrial city as a distinct entity links to very particular conceptualizations of cities as operating within the capitalist worldview, being essentially modern and industrial (see Penrose, Chapter 8 and González-Ruibal, Chapter 7). Of course, archaeologists are aware that urbanization pre-dates the Industrial Revolution by a considerable margin, but many of our ideas about the contemporary city stem from the reconceptualization of the city as a result of the massive industrialization of eigtheenth- and nineteenth-century North America and Western Europe. A significant refocus from the viewpoint of contemporary archaeology is the understanding that cities are modern entities that have been created, shaped, and marked by rapid growth, and even swifter decline, through processes of global industrialization and super modernity that, in many cases, are still ongoing and unresolved (González-Ruibal 2008).

One aim of this volume is to problematize how central industrialization (and its decline) is in understanding contemporary cities. Not all cities were formed or defined by industrialization. Even in those cities self-conceived as essentially 'industrial', the position industry holds in both their imaginary and material reality can be complexified. Likewise, for those contemporary cities that were formed and shaped by industrialization but have eradicated it from their current persona, their material reality may still survive. As Penrose (Chapter 8) argues, *creating* the post-industrial service economy entails some destruction of the previous industrial economy and its workers. Industrialization was not a monolithic process that shaped all urban environments at the same time and in equal measures. The form, extent, and location of industrialization greatly directed the development but also decline of cities in a process that remains individual to each city in its exact formulation and materialization. In this volume alone there are a number of contrasting perspectives on what constitutes a post-industrial city and how the city continues to engage with industrial memories, evolutions or declines. González-Ruibal highlights the dominance of the 'Global North' (Brandt 1980) in his discussion of how conceptions of industrial ruination have skewed our understandings of other realities. He argues that such worldviews deny the postcolonial materiality of industrialization and post-industrial destruction in South America. Penrose argues that industrial spaces in the UK do not so much decline but rather transition to neoliberal, post-industrial spaces. McAtackney reflects on how cities can be both a node of globalized industrialization while being shaped by decidedly local expressions, such as the entwining of industrialization with sectarianism in Belfast.

The conception of the post-industrial city as a neoliberal space that materially plays out naturalized policies, including explicit attempts to rebrand cities, is also central to many of the chapters (see White and Seidenberg, Chapter 1, for a discussion of 'creative cities'). In her edited volume on 'reanimating' industrial spaces, Hilary Orange highlights the increasingly common experience of industrial cities being actively transitioned into places of heritage and considers how they link to local identity and authenticity (Orange 2014). This volume adds to those concerns with its consideration of how rebranding efforts often connect to deliberately partial renderings of cities' pasts (including Detroit as 'Motor City') or make statements of intent for the future of cities in ways that can misrepresent and disconnect from the present (Berlin as a 'Creative City').

Using Penrose (Chapter 8) as a point of departure, one might question how appropriate the term '*post*-industrial' is in considering the living, evolving contemporary city. All cities are in varying but constant states of change and flux, so while the tangible loss of what have been called 'traditional' heavy industries without replacement (in terms of employment and *in situ*) is an experience of many modern, Global North cities, it is not a total experience or locatable in *all* contemporary cities. As industrialization changes form and moves from places of mass-manufacturing to sites of new industry so too does it continue to reproduce in new ways in which decline and complete destruction is not inevitable. Loss of traditional manufacturing industries is often counterbalanced by the introduction of new, usually service and technology sector, industries located in the same place as older industrial operations. Indeed 'traditional' industries are not so much lost, but are often displaced to new, developing markets. However, this transition does not necessarily result in an even equilibrium of redistribution. A useful comparison of two chapters in this volume—Penrose's discussion of neoliberal transition in London Docklands, Liverpool Docks, and Salford Quays and McAtackney's case study of the shipyards of East Belfast—reveals that even within the British state there is little evidence of commonality of experience. Whereas deindustrialized zones can transition—over varying temporal scales—to vibrant nodes of activity, industrial renewal; transition, or even long-term stasis is not the uniform experience of other historically industrialized zones in the same geopolitical entity.

I.4.2 Conflicted Cities

By their very nature cities are inherently conflicted spaces. Containing a multitude of individuals and communities in competition for space, resources, and meaning, the demarcation of space in the city directly relates to issues of access, control, and power (Marcuse 1994). Within the definition of conflicted cities, conflict is not delineated solely in terms of explosive, violent interactions. At its most basic level conflict relates to divergent ideas about the meaning and political economy of the city—who has access to or ownership of particular spaces in the city, and how the city moves forward.

At some level all of the volume contributors present conflicting ideas about what the city means in contemporary society and how it positions itself to move forward at the expense of marginalized or less empowered communities and their histories. Conflicts can be made to appear naturalized, particularly when they stem from significant issues of meaning, identity, memory, ownership, and belonging. Indeed, it is telling that the interconnection between conceptions of the past, power relations in the present, and divergent aims for the future largely determines the nature of these conflicts. In Istanbul (Russell, Chapter 2) and New York City (Beisaw, Chapter 6) these conflicts fluctuate but often centre on ideas of private versus public ownership of, and access to, public spaces and 'natural' resources. In Berlin, White and Seidenberg (Chapter 1) argue that artists' access to working spaces is determined by the availability of cheap accommodations, which can lead to conflict with local communities in areas that are often associated with low paid workers and new migrants.

Conflict can also take a much more explicit form and can range in severity and scale. Cities are often focal points for civil conflict arising from different worldviews among citizens that in extreme circumstance can lead to mass destruction and death. Violent conflict can result in cities rapidly transforming into 'traumascapes' for those who must continue living in them (Tumarkin 2005). Various scales of contemporary materializations of conflict are referenced in the chapters in this volume. González-Ruibal (Chapter 7) argues that industrialization—and its ruination—in 'the South' differs considerably from 'the North' in both how it is materialized and who is implicated in it. Not only do the processes of ruination often occur outside of cities—including scarring the Amazonian rainforests—they also reveal the reliance on the violence of slave labour to maintain and refocus industry at the whim of global markets. Russell (Chapter 2) demonstrates how contestation of ownership and meaning of public spaces in Istanbul has resulted in violent confrontations during street protests, as well as in more subtle ways. His discussions of Pamuk's *Museum of Innocence* reveal how this cultural space has constructed a narrative of everyday life in Istanbul in ways that defy increasing controls on Turkish freedom of expression. Within the museum, the ordinary material culture related to the mundane but inherently political lives of historic and contemporary inhabitants of the city was used to craft a multitude of emergent narratives. By engaging with issues of gender, class, and illicit love the *The Museum of Innocence* powerfully reveals real communities in Istanbul and quietly disrupts attempts at totalizing, official narratives.

I.5 THEMES AND CONTRIBUTIONS

Contemporary Archaeology and the City is organized around three themes that highlight key characteristics of urban transitions in contemporary cities—creativity, ruination, and political action. The contributions in each section focus on the social, political, economic, and cultural material realities of 'now' while engaging with the latent agency of post-modern and post-industrial cities to creatively re-emerge, transform, and reposition themselves in the near future. The focus on these three themes within the broader study of the contemporary city redirects parts of the contemporary archaeology research agenda firmly away from 'ruin porn' (critiques include Mullins 2014, 2012; Ryzewski 2014) and modernist-influenced approaches to the past (see Harrison 2011). In addition, the themes connect contemporary archaeological conceptions of the city as a palimpsest with methodological challenges specific to particular cities. As a result, multiple contemporary realities are explored in ways that position cities as places of long-term urban transformation, simultaneously engaged with the impact of decline and the potentialities of transformational movements.

This volume's case studies expose two distinct but overlapping strands of contemporary archaeological practice. Some studies illustrate the *making* of contemporary cities through creative interventions in the present, compositional processes, or the presencing of the past through material remains. Others follow more closely a second strand of practice, which involves *extending* archaeologies of modernity into the contemporary world. Avoiding the tendency of one strand of practice to criticize or usurp the other, the volume contributions maintain a collegial diversity of contemporary archaeology in ways that expose productive tensions between aestheticization and an active engagement with poverty, politics, and social justice.

I.5.1 Creativity

The first section presents case studies on the theme of creative engagements in contemporary cities. Rather than framing cities such like Berlin or Detroit as places of failure, this thematic focus highlights the ways in which contemporary archaeology engages creatively with the transitioning city as a place of potential, collaboration, innovation, and change. Case studies by Carolyn White and Steven Seidenberg (Berlin), Ian Alden Russell (Istanbul), and Krysta Ryzewski (Detroit) detail actions in everyday urban life that fall outside of textual forms of knowledge through collaborations with artists, museums, heritage practitioners, musicians, non-profits, and sound conservators.

While creative engagements have always been part of contemporary archaeological studies, particularly those involving collaborations with artists and filmmakers or mixed media outcomes, (e.g. film, art installations, museum exhibits; Holtorf and Piccini 2009; Russell and Cochrane 2014; Dixon forthcoming), creative engagements have less commonly been employed in studies with specific interests in contemporary urban environments and transitioning patterns of urbanization. By actively exploring and analysing emerging and counter-hegemonic artistic responses to the city, the contributors articulate contemporary archaeological understandings of creative responses to civic re-imaginings. Together, their case studies convey the diversity of contemporary archaeological interests in art and heritage as creative, community-oriented practices that explore new terrain, incorporate marginalized stakeholder groups, and participate in the documentation of histories that fall outside of established approaches and challenge prevailing discourses (Smith 2006).

Creativity is a concept that has been at the fore of urban policy, planning, and theoretical debates in the fields of economic geography and urban studies for over a decade now, particularly as creative economies have been increasingly, and often controversially, enlisted as catalysts for urban redevelopment (see Scott 2014; Florida 2002). The growing connection between creativity and overtly capitalist enterprises is a characteristic of many contemporary cities. As demonstrated by the authors in this section, creative archaeological and cultural heritage engagements require circumspection among practitioners, demanding particular attention to and critical awareness of the ways in which our creative work might productively or adversely affect policy decisions, heritage narratives, or local stakeholder groups.

In a city often described as a living ruin, post-industrial Berlin is home to a thriving international community of artists. Carolyn L. White and Steven Seidenberg employ an archaeological gaze method to analyse the physical elements of five artists and their studios and to examine the placement of artist communities across Berlin. Although the physical spaces that artists occupy are the primary focus of the chapter, the authors' work also engages directly with artists living and working in the studios, combining the physical and personal elements of artists' work and dwelling spaces into a broader consideration of the role of creative processes in contemporary Berlin. White and Seidenberg illustrate the innovative ways that artists use and repurpose the physical environment of the post-Berlin Wall environs in temporary, permanent, physical, and conceptual 'project spaces'. Exploring the meanings of space and community in the broader context of Berlin's extant built environment, White and Seidenberg call attention to issues of physicality, ephemerality, and durability in the contemporary archaeological record, as well as to the fruitful intersections between archaeology and art in practice.

The role of the contemporary past in forming understandings of heritage that are socially engaged and attentive to place-specific political ecologies is central to Ian Alden Russell's chapter (see also Buchli in González-Ruibal et al. 2014: 268). Russell draws inspiration from artists, in creating *An Innocent City*, a socially engaged and collaborative heritage exhibition that is a notable model of participatory practice. Launched in the summer of 2014, *An Innocent City* was an exhibition at Koç University's Research Center for Anatolian Civilizations in Istanbul. Russell and his collaborators, (artists, local communities, and students), selected objects on display in the Museum of Innocence and charted the lives of these objects, which have been on display in the Museum since the 1970s, in present-day Istanbul. The participatory processes of research, narrative creation, and exhibit design create maps of the lives of everyday objects in Istanbul in ways that enfold the local community and exhibition audiences into the development and interpretation of the contemporary objects' stories. Russell offers *An Innocent City* as an example for how heritage may be used creatively in contemporary archaeological and artistic practices to open up new platforms for engagement and dissemination. Drawing relevant parallels between socially engaged arts and heritage practices in Istanbul with those in Detroit, Russell highlights particular forms of practice and addresses disparities within the political ecologies of urban places that, if addressed by practitioners, may result in closer collaborations between individuals and the constitution of heritage.

Krysta Ryzewski presents the 'Making Music in Detroit' project, a contemporary archaeology and digital storytelling exercise focused on popular music assemblages and their placemaking power in Detroit. Similar to Russell's socially engaged practice in Istanbul, 'Making Music' is a collaborative project that contributes to a grassroots and place-based heritage discourse about Detroit and other post-industrial cities through creative archaeological documentation and dissemination. Incorporating popular music, urban geography, archaeological, and heritage research, Ryzewski explores connections between places and the physical remains of creative production, music consumption, and memories associated with Detroit's twentieth-century popular music industry. The 'Making Music' project confronts head-on the challenges of working with a rapidly changing urban setting by creating brief digital engagements with meaningful places, most of which are either derelict, slated for demolition, or already demolished. Ryzewski's design of the 'Making Music' project injects dimensions of temporality and materiality into discussions of creativity and argues that contemporary archaeologists have important contributions to make in understanding how creativity differs over time and how archaeological and multimedia approaches to documenting music-based histories (and histories of other generative movements) might contribute productively to the redesign and heritage narratives of future cities.

I.5.2 Ruination

The second thematic section of *Contemporary Archaeology and the City* engages with ruination—the most widespread, visually prominent, and publicly noticeable material manifestation of urban decay explored in contemporary archaeology. Some of the cities discussed by this section's contributors, including Belém, are landscapes composed of empty factories, decaying infrastructure, and abandoned homes; largely bereft of people they are settings of expansive post-industrial ruination (González-Ruibal). Others, as in the cases of Melbourne and Chicago, demonstrate how ruination and memorialization are still integral components of the physical fabric and social memories of places and people in contemporary cities that are less affected by processes of deindustrialization (Shanahan and Shanahan, Graff). Beisaw and González-Ruibal introduce nuanced conceptions of urban ruination by focusing on rural places, in New York state and Brazil, that, despite their distance from metropolitan areas, have experienced the effects of displacement and landscape transformation as a direct counterpoint to and consequence of urban, industrial expansion. Though diverse in temporal, geographic, and topical scope, the authors in this section contribute important new perspectives on ruination to contemporary archaeological scholarship. In their engagements with the specificity of ruin in the contemporary urban environment the authors avoid the tendency to engage uncritically in 'ruin porn'—especially the selective and overly aesthetized objectification of ruination—and instead focus on the transition of modern ruins as living, transformative places (for discussions on ruin porn in contemporary archaeology, see Pétursdóttir and Olsen 2014 and accompanying comments).

Rebecca S. Graff's chapter introduces the power of ruins to invoke a material past that is cared for, conserved, and maintained by civic narratives and social memory. Graff discusses two cases involving the creative reuse of architectural and building materials in Chicago, one still-extant building and the other demolished. The Chicago Tribune Tower is a building on Chicago's 'Magnificent Mile' with a façade composed of 138 architectural fragments of buildings ('Famous Stones') collected from the world's most recognizable and esteemed cultural heritage sites beginning during World War I. Graff argues that the Famous Stones allow those who view them to locate Chicago within a narrative of ancient and modern human accomplishments by interfacing with the world in the space of a building façade. The second case considers a demolished building, the Relic House, built in 1872 from ruins of the 1871 Chicago Fire and repurposed several times during the course of its history before its demolition and gradual erasure from social memory. In her analysis of these two sites Graff interrogates the relationships between architectural fragments and social memory, the role of fragmented ruins in creating and sustaining Chicago's narrative history, and the processes by which narratives are institutionalized and incorporated into an urban built environment.

Drawing on similar themes of narrative history, social memory, and temporal fragmentation, city parks in Melbourne, Australia, provide the setting for Madeline Shanahan and Brian Shanahan's chapter. They explore how public memorials and monuments commemorating Australia's colonial legacies serve as locations for engaging with the negotiations, contestations, and discourses that shape Melbournians' present-day post-colonial and urban identities. Four case studies illustrate the changing relationships that citizens have with the city's colonial and pre-colonial past; two British-Australian sites (Cooks' Cottage and LaTrobe's Cottage) and two Aboriginal memorials (The Kings Domain Resting Place and The Fitzroy Gardens Sacred Tree). The comparisons made between the pre-colonial and colonial sites highlight significant contrasts in how material expressions of memory and commemoration are differentially asserted in public urban spaces. The British-Australian cottages are remembered as physical connections to individual white, male, elite historical figures, whereas the Aboriginal sites are gender-neutral places of tangible and intangible cultural heritage that focus on collective identities. For Shanahan and Shanahan, Melbourne's public parks are places for reflection on and recontextualization of urban foundation stories via material expressions.

Expanding upon the ecologies of urban infrastructure and landscapes of ruination, April M. Beisaw explores the long-term processes of ruination, displacement, and abandonment that were created over 150 years to accommodate water demands from an increasingly prosperous New York City. Beisaw's archaeological survey of the remains of New York City's water system, located in rural areas well beyond the city's limits, documents the process by which the modern city's growing need for water created ruins in and displaced communities from rural and suburban landscapes. As previous water supplies were exhausted, residents living in proximity to new water sources were displaced and their homes replaced with hydraulic infrastructure. The results of Beisaw's archaeological research detail the historical processes that set ruination in motion with particular attention to recent decisions that have encouraged, if not escalated, the continued abandonment of lived landscapes in New York City's watershed regions. In comparing New York City's water management struggles with Detroit's current water crisis and historic infrastructure issues, Beisaw highlights how comparable policies ensure the continuation of the process of urban and rural ruination related to urban infrastructure and resource maintenance in contemporary and future cities.

The second section concludes with a shift in perspective to the ruins of the South in the chapter by Alfredo González-Ruibal. The ruins of modernity, González-Ruibal argues, are inevitably the ruins of the North, particularly in the industrial and post-industrial metropolises of Europe and North America. González-Ruibal proposes the concept of 'ruins of the South' as a way to understand forms of post-industrial ruination that are not congruent with contemporary archaeological and other perspectives developed in reference to the North. In presenting multiple cases of urban and rural ruination in Brazil, a country that has generated a tremendous volume of modern ruins, González-Ruibal critically reflects upon the intersections of ruination, capitalism, colonialism, and other modernities as a logical conclusion to high capitalist exploitation of the Global South. Importantly, González-Ruibal's concept of the South is not restricted to a particular global region, but refers instead to a political-economic geography, which is perhaps most prominent in Latin America and Africa, but also includes cities like Detroit.

I.5.3 Political Action

The third and final section builds on the socially and politically engaged aspects of the first two themes, creativity and ruination, by overtly considering archaeological approaches to radical change, political (dis)enfranchisement, and social activism in contemporary settings. Contemporary archaeology has often combined the study of material culture with social justice and political issues, including studies of abandonment of social housing (Buchli and Lucas 2001) and the lived experiences of homelessness (Zimmerman et al. 2010) and prisoners (McAtackney 2014). To some extent, however, discussions of politics and ethics in practice, and direct involvements of archaeologists with political engagements or social movements, have been less prominent in contemporary archaeological practice to date.

Contributors to this section demonstrate why it is both improbable and generally undesirable for contemporary archaeologists to maintain detachment from their research subjects. As such, the volume concludes with an explicit link to the growing role of archaeologists as political commentators, and even activists in the contemporary city (see Crea et al. 2014; Singleton, Chapter 11). Through five different case studies, including explorations of homelessness, the negative impact of deindustrialization, post-apartheid struggles, and the politics of absences, the section's authors use archaeological methodologies and theories to critique under-discussed and even deliberately hidden aspects of cities. The authors engage directly with and mobilize controversial socio-political topics relevant to understanding contemporary cities by recording, understanding, and articulating dissent and exploitation. They also suggest how contemporary archaeology might contribute to the power of grassroots movements and ongoing governmental processes to generate positive change in civic policies, social movements, and public memory. Archaeology has always had the potential to show how interpreting material realities can reveal different and even deliberately obfuscated narratives of recent history (see Hall 2000), and so it is fitting that the socio-political commentary that remains central to much contemporary archaeology should conclude this volume.

Sefryn Penrose's opening chapter provides an intriguing counterpoint to the perspective on ruins provided by González-Ruibal in the preceding section through a very different exploration of the afterlife of industrialization in the 'Global North'. Penrose contends that ruin studies within contemporary archaeology often present an overtly anti-capitalist critique within a particular focus on the aestheticization of things and places. In continuing to treat ruins as stationary objects 'from the ground', archaeologists run the risk of eluding processes of movement and change that are central to fully situating sites and places of ruin. In her discussions of deindustrialized sites in London's Docklands and Canary Wharf, and in the North of England extending from the Liverpool Docklands to Salford Quay, Penrose evaluates 'the winners' of neoliberal capitalist landscapes and considers the extent to which the current emphasis on ruination in contemporary archaeology has disqualified them from analysis. Penrose's case studies call attention to creative destruction—the process of continuous reinvention within capitalist markets—and the large-scale landscape transformations of deindustrialized areas that have been swiftly altered by neoliberal government policies to accommodate new service economies.

Contrasting with the previous chapter, which focuses on the relatively positive political outcomes of deindustrialization, Laura McAtackney focuses on the negative impacts of urban deindustrialization processes specific to the historically conflicted city of Belfast. Belfast and other cities in Northern Ireland continue to be determined in how they are understood and engaged with by legacy issues from 'the Troubles', a period of sectarian conflict spanning from the late 1960s to the signing of the Belfast Agreement in 1998. Many of the period's tensions have subsided from widespread violence but have remained unresolved among present-day local communities, particularly in community heritage discourses and governmental policies. McAtackney considers how these legacies of the past affect Belfast's contemporary urban landscape and community identities through examples of civic memorialization practices (e.g. murals, sculptures) and other material interventions (e.g. walls, graffiti, memorials) in the historically loyalist and industrial area of East Belfast. McAtackney demonstrates how abnormal societal relations with deep historical roots continue to materialize in contemporary society, although not always in ways one would expect. Her work encourages other researchers to examine these materialities in an effort to question why Belfast's contentious relations were accepted and permitted to proliferate, as well as contextualize how the city links global political-economic processes.

Christian Ernsten moves the section's conversations about political action to focus on poignant questions of loss and violent pasts in his explorations of the ruins in District One and District Six of Cape Town, South Africa. Post-apartheid Cape Town continues to undergo large-scale redevelopments designed to bolster its recent status as a world-class tourist destination. These urban transformations, Ernsten argues, are imbued with a hopeful rhetoric of reinvention that fails to access the others—the people, their histories, the violence of segregation, and other absences—that continue to inhabit the negative spaces of the city's modernity and public memory. Ernsten's discussion is divided into multiple themes (land, homage, witness, truth, percolate, scar, and drama), each of which contains theoretically informed introspections on how the materialities of Cape Town's ruined landscapes offer ways of experiencing degraded personhoods, past and present. The controversial removal, reinternment, and subsequent commoditization of the Prestwich Street dead is a central case study undergirding Ernsten's reflections and powerful images. The themed vignettes structuring the chapter effectively capture the complex transformations of the two districts and the scars that their treatments continue to leave on a shapeshifting contemporary Cape Town.

Thousands of miles away in Indianapolis and New York City, Courtney Singleton's multisited discussion about the archaeology of contemporary urban homelessness connects with themes articulated by Ernsten, Penrose, and McAtackney about how government policies and public conceptions of urban citizenship work against the attempts of marginalized, local communities to assert attachments to place. In Singleton's case studies these processes are manifest among the homeless populations' attempts in New York City and Indianapolis to create and maintain spaces of living in public venues. Singleton's discussion of the homeless community during the 2011 Occupy Wall Street Protests at Zuccotti Park in New York City and her study of the Davidson Street Bridge Encampment in Indianapolis use contemporary archaeological methods to illustrate how cycles of dispossession and violence continuously rupture homeless communities' practices of homemaking and personhood within contemporary North American cities.

Paul R. Mullins' concluding chapter offers a comprehensive focus on landscape absences in ways that resonate with many of the volume's previous discussions of displacement, heritage, conflict, and the materialities of the recent past and present. Mullins foregrounds two distinct case studies in his discussion, an African-American community from the near-Westside of

Indianapolis which was displaced by urban renewal programmes during the mid–late twentieth century, and Oulu, Finland, a city that was the base for Nazi co-belligerents during World War II. In each case Mullins examines how the material remains of removal and warfare were effaced by differently enacted processes of displacement, both of which left behind absences in urban spaces that reflect the intentional and near wholescale removal of landscapes of conflict and contestation. Like ruined buildings, Mullins argues that absences on urban landscapes are grounds for recognizing the extent to which contemporary communities grapple with conflicted histories, particularly through attempts to confront, resolve, or erase contested places of heritage.

I.6 DETROIT AS TOUCHSTONE

Detroit is a recurring frame of reference throughout the volume, owing in part to the Wenner-Gren workshop's location but also due to the heightened role Detroit plays in public renderings of a transitionary contemporary city. The city is a timely and relevant reference point for connecting and contrasting major aspects of urban transformations with other contemporary cities (e.g. deindustrialization, grassroots initiatives, creative destruction, rebranding, population movement, the consequences of post-Fordism/Reganism/Thatcherism). Its materiality is exceptional in comparison with other contemporary post-industrial cities because of the unprecedented scale and speed of ruin and abandonment across its landscape. Over 70,000 structures sit derelict throughout the city's 139 square-mile expanse (Data Driven Detroit 2014). Detroit in its present state fits the definition of what anthropologist Maria Tumarkin (2005) refers to as a 'traumascape', a place marked by loss, violence, and dispossession that nonetheless remains an important cultural landmark in contemporary memory. Jerry Herron argues that Detroit is an essential case for understandings of contemporary cities; as the 'first urban domino to fall' it is representative of an America and a global modernity that is over; it also signals the failure of modern institutions to 'realize their utopian promises' (1993: 15, 77, 203; see also 2007).

Countless other post-industrial cities of varying sizes—Cleveland, Hull, Buffalo, Manchester, Łódź, to name but a few—share similar plights with present-day Detroit, if at different times and on a lesser scale. Whilst expansive factory ruins, industrial decline, and political struggles have cast Detroit into the spotlight in recent years, such post-industrial malaise is not singular to any one city or even to the contemporary. As noted by González-Ruibal (Chapter 7), post-industrialization has occurred in other places and in earlier times. Our fixation with contemporary post-industrialization must not overlook its antecedents both in terms of the different material forms of previous waves of deindustrialization or in their various short and long term consequences. Likewise, as Penrose (Chapter 8) notes, we should recognize that the transformations in Detroit have 'occurred within a globalized network of capital ownership' that materialize differently in other contexts. In this sense Detroit is in Michigan, but also can be located in Sweden, Northern Ireland, Germany, and Brazil. It is with this global comparative perspective in mind that the following contributions consider how creativity, ruination, and political action accompany the materialities and people in urban post-industrial settings worldwide.

REFERENCES

Beaudry, Mary C. and Travis Parno (eds). 2013. *Archaeologies of Mobility and Movement*. New York: Springer.

Biehl, Peter F., Douglas C. Comer, Christopher Prescott, and Hilary A. Soderland (eds). 2014. *Identity and Heritage: Contemporary Challenges in a Globalized World*. New York: Springer.

Brandt, Willy. 1980. *North/South: A Programme for Survival: The Brandt Commission Report*. London: Macmillan.

Buchli, Victor, and Gavin Lucas. 2001. 'Introduction'. In *Archaeologies of the Contemporary Past*, edited by Victor Buchli and Gavin Lucas, London: Routledge, pp. 158–67.

Cantwell, Anne-Marie, and Diana diZerega Wall. 2001. *Unearthing Gotham: the archaeology of New York City*. New York: Yale University Press.

Casella, Eleanor C. and Sarah Croucher. 2010. *The Alderley Sandhills project: an archaeology of community life in (post) industrial England*. Manchester: Manchester University Press.

Casella, Eleanor C. and James Symonds. 2005. *Industrial Archaeology: future directions*. New York: Springer.

Cherry, John F., Krysta Ryzewski, and Luke Pecoraro. 2013. '"A Kind of Sacred Place": The Rock and Roll Ruins of *AIR Studios*'. In *Archaeologies of Mobility and Movement*, edited by Mary C. Beaudry and Travis Parno, New York: Springer, pp. 181–98.

Clark, Bonnie L. 2010. 'When the Foreign is Not Exotic: Ceramics at Colorado's WWII Japanese Internment Camp'. In *Trade and Exchange: Archaeological Studies from History and Prehistory*, edited by Carolyn Dillian and Carolyn L. White, New York: Springer, pp. 179–92.

Council of Europe. 2005. *The Framework Convention of the Value of Cultural Heritage for Society (Faro Convention)*. Treaty Series No. 199.

Crea, Gillian, Andrew Dafnis, Jane Hallam, Rachael Kiddey, and John Schofield. 2014. 'Turbo Island: excavating a contemporary homeless place', *Post-Medieval Archaeology* 48(1): 133–50.

Crossland, Zoë. 2002. 'Violent spaces: conflict over the reappearance of Argentina's disappeared'. In *Matériel culture: the Archaeology of Twentieth Century Conflict*, edited by Colleen M. Beck, William G. Johnston, and John Schofield, London: Routledge, pp. 146–59.

Data Driven Detroit. 2014. http://datadrivendetroit.org/ (accessed 28 July 2016).

Dawdy, Shannon. 2008. *Building the Devil's Empire: French Colonial New Orleans*. Chicago: University of Chicago Press.

Dawdy, Shannon. 2010. 'Clockpunk anthropology and the ruins of modernity', *Current Anthropology*, 51(6): 761–93.

Dawdy, Shannon. 2015. 'Profane archaeology and the dialectics of the city', *Journal of Social Archaeology*, 16(1): 1–24.

Dawson, Richard, Annemie Wyckmans, Oliver Hiedrich, Jonathan Koher, Stephen Dobson, and Efren Feliu (eds). 2014. *Understanding Cities: Advances in Integrated Assessment of Urban Sustainability*. Newcastle upon Tyne: Centre for Earth Systems Engineering Research.

DeSilvey, Caitlin. 2006. 'Observed decay: telling stories with mutable things', *Journal of Material Culture*, 11(3): 318–38.

Dickens, Roy S. (ed.). 1982. *Archaeology of Urban America: The Search for Pattern and Process*. New York: Academic Press.

Dixon, James. 2007. 'Bristol Broadmead: art and heritage in urban regeneration', *English Heritage Conservation Bulletin*, Issue 56. Autumn.

Dixon, James. 2013. 'Two riots: the importance of civil unrest in contemporary archaeology'. In *The Oxford Handbook of the Archaeology of the Contemporary World*, edited by Paul Graves-Brown, Rodney Harrison, and Angela Piccini, Oxford: Oxford University Press.

Dixon, James (ed.). forthcoming. *Fragmenting Archaeology, or Taking a Leaf Out of Shanks and Tilley's Book*. British Archaeological Reports.

Edgeworth, Matt. 2012. 'Follow the cut, follow the rhythm, follow the material', *Norwegian Archaeological Review*, 45(1): 76–114.

Florida, Richard. 2002. *The Rise of the Creative Class: And How It's Transforming Work, Leisure, Community and Everyday Life*. New York: Basic Books.

Fortenberry, Brent and Laura McAtackney (eds). 2012. *Modern Materials: papers from CHAT Oxford (2009)*. Oxford: Archaeopress.

Fortenberry, Brent and Adrian Myers (eds). 2010. 'CHAT @ TAG: In Context', *Archaeologies*, 6(1): 1–4.

González-Ruibal, Alfredo. 2006. 'The Past is Tomorrow. Towards an Archaeology of the Vanishing Present', *Norwegian Archaeological Review*, 39(2): 110–25.

González-Ruibal, Alfredo. 2008. 'A time to destroy: an archaeology of supermodernity', *Current Anthropology*, 49(2): 247–79.

González-Ruibal, Alfredo (ed.). 2013. *Reclaiming archaeology: beyond the tropes of modernity*. London: Routledge.

González-Ruibal, Alfredo, Rodney Harrison, Cornelius Holtorf, and Laurie Wilkie. 2014. 'Archaeologies of the Contemporary Past: an interview with Victor Buchli and Gavin Lucas', *Journal of Contemporary Archaeology*, 1(2): 265–76.

Gould, Richard. 2007. *Disaster Archaeology*. Salt Lake City: University of Utah Press.

Gould, Richard and Michael Schiffer (eds). 1981. *Modern material culture: the archaeology of us*. New York: Academic Press.

Graves-Brown, Paul (ed). 2000. *Matter, materiality and modern culture.* London: Routledge.

Graves-Brown, Paul. 2009. 'The privatization of experience and the archaeology of the future'. In *Contemporary archaeologies: Excavating now,* edited by Cornelius Holtorf and Angela Piccini, Frankfurt: Peter Lang.

Graves-Brown, Paul, Rodney Harrison, and Angela Piccini (eds). 2013. *The Oxford Handbook of the Archaeology of the Contemporary World.* Oxford: Oxford University Press.

Green, Adrian and Roger Leech. 2006. 'Introduction; Urban Historical Archaeology: Challenging Ambivalence'. In *Cities in the World 1500–2000: Proceedings of the Society for Post-Medieval Archaeology Conference,* edited by Adrian Green and Roger Leech, London: Maney Publishing.

Hall, Martin. 2000. *Archaeology and the Modern World: colonial transcripts in South Africa and the Chesapeake.* London: Routledge.

Harrison, Rodney. 2011. 'Surface assemblages, Towards an archaeology of and in the present', *Archaeological Dialogues,* 18(2): 141–61.

Harrison, Rodney. 2012. *Heritage: Critical Approaches.* London: Routledge.

Harrison, Rodney. 2015. 'Beyond "Natural" and "Cultural" Heritage: Toward an Ontological Politics of Heritage in the Age of Anthropocene', *Heritage and Society,* 8(1): 24–42.

Harrison, Rodney and John Schofield. 2009. 'Archaeo-Ethnography, auto-archaeology: Introducing archaeologies of the contemporary past', *Archaeologies,* 5(2): 185–209.

Harrison, Rodney and John Schofield. 2010. *After modernity: archaeological approaches to the contemporary past.* Oxford: Oxford University Press.

Harvey, David. 2012. *Rebel Cities: From the Right to the City to the Urban Revolution.* London: Verso.

Herron, Jerry. 1993. *After Culture: Detroit and the humiliation of history.* Detroit: Wayne State University Press.

Herron, Jerry. 2007. 'Detroit: disaster deferred, disaster in progress', *South Atlantic Quarterly,* 106(4): 663–82.

Herzfeld, Michael. 2015. 'Heritage and the Right to the City: When Securing the Past Creates Insecurity in the Present', *Heritage and Society,* 8(1): 3–23.

Hewitson, Chris. 2012. '"The workman laid down his tools": approaches to recording and analysis of artefactual remains in 19th and 20th century workshops'. In *Modern Materials: Contemporary and Historical Archaeology 8,* edited by Brent Fortenberry and Laura McAtackney, Oxford: Archaeopress (British Archaeological Reports International Series 2363), pp. 37–50.

Hicks, Dan, Laura McAtackney, and Graham Fairclough (eds). 2007. *Envisioning Landscape: Situations and Standpoints in Archaeology and Heritage.* Walnut Creek: Left Coast Press.

Holtorf, Cornelius. 2007. *Archaeology is a Brand! The Meaning of Archaeology in Contemporary Popular Culture.* Oxford: Archaeopress and Walnut Creek: Left Coast Press.

Holtorf, Cornelius and Angela Piccini (eds). 2009. *Contemporary Archaeologies: Excavating Now.* Frankfurt: Peter Lang.

Lefebvre, Henri. 1996. *Writing on Cities.* Oxford: Blackwell.

Lefebvre, Henri. 2003. *The Urban Revolution*. Minneapolis: The University of Minnesota Press.

Leone, Mark P. 2006. *The Archaeology of Liberty in an American Capital: Excavations in Annapolis*. Berkeley: University of California Press.

Lewis, Ann-Eliza (ed.). 2001. *Highway to the Past: The Archaeology of Boston's Big Dig*. Boston: Massachusetts Secretary of the Commonwealth, Massachusetts Historical Commission.

McAtackney, Laura. 2014. *An Archaeology of the Troubles: the dark heritage of Long Kesh/Maze prison, Northern Ireland*. Oxford: Oxford University Press.

McAtackney, Laura, Matthew Palus, and Angela Piccini (eds). 2007. *Studies in Contemporary and Historical Archaeology 4: Contemporary and Historical Archaeology in Theory Papers from the 2003 and 2004 CHAT Conferences*, British Archaeological Reports S1677.

McAtackney, Laura, and Sefryn Penrose. 2016. 'The contemporary in post-medieval archaeology'. *50th Anniversary (special edition) Post-Medieval Archaeology*.

McNamara, Kevin R. (ed.). 2014. *The Cambridge Companion to the City in Literature*. Cambridge: Cambridge University Press.

Marcuse, Paul. 1994. 'Walls as Metaphors and Reality'. In *Managing Divided Cities*, edited by Seamus Dunn, Keele: Keele University Press, pp. 41–52.

May, Sarah, Hilary Orange, and Sefryn Penrose (eds). 2012. *The Good, the Bad and the Unbuilt: Handling the Heritage of the Recent Past. Studies in Contemporary and Historical Archaeology 4: Contemporary and Historical Archaeology in Theory Papers 7*, British Archaeological Reports S2362 2012.

Mayne, Alan and Tim Murray. 2001. *The Archaeology of Urban Landscapes: Explorations in Slumland*. Cambridge: Cambridge University Press.

Millington, Nate. 2013. 'Post-industrial imaginaries: Nature, Representation and Ruin in Detroit, Michigan', *International Journal of Urban and Regional Research*, 37(1): 279–96.

Mrozowski, Stephen. 2006. *The Archaeology of Class in Urban America*. Cambridge: Cambridge University Press.

Mullins, Paul R. 2006. 'Racialising the commonplace landscape: an archaeology of urban renewal along the color line', *World Archaeology*, 38(1): 60–71.

Mullins, Paul R. 2012. The Politics and Archaeology of 'ruin porn'. http://paulmullins.wordpress.com/2012/08/19/the-politics-and-archaeology-of-ruin-porn/ (accessed April 2015).

Mullins, Paul R. 2014. 'Imagining Ruin Images: The Aesthetics of Ruination', *Journal of Contemporary Archaeology*, 1(1): 27–9.

Murray, Tim and Penny Crook. 2005. 'Exploring the Archaeology of the Modern City: Issues of Scale, Integration, and Complexity', *International Journal of Historical Archaeology*, 9(2): 89–109.

Olivier, Laurent. 2001. 'The archaeology of the contemporary past'. In *Archaeologies of the contemporary past*, edited by Victor Buchli and Gavin Lucas, London and New York: Routledge, pp. 175–88.

Olsen, Bjørnar and Þóra Pétursdóttir (eds). 2014. *Ruin Memories: Materialities, Aesthetics and the Archaeology of the Recent Past*. London: Routledge.

Olsen, Bjørnar, Michael Shanks, Timothy Webmoor, and Christopher Witmore. 2012. *Archaeology: the discipline of things*. Berkeley: University of California Press.

Orange, Hilary (ed.). 2014. *Reanimating Industrial Spaces: Conducting Memory Work in Post-industrial Societies*. Walnut Creek: Left Coast Press.

Pardo, Italo and Giuliana B. Prato (eds). 2012. *Anthropology in the City: Methodology and Theory*. Basingstoke: Ashgate.

Pearson, Michael and Michael Shanks. 2001. *Theatre/archaeology*. London: Routledge.

Penrose, Sefryn (ed.). 2007. *Images of change: an archaeology of England's contemporary landscape*. Swindon: English Heritage.

Perry, Sara and Nicole Beale. 2015. 'The Social Web and Archaeology's Restructuring: Impact, Exploitation and Disciplinary Change', *Open Archaeology*, 1: 153–65.

Pétursdóttir, Þóra and Bjørnar Olsen. 2014. 'Imaging Modern Decay: the Aesthetics of Ruin Photography', *Journal of Contemporary Archaeology*, 1(1): 7–23.

Pilling, Arnold R. 1967. 'Skyscraper Archaeologist: The Urban Archaeologist in Detroit', *Detroit Historical Society Bulletin*, 38(2): 4–9.

Praetzellis, Mary and Adrian Praetzellis (eds). 2004. *Putting the 'there' there: historical archaeologies of West Oakland: I-880 Cypress Freeway Replacement Project*. Anthropological Studies Center, Sonoma State University: Department of Transportation, District 4, Cultural Resource Studies Office.

Rathje, William. 1979. 'Modern material culture studies', *Advances in archaeological method and theory*, 2: 1–37.

Rothschild, Nan A and Diana diZerega Wall. 2014. *The archaeology of American cities*. Gainesville: University Press of Florida.

Russell, Ian Alden and Andrew Cochrane (eds). 2014. *Art and Archaeology: Collaborations, Conversations, Criticisms*. New York: Springer.

Ryzewski, Krysta. 2014. 'Ruin Photography as Archaeological Method: A Snapshot from Detroit', *Journal of Contemporary Archaeology*, 1(1): 36–41.

Ryzewski, Krysta. 2015. 'No home for the "oridinary gamut": A historical archaeology of community displacement and the creation of Detroit, City Beautiful', *Journal of Social Archaeology*, 15(3): 408–31.

Ryzewski, Krysta. 2016. 'Reclaiming Detroit: Decolonizing Archaeology in the Post-Industrial City'. *Savage Minds*, blog post, 5 July. http://savageminds.org/2016/07/05/reclaiming-detroit-decolonizing-archaeology-in-the-postindustrial-city/ (accessed 28 July 2016).

Scott, John A. 2014. 'Beyond the Creative City: Cognitive-Cultural Capitalism and the New Urbanism', *Regional Studies*, 48(4): 565–78.

Sennett, Richard. 2006. 'The Open City', *Urban Age*, Berlin, pp. 1–5.

Shanks, Michael, David Platt, and William Rathje. 2004. 'The perfume of garbage: modernity and the archaeological', *Modernism/Modernity*, 11(1): 61–83.

Smith, Laurajane. 2006. *Uses of Heritage*. London: Routledge.

Symonds, James. 2004. 'Historical archaeology and the recent urban past', *International Journal of Heritage Studies*, 10(1): 33–48.

Tumarkin, Maria M. 2005. *Traumascapes: the power and fate of places transformed by tragedy*. Melbourne: Melbourne University Press.

Unearthing Detroit: Collections-based research at Wayne State. https://unearthdetroit. wordpress.com/ (accessed 25 April 2015).

UNESCO. 2013. 'Creative Cities Network Mission Statement'. http://www.unesco.org/ new/fileadmin/MULTIMEDIA/HQ/CLT/pdf/Mission_statement_Bologna_creative_ cities_meeting.pdf (accessed 25 April 2015).

UNESCO. 2015. 'Creative Cities Network'. http://en.unesco.org/creative-cities/ (accessed 8 Jan 2017).

Voss, Barbara L. 2012. 'Curation as Research. A Case Study in Orphaned and Under-reported Archaeological Collections', *Archaeological Dialogues*, 19(2): 145–69.

Wall, Diana diZerega. 1994. *The archaeology of gender: separating the spheres in urban archaeology*. New York: Plenum Press.

White, Carolyn. 2013. 'The Burning Man Festival and the Archaeology of Ephemeral and Temporary Gatherings'. In *Oxford Handbook of Contemporary Archaeology*, edited by Rodney Harrison, Paul Graves-Brown, and Angela Piccini, London: Oxford University Press, pp. 591–605.

Wilkie, Laurie. 2014. *Strung Out on Archaeology: An Introduction to Archaeological Research*. Walnut Creek: Left Coast Press.

Witmore, Christopher. 2012. 'The Realities of the Past: Archaeology, Object-Orientations, Pragmatology'. In *Modern Materials: papers from CHAT Oxford (2009)*, edited by Brent Fortenberry and Laura McAtackney, Oxford: Archaeopress.

Yamin, Rebecca. 2001. 'Becoming New York: The Five Points Neighborhood', *Historical Archaeology*, 35(3): 1–5.

Zimmerman, Larry, Courtney Singleton, and Jessica Welch. 2010. 'Activism and creating a translational archaeology of homelessness', *World Archaeology*, 42(3): 443–54.

Section I

Creativity

1

Artist Spaces in Berlin

Defining and Redefining a City through Contemporary Archaeology

Carolyn L. White and Steven Seidenberg

The contemporary city of Berlin is known for its art and for its community of practising artists, along with its 'weirdness, perpetual incompleteness, and outlandishness...and the liveliness inherent in these qualities' (Schneider 2014: 7). One of Berlin's primary energy currents comes from the role of artists and the creative verve that abounds in the city. Artists use and reuse the physical environment of the post-Berlin Wall city and the surrounding environs (the Wall was officially taken down in 1989, although parts of it still remain) in temporary and permanent project spaces. The buildings and project spaces artists occupy are entwined with the history of the city— a history manifest in the city's form, aesthetics, and economics. A similar dialectic exists inside artist spaces; artists actively define and redefine studio spaces through their practices as their manners and methods are simultaneously defined, confined, and reflective of the restrictions and allowances that interiors provide. This chapter is a contemporary archaeological analysis of the physical elements of four artists' studios and buildings, the placement of artist communities within the city, and an exploration of the meanings of space and community in broader context. We highlight the reuse of historically significant buildings and the materiality and physicality of artists' spaces within a broader context of the political economy of creativity.

The use of Berlin for creative practice reflects many of the problems associated with the 'Creative City' and so-called creative economy. The art practices inside studios are reflective of the political economy of the world of art. The placement, availability, and tenuousness of the buildings themselves attest to problems associated with the adoption of creative capital by neoliberal capitalist agendas. The archaeological project can be used to document the micro and the macro—the interior and the exterior—of the economically circumscribed worlds of the artist, documenting an important moment in the development of a global cultural hotspot.

The chapter considers project spaces as both physical places and conceptual spaces among Berlin artists focusing on the geographic, ephemeral, and enduring spaces of artist studios. What do project spaces in Berlin look like? How do individual artists create their spaces? How does the physical space reflect artistic practices? How is the idea of the ruined city embraced, rejected, or ignored in artists' spaces? How does the idea of the creative city as exported by economists mesh with the reality of Berlin's metropolis of artists? Can the 'creative' survive in the new creative city?

1.1 THE ARCHAEOLOGY OF THE ARTIST STUDIO

Many artists have considered the relationship between art and archaeology as part of contemporary artistic practice (see Russell, Chapter 2). Artists have used archaeological techniques and tropes in their practice to comment on and question multitudinous themes, among them ideas of scientific authority; modes of collecting, sorting, and describing; and narrative creation. Mark Dion, Mike Kelley, and Simon Fujiwara are just three major artists who have explored these themes and garnered significant attention in doing so (for a more expansive discussion on this theme and the relationship today between art and archaeological practices, see Bailey 2014). More recently, archaeologists have begun to engage with aspects of art making from an array of angles (including contributors to Russell and Cochrane 2014). This project shares ideas and influences with recent scholarship that reaches between the two worlds in various forms and practices.

In particular, the highly influential removal and reinstallation of Francis Bacon's studio from London to Dublin using archaeological methodologies can inspire us to explore the physical world of the artist (O'Connor 2014). We admired the use of archaeology as a recording method in service to curation, but wanted to understand artist spaces as active and continuously changing places. A confluence of factors surrounding the artist Simon Fujiwara was key to the project. Harrison's illuminating use of Fujiwara's Frozen City as an illustration of the impact of archaeological tropes (2011: 149) catalysed our thinking about the intersection between art and archaeology from the side of the artist. A fortuitous personal encounter with Mr Fujiwara resulted in an invitation to his Berlin studio as he invited us to turn the trope on its head by doing an archaeology of his studio (White 2013b). Finally, one of our projects on temporary spaces and the role that art plays in Black Rock City led us to apply archaeological fieldwork techniques developed in one urban, art-oriented environment to another (White 2013a).

In 2013 we conducted archaeological fieldwork consisting of survey, mapping, and photographic documentation (both artistic and archaeological; White 2013b) along with personal interviews at nineteen artists' studios ranging from temporary spaces to large properties owned by world famous artists. Five are taken up in this article—Tacheles, GlogauAIR artists Lauren Chipeur and Emma Dixon, Wolfgang Ganter, and Elmgreen and Dragset. The physical spaces that were occupied by these artists varied considerably, dependent on length of time in the city and the success level of the individual artist although all of the selected studios were located in historic or formerly industrial buildings repurposed for artistic production.

1.2 OCCUPIED SPACE IN PAST, PRESENT, AND FUTURE

The city of Berlin is a place of decay, of open spaces, and of painful memory hybridized with around-the-clock vibrancy and vitality (see Ernsten, Chapter 10, for Cape Town as a comparative). The monolithic architecture covered in graffiti is alien to many outsiders' eyes, but to a Berliner (temporary or permanent) the indecipherable scribble on every building façade and exposed wall is a reflection of the mutability, irreverence, and participatory nature of life in the city. The city is marked by human hands; emblematic of the embracement of decay, discovery, and adventure in post-Wall Berlin. This creativity extends to the manipulation of interior space as Berlin's artists' project spaces embody the same creativity and manipulation of place.

The role of temporariness in artists' lives, issues of subject selection and the effect of timing on data collection and results, the fluidity of the present, and the 'presencing of absence' (Buchli and Lucas 2001: 122)—what exists in the present but not in the past—along with the ways that active spaces are both full and empty (see also Fowles and Heupel 2013) and left vacant when active are accessible in these project spaces. Interviews with current artists (permanent and temporary residents of Berlin) helped to understand the relationship between past, present, and future as enacted in the city.

The four project spaces discussed here are located across the city of Berlin, a city of 3.5 million people in a space that could hold 4.5 million. The inverse relationship between people and space means that real estate does not have the same premium that it does in other world capitals (London, Paris, New York, Tokyo). Housing is relatively cheap, and artists are able to live in Berlin inexpensively, even as they work to sell their art in other countries since the local art market is poor. The setting of Berlin offers an opportunity to build on important early work in contemporary archaeology as it bridges the divide between archaeology and ethnography.

The archaeology of artist studios in Berlin is firmly an archaeology *in* and *of* the present (vis-à-vis Harrison 2011). At the same time this project is also an ethnographic one, in which the techniques of the cultural anthropologist (participant observation, semi-structured interviews) are used nearly as much as those in the archaeologist's arsenal. A primary aspect of this research centres on time, developing 1) an archaeology of the present that focuses on occupied spaces, and 2) an ethnography of the material past, considering both the temporary and enduring aspects of the community of artist squats and reused industrial buildings. In engaging with sites that are not yet abandoned, we join the ranks of other scholars interested in actively occupied places (see also Yaneva 2013; Schofield 2013; Holtorf 2013). Projects like this one stand apart from those that examine abandoned places and the multitudinous meanings bound up in derelict spaces and 'ruin' more generally (e.g. Olsen and Pétursdóttir 2014; Lucas 2013; contributions to this volume). The cyclical nature of artist resident communities and the fluid nature of artist lives— many artists stay for short periods of time and others linger and become permanent residents of Berlin—allows a consideration of the relationship between past, present, and future permutations of the same space.

1.3 IS THE RISE OF THE 'CREATIVE CITY' THE FALL OF *ZWISCHENNUTZUNG*?

Much of the vibrancy of Berlin emerges from its irreverent attitudes toward Western capitalism and mainstream culture. Known for its artist squats, lo-fi aesthetic, techno music, re-use of industrial spaces, and temporary use projects— *Zwischennutzung* in German—Berlin hosts creative practitioners that take many paths toward self-expression. The gritty and alternative aesthetic is bound up with an 'anything goes' attitude and the imaginative energy in the city is palpable.

Artist spaces reflect many of the modes of creativity that characterize Berlin. The placement of the artist communities, the kinds of spaces created, and the changes seen today in those places reflect a number of historical trends in Berlin. As we discuss in the following pages (see the discussion of Jakob's work in particular), those trends raise questions about the role of gentrification, capitalism, and corporatization bound up with the creative class in urban development.

Berlin's development reflects the bright and dark sides of the 'Creative City', an idea conceptualized by Richard Florida and Charles Landry. Richard Florida's vision of productivity and generation of capital (Florida 2003, 2002) is well known in urban studies circles, but less so in archaeological scholarship. Florida positions 'creative people' as the catalysts for economic growth; industry follows creative people or is created by them in places where creative people cluster. 'Creative centres provide the integrated ecosystem or habitat where all forms of creativity—artistic and cultural, technological and economic—can take root and flourish' (Florida 2003: 9). Bohemians (artists, musicians, and writers) form an important part of the creative tissue that generates the attractiveness of a city as a place to live. According to Florida, 'The Bohemian Index turns out to be an amazingly strong predictor of everything from a region's high-technology base to its overall population and employment growth' (2003: 13).

Florida's work is controversial, and critics question almost every facet of his creative class model (Lang and Florida 2005 and Peck 2005 summarize these critiques). A thorough evaluation of the work is beyond the scope of this piece, but scholars have raised important questions about the validity of statistics gathered to construct his quantitative measurements and the problems with correlation vs causation in his model more generally. Others accuse Florida of more insidious intentions: that his work trivializes what economic development is and that it fails large swaths of society by replacing ideas of serving populations with simplistic and disingenuously positive solutions to deeper problems. Despite this controversy, Florida's work has been heralded by planners and civic chambers of commerce to bolster urban growth around the world (cf. Peck 2005). Its impact has been seismic.

Building on Florida's work, Charles Landry and Franco Bianchini developed the concept of the 'Creative City' for urban planners to nurture creativity in cities so as to engender urban vitality and its economic benefits (Landry and Bianchini 1995). Their initiatives included streamlining bureaucracies, creating more opportunities for creativity, greening cities, and encouraging community participation. In 2004 UNESCO developed the UNESCO Creative City network formed on the concepts popularized by Landry and Bianchini. The aim of the network is to 'develop international cooperation among cities that have identified creativity as a strategic factor for sustainable development' (UNESCO 2013). Thematic groupings of literature, film, music, crafts and folk art, design, media arts, and gastronomy are used to connect cities seeking to emphasize the creative economy, to push their cultural products outward, and to work with other urban centres to exchange knowledge. Berlin became a UNESCO Creative City in 2005 as part of the design network (UNESCO 2015) and Berlin is widely touted now as a Creative City. With this moniker, government officials and city planners have embraced what is often characterized as a neoliberal attitude toward inviting investment through a commodification of creativity (see Harvey 2005).

Jakob has written eloquently of the corporatization of creativity in Berlin, noting in particular the ways that the city has been working to 'reframe and repackage an entrepreneurial model of urban governance and development geared towards attracting highly mobile capital and professional elites with environments to live and work in as well as to consume and invest into that are lively yet safe, diverse yet controlled, and artistic yet profit-driven' (Jakob 2010: 194). She describes the ways government officials have marketed the creativity of Berlin rhetorically while clearing the way for major urban development at the expense of city residents, particularly those of lower socio-economic sectors.

The place of artists' spaces in Berlin, then, is reflective of the lightness and of the shadows of the creative city. Many of the artist spaces in Berlin discussed below come out of 'conditions of *Zwischennutzung*—the temporary, in-between use of abandoned space for little to no rent' (Jakob 2010: 195). Such spaces are generally embraced by local governments, but only until there are more lucrative opportunities for city development. The creative communities in Berlin foretell the future of the neighbourhood—as more artists move into a neighbourhood, that part of the city draws additional commerce—the countdown toward increased desirability and an infusion of capital begins. The artists, then, pave the pathway to their own expulsion unless their own international reputation and marketability rises synchronously with property values.

1.4 THE HISTORICAL CIRCUMSTANCES OF *ZWISCHENNUTZUNG*

Berlin is a haven for artists because of its cheap rent and low cost of living as well as the existing liveliness of the art scene. Described as 'poor but sexy' (*Berlin ist arm, aber sexy*) by its mayor Klaus Wowereit in 2004, the allure of the ruin and the bargain still drives life in the city. The places occupied by artists range from converted schools, light industrial buildings, apartment buildings, municipal spaces, and larger industrial spaces. The historical trajectory of Berlin and the impact of the history on its physical form are important factors in its current place as a centre for artistic practice. Berlin's history is raw, made visible through formal monuments and memorials and through the extant scars and marks on the landscape. As Huyessen noted, Berlin is a 'historical text, marked as much, if not more, by absences as by the visible presence of its past, from prominent ruins such as the Kaiser-Wilhelm-Gedichtniskirche...to World War II bullet and shrapnel marks on...its buildings' (1997: 60). The absences and presences result from two recent periods in its history: World War II/Nazi Berlin and the Cold War period and subsequent reunification directly intersect with artist spaces throughout the city.

While World War II and the Cold War period are not the subject of this paper (see Huyessen 1997 for more on the subject of voids and Berlin's history), these historical periods directly impact the built environment of the city. The extensive bombing during World War II, in concert with the Third Reich's own architectural agenda which demolished buildings to make way for large scale boulevards and monuments, resulted in a city of rubble and ruin (basements, abandoned buildings, and any available voids were used to remove what was ultimately 55 million cubic metres of rubble created during the bombing of the city; Diefendorf 1993: 15). Clearing the rubble took many years, and recovery was slow. The forcible removal and murder of large swaths of the population meant that after World War II the title of much of the property was unknown, and it took many years for ownership claims of central areas of Berlin real estate to be resolved. In the 1950s urban renewal resulted in the razing of additional stretches of Berlin buildings to make way for modern architecture (Huyessen 1997: 63–4).

During the Cold War period of Berlin's history, when the city was divided into East and West, the Wall that sliced the city into two created voids in Berlin on either side of it. On the eastern side, the large expanse that was no man's land behind the Wall itself was empty. On the western side of the Wall, adjacent buildings were uninhabited on account of their proximity and associated stigma and danger. Huyessen described the space of the Wall after it came down in 1989/90:

> For a couple of years, the very center of Berlin, the threshold between the Eastern and the Western parts of the city, was a seventeen-acre wasteland that extended from the Brandenburg Gate down to Potsdamer Platz and Leipziger Platz, a wide stretch of dirt, grass, and remnants of pavement under a big sky that seemed even bigger given the absence of a high-rise skyline that is so characteristic of this city. Berliners called it affectionately their 'wonderful city steppes,' their 'prairie of history.' (1997: 64)

Almost twenty-five years later, redevelopment has filled in and transformed many of the holes, often on a massive commercial scale by large developers. There remain many blocks throughout the city that are as yet undeveloped, and empty disused spaces have been colonized for *Zwischennutzung* (temporary use) by 'space pioneers' (Overmeyer 2007)—people who create alternative spaces in otherwise abandoned spaces. In Berlin, there has been some success in blocking massive commercial redevelopment through demonstrations and protests, often led by 'creatives' or cultural producers, including artists (Novy and Colomb 2013; Harvey 2001). The alternative uses of space and the prominence of creative activity have been critical in the rise of Berlin as a creative place.

The popular press contains myriad articles about the impending end of Berlin as a place for creativity and for cultural alternativity (e.g. 'Berlin is

"Over," But So What?' [Pitu 2014] or 'Is Berlin "Over?" Yawn' [Pearson 2014]). Although these articles have just as many counterpoints, the role of gentrification and its associated ills cannot be ignored (e.g. there has been an 80 per cent increase in rent in some Berlin neighbourhoods since 2008; see Ernsten, Chapter 10, on critiques of gentrification in Cape Town). How will these changes affect the world of artist's spaces? Is the city of Berlin at a turning point in respect to its alternative use of space? Is the vivacity of the city threatened by new strains of urban development? The impact of development has meant that many of the buildings and spaces that were used and inhabited by artists have been reclaimed for development and as buildings are renovated, rents rise. The creatives on the front edge of the space frontier, the 'settlers' in both a positive and negative sense, are pushed aside, victims of infusions of new capital.

1.4.1 Tacheles

One of the most iconic examples of Berlin's art squat past is that of Tacheles, located in Mitte, formerly in East Berlin. Tacheles was occupied by artists after the fall of the Berlin Wall in 1989. The building is very close to the location of the former Wall and the spaces near the Wall were undesirable in the divided city. After the Wall fell, many of the buildings along the Wall were unoccupied and thus were taken over by squatters. There were many buildings like Tacheles throughout Berlin, but Tacheles is the most well-known and serves as an important case study. Its location in central Berlin, on Oranienburger Straße, made the squat a prominent icon, an emblem of the edginess and artistic nature of Berlin. But it also made the squat vulnerable to displacement, as the property was deemed valuable for development, and ultimately the demise of the squat lay in seeds planted early in its existence.

The physical space of Tacheles is on a large scale. The building was constructed as a department store in 1908, but the venture was unsuccessful and the company filed for bankruptcy in August of that year. Wolf Wetheim rented the space in 1909 and opened a department store called Friedrich-straßenpassage that operated until 1914.

The use of the building between 1914 and 1924 is not easily traceable but in 1928 the building was sold to the German Engineering Company, AEG, where it was renamed Haus der Technik (http://www.kunsthaus-tacheles.de/institu tion/history/). In 1934 it was taken over by the Nazi Party where it served as administrative offices. During the war it housed French prisoners of war used as a human shield for German communications (http://www.kunsthaus-tacheles.de/institution/history/). The building was damaged in the bombing of Berlin, but not irrevocably.

After the war it was owned by the German Democratic Republic (GDR); it was in poor condition and close to the Wall therefore only small portions of the building were utilized. It housed several stores and an art school briefly. The government conducted engineering surveys in 1969 and 1977 and determined that the building should be demolished and the property redeveloped. Large pieces of the building were torn down but the construction never commenced due to lack of funds.

After the fall of the Wall, many buildings like Tacheles were unoccupied in central Berlin. One artist described the post-Wall atmosphere: 'You went into a house, doors were open, and you just lived there' (Martin Reiter, pers comm, 2013). Development was slow after the unification of the city, with titles being difficult to resolve given the extermination of many property owners in what had been the Jewish neighbourhood of Berlin. The building was planned for demolition, but two months before it was to take place, the building was occupied by a group of artists and musicians, who formed a collective called TACHELES (Yiddish for 'straight-talking') on 13 February 1990. A last minute injunction by the Berlin Round Table delayed demolition. The artists commissioned a new engineering survey, and the structure was deemed to be sound. It was officially declared a historic landmark in 1992.

In the mid-1990s the developer Fundus Group purchased the property from the city. In 1998 the developer gave the artists squatting in the building a 10-year lease at a nominal fee. As part of this agreement, renovations to the building were undertaken (discussed in §1.4.1.1). The renovation created new livable space, new studio spaces, and a new gallery. The garden house was taken down during this renovation.

Following an extension of the lease for one year, the contracted lease expired in 2009, so the residents were squatters once again. The Fundus Group was bankrupt at this time, and in 2011 they sold it to HSH Nordbank in partial payment for debts. HSH Nordbank in 2011 put up the property for auction and began proceeding to remove the artists from the space by scheduling evictions. At the time of the sale, extant internal divisions in the arthouse crystallized and a portion of the group accepted a €1 million payment for vacating the property. The rest of the collective continued to stay in the property, seeking a long-term solution. Although the residents fought the eviction in court and through prominent demonstrations, they were ultimately unsuccessful. The squat was finally cleared on 4 September 2012. In spring 2013 the core organizers had relocated to Potsdam, moving the Tacheles archives and some of the artwork associated with the collective.

1.4.1.1 The Space of Tacheles

Initially, the space of Tacheles was conceived as a counterpoint to established cultural practices in Berlin (http://www.kunsthaus-tacheles.de/institution/history/).

The intent of the collective was as an experimental, young, creative, international alternative art scene. The space was used for exhibitions, music events, theatre performances, open studios and workshops, music studios, and other perform-ances. Contrary to popular perception, artists did not live in the house, but used it for working space (Martin Reiter, pers comm, 2013).

The physical form of the building was dilapidated, and the ruinous charac-ter of the building was intrinsic to its identity. When the artists worked with the building owners to renovate the building in 2000, they chose a design that retained the 'ruin' character. Prior to its renovation, the back of the building was missing, exposing the interior spaces, rendering them uninhabitable. Many of the windows were broken and missing, and portions of the structure appeared to be crumbling. The renovations retained the crumbling, ragged character of the masonry, using glass to encase the ruin, preserving the exposed interior while making the spaces inhabitable. The preserved ruin references the processes of both disintegration and regeneration, crystallizing what DeSilvey describes as 'simultaneous resonances of death and rebirth, loss and renewal' (2006: 328).

When the building was first occupied, artists simply opened doors and moved into unoccupied rooms. Most of the ground floor and basement rooms were full of dirt deposited during rubble clearing following World War II. If someone wanted to occupy the space, they simply removed the dirt and moved into the space. In the early years artists used multiple studios. As time passed, the collective became more well-known and space became more limited. Some of the artists stayed at Tacheles for many years, but many stayed for one or two years. There were thirty-one artist studios that were leased to artists who applied to join for six—twelve months.

The building was open to the public twenty-four hours a day. Most of the space was dedicated to studio floors, which were relatively open. The artists worked in these spaces and tourists and visitors could interact with them. On the third floor there were music studios and an exhibition gallery. On the first floor there was a cinema, a theatre for exhibits and performances, and a restaurant. There were also workshops—a screen-printing workshop, a metal shop, a music studio, and small jewellery shops. On the top floor, was the 'Blue Salon' used for exhibits and as an experimental space as well as an open studio (http://www.kunsthaus-tacheles.de/institution/history/). The basement was cleared by the inhabitants in the early 1990s to house a disco. Between 1994 and 2000 there was a garden house outside that was placed in the former storage spaces. This connected the large open garden space with the house and there was a bar as well as a dance floor and exhibits in the space.

Martin Reiter described the atmosphere as 'very free' from 1990 to 1995. After 1995 factions began to develop, and these factions were divided along the lines of physical space. The tensions between the groups were polemical, and issues of jealousy, political differences, and disorganization began to plague the collective. The space was roughly divided into an 'Upstairs' and a 'Downstairs'. The Upstairs group consisted of the space in which the artists lived, with artists and their studios. The Downstairs group consisted of a range of business—most prominently the Café Zapata, a restaurant, and High End 54, a cinema. These businesses gradually became more independent from the artist collective and ultimately broke away, accepting payment to leave the space in 2011.

Interviews with former members of Tacheles bring forth many threads relating to issues of Berlin's development. The history of the site is entwined with politics, privatization of space, and secret deals. The future of the building today is unknown. Since it is a listed building, it cannot be torn down easily, and the interior cannot be altered. But, as Martin Reiter stated in 2013, 'if Berlin isn't interested in this place, then why bother? There is no point to having a squat just to have a squat.' Despite the successful eviction of its members, the property remained undeveloped in 2017.

1.4.2 GlogauAIR Studios

GlogauAIR Studios is located in Kreuzberg. Although formerly in West Berlin, Kreuzberg was historically one of poorest districts of the divided city; its development was checked by controlled rent policy and it was isolated since it was surrounded on three sides by the Wall. Historically it has been home to a large immigrant population (particularly Turkish), and to Berlin's alternative music and art scene.

GlogauAIR is housed in a modernist building designed as a school by the architect Ludwig Hoffmann, built in 1896. The main portion of the school was destroyed in bombing during World War II, and that space remains as an empty green space.

The space houses ten artists in live/work spaces, and artists occupy those spaces for periods of six to nine months. The population is international, and when we visited in 2013 artists from Greece, Argentina, Canada, England, America, Spain, and Japan were in residence (Irene Pascual, pers comm, 2013).

Lauren Chipeur, a Canadian, had very recently moved into her studio and was just beginning to work in the space when we visited her studio. She is a sculptor and performance artist, and the two media are usually integrated. Her space was sparse but also divided into her working and living space. She reported that she moved into the space as arranged, rearranged it, and moved it back to the way it was originally. She tries to keep the living space confined to a small area, and to keep the 'food situation' in one half of the room. The desk, in fact, held many pieces of paper, notebooks, drawing ideas, writing implements, but also held a coffee maker, bread, olives, and a ketchup bottle. Lauren's work had an archaeological character in that she was working with ideas of exchange (e.g. exchanging rocks for labour). She was also working with idea of a 'peelpal', where a person at distance would command an actor to peel away layers of a wax ball. When we visited her studio the first time she was working on the prototype and there was a small wax ball with associated debitage surrounding it. A subsequent visit displayed the finished piece in action during the open studio exhibition (held biannually at GlogauAIR). Many of the materials recorded during the first visit two months previous were redistributed around the room. The peelpal was used by visitors, and was placed in the middle of the space. All evidence of living in the space was hidden.

A second GlogauAIR artist underscores the self-awareness that artists have about the use of space, as well as the ways that their *actual* use contradicts their *ideas* about use. Emma Dixon is a performance artist from England. Her use of space is particularly self-conscious in that she clearly demarcated her living space from her working space by marking that division on the wall. Her space was divided into live and work areas, marked on the wall as art and life. She had taken the two water pipes that ran parallel on the wall and used these as an imposed boundary, labelling each side. At the time of our visit, her artistic practice was focused on dualisms, in particular on the distinctions between presence and absence. This work was manifest in multiple ways in her working space, though graphic representations, text posted on the wall, and through the organization of the space. Despite such cognizance, these lines blurred in practice—for example her laundry was drying on the 'art' side of the room.

The spaces at GlogauAIR are small, and artists can choose the ways that they use the space. The rooms are painted white (although artists can modify the colour). Furnishings are provided. But the neutrality of the spaces is designed to be easily changeable and to provide a backdrop for the different kinds of work that the visiting artists undertake. Over the course of the six-month residency, the workspace becomes more 'lived in', but generally the spaces are not modified very heavily. As one-room spaces, the artists made attempts to separate their 'work/art' space from their living spaces, but the actual use of the space was largely given over to the work. As artists stayed longer in these spaces, it was increasingly blended, even when the artist attempted to make the boundaries between those spaces distinct. Each artist is given the same furniture, so the rooms are furnished with similar objects, but arranged differently by each resident.

1.4.3 Wedding: UferHallen

Wolfgang Ganter's studio is located in the neighbourhood of Wedding. This district in the former West Berlin is one of the city's poorest and has not experienced noticeable gentrification to date. The neighbourhood is also home to many immigrant communities and its low rent has made it attractive to many artists. The space in which Ganter lives and works was transformed into artist spaces in 2008.

Today UferHallen is located in a large complex of historic buildings that were originally built between 1926 and 1931. These buildings were part of the Great Berlin Horse Railway and operated as a depot. After World War II, the Berliner Verkehrsbetriebe (Berlin Transport Organization, BVG) used the workshops for repairing their buses. In 2008 UferHallen GmbH leased the buildings for twenty-five years and they were renovated for use by artists. They are desirable and inexpensive places, housing artists, musicians, and other creative practitioners.

One of those residents is Wolfgang Ganter, a photographer. Ganter was one of the first residents in the studios. He rents a studio space and lives in a separate apartment. Ganter's art practice is multi-staged and the physical space that he occupies reflects different stages of practice. Ganter takes slides with images that he has captured or obtained from others and injects the slide with bacteria that he incubates. The bacterium affects the slide in different ways, degrading the image or transforming it, creating a decayed aesthetic. These slides are then scanned, enlarged, digitally stitched together, and printed in large format. Ganter builds a large frame from wood, attaches the image to the frame, and lacquers the surface.

The spatial division of tasks is largely determined by the kind and quantity of mess that they produce. As such, Ganter moves between three distinct areas in his spaces. There is an 'outside' space in the studio (Colour plate 1), an 'inside' space in the studio (Colour plate 2), and his living space. The area outside his living space in the courtyard operates as a seasonal fourth space.

Although each of these spaces has its own set of practices associated with it, the use of the space is nonlinear. For example, the outside space has multiple uses: it is used to build the frames for the artwork, to store finished pieces, and to coat the framed pieces with resin. Although it was also described as the 'dust' space since it is often given over to framemaking and its associated sawdust, when the space is used to apply the resin to the finished work, it must be free of dust, so the space is cleaned thoroughly. The 'outside' area is also used to stage artwork before it is taken to exhibitions.

The 'inside' space serves many functions. It is separated from the 'outside' space by plastic sheeting (still the original piece; Colour plate 1). Like most of the studio, it is packed from floor to ceiling with all manner of art supplies and chemicals, but the primary use of the space is to examine slides on the light tables and to inject and incubate the bacteria (Colour plate 2 and Figure 1.1). Much of this work is dirty and odiferous, and although it is described as free of dust, it is in many ways the dirtiest space in the

Figure 1.1. Wolfgang Ganter's studio 'inside space'; detail of syringes and film in the studio. Photo by Steven Seidenberg.

studio.[1] Although Ganter works in the space frequently in winter, in the summer, he spends time outside examining slides to move away from the smells associated with the bacteria incubation. The intensity of the use of each of the spaces varies depending on the stage of his practice for individual pieces.

Ganter was the first person to rent a studio, and like many other artists, he has modified his space considerably. He described it as a submarine, in that no vacant space was unused. He built the 'inside' space in the studio using recycled wood, and other found materials. Within that space he built the shelving. He also modified the space to create storage around the perimeter of the studio as well as above the 'inside' studio.

[1] In fact, the space was described by Ganter as containing bacteria that could cause infection, so we were instructed not to touch anything and to wash our hands immediately after the visit.

Ganter's workspace and artistic practice aligns with many others in Berlin. He makes a living, but it is a modest one and it is made possible by the low rent in Berlin and his success in showing and selling his work outside Berlin. His space, and his daily life, is given over to his artistic practice, blending the working space with the living space and vice versa.

1.4.4 Neukölln: Elmgreen and Dragset

The studio of Elmgreen and Dragset operates at a massive scale. Elmgreen and Dragset are installation artists of international renown. Their live/work space is in a renovated Neukölln water-pumping station (Colour plate 3, top). Like many of the districts discussed in this paper, the neighbourhood is largely comprised of non-German residents, but it has also been the locus for significant gentrification as artists and students have moved into the area, rents have increased and tensions have emerged between the two populations (Mendoza 2011).

The Elmgreen and Dragset space is colossal at 1,000 square metres. The building was a water pumping station that was abandoned in 1990, replaced by the station that sits next to it today. The duo purchased the building in 2008 and renovated it, using the space as studio, office, and living space. Since then, they have both moved out, and the space no longer serves as a full-time living space, rather it serves multiple functions and is the workspace for a large team of people.

Beginning on the main floor, the large central volume of the space is visible immediately on entry (Colour plate 3, bottom). The ground floor has a very large open space that is the main area of the building, and is four storeys tall. This space has multiple functions. It is used to stage exhibition work that is under construction (when we visited two areas were used for planning the *Tomorrow* exhibition at the Victoria and Albert Museum, London). A set of shelves on the eastern edge of the main space was used to store catalogues, media, and pieces from various installations. There are other pieces of installations distributed around the space as well, stored and displayed at the same time. Finally, this space serves as entrance and egress to the building. Near the door a bike was stored, and just to the side of the front door there was domestic refuse waiting to be brought outside.

The second and third floors are carved out of a portion of the building in the back. On the ground floor, at the back is a kitchen and dining room that also functions as a meeting room. This is a communal kitchen space used by the seven people that comprise the Elmgreen and Dragset staff. The staff eat lunch together on a regular basis, and the food is prepared and consumed in that space.

Just above the kitchen on the third floor is the working space of the staff. The space has seven desks distributed throughout, most are dedicated full time to a single person. Some of the desks are shared. This space is used as a

Figure 1.2. Fourth floor of Elmgreen and Dragset studio. Photo by Steven Seidenberg.

workspace only in the winter. In the summer the staff move to the mezzanine that overlook the main space (Colour plate 3, bottom). The mezzanine is used as workspace for half of the year, with staff desks located in the space. The large space is cold in winter, so the staff move to the smaller room, which can be heated more effectively. The mezzanine also houses books and other materials tucked into some of the interstitial spaces, but is largely empty.

The fourth floor is another full floor and is a large apartment with a small bedroom, kitchen, and bathroom along with a vast living space. The space is dramatically and sparingly furnished with clusters of furniture that create small sitting areas (Figure 1.2). In addition to these areas, there are taxidermied animals, large pieces of sculpture, photographs, and stereo equipment spread throughout the space. A small apartment is located in the back portion of the building. The space is no longer the 'live' space of the studio, but is used for functions, for meetings, and for staff yoga classes. Ingar Dragset uses the space to read and think, since there is no computer there (pers comm, 2013). In the rear of the first floor is a small workshop where some of the more messy artistic practices are undertaken. At the time of my visit, a staff person who was gold plating a sculpture used the space.

The space of Elmgreen and Dragset is more than simply a place to make art. Like the work the artists produce that offers commentary on museums, collectors and the art of spectacle, the space is a showplace of the team. Although designed as a live/work space, neither of the artists lives in the space, but it functions as an office for the many employees they have to fabricate and conceptualize their work.

1.5 THE VALUE OF EXAMINING ARTISTS' STUDIOS

The archaeology of artists' studios in Berlin intertwines standard archaeological practices and ethnographic techniques to explore the world of artistic practices in contemporary Berlin. As such, the micro-scalar approach of detailed mapping and photography of the studios highlights the layered actions of their activity, rendering their often-unconsidered actions visible. In addition, semi-structured interviews and participant observation permit a deeper level of engagement with the people who make the spaces, drawing connections between the artists' intent (or lack thereof) and the physical spaces. We look intensively into the intentionality around the production of space on a personal scale while simultaneously observing how the actions and products of the artists connect to the broader world of the city and of the art market. The process of engaging directly with the inhabitants of these spaces as the process of mapping and documenting the space occurs, allows for a nuanced understanding of how these spaces are invested with meaning by their inhabitants. This project focuses on one spatial niche, artist studios, but it models an approach that can be applied to many living and working spaces.

Ranging from the very temporary to the more permanent, the spaces occupied by these artists are housed in historical buildings that are reused in innovative ways. Department stores, bus depots, school rectories, and water pumping stations are but a few of the sorts of spaces that have been taken up by artists working in Berlin. International in flavour, diverse in artistic practice, and blending public and private, living and working, the materiality and physicality of these spaces are but a mere few of thousands extant in contemporary Berlin.

The examples presented attempt to show what some of the spaces look like and help us recognize how such spaces are transformable, ephemeral, permanent, and contested. The four spaces discussed in this chapter offer a slice of artistic life at a particular moment in Berlin's history. They range from the small and temporary, as seen at the GlogauAIR studios, to the colossal and established, as seen by the Elmgreen and Dragset space. Of course the largest and seemingly most permanent was Tacheles; while the building is still extant, it is now an empty and hulking reminder of the post-Wall past of the Mitte district. It acts as proof that the most enduring space can become the most ephemeral. Tacheles is but one of many spaces directly transformed by major redevelopment in the ongoing conflict between grassroots creativity and governmental visions of economic vitality.

This archaeological project examines single sites of artistic practice and in doing so records the spatiality and materiality of a day, a week, or a month in the life of the space. The actual people, the actual work, and the actual spaces in action are documented through the project. The relationship between space, practice, and political economy is too often vague and faceless. Who are the artists that make the city turn? Who are the people who are behind the numbers in a Floridian Bohemian index? In addition to the important task of putting faces on people (see Tringham 1991), in detailing people in their spaces, the diversity of life is made visible.

Finally, in documenting the spaces used by artists in a place like Berlin, the relationship between the broader economic trends that occur outside the artist walls and those that happen within comes into sharper focus. At a prosaic level: the larger the studio, the bigger the work that can come out of the studio. More marginal artists live in peripheral areas, share space, and make physical innovations that condition their art practices. The political economy of scale directly impacts the practices of working artists, and the most successful artists—those with a market—are able to support themselves and others even as the urban space around them moves through processes of gentrification and commercialization.

At the beginning of this piece we posed the question, 'Can the creative survive in the new "Creative City"?' Our work highlights the fact that the success of the creative city ultimately jeopardizes many who build it (for parallels in Detroit, see Ryzewski, Chapter 3). Many artists who founded the creative culture, particularly after the fall of the Wall in 1989, have been forced to move out and on. Tacheles is the most visible of many instances of gentrification and corporate redevelopment. Each of the spaces documented in this project attest to the ways that Berlin's project spaces are embodied within the creative city concept. They also foretell the future of their neighbourhoods, breaking ground for impending capital investment at an approaching but unknown date. This project documents these spaces in anticipation of their inevitable disappearance.

REFERENCES

Bailey, Doug. 2014. 'Art//Archaeology//Art: Letting-Go Beyond'. In *Art and Archaeology: Collaborations, Conversations, Criticisms*, edited by Ian Alden Russell and Andrew Cochrane, New York: Springer, pp. 231–50.

Buchli, Victor and Gavin Lucas. 2001. *Archaeologies of the Contemporary Past*. London: Routledge.

DeSilvey, Caitlin. 2006. 'Observed Decay: Telling Stories with Mutable Things', *Journal of Material Culture*, 11: 318–38.

Diefendorf, Jeffrey M. 1993. *In the Wake of War: The Reconstruction of German Cities after World War II*. Oxford: Oxford University Press.

Florida, Richard. 2002. *The Rise of the Creative Class: And How It's Transforming Work, Leisure, Community and Everyday Life*. New York: Basic Books.

Florida, Richard. 2003. 'Cities and the Creative Class', *City & Community*, 2: 3–19.

Fowles, Severin and Kaet Heupel. 2013. 'Absence'. In *Oxford Handbook of Contemporary Archaeology*, edited by Rodney Harrison, Paul Graves-Brown, and Angela Piccini, Oxford: Oxford University Press, pp. 178–91.

Harrison, Rodney. 2011. 'Surface Assemblages: Towards an archaeology in and of the present', *Archaeological Dialogues*, 18(2): 141–61.

Harvey, David. 2001. *Spaces of Hope*. Berkeley: University of California Press.

Harvey, David. 2005. *A Brief History of Neoliberalism*. Oxford: Oxford University Press.

Holtorf, Cornelius. 2013. 'Material Animals: An Archaeology of Contemporary Zoo Experiences'. In *Oxford Handbook of Contemporary Archaeology*, edited by Rodney Harrison, Paul Graves-Brown, and Angela Piccini, Oxford: Oxford University Press, pp. 627–41.

Huyssen, Andreas. 1997. 'The Voids of Berlin', *Critical Inquiry*, 24(1): 57–81.

Jakob, Doreen. 2010. 'Constructing the creative neighborhood: Hopes and limitations of creative city policies in Berlin', *City, Culture, and Society*, 1: 193–8.

Kunsthaus Diaspora. 2017. 'History'. http://www.kunsthaus-tacheles.de/institution/history (accessed 16 January 2017).

Landry, Charles and Franco Bianchini. 1995. *The Creative City*. London: Demos.

Lang, Robert E. and Richard Florida. 2005. 'Review Roundtable: Cities and the Creative Class/Discussion/Response', *Journal of the American Planning Association*, 71(2): 203–20.

Lucas, Gavin. 2013. 'Ruins'. In *Oxford Handbook of Contemporary Archaeology*, edited by Rodney Harrison, Paul Graves-Brown, and Angela Piccini, Oxford: Oxford University Press, pp. 192–203.

Mendoza, Moises. 2011. 'Foreigners feel accused in Berlin Gentrification Row', *De Spiegel*, 3 November.

Novy, Johannes and Claire Colomb. 2013. 'Struggling for the Right to the (Creative) City in Berlin and Hamburg: New Urban Social Movements, New "Spaces of Hope"?', *International Journal of Urban and Regional Research*, 37(5): 1816–38.

O'Connor, Blaze. 2014. 'Dust and Debitage: An Archaeology of Francis Bacon's Studio'. In *Art and Archaeology: Collaborations, Conversations, Criticisms*, edited by Ian Alden Russell and Andrew Cochrane, New York: Springer, pp. 131–9.

Olsen, Bjørnar and Þóra Pétursdóttir (eds). 2014. *Ruin Memories: Materialities, Aesthetics and the Archaeology of the Recent Past*. Abingdon: Routledge.

Pearson, Joseph. 2014. 'Is Berlin "Over?" Yawn'. http://needleberlin.com/2014/03/08/is-berlin-over (accessed 12 July 2014).

Peck, Jamie. 2005. 'Struggling with the Creative Class', *International Journal of Urban and Regional Research*, 29(4): 740–70.

Pitu, Lavinia. 2014. 'Berlin is "Over," But So What?'. http://www.dw.de/berlin-is-over-but-so-what/a-17492413 (accessed 12 July 2014).

Russell, Ian Alden and Andrew Cochrane. 2014. *Art and Archaeology: Collaborations, Conversations, Criticisms*. New York: Springer.

Schneider, Peter. 2014. *Berlin Now: The City After the Wall*. New York: Farrar, Straus and Giroux.

Schofield, John. 2013. '"A Dirtier Reality?" Archaeological Methods and the Urban Project'. In *Oxford Handbook of Contemporary Archaeology*, edited by Rodney Harrison, Paul Graves-Brown, and Angela Piccini, Oxford: Oxford University Press, pp. 466–78.

Tringham, Ruth. 1991. 'Households with Faces: The Challenge of Gender in Prehistoric Architectural Remains'. In *Engendering Archaeology: Women and Prehistory*, edited by Joan Gero and Meg Conkey, Oxford: Blackwell Publishers, pp. 93–131.

UNESCO. 2013. 'Creative Cities Network Mission Statement'. http://www.unesco.org/new/fileadmin/MULTIMEDIA/HQ/CLT/pdf/Mission_statement_Bologna_creative_cities_meeting.pdf (accessed 15 March 2015).

UNESCO. 2015. 'Creative Cities Network'. http://www.unesco.org/new/en/culture/themes/creativity/creative-cities-network/design/ (accessed 15 March 2015).

White, Carolyn. 2013a. 'The Burning Man Festival and the Archaeology of Ephemeral and Temporary Gatherings'. In *Oxford Handbook of Contemporary Archaeology*, edited by Rodney Harrison, Paul Graves-Brown, and Angela Piccini, Oxford: Oxford University Press, pp. 591–605.

White, Carolyn. 2013b. 'The Archaeology of Art in Berlin'. Paper presented at the Contemporary and Historical Archaeology in Theory Conference, London, England.

Yaneva, Albena. 2013. 'Actor-Network-Theory Approaches to the Archaeology of Contemporary Architecture'. In *Oxford Handbook of Contemporary Archaeology*, edited by Rodney Harrison, Paul Graves-Brown, and Angela Piccini, Oxford: Oxford University Press, pp. 121–34.

2

Cultural Heritage and Political Ecology

A Modest Proposal from Istanbul via Detroit

Ian Alden Russell

2.1 REFLEXIVE ACKNOWLEDGEMENT

I am a white, middle-class, man born in Richmond, Virginia, educated in Dublin, Ireland, and who has worked in Istanbul. In Turkey, I was a *yabancı*—a foreigner. It was with an outsider's perspective that I worked to develop the curatorial sensibilities and sensitivities around the project presented here. I do not speak *for* those in Turkey, nor do I speak for those living in Detroit. I only hoped to speak *with* those in Turkey and offer an honest reflection on my experiences in Detroit. In as far as I am able, I hope to lend my voice and my care to sharing experiences and issues which I can only make limited claims to understand but which I feel are profoundly urgent.

2.2 AN UPTURNED CUP OF TURKISH COFFEE

A ritual that happens every day at countless café tables throughout Istanbul. This is the moment of anticipation—the moment before the amateur tasseo-grapher turns over the cup and reads your fortune in the coffee grounds. In my walks around the streets of Istanbul, I've paused to witness friends peer into each other's futures, and I've wondered if one question many are asking is: 'İstanbul'un kısmetinde ne var? What's in Istanbul's fortune?'

There is a vital connection (and tension) between the past and the future. They are both entangled in our encounters with material things. What is this thing's story, how did it get here, and what should we do with it? How do we negotiate these tensions—to save or discard, to record or omit, or simply to consume? More broadly, how do we establish consensus on how we should handle, order, and pass on our material world? These are moral and political questions. They are questions about heritage and inheritance. What do we determine to be heritage, who are determined to be the stewards, and who are the inheritors?

2.3 A POLITICAL ECOLOGY

During the summer of 2013, different visions for the futures of Istanbul came into conflict. The events that began on 28 May 2013 in Gezi Park started with the defence of trees that were being removed in a planned demolition of the park for the development of a pseudo-historical Ottoman-era barracks and a shopping centre. It was reported widely in the media that Gezi Park was 'the last straw' in a long line of grievances against the government. The Gezi Park demonstrations and the ensuing protests speak, however, to a broad, shared issue in contemporary urban politics, one experienced not only in Istanbul but in many cities throughout the world. It concerns political ecology and the impact of neoliberal trends towards the privatization of public space on the integrity of civic life.[1]

In the words of archaeologist and theorist Ömür Harmanşah (2013):

> ...political ecology concerns the place- and space-based struggles of local com-
> munities across the world in coming to terms with development projects and the
> effects of globalization. It is about people's very human claims to their rights to
> local resources such as water, land, clean air, biodiversity, and cultural heritage.

Both Istanbul and Detroit are cities that span vast areas. Where Istanbul has been an increasingly overpopulated megalopolis shooting from a population of about two million in 1980 to nearly fifteen million (officially) today, Detroit has been rapidly depopulating from nearly two million residents in 1950 to just under 700,000 today. This divergence in population density makes the physical experience of these two cities vastly different; however, there are compelling similarities in the material semiotics of these tensions. In Istanbul there is protest over the governance and planning for shared public spaces, private development, and housing. Space is a scarce resource. In Detroit, there

---

[1] Political ecology is a broad, multidisciplinary field that has grown in influence and profile over the twentieth century since its introduction in the 1930s (see Thorne 1935: 14). Traditionally associated with the fields of human geography and human ecology, political ecology has become a discursive focus for a range of disciplines across the sciences and humanities concerned with the politicization of complex relationships between humans and the forces and dynamics of the material world. Most recently, critical theorist Bruno Latour (2004) addressed the term in his *Politics of Nature*.

is abundant space, but protest addresses the governance of shared resources and how they are distributed within that space. In material terms, in Istanbul, the debate began with saving trees, and in Detroit, it continues about water.

In both Detroit and Istanbul, the core political issue is that the systems that govern finite material and spatial resources are not directly accountable to the people who are subject to them. In Istanbul, police detain individuals and shut down public spaces in response to peaceful demonstrations against private developments (such as commercial malls or high-end apartments) that displace low-income communities. In Detroit, the city has shut off residents' water for lack of payment while private corporations who have also not paid their water bills are untouched. In response, in both cities, there are urgent calls for more direct, deliberative approaches to the management of and access to materials crucial to human life—water, space, and housing.

In Detroit in the summer of 2014 as part of a workshop, we spent time meeting people such as Olayami Dabls and visiting places such as Heidelberg Project or the Oakland Avenue Farmers Market where the tensions and opportunities in engaging political ecology in civic life are made visible through daily acts of creativity and sustained commitment to a sense of interdependency and community. These acts echo Isabelle Stengers's (2010) call for a treatment of 'cosmopolitics', shifting away from a politics of modernization to a politics of composition. Focusing on the process of building (or composing) democratic consensus rather than a fixed product, this compositional approach to the politics of things points not only to the possibility for a different frame for considering and arbitrating competing political ideologies but also to the need for an appreciation of the integrity of material things themselves and the dignity of our relations with these things within our political discourses.

2.4 CULTURAL HERITAGE AS A PLACE OF POSSIBILITY

Cultural heritage plays a crucial role within these political discourses because it frames and structures power relationships that determine access to space, financial resources, and material resources for expression and affective experience (see also Shanahan and Shanahan, Chapter 5, regarding some of these issues in Melbourne's public spaces). Dominant models of heritage and inheritance have supported top-down systems of governance that distance individuals from being directly engaged in deliberations over the constitution of heritage. This model of heritage is of a tree. The many branches are the people alive today who share a common lineage to a single trunk of identification (religion, ethnicity, language, etc.). This trunk connects to roots which are grounded in specific places. This vertical structure of inheritance is what most heritage legislation uses to determine ownership of cultural objects, sites, and land and is the basis of empowerment of certain cultural identities to govern (determine the future of) these resources and spaces.

Due to the complexity of the many tree branches, government and non-government institutions are created to govern the definition of the identifications that determine who are members of the tree. In turn, these identifications empower the institutions to make decisions for the future of the material and immaterial heritage of this entire group. They also inevitably lead to individuals and groups being disempowered and treated as others, outsiders, and non-citizens. In practical terms, people can be cut off from deliberations over the composition of the tree. Hierarchies of both temporal age and social position effect power disparities and competitions over authenticity of agency. Although there can be many different trees, this only effects a proliferation of competing hierarchical systems of control, entitlement, and power. There may be a pragmatic usefulness of tree-models for power hierarchies in governance; however, if we wish to create communities that are not in eternal conflict or where there are always outsiders or losers, there is a need to move away from dialectics of self and other (us/them).

An alternative to the tree model was described by Carl Jung and developed upon by Gilles Deleuze and Félix Guattari (1980)—the rhizome.

> Life has always seemed to me like a plant that lives on its rhizome. Its true life is invisible, hidden in the rhizome. The part that appears above the ground lasts only a single summer. Then it withers away—an ephemeral apparition. When we think of the unending growth and decay of life and civilizations, we cannot escape the impression of absolute nullity. Yet I have never lost the sense of something that lives and endures beneath the eternal flux. What we see is blossom, which passes. The rhizome remains.   (Jung 1965: 4)

In Jung's metaphor the rhizome (e.g. ginger root) is a capricious, undulating coalescence of existential possibility from which our perceptible phenomena emanate and return. The Jungian rhizome allows us to leave behind linear logic and arborescent (tree-like) knowledge structures and instead suggest that heritage is a rhizomatic constellation of sentiments.

This reconceptualization of the structure of cultural heritage has significant implications in terms of the deliberations of political ecology. It locates heritage not as a distant thing to be cared for and stewarded through our present moment. Rather, it sees heritage as a common, shared space where we engage in deliberations over how we will share the burdens and distribute the resources of our places both today but also to make a better world for us all tomorrow. Heritage discourse invokes both the past and the future simultaneously, and it is the potency of our expectations for the past and the future that lead to heritage becoming a proxy site both for the control of political ecologies and the site for contesting this control. In this way, the past and future senses of heritage make it a space for consultation, deliberation, negotiation, and constitution.

2.5 ALTERNATIVE PLATFORMS FOR PARTICIPATION

In both Detroit and Istanbul, we witness a persistence by people to call into question the systems that govern their access to shared resources and spaces. There is also resilience in how people—where these systems fail or suppress them—work together to build their own deliberative systems or make their own spaces that treat people with dignity and respect the integrity of not only practical needs for food and water but also affective needs for senses of belonging, participation, and presence. This integrity and dignity of relations, I argue, is the basis for a constitutional treatment of cultural heritage. It is not simply a politics of humans' power over things but an issue of human and civil rights to be with and amongst material things, equally participating in the manifestation of these relations through acts of social sculpture.

In Detroit, I was inspired by the achievements of local communities such as the Oakland Avenue Farmers Market to realize their own food-systems through community gardening and urban agricultural projects. I was also moved by the resilience of individuals and artists such as Olayami Dabls of the African Bead Museum or Tyree Guyton of Heidelberg Project who continue to open up new platforms for witnessing and participating in cultural expression despite many obstacles—practical, financial, political, and social. Whilst this is not the place to critically evaluate these projects, I feel it is important to offer some brief words gesturing towards possible ways of thinking critically about these types of projects. I take inspiration from the cautious efforts of Pablo Helguera (2011) in his short publication *Education for Socially Engaged Art* in which he built upon Suzanne Lacy's (1995: 178) sketch of participatory structures in the arts. Helguera (after Lacy) presents a four-fold structure for thinking about the forms of socially engaged arts practice. *Nominal participation* refers to practices that result in a passive experience for viewers/visitors whose participation is mostly limited to the experience of seeing the artwork. *Directed participation* refers to practices which involve the artists directly addressing the visitor/viewer and asking them to undertake an action that completes the experience of the work but does not alter the fundamental material or spatial forms of the work. *Creative participation* refers to practices where the artist involves the visitor/viewer in an action that generates new materials or may alter the spatial form of the work; however, the fundamental platform, structure, and terms of participation for the work are determined by the artist. Finally, *collaborative participation* refers to practices where visitors/viewers share responsibility with the artist for the developing the platform, structure, and form of the work itself.

If we have an aspiration to open up cultural heritage to a deliberative constitutional process, then we must be mindful of how we structure this process and how these structures can both empower and disempower people. For the most part, heritage experiences operate under nominal participation in which experts or government employees structure a space or experience in which a member of the public can view heritage sites at a distance. There are moments of directed participation, such as educational programmes or public events where visitors can interact within a space or site but only under certain terms and in ways that do not threaten the integrity of the heritage site. Community engagement work around heritage sites may involve forms of creative participation in so far as it involves community members in the development of thinking and planning; however, the final decisions and all power still resides with a central authority or expert. This is not to say that there are not projects that employ nominal or directed participation but which also allow for sub-projects/events that involve creative or collaborative participation. In practice, cultural heritage requires many different moments of participation, some of which call for specialist training (e.g. the teaching of specific technical skills or requisite safety procedures). What is important, and difficult, is to be continually mindful of our aspirations for deliberative and participatory models of heritage and of how slight variations in structure can open up or close down opportunities for participation in the making of new platforms.

Over the 2013–14 academic year, I had the opportunity to lead a group of students from Koç University, museum staff, designers, and artists in an effort to open up a new platform for considering the constitution of heritage in Istanbul. Responding to Turkish author Orhan Pamuk's Museum of Innocence, *An Innocent City* was the result of collaborative and participatory process whose modest goal was to tell the stories of the lives of everyday objects in Istanbul and to enfold the local community and the exhibition's audiences into the ongoing unfolding of these stories. In dialogue with the museum, novel, catalogue, and manifesto that constitute Pamuk's parafictional project, *An Innocent City* was one example of how heritage can be used creatively to open up new platforms, simply by pausing to collect everyday material things from a neighborhood in Istanbul and taking time to tell their stories together (Colour plate 4, top and Figure 2.1).

Figure 2.1. Installation view of *An Innocent City*. July 2014. Photo by Ian Alden Russell.

2.6 THE MUSEUM OF INNOCENCE

The Museum of Innocence in Cihangir, Istanbul opened in the summer of 2012. It houses a collection of everyday objects that were collected over two decades by the Nobel Prize-winning author Orhan Pamuk. Pamuk used the objects as inspiration for the creation of the characters, scenes, and stories of his novel of the same name (Pamuk 2009), which tells the tale of the intimate affair of a mid-thirties, bourgeois man named Kemal, and a younger, working-class woman named Füsun in 1970s Istanbul.

The narrative structure of the novel revolves around objects, their details, and how they evoke memories of times gone by. The character Kemal collects the objects that testify to his love for Füsun (and her innocence), and in the culmination of the novel, asks Pamuk to build a museum—collapsing the boundary between the imagined world of nostalgia in the novel and the real life nostalgia of Pamuk as a collector and curator of a museum.

In the museum today, what can be seen is a series of more than seventy wooden exhibition cabinets—one for each chapter in the novel. The cabinets hold carefully curated displays of the everyday objects that Pamuk has collected. There is little to no text so that the objects, at one time, both index the story of the novel and present an ambiguous, nostalgic archive of 1970s

Istanbul. As collector/curator, Pamuk (2012: 28–9) says that his efforts were an attempt to preserve some part of the rapidly changing neighbourhoods of Çukurcuma and Cihangir in Beyoğlu, Istanbul:

> More important was my growing attachment to the streets of Tophane, Cukur-cuma, and Cihangir, and my desire to preserve them somewhat but also to become involved in their daily life. My route going back to my studio from my daughter's school lengthened, and I explored streets I'd never seen before. Breathing in the smell of sesame bread and pastry wafting out of bakeries, buying the newspaper at the corner shop as it opened in the morning, purchasing a piece of fruit from the grocer for the working day, and watching schoolchildren running about—all these things made me happy. On days when I followed the same route, it pleased me to see the same office workers and shopkeepers going to work at the same time; I felt that I was part of a community. If I returned in the afternoon, these streets would be teeming with children playing ball, itinerant salesmen (scrap dealers, potato and onion mongers, meatball and liver sellers), women killing time sitting on steps and chairs in their doorways, and cats. But in the morning the streets were quiet. The things displayed in the shop windows (packets of soap and detergent, socks, knitting yarn for housewives, soda bottles, pastures, and jars of pickles) looked lovely in the first light of day and awakened in me the desire to touch those objects, to feel their purity and innocence.

All the objects were collected by Pamuk on walks around the neighbourhoods near his studio from the 1980s onwards—exploring junkshops, antique sellers' wares, corner shops and the objects and mementos in friends' and acquaint-ances homes. Originally, Pamuk had planned to write a novel in the format of a museum catalogue—writing catalogue entries for a large series of objects.

> I wanted to collect and exhibit the 'real' objects of a fictional story in a museum and to write a novel based on these objects. At the time, I did not know what sort of place the museum would be, and neither did I know the shape the novel would take. But I had the feeling that focusing on objects and telling a story through them would make my protagonists different from those in Western novels—more real, more quintessentially of Istanbul. What I had in mind was a sort of encyclopedic dictionary in which not only objects (a radio, a wall clock, a lighter) and places (an apartment block, Taksim Square, Pelur Restaurant) but also concepts (love, impa-tience, panic) would be the subject headings.   (Pamuk 2012: 15)

In reading through all the catalogue entries and paying attention to each thing in turn, a narrative would emerge.

Placing the objects collected from his wanderings on his desk, these things began to play a role not dissimilar to Sigmund Freud's antiquity collections that occupied his desk and haunted his writings almost a century ago.[2]

---

[2] For photographs of the antiquity collections of Sigmund Freud, see Engelman 1976. For an excellent introduction to the antiquity collections of Sigmund Freud and their relationships with his thought, work, and writing, see Marinelli 1998.

The more I looked at the objects on my desk next to my notebook—rusty keys, candy boxes, pliers, and lighters—the more I felt as if they were communicating with one another. Their ending up in this place after being uprooted from the places they used to belong to and separated from the people whose lives they were once part of—their loneliness, in a word—aroused in me the shamanic belief that objects too have spirits.

When I found a particular object in a shop and realized, with a sudden burst of inspiration, that I might be able to weave it into my story, I would be happy.... I would place it on my desk, believing optimistically that its role in Kemal and Füsun's story would simply come to me unbidden.   (Pamuk 2012: 52)

Over time, the collection of objects grew and the story took on a life of its own. Eventually, the decision was made to realize a real museum space rather than only a catalogue—an archive of Istanbul nostalgia, cast with an aura of innocence, love, and loss from a novel.

2.7 THE MUSEUM AS PARAFICTION

Whilst distinct efforts, the two worlds of text and objects are faces of the same artwork that is both a novel and a museum.

There is, of course, a strong bond that holds the novel and the museum together: both are products of my imagination, dreamed up word by word, object by object, and picture by picture over a long period of time. This is perhaps also why the novel and the museum each tell a story. The objects exhibited in the museum are described in the novel. Still, words are one thing, objects another. The images that words generate in our minds are one thing; the memory of an old object used once upon a time is another. But imagination and memory have a strong affinity, and this is the basis of the affinity between the novel and the museum.

(Pamuk 2012: 18)

The two worlds poetically converge in the only visual illustration in the novel—a simple graphic of a ticket for entry to the museum. The reader can take their copy of the book with them to the Museum in Cihangir, and have it stamped for free admission—implicating the reader in the dissolution of the boundary between object and story, between fact and fiction. The novel-with-museum extends the narrative device of a plausible reality in the story of the novel into the realm of what Carrie Lambert-Beatty (2009: 54) calls parafiction:

... a parafiction is related to but not quite a member of the category of fiction as established in literary and dramatic art. It remains a bit outside. It does not perform its procedures in the hygienic clinics of literature, but has one foot in the field of the real. Unlike historical fiction's fact-based but imagined worlds, in parafiction real and/or imaginary personages and stories intersect with the world as it is being lived.

The Museum of Innocence does not stand alone in this parafictional realm, but is joined by a number of artist–museum projects that have explored the imaginative domain of the museum as platform. Mark Dion's artworks and projects have long occupied the imaginative space between the museum as object and the museum as medium. Often working with and through museums and educational institutions, he has interrogated and explored the methods and methodologies of disciplines such as natural science and archaeology and the possibilities for aesthetic and creative display of the output of these methods. As a contribution to *An Innocent City*, Dion wrote a modest postcard to the Museum of Innocence on behalf of The Jenks Society for Lost Museums. Moved by the death of Kemal Basmacı—the parafictional collector behind the Museum of Innocence—Dion shares the tale and fate of the Jenks natural history collection in Providence, Rhode Island, and the effort of the Jenks Society—collaboratively formed by Dion and students and faculty from Brown University—to preserve the memory of a lost collection and its founder. Writing a postcard form a collection that no longer survives, the *The Lost Museum* presented by the Jenks Society in some becomes an inverted parafiction where the truth of the story becomes a platform for presenting constructed objects and new fictions. Dion's modest missive, prompted by the feeling of loss for the character Kemal Basmacı and his collection in the Museum of Innocence, deepens the parafictional bound between the novel and museum.

Despite their paraficational union, Pamuk (2012: 18) maintains that the novel and the museum can be experienced independently of one another:

> And yet just as the novel is entirely comprehensible without a visit to the museum, so is the museum a place that can be visited and experienced on its own. The museum is not an illustration of the novel, and the novel is not an explanation of the museum.

If the Museum can be experienced without the novel—perhaps by someone who has never read the novel or may be unaware or unsure if it is or is not fiction—might a visitor choose to experience the Museum as an archive? What might the implications of these objects be if treated as artefacts of a true story? Lambert-Beatty (2009: 82) suggests that, 'this is precisely the territory of parafiction, which at once reveals the way things are and makes sensible the way we want them to be; and which offers experiences of both skepticism and belief'. In the ambiguous space between the novel and the material reality of the Museum, an imagination takes hold that is at once both permissive and subversive.

2.8 A RADICAL INNOCENCE

In contemporary Turkey, there are modes of speech and expression that are actively suppressed—the recent banning of Twitter and YouTube are just two examples. At a time when speech and expression can be censored, when political assembly and demonstration can be suppressed, are there alternative strategies? Might the act of archiving and presenting everyday things present a way of speaking through things that, due to their apparent innocence or silence, is in some ways less mutable? This, I propose, is core to Pamuk's project with the physical archive and museum. The legal requirement for any institution in Turkey that carries the title museum is that they are overseen and approved by a statutory museum and that their collection is archived and listed as cultural artefacts within the state's care. Thus, in establishing a Museum of Innocence, Pamuk has inscribed a parafictional archive testifying to the dignity of everyday life in Istanbul—a sensibility increasingly isolated by recent cultural and political shifts—into the state's official material record. It was, in this sense, a radical political act to insert counter-narratives challenging established and emerging master narratives of the Turkish state.

Pamuk personally experienced political suppression of acts of free speech almost a decade ago, when faced by troubling legal proceedings as a result of public comments he made in a Swiss newspaper that ran counter to the historical perspectives of the Turkish state.[3] Where his words were quickly politicized and targeted for suppression, I suggest that in the making of this museum he may have found solace in the persistence of material things and their immutability. This element of Pamuk's museum brings to mind the words of Bruno Latour (1993: 76):

> If there are more of us who regain the capacity to do our own sorting of the elements that belong to our time, we will rediscover the freedom of movement that modernism denied us—a freedom that, in fact, we have never really lost.

Perhaps, the museum is where Pamuk found an alternative political voice in the acts of archiving and display—allowing things to speak for him, by letting them speak for themselves.

Though it was assembled through the authoring of one narrative, the absence of text in the museum helps his archive avoid semiotic closure. The assemblages are open-ended, parafictional platforms from which one is free to imagine, remember, recollect. For example, the red –and-white floral dress of Füsun in box 73 of the Museum (and all its associations with femininity and its

---

[3] Pamuk was charged under Article 301 of the revised penal code, which criminalizes criticism of 'Turkishness' and of state institutions. See Anonymous 2005; Kinzer 2005; and Reuters 2005.

captivity within a masculine gaze) is difficult to dissociate from another image of another young woman in a red dress defying a different chauvinism this past summer—known to us as the 'Lady in Red' from the photograph of Osman Orsal.[4] Of course, the spectre of Pamuk and his characters are everywhere in the archive, but so too are the spectres of the streets of Çukurcuma. His authorial intention is reflexively present—allowing for the opening of a conversation between things and visitors—one that requires neither concord nor resolution, only presence.

2.9 THE MANIFESTO

Pamuk (2012: 54–7) extends this ongoing conversation in his *Modest Manifesto for Museums*. Broadly concerned with the increasing development of large museums and state institutions around the world, which propagate master narratives, Pamuk calls for modest museums.

> 7. The aim of present and future museums must not be to represent the state, but to re-create the world of single human beings—the same human beings who have labored under ruthless oppression for hundreds of years.

Pamuk does not wish for his museum to remain isolated as a sole counterpoint. Rather, he works to foster conversations with others around establishing small museums that present alternative narratives, everyday stories.

> 10. Monumental buildings that dominate neighborhoods and entire cities do not bring out our humanity; on the contrary, they quash it. Instead, we need modest museums that honor the neighborhoods and streets and the homes and shops nearby, and turn them into elements of their exhibitions.

At a moment when Turkey is witnessing the establishment of new master narratives of neoliberal, economic, and imperial ambition under a policy of Neo-Ottomanism, Pamuk's manifesto and museum urge the validation of the everyday, the common, perhaps the subaltern, through an empowered, democratic archival practice.

In the absence of a museum of civic life in Istanbul, there is a certain degree of pressure on, or perhaps expectation for, the museum to represent not only the collector and author's nostalgia but also a view of the everyday life of the city of Istanbul. Therein lies a tension between authorial voice and the

---

[4] On 28 May 2013, Osman Orsal took a photograph of a policeman spraying tear gas directly into the face of a young woman in a red dress standing alone on a patch of grass in front of a line of riot police in Gezi Park, Istanbul. The photograph quickly became one of the iconic images of the Gezi Park demonstrations and considered evidence of the excessive force used by police to disperse demonstrators.

multi-vocality of interpretations of everyday life. The parafictional archival practice that Pamuk uses offers us, however, is a way to negotiate this tension—expanding the representational possibilities of everyday things beyond the binary dialectics of inclusion/exclusion or authentic/fabricated. The Museum of Innocence becomes a parafictional platform. One can linger a while in liminal spaces—between, before, and after.

To build this platform, Pamuk collected objects from everyday life to create an archive to tell an intimate story. What if we reversed this process—selecting objects from the museum and following them back out into the city? We could tell new stories of the lives of everyday objects as they unfold in the streets of Istanbul today. Visitors to the museum could, perhaps, find new ways of discovering the city through the objects and write new stories, offering an alternative way to participate in the archiving and authoring of the city.

2.10 MODEST MUSINGS

For *An Innocent City*, Bilge, Emily, Fatma, Jenna, Pınar, and I selected things from the museum's cases, drawn to each for various reasons. We then stepped out into the streets of Istanbul to try to find these things, to dignify the stories of these everyday things as they live with and amongst us. Each object led us on different paths through the city. A tea glass led to a back alley tea shop in Eminönü and the hidden economy of tea production that saturates the city. A coffee cup led to encounters with Turkish fortune tellers and questions about our city's future (Figure 2.2). A lost hairpin indexed, perhaps, the presence of a women often overlooked and unrepresented in the story of the city. A bottle of *gazöz* glass revealed a nation-wide heritage of locally made fruit-flavoured soda eclipsed by the introduction of major Western, multinational brands from the 1960s onwards (Figure 2.3). Photography, oral historical interviews, cartography, video, and narrative writing were techniques. The result was a collection of twelve stories about material things and how they connect us with each other throughout the city. *An Innocent City* was held at the gallery of the Research Center for Anatolian Civilizations on İstiklal Caddesi in the summer of 2014. As a collaborative endeavour, the exhibition presented these stories with illustrations designed by the students and our designer Ayşe Karamustafa and photographer Hasan Deniz amongst others.

As an effort to address the political ecology of constitutional heritage, we were inspired by Pamuk's *Modest Manifesto for Museums* and its call for modest museums of everyday life, honouring neighbourhoods and streets and the lives that constitute those spaces. Our aspiration was to open up a participatory platform where visitors and the local community could share

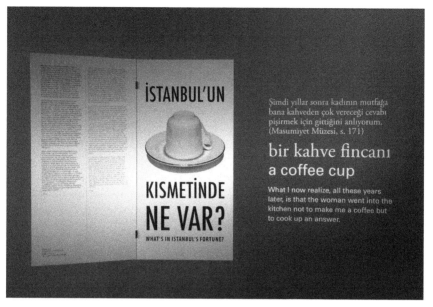

Figure 2.2. Installation view of 'a coffee cup' from *An Innocent City*. July 2014. Photo by Ian Alden Russell.

Figure 2.3. Installation view of 'a gazoz bottle' from *An Innocent City*. July 2014. Photo by Ian Alden Russell.

their own modest musings on the lives of the objects in Istanbul. We achieved this in two ways. The first was by inviting temporary loans for the exhibitions from local community members of examples of the everyday objects about which both we and Pamuk wrote (Colour plate 4, bottom). The second was by producing a run of twelve postcards, a few hundred of each type, each with the names of a different object from our exhibition. We displayed them in stacks on a table at the entrance to the exhibition with a prominent wall-vinyl saying 'Take a postcard. Leave a Story' with pens and pencils (Colour plate 5, top). We hoped that visitors would offer some of their own stories or reflections about what these objects mean to them. The technicians installed wires across the wall with bulldog clips onto which visitors could attach their postcards. The results overwhelmed us. Within a week the wall was covered with stories, and visitors spent as much time reading the stories written by fellow visitors as they did viewing the rest of the exhibition.

In the pages of a book published by Yapı Kredi Publishers (Russell 2014), you will find some of these stories. As well as a guide for how to create your own 'modest musings' (Figure 2.4). Our hope is that our inversion of the museum's parafictional archive may offer a model for public and educational programming—where members of the public in Istanbul can find their own personal, intimate or political voices and express them through the material things they hold dear. The underlying intention is to undercut the divisions that have emerged in recent Turkish cultural politics, to find shared spaces between the things in our city. How many of us share the same tea glasses that are used, washed, used, and washed again at cafés every day? Or touch the same doorknobs? Rather than flatten the narrative of any one thing into a singular consensus of what it may or may not mean—a semiotic closure—we invite an open, participatory archival practice within Istanbul—where the many fortunes for the city's future can be enjoyed equally. And perhaps, just as we share coffee with each other, we may anticipate fortunes we can all share from our upturned coffee cups.

2.11 APPROACHING SOCIALLY ENGAGED HERITAGE

Recalling the thoughts of Isabelle Stengers and Pablo Helguera mentioned earlier, our approach to *An Innocent City* was inspired by the growing number of artists working under the banner of socially engaged arts practice to address disparities within the political ecologies of place. Just as some artists have moved on from models of institutional critique to models of participatory practice and collaborative art to engage the issues of our time, we hope that our work on *An Innocent City* is a contribution towards a practice of socially engaged heritage. More than a presentation or discourse of objects with

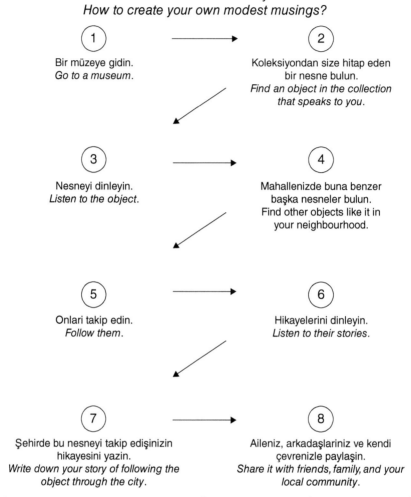

Figure 2.4. How to create your own modest musings. Design by Ayşe Karamustafa and Ian Alden Russell. Photo by Ian Alden Russell.

passive or nominal participation, we are looking for ways of approaching heritage as a process of composition that engages publics in directed, creative, and collaborative ways. Detroit is not a fixed site. Istanbul is not a laboratory. These cities, and many more, are slippery spaces where survey, documentation, and interpretation are less technique or method and more practice and process. Approaching socially engaged heritage as a creative practice, heritage can be opened up to a wider community of participants. Creating platforms of access and support that widen participation in composing heritage, we resist the tendency for heritage to be a method of control of political ecologies.

Instead, heritage becomes a commitment to ongoing consultation and deliberation over and constitution and composition of our shared places.

ACKNOWLEDGEMENTS

I would like to thank Laura McAtackney and Krysta Ryzewski for the invitation to visit Detroit and to contribute to this volume. I would also like to thank Chitra Ganesh and Mariam Ghani for the invitation to present a version of this paper at the Radical Archives conference at New York University in April 2014. I am deeply grateful to Esra A. Aysun, without whose support during the early stages of this project, it may not have occurred. I would also like to thank Onur Karaoğlu and all the staff at the Museum of Innocence and the wonderful people at Yapı Kredi Publishers for your belief in and support of the project. And a special thank to my dear colleagues Buket Coşkuner, Şeyda Çetin, and Esra Ebru Satıcı at the Research Center for Anatolian Civilizations for their steadfast and continuing support and belief in not only me and this project, but also in the value and importance of exhibition-making in education, research, and public engagement.

REFERENCES

Anonymous. 2005. 'The Turkish Identity', *New York Times*, 11 September.

Deleuze, Gilles and Félix Guattari. 1980. *A Thousand Plateaus: Capitalism and Schizophrenia*. Minneapolis: University of Minnesota Press.

Engelman, Edmund. 1976. *Bergasse 19: Sigmund Freud's Home and Offices, Vienna 1938: The Photographs of Edmund Engelman*. London: University of Chicago Press.

Harmanşah, Ömür. 2013. 'Urban Utopias and How They Fell Apart', *Jadaliyya*. http://www.jadaliyya.com/pages/index/12456/urban-utopias-and-how-they-fell-apart (accessed 13 July 2013).

Helguera, Pablo. 2011. *Education for Socially Engaged Art*. New York: Jorge Pinto Books Inc.

Jung, Carl G. 1965. *Memories, Dreams, Reflections*. New York: Vintage Books.

Kinzer, Stephen. 2005. 'In Turkey, the Novelist as Lightning Rod', *New York Times*, 23 October.

Lacy, Suzanne. 1995. *Mapping the Terrain: New Genre Public Art*. Seattle: Bay Press.

Lambert-Beatty, Carrie. 2009. 'Make-Believe: Parafiction and Plausibility', *October*, 129: 51–84.

Latour, Bruno. 1993. *We have never been modern*. Cambridge: Harvard University Press.

Latour, Bruno. 2004. *Politics of Nature: How to Bring the Sciences into Democracy*. Cambridge: Harvard University Press.

Marinelli, Lydia (ed.). 1998. *'Meine... alten und dreckigen Götter': Aus Sigmund Freuds Sammlung*. Vienna: Sigmund Freud-Museum and Stroemfeld Verlag.

Pamuk, Orhan. 2009. *The Museum of Innocence*. New York: Alfred A. Knopf.

Pamuk, Orhan. 2012. *The Innocence of Objects*. New York: Abrams.

Reuters. 2005. 'Popular Turkish Novelist on Trial for Speaking of Armenian Genocide', *New York Times*, 16 December.

Russell, Ian Alden (ed.). 2014. *An Innocent City: Modest Musings on Everyday Istanbul*. Istanbul: Yapı Kredi Publishers.

Stengers, Isabelle. 2010. *Cosmopolitics I*. Minneapolis: University of Minnesota Press.

Thorne, Frank. 1935. 'Nature Rambling: We Fight for Grass', *The Science Newsletter*, 27: 717.

3

Making Music in Detroit

Archaeology, Popular Music, and Post-industrial Heritage

Krysta Ryzewski

Detroit's popular music-making legacy has remained a foundation for the city's symbolic identity throughout the twentieth century and into the present. For over a century music production in Detroit has been part of a thriving local industry and global enterprise, with different genres and styles of music measuring the city's changing composition over the years (Holt and Wergin 2014). The sounds emerging from the city, coupled with its built environment and physical landscape, tell the stories of a creative, shapeshifting industrial and post-industrial centre defined by melodies, artists, and sounds that are distinctly Detroit—The Hucklebuck, Martha and the Vandellas, Cybortron. Attention to the assemblages of buildings, landscapes, people, and the soulful sounds associated with them reveal the underlying power of the city's creative accomplishments to unite disparate communities, call attention to issues affecting urban well-being, and preserve memories of Detroit's rich musical heritage.

In its expansive repertoire of recording history and in its vast contemporary terrain of decay and ruination, Detroit's musical heritage holds tremendous potential for archaeological research and cultural heritage initiatives. Through creative documentation platforms and dissemination practices contemporary archaeological approaches are particularly well suited for engaging place-based and thematic heritage discourses about Detroit and other post-industrial cities. This chapter presents the 'Making Music in Detroit' project, a contemporary archaeology and digital storytelling exercise focused on popular music assemblages and their placemaking power in Detroit, a city that is simultaneously defined and encumbered by the traumatic and festering post-industrial wounds of poverty, mismanagement, and ruination. In a series of twenty-four videos and web texts, 'Making Music in Detroit' illustrates how archaeologists might use digital storytelling to involve music-making places and their physical remains (some ruined, others intact) in communicating present-day senses of place as they relate to urban histories of creativity. These stories are part of a substantially broader and more formal multidisciplinary digital humanities effort to map Detroit's transformations over the course of the past century, as it transitioned first from a thriving, wealthy, and innovative centre of manu-facturing industries to an epicentre of post-industrial struggle, and more recently, from a bankrupt city into a stage for selective, privatized, and creative revitalization efforts (Ethnic Layers of Detroit project 2016; on creative cities, see White and Seidenberg, Chapter 1).

Drawing on research into popular music, urban geography, and heritage management conducted by archaeologists and other scholars, this chapter explores connections between places and the physical remains of creative production, music consumption, and memories associated with Detroit's twentieth-century music-making landscape (Brace VI 2016; Cherry et al. 2013; Darvill 2014; Graves-Brown 2012; Ouzonian 2013; Parkman 2014; Roberts 2014; Schofield 2014a). Following an overview of Detroit's popular music landscape, the 'Making Music' digital storytelling project is presented. The discussion then turns to evaluate the challenges involved with digital storytelling as a technique for gathering and disseminating archaeological information about popular music and its place-production in cities. The con-cluding section reflects upon the future-making possibilities of such practices with regards to foregrounding legacies of creativity and in composing discourses about urban heritage that involve the archaeological record of the recent past.

3.1 A MUSIC-MAKING HISTORY OF THE MOTOR CITY

In the short space of a half-century, Detroit's popular music scene transitioned from the swinging, bluesy jazz music of Paul Williams in the 1940s to the upbeat and carefully scripted sounds of Motown in the 1950s and 1960s. Alongside the political, labour, and racial struggles of the 1960s and 1970s emerged the aggressive rock music of MC5 and the proto-punk band Death. Shortly thereafter, during a period of prolonged economic downturn, new instrumentation technologies gave rise to the first synthetic sounds of techno music in the 1980s and 1990s.

Detroit's twentieth-century musical heritage maps closely onto the rise and fall of various local manufacturing industries and the lasting effects of the 1960s urban crisis; in its totality this heritage is an acoustic arrangement that charts the city's unprecedented urban transformations over several decades (Sugrue 2014). Today the city's present physical landscape is comprised of a combination of intact historic buildings, repurposed structures, monumental ruins, and vast empty spaces. Many of Detroit's significant places of popular music production and consumption have transitioned between these forms of existence in ways that mirror the city's twentieth-century industrial tempo. For instance, the Packard Automotive Plant, designed by architect Albert Kahn, gradually fell into ruin after the factory closed in 1958. During the 1980s and 1990s the space was reclaimed by the city's pioneering techno musicians, who used the empty buildings to host raves. A similar overlap between Detroit's motor vehicle and music industries exists downtown at the site of the Michigan Theatre, which stands at the exact location of Henry Ford's garage at 58 Bagley, where he assembled his first experimental car in 1896. The Michigan Theatre was constructed in 1926 and in its heyday boasted capacity for over 4,000 patrons and was the city's premiere venue for motion pictures, Wurlitzer organ, and other performances. The theatre fell victim to competing suburban venues and the massive out-migration of residents from Detroit in the 1970s. It closed in 1976 and was soon thereafter gutted to accommodate a multistorey car park, a conversion that served to accommodate motor vehicles once again (Colour plate 5, bottom).

Popular music production in Detroit has long been a response to the call of local industries, from the lumber boom of the late nineteenth century that made the mass production of Grinnell pianos possible, to the dominance of motor vehicle manufacturing in the first half of the twentieth century. In his 1994 autobiography *To Be Loved*, Berry Gordy, Jr, founder of Motown Records, recounts how during his brief stint as a Lincoln-Mercury autoworker in the 1950s he drew musical inspiration from the repetitive sounds and tasks of the factory's machinery. True to the spirit of Fordism, Gordy soon thereafter transferred the process of mass motor vehicle manufacture to his redesign of the Detroit music industry, which he operated out of an unassuming row of repurposed homes on West Grand Boulevard, known as Hitsville USA. Gordy's application of factory techniques to music production allowed Motown Records to function as a multi-component assembly line that churned out a steady stream of polished, tightly managed, and strategically marketed chart-topping artists from 1959 onwards, including The Supremes, Stevie Wonder, The Temptations, and Marvin Gaye, among many others.

A generation later, as the repetitive sounds of motor vehicle production slowed inside of Detroit's factories, they re-emerged in techno, a new genre of music created with electronic instrumentation—synthesizers, drum machines, and mixing stations. By the early 1980s DJ Juan Atkins and his protégés Derrick May and Kevin Saunderson were introducing techno to the world via a local Detroit network of underground clubs, recording studios, and record shops. In the 1996 French documentary *Universal Techno*, Atkins reflects upon the development of the genre and credits the depressed city of Detroit with 'lend [ing] to the creative juices' of his technology-influenced sound. Linking the genre's inspiration to Detroit's extreme post-industrial conditions, Atkins alleges that techno 'wouldn't have developed...in any other city in America' (Deluze 1996). More than any other variety of Detroit-based music, techno's sounds and its associated places of performance fed off of the city's post-industrial and urban setting; the most popular techno venues of the 1980s and 1990s were the abandoned factories across Detroit that stood as monuments to the city's failed industrial manufacturing projects (Moreno 2014).

Accompanying the socio-economic changes facing Detroit during the twentieth century were shifts in the city's acoustic terrain—the places where people gathered to make and enjoy popular music. Performance spaces and the sounds of the city moved from the Graystone, Grande, and Vanity, the ornate art deco ballrooms and theatres of the early Ford era, to concert halls, factories, and pop-up clubs (Sicko 2010; on the concept of acoustic terrain, see Gandy and Nilsen 2014: 6). These radical changes in the soundscape of music making did not, however, disrupt the continuous musical pulse anchoring a fundamental component of Detroit's cultural identities. Instead, the Packard Plant, Michigan Theatre, Hitsville USA, and other music venues across the city are lenses through which to view the continuities and changes in the rhythms of post-modern, contemporary Detroit. These music-making places allow archaeologists to evaluate how different actions and memories within the urban landscape link the overlapping pasts and presents of post-industrial spaces together, both physically and imaginatively (see Herron 1993).

3.2 DETROIT'S POST-INDUSTRIAL MUSIC-MAKING LANDSCAPE

In its mid-century heyday, Detroit's music scene was everywhere: in theatres, nightclubs, barber shops, on the radio, and on street corners (Gordy 1994). Neighbourhoods like Paradise Valley were home to vibrant and nationally prominent African American music venues, including the Flame Show Bar, Chesterfield Lounge, Garfield Lounge, and Frolic Show Bar (Gordy 1994). These establishments were demolished alongside entire neighbourhoods, (e.g. Paradise Valley), during urban renewal projects of the 1960s and 1970s.

Despite the widespread losses over the past fifty years of places important to the city's musical heritage because of urban renewal projects, blight management efforts, and the mass exodus of residents to the suburbs, Detroit's music-making legacy still exists in innumerable remains across the city's landscape. Unfortunately, the vast majority of these places are in a state of irreparable decay or in danger of demolition by neglect. Preservationists have documented the architectural significance of many high profile historic venues, but in general, comprehensive histories and accounts of the exteriors and inner spaces of Detroit's former recording studios and performance venues survive only in the scattered photographs, oral histories, and memories of former patrons or musicians. The material culture associated with music making is also widely dispersed among private individual collections of records, ticket stubs, and instruments.[1] Few written histories extend their focus beyond a single musical genre, era, venue, or artist.[2] Nevertheless, the places of music production and consumption, the material culture of popular music, and the memories of past producers, musicians, and fans remain vital points of connection for many Detroiters (and non-Detroiters). They are direct, physical links to the places associated with innovative music, creative spirit, and past memories of the city. For Detroiters, this connection is a matter of place-based pride and is essential for promoting the city's unique cultural heritage and defining its collective identity (O'Keeffe 2013).

At the time that the 'Making Music in Detroit' project was developed in 2014 no prior archaeological studies had been conducted on places associated with popular music production or consumption in Detroit. As a result, the 'Making Music' project was inspired in large part by a parallel contemporary archaeology project I co-directed at the AIR Studios on the Caribbean island of Montserrat (Cherry et al. 2013). The archaeological documentation of AIR Studios enabled a scholarly and multisited consideration of the global movement of songs, the reciprocal power they held for a generation of music listeners, and their role in defining a legacy of musical heritage on, and associated with, Montserrat. Through examples of songs recorded at the studios, graffiti left by artists, and material culture scattered throughout the complex, connections were made between Montserrat's musical legacy at multiple scales of attachment to the studio's memories, experiences, and material remains. These same foci guided the place-based contemporary archaeological study of Detroit's music heritage in the design of the 'Making Music' project.

Like AIR Studios, Detroit's spaces of music making, from the ornate 1920s Vanity Ballroom to the Techno Boulevard of the 1980s, attest to the

---

[1] Examples of oral history and archival projects include: the Detroit Stories Project, https://digitaldetroitstories.wordpress.com/; Windsor-Detroit Oral History Music Project, http://windsordetroitmusic.blogspot.com/; Detroit Sound Conservancy Oral Histories, http:// detroitsoundconservancy.org/oral-history/ and the Living Music Project, http://sitemaker.umich. edu/livingmusic/home, and Friends of the Grande (Ballroom) http://thegrandeballroom.com/ (all accessed 23 January 2017).

[2] With few notable exceptions (see Miller 2013), the result is a tendency to focus on an individual venue or person and a musical genre or time period associated with it; recent examples include 'Louder than Love', a 2012 documentary of the Grande Ballroom during its 1960s rock heyday, 'Searching for Sugarman', a 2012 Oscar award-winning biographical film about forgotten folk singer Sixto Rodriguez, and heavily illustrated *Images of America* thematic series, with titles like *Motor City Rock and Roll: The 1960s and 1970s* (Harris and Peters 2008).

archaeological significance of the physical remains of musical heritage in crafting the identity of a local community. In contrast to AIR Studios, which was only active between 1979 and 1989, Detroit's popular music-making history spans a century and includes vastly different genres of music, from jazz to rap. The physical remains of Detroit's musical legacy comprise an extraordinary range of structures scattered across the city's landscape: single-family houses converted into recording studios (e.g. Hitsville USA and United Sound Systems), ornate art deco ballrooms, small record shops, and abandoned factories. One of the biggest challenges to mapping Detroit's music-making heritage archaeologically is that the city is a vast 139 square mile landscape marked by urban blight, with over a third (upwards of 70,000) of its structures derelict and earmarked for demolition (Data Driven Detroit 2014). The rapid pace of decay plaguing many of the city's historically significant properties and landmarks introduces a sense of urgency into archaeological documentation projects (Ryzewski 2016a). In Detroit, efforts to preserve decaying or abandoned historic landmarks often run counter to residential communities' desire to eradicate neglected properties as a vital first step towards the city's revitalization. In these instances, issues of maintenance and continuity that are foundational to heritage management practices can come into direct conflict with the present reality of Detroit's post-industrial landscape and the desires of the people who live within it.

3.3 ARCHAEOLOGY AND POPULAR MUSIC

For music makers and consumers alike, popular music and the memories associated with it relate to particular experiences associated with places on Detroit's urban landscape (Long 2014; Keeling 2011). These lasting connections between ephemeral sounds, personal or collective histories, and physical remains are powerful inspirations for studies that address archaeology, heritage, and popular music, and for revitalization strategies in post-industrial cities. In recent years city planners and heritage agencies in the UK cities of Sheffield, Liverpool, and Birmingham have capitalized on popular music heritage through tours, exhibits, and interactive experiences that emphasize local uniqueness in relation to global pop music phenomena (Long 2014; Roberts 2014; Lashua et al. 2010). Archaeologists of the recent past have also contributed to the emergent conversations on popular music heritage by employing various efforts, from mapping changes across decades in musical styles, themes, and settings in Berlin (Schofield 2014a) to enlisting various strategies of place production in charting popular music heritage across expansive landscapes (Darvill 2014). As Schofield notes, this work has effectively demonstrated how archaeology can valuably contribute to documenting recent music making by building from the multiple scales and sources within the archaeological record, particularly when knowledge from or access to other written, oral historical, or material remains are lacking (2014b: 290).

The relationships between archaeology and popular music are manifest in material, acoustic, human, and intangible traces and therefore hold possibilities for pursuing archaeological studies from several different points of departure. O'Keeffe suggests three suitable entry points for conducting such studies. Relationships between archaeology and popular music might be examined by: focusing on music's materiality (e.g. record collections, recording devices); exploring music as a dimension of cultural heritage; or recognizing music as a communicative medium (2013: 91–2). The digital stories from the 'Making Music in Detroit' project pursue each of these entry points to various degrees in their documentation processes and place-based engagements as described below.

In an effort to map and understand music-making landscapes and popular music heritage, Paul Graves-Brown warns that archaeologists must be cautious of monumentalizing music as if it were a static, physical thing (2009: 220; see also Connor 2014; Ceraso 2010). The challenge in understanding a particular place of importance to popular music history should not be confused with defining and fixing that place in history. Instead, place-based studies of popular music heritage benefit most from recognizing the fluidity of cultural landscapes and making multisited connections that have strong genealogical links between particular places (Graves-Brown 2009; Penrose 2007; Ryzewski 2012).

One might reasonably argue that an inherent contradiction also exists between the semi-permanence of the physical traces associated with music making and the short-lived fame of most popular music, which is often produced with the intention of achieving a momentary, chart-topping hit (Mullins 2014). Though it is certainly possible to map a chronological progression between short-lived musical styles and trends in Detroit, it is equally important to appreciate the extent to which the city's different musical genres are interrelated with one another, with each drawing inspiration from and overlapping with earlier forms. Desires for profit and popularity unquestionably drove the high-speed output of music producers in Detroit, especially during the Motown era, but local popular music also had deep roots in and was widely repurposed from earlier styles and songs. This practice lends an important and often unappreciated perspective of longevity to the creative process of popular music production. The process of passing music between cultures and generations of musicians is reflected in Jon Savage's notion of 'double refraction', whereby emergent subcultures of music are a new component of an existing pop music scene and are influenced by contributions from other genres, such as R&B, disco, and soul in the case of techno (Sicko 2010). An understanding of popular music development as a process of sharing, copying, and influencing acts to temper the notion that Detroit's

popular music was ephemeral by design, and instead reflects the perspective
of music creators like Paul Williams, Berry Gordy, Jr, and Juan Atkins, who
consciously crafted their works in hopes of contributing to the city's existing
musical legacy and heritage. This legacy-oriented perspective also directly
lends itself to viewing Detroit's urban and acoustic landscapes archaeologically
in a long-term framework that recognizes the fluidity of music making places
and resists monumentalizing particular episodes in music history. It is with
these circumstances and perspectives in mind that the 'Making Music in
Detroit' project was developed.

3.4 'MAKING MUSIC IN DETROIT', A DIGITAL STORYTELLING EXERCISE

'Making Music in Detroit' is an urban archaeological digital storytelling tour
of landmarks, artefacts, places, and soundscapes associated with Detroit's rich
musical history over the past century. The tour includes twenty-four short
2–3 minute videos, viewable through YouTube or the geolocational web
platform Geostoryteller (Table 3.1).[3] The stories may be accessed remotely,
as stand-alone videos with accompanying text, or they may be watched as
geostories at specific locations on handheld mobile technology devices.
I developed the design and objectives for the 'Making Music in Detroit' project
during my Urban Archaeology course in 2014. Students were divided into
pairs and assigned a particular genre of music affiliated with Detroit's local
industry. Each group of students selected story locations associated with their
musical genre from a list of places provided to them. Under supervision, the
class then visited and researched each location, documenting its physical
elements, researching site histories, identifying connections to other places
within the genre, and recognizing the locations' broader importance to understanding Detroit's musical heritage. In creating digital outputs for each music-
making place, information collected during a month's worth of research was
combined into short video and narrative text summaries. Design decisions,
such as text size and format, background music, voice-over narration, and the
balance between text and video were made by the students. Each student
group produced four of the twenty-four stories in the 'Making Music' project
repertoire (Figure 3.1).

The musical genres and associated places featured in the digital stories were
organized chronologically: the city's early instrument manufacturing industry

---

[3] For 'Making Music in Detroit' videos, see: https://www.youtube.com/channel/
UCInEMiEsDwrpZXkZ_CH3p0w and http://www.geostoryteller.org/mobile_all.php?usePortal=
soundscape (both accessed 23 January 2017).

Table 3.1. The 'Making Music in Detroit' digital stories organized by genre and chronology. Story authors are listed underneath each section title

Genre, Time Period and Authors	Music-Making Site	Link to Digital Story
INSTRUMENT PRODUCTION late nineteenth–early twentieth century C. Harvey and K. Korth	Wurlitzer Building Grinnell Piano Factory Grinnell Brothers Music Building Grinnell Piano Warehouse	https://tinyurl.com/k3v92a4 https://tinyurl.com/l6zbsed https://tinyurl.com/m4zqjmw https://tinyurl.com/n85cmlk
BALLROOMS & VAUDEVILLE 1910s–1930s S. Godfrey	Vanity Ballroom National Theatre Michigan Theatre Graystone Ballroom	Video not available. See: https://tinyurl.com/m5h4jok https://tinyurl.com/mztbgno https://tinyurl.com/n66zzhn Video not available. See: https://tinyurl.com/mqdbwfo
JAZZ & BLUES 1930s–1950s S. (Malette) Ellens and K. Mutch	Blue Bird Inn Paradise Theatre Baker's Keyboard Lounge United Sound Systems	https://tinyurl.com/n886mrh https://tinyurl.com/mmzn6vl https://tinyurl.com/lp6ub8a https://tinyurl.com/mk2yyna
MOTOWN 1950s–1970s C. Donnelly and B. Doucet	Hitsville, USA Donovan Building Motown Mansion Brewster-Douglass Homes	https://tinyurl.com/m7mho9a https://tinyurl.com/lfrtzq7 https://tinyurl.com/kohco3b https://tinyurl.com/mx824qh
ROCK 1960s–1980s B. Moloney and J. Pajor	Cobo Hall Grande Ballroom Eastown Theatre St. Andrew's Hall	https://tinyurl.com/kuwy2m4 https://tinyurl.com/lfbsnjq https://tinyurl.com/lmk8n98 https://tinyurl.com/lvopf8j
TECHNO & PUNK 1970s–2000s C.L. Brace VI and K. Zimmerman	1217 Griswold Techno Boulevard Bookie's Club 870 Submerge Records	https://tinyurl.com/k95hba7 https://tinyurl.com/jvtt3ck https://tinyurl.com/n86sxex https://tinyurl.com/jwvepvn

(turn of twentieth century); theatres and ballrooms (1920s–40s); jazz and blues venues (1930s–50s); Motown-related locations (1950s–60s); (in)famous rock-and-roll clubs (1960s–80s); and pioneering punk and techno performance and production spaces (1970s–90s) (Table 3.1).

The purpose of grouping the twenty-four digital stories into genres was to gather a representative sample of the acoustic terrain of the city over the past century. It was understood that whenever such information is categorized chronologically or thematically, the degree to which the editors of information are controlling and constraining the resulting experience always comes into question.

The 'Making Music' digital stories were intentionally packaged into organizational units, at least insofar as their titles suggest. However, the archaeological

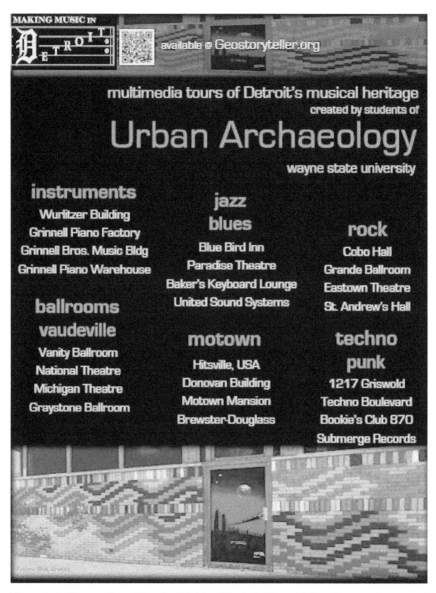

Figure 3.1. Poster advertising the 'Making Music in Detroit' digital stories by musical genre. The exterior of Submerge Records on Detroit's 'Techno Boulevard', Gratiot Avenue, is the featured image. Photo by K. Ryzewski, 2014.

perspective incorporated into the storytelling allowed the conveyance of the depth and breadth of each place, moving beyond chronological boundaries by recognizing overlaps with other social networks of musicians, types of music, histories of performance spaces, and origins of certain sounds. For example, to convey the reciprocal impact of popular music in shaping all parts of the city's urban fabric and to emphasize connections and alternative histories of music making places, students Caitlin Donnelly and Brendan Doucet created a group of Motown genre-specific stories. They included the original home of Motown Recording Studios at Hitsville USA, the Boston Edison-neighbourhood mansion where the label's founder Berry Gordy, Jr lived, the Brewster-Douglass housing projects where several Motown stars were discovered (e.g. The Supremes, Smokey Robinson; Mullins, Chapter 12), and the empty lot in the lower Cass Corridor where the Donovan Building (the later Motown headquarters) once existed before operations were relocated to Los Angeles (Figure 3.2).

Research into Detroit's popular music locales quickly revealed that many places famously associated with one performer or a particular type of music had much deeper connections to earlier decades and musical genres. Such was the case at the Grande Ballroom, most famous today as the venue where the epic rock acts of the 1960s came to play (e.g. The Stooges, The Who, Led Zeppelin, MC5, Pink Floyd, Cream). Historical research revealed that the Grande Ballroom was also a state-of-the art entertainment venue during the late 1920s to the 1940s where patrons drawn largely from the city's nearby Jewish neighbourhood were treated to the sounds of the era's famous big band and swing ensembles (Colour plate 6, top).

Figure 3.2. Places featured in the Motown genre digital stories include a) Hitsville USA, the original Motown recording studios; b) The Donovan Building, now demolished; c) the Motown Mansion, Berry Gordy's former residence; and d) the Brewster-Douglass Homes, the African American housing projects that was home to several Motown stars, now demolished. Photos by K. Ryzewski and Wikicommons, 2014.

Similarly, the history of the Paradise Theatre on Woodward Avenue resists relegation to one genre or period of music making in Detroit. Originally constructed in 1919 to house the Detroit Symphony Orchestra (DSO), the theatre became a centre of Detroit's African American entertainment and jazz scene during the 1940s after the DSO moved out of the facility in 1939. During the 1940s the surrounding African American neighbourhood was known as Paradise Valley. After the entire neighbourhood was demolished by urban renewal efforts, the Paradise Theatre fell into ruin. The building sat abandoned for decades until donors in the 1980s funded its rehabilitation and returned the DSO to the building, which is now known as Orchestra Hall.

These examples illustrate how the topic of each 'Making Music' digital story was an entry point for exploring deeper histories of places associated with the city's creative heritage. The points of connection that the stories make with Detroit's contemporary landscape illustrate the everyday lives, creative energies, and inspirations of the city's music makers, producers, and consumers. Emergent connections map meaningful movements by linking music-making places to histories of what remains (or not) on the urban landscape today (Figure 3.2). Places like the Donovan Building (Motown Headquarters) in Cass Corridor and the Brewster-Douglass projects are now empty lots. Others, like the Wurlitzer Building, the Blue Bird Inn, and the Vanity Ballroom sit empty, awaiting their fate. A fortunate few, including St Andrew's Hall, Submerge Records, and the Paradise Theatre are still active participants in the city's vibrant music scene (Table 3.1). In the digital stories all of these places, occupied or not, continue to exist as active spaces of musical heritage and memory.

In its capacity to communicate the power of place across boundaries of age, race, and economics, and in its ability to assemble different genres of music into a collective urban heritage, digital storytelling holds potential as a creative practice for archaeologists to present and re-imagine certain experiences of the city's acoustic terrain (Ouzonian 2013: 54; Gandy and Nilsen 2014: 6). The 'Making Music' digital stories convey how Detroit's musical heritage is a series of movements in which people, ideas, and places benefit from contact and collaboration with one another. Detroit's music scene is not and never has been segregated according to isolated trends or groups of musicians. This is a city where audiences can still enjoy collaborative performances of seemingly disparate musicians like Melvin Davis, godfather of Northern Soul, and Wayne Kramer, founder and guitarist of rock group MC5 (Detroit Concert of Colors, July 2014).

From the Mesoamerican-inspired art deco elements of the big band-era Graystone and Vanity ballrooms, to the less glamorous punk venue of Bookie's, and the memories of the underground techno scene born at Submerge Records, the material remains of musical production and performance spaces convey the impact that popular music had on physically shaping the design and use of certain buildings and landscapes across the city. The resulting assemblage of digital stories in the 'Making Music' project succeeds in communicating the sonic profile and terrain of the city, its layers of creativity, different uses of space, and the changing sounds that cumulatively shaped the cultural heritage of Detroit and popular music history worldwide.

3.5 POPULAR MUSIC HISTORY AND ARCHAEOLOGY IN POST-INDUSTRIAL DETROIT: A DIGITAL FUTURE?

The process of integrating an archaeological perspective into the digital mapping and storytelling of popular music-related places in Detroit is uncharted methodologically and is also bound up with the challenges of the city's present struggles (e.g. scale of abandonment, decay, hyper-localism, resource allocation), all of which required careful consideration during the course of the project. Following the completion of the 'Making Music' stories I evaluated the extent to which digital storytelling was an appropriate and effective method for archaeologically documenting places associated with popular music and for communicating the significance of its heritage more broadly. In particular, there was the issue of whether the brief stories and their chronological organization risked oversimplifying place-based histories or whether they presented enough content to inspire viewers to visit the sites, either at a distance or in person, and to further engage with them. Indeed, such challenges are present in any situation that involves crafting narratives via brief engagements with digital content and mobile technologies. I concluded that this was a risk worth taking in Detroit. In a city where access to the places featured in the digital stories can be difficult, a heritage tourism industry is non-existent, and preservation of historic buildings rank among the lowest priorities of city management, digital storytelling is a viable alternative for connecting people to the city's musical heritage and for encouraging its connections to be part of the city's future redevelopment agenda (Sicko 2010: 86).

Shortly after the 'Making Music' stories were submitted in April 2014, the roof of one of the sites, the Eastown Theatre, caved in, totally destroying the ornate theatre and much of the material remains at the heart of the digital story created just days beforehand (Moloney and Pajor 2014). In November 2015 the Eastown Theatre was demolished. In fact, between the time the stories were created in April 2014 and the final editing of this chapter in July 2016, the Brewster-Douglass projects (home to many Motown recording artists) have been demolished, the Grande Ballroom has been slated for demolition, the musicians living in the 1217 Griswold Lofts (a centre of the underground techno scene) have been evicted to make way for a multi-million dollar luxury loft development (for artists), the Blue Bird Inn jazz club's roof is decaying, and the United Sound Systems studio (the oldest Jazz and R&B recording studio in the US) continues to fight to be spared from the expansion of the adjacent interstate highway. Seven of the twenty-four places initially documented by the urban archaeology group during the 'Making Music' project have already or will soon disappear from Detroit's physical landscape.

In the midst of this alarming rate of loss, one of the direct and positive results of the 'Making Music' project was the ability of the digital stories to advocate for the potential of archaeology to assist in the documentation of endangered contemporary and historic places associated with popular music. In the aftermath of the 'Making Music' story releases Wayne State University archaeologists began a fruitful collaboration with the Detroit Sound Conservancy (DSC), a grassroots organization that aims to preserve all traces of the city's music history. Through this ongoing collaboration, Wayne State archaeologists have since conducted thorough surveys, excavations, and research at the Grande Ballroom, the Blue Bird Inn jazz club, and the United Sound Studios, three of the aforementioned endangered buildings featured in the digital stories. The results of this work appear in conventional archaeological reports (Ryzewski 2016b), conference presentations, and a Master's thesis (Brace VI 2016), as well as in blog posts and podcasts oriented to popular audiences (Early 2016; Brace VI and Ellens 2015; Ryzewski 2014). Inspired by our earlier archaeological suveys, during the summer of 2016 the National Park Service's Urban Agenda initiative used the United Sound Studios and the Blue Bird Inn as two case studies in their Park Break graduate training programme in historic preservation (George Wright Society 2016). Although ongoing collaborative work with various local and national preservation groups offers many opportunities in Detroit to expand archaeology's role in documenting the city's contemporary creative past, it remains impossible and unrealistic for archaeologists to attempt to document every relevant endangered building in Detroit through conventional survey or excavation methods. With such a remarkable number of places at risk of total loss, there is a matter of urgency that demands an active and accessible approach to documenting place-based histories digitally, at least in the first instance.

The ability of digital stories to offer virtual access to transformed buildings like the Vanity Ballroom or the Michigan Theatre may also be valuable in delivering a wake-up call to those who remain disengaged from, or unaware of, the city's rich archaeological and cultural heritage. These experiential sound bites provided by the 'Making Music' project offer an opportunity for archaeologists and others to think about whether it might be worth integrating or curating ruins as part of the city's place-based music history and revitalization movements. Such sentiments were perhaps best articulated by techno artist Derrick May, in the documentary *Universal Techno*. As he stands inside the ruins of the Michigan Theatre, May proclaims:

I totally believe in the future, but as well I believe in a historic and a well kept past. I believe that there are some things that are important. Now maybe this [the Michigan Theatre ruins] is more important like this because in this atmosphere you can realize just how much people don't care—how much they don't respect, and it can make you realize how much you should respect it.

(*Universal Techno*, Deluze 1996)

Detroit's musical heritage and the places related to it form a strong base of collective symbolism that the city has yet to organize or curate to its advantage (Owens 2015). Although it is clear that archaeological studies of the recent past have much to contribute to the documentation and dissemination of popular music heritage in Detroit, it remains to be seen how music heritage will fit into the city's future-making and revitalization efforts. However, the built environment of the city's musical past holds potential for contributing to the future of Detroit's urban social space; if the city is indeed moving towards development strategies affiliated with creative capitalist policies.

Detroit's present urban setting is not (yet) conducive to the examples of place-production that Darvill (2014) suggests as ways in which the places of musical heritage might be experienced, maintained, and sustained: linear routes like Route 66, marker plaques on London's historic buildings, or explorations of music-rich cities like Memphis and Liverpool. Owing to Detroit's widespread poverty, rampant crime, extensive urban blight, and woefully inadequate public transit system, the city currently offers limited options for investing in or maintaining routes, buildings, or neighbourhoods that showcase the city's places of popular musical significance for the sake of either historic preservation or tourism. However, as privatized redevelopment efforts become increasingly prevalent in downtown neighbourhoods of the city, entrepreneurs, preservationists, and the tourism industry have the opportunity to connect with Detroit's rich musical legacy by mobilizing the city's civic engagement efforts and attempts to rebrand itself as a creative city with a globally significant local history (Harvey 2001; Novy and Colomb 2013; UNESCO 2011, 2013; on creative cities, see White and Seidenberg, Chapter 1). The recent emergence of the Detroit Institute for Music Education (DIME) in 2014 and collaborative advocacy groups like the Detroit Sound Conservancy (DSC) in 2012 have been instrumental in spearheading heritage discourse related to the city's musical past. Through performances, community events, oral history projects, collaborations with archaeologists (in the case of the DSC), and web-based wikis, these groups have asserted an active presence in gathering and publicizing information about Detroit's creative legacy, and they are encouraging indicators that music-related heritage may eventually be included within the city's redevelopment strategies.

3.6 CONCLUDING THOUGHTS

In a Detroit where revitalization and repopulation are primary goals, not every historically significant structure can or should be saved. Likewise, the enormous scale of the city and the countless places associated with popular music production and consumption means that every individual location cannot be studied archaeologically. The overwhelming expanse of contemporary material remains is a familiar reality facing archaeologists of the present and recent past, especially in post-industrial cities (see Introduction). In the absence of safe or sustainable alternatives to carefully planned heritage management strategies, grassroots initiatives to documenting place-based histories archaeologically, as with the 'Making Music' digital storytelling project and emergent non-profit groups, offer an alternative creative participatory platform to the total and undocumented loss of the city's tangible music history and heritage (on participatory platforms in heritage, see Russell, Chapter 2).

An undercurrent of creative music-making energy has set the rhythm for Detroit's response to the unprecedented scale and pace of the industrial and post-industrial change it has faced since its branding as the Motor City a century ago. Unlike the place-based documentaries or music-related landmark inventories that are increasingly emerging from journalists, film producers, and preservationists' mapping efforts, the 'Making Music in Detroit' project's digital stories are meant to convey a broader and longer term understanding of Detroit's musical heritage and urban landscape. They connect overlapping spaces and genres of music with each other, and in doing so, trace routes and assemblages of music making across the city's landscape in various configurations and trajectories. In doing so, special attention is paid to the spatial and material landscape of music making, the places were Detroit's own music was inspired, created, and performed, and what these places meant, how they changed in meaning and continue to be meaningful in shaping the city's narrative history and identity—both for residents and for visitors.

The 'Making Music in Detroit' project confronts head-on the challenges of working with cultural and archaeological heritage in a rapidly changing urban setting by creating a digital storytelling platform to engage material remains and the public in a timely manner with meaningful places in Detroit's music industry's history. These are more than memorable places where popular music was made. They are places that created the soundtrack of a city and shaped its cultural identity over the course of the twentieth century, and they continue to change with the city today. Some of the venues that are in good condition or located in downtown neighbourhoods have the potential to contribute to and benefit from revitalization efforts, but many others are decaying, derelict, or already demolished. Several of these places hold little potential to survive beyond the time it takes to publish this book. Regardless of whether individual music-making places will endure as physical traces of the city's musical heritage or transition into the realm of intangible heritage, the assemblages that now exist in the 'Making Music' videos, web texts, and other local oral history repositories serve to steady the beat of Detroit's music-based legacies, past and future.

ACKNOWLEDGEMENTS

Special thanks to the students of ANT5565 Urban Archaeology (2014) for their willingness to make their digital stories public: Erica Atkinson, C. Lorin Brace VI, Caitlin Donnelly, Brendan Doucet, Sarah Godfrey, Cecelia Murrell-Harvey, Samantha (Malette) Ellens, Brenna Moloney, Kathy Mutch, Kate E. Korth, Jeri Pajor, and Keith Zimmerman.

REFERENCES

Brace VI, C. Lorin. 2016. *'Nothing Phony About it in Any Way': Archaeological Analysis of the Blue Bird Inn Jazz Club in Post-War Detroit*. MA Thesis, Department of Anthropology, Wayne State University, Detroit, MI.

Brace VI, C. Lorin and Samantha Ellens. 2015. 'Archaeology at the Blue Bird'. *Detroit Sound Conservancy blog post*, 7 November. http://detroitsoundconservancy. org/archaeology-at-the-blue-bird/ (accessed 1 August 2016).

Ceraso, Steph. 2010. 'The Sight of Sound: Mapping Audio'. *Hastac blog post*, 5 October. https://www.hastac.org/blogs/stephceraso/2010/10/05/sight-sound-mapping-audio (accessed 27 January 2017).

Cherry, John F., Krysta Ryzewski, and Luke Pecoraro. 2013. '"A Kind of Sacred Place": The Rock and Roll Ruins of AIR Studios, Montserrat'. In *Archaeologies of Mobility and Movement*, edited by Mary C. Beaudry and Travis G. Parno, New York: Springer, pp. 181–98.

Connor, Steven. 2014. 'Rustications: Animals in the Urban Mix'. In *The Acoustic City*, edited by Matthew Gandy and B. J. Nilsen, Berlin: Jovis, pp. 16–22.

Darvill, Timothy. 2014. 'Rock and Soul: Humanizing Heritage, Memorializing Music, and Producing Places', *World Archaeology*, 46(3): 462–76.

Data Driven Detroit. 2014. http://datadrivendetroit.org/ (accessed 28 July 2016).

Deluze, Dominique. 1996. *Universal Techno*, Documentary Film. https://www. youtube.com/watch?v=SZaUCYLoEks (accessed 28 July 2016).

Early, Leo. 2016. *October 5, 2016 Grande Ballroom Inspection*. Grande Ballroom Blog, October 21. http://thegrandeballroom.com/october-5-2016-grande-ballroom-inspec tion/ (accessed 22 October 2016).

Ethnic Layers of Detroit. 2016. http://www.fltc.wayne.edu/eld/ (accessed 28 July 2016).

Gandy, Matthew and B. J. Nilsen (eds). 2014. *The Acoustic City*. Berlin: Jovis.

George Wright Society. 2016. *More than Motown: Park Break Students Document Diverse Detroit Music Heritage Sites*. 26 September. http://www.georgewright.org/node/13414 (accessed 2 October 2016).

Gordy, Berry. 1994 [2013]. *To Be loved: The Music, the Magic, the Memories of Motown: an Autobiography*. New York: Warner Books.

Graves-Brown, Paul. 2009. 'Nowhere Man: Urban Life and the Virtualization of Popular Music', *Popular Music History*, 4(2): 220–41.

Graves-Brown, Paul. 2012. 'Where the Streets Have no Name: A Guided Tour of Pop Heritage Sites in London's West End'. In *The Good, the Bad and the Unbuilt: Handling the Heritage of the Recent Past* (Studies in Contemporary History and Archaeology 7), edited by Sarah May, Hillary Orange, and Sefryn Penrose, Oxford: Archaeopress (British Archaeological Reports International Series 2362), pp. 63–76.

Harris, Bob and John Douglas Peters. 2008. *Motor City Rock and Roll: The 1960s and 1970s*. Charleston: Arcadia Press.

Harvey, David. 2001. *Spaces of Capital: Towards a Critical Geography*. New York: Routledge.

Herron, Jerry. 1993. *After Culture: Detroit and the Humiliation of History*. Detroit: Wayne State University Press.

Holt, Fabian and Carsten Wergin (eds). 2014. *Musical Performance and the Changing City: Post-Industrial Contexts in Europe and the United States*. New York and London: Routledge.

Keeling, David J. 2011. 'Iconic Landscapes: The Lyrical Links of Songs and Cities', *Focus on Geography*, 54: 113–25.

Lashua, Brett, Sara Cohen, and John Schofield. 2010. 'Popular Music, Mapping and the Characterization of Liverpool', *Popular Music History*, 4(2): 126–44.

Long, Philip. 2014. 'Popular Music, Psychogeography, Place Identity and Tourism: The Case of Sheffield', *Tourist Studies*, 14(1): 48–65.

Miller, Steve. 2013. *Detroit Rock City: The Uncensored History of Rock 'n Roll in America's Loudest City*. Boston: Da Capo Press.

Moloney, Brenna and Jeri Pajor. 2014. *Making Music in Detroit: Rock and Roll Digital Stories*, Created for ANT5565 Urban Archaeology, Prof. K. Ryzewski, Wayne State University, Detroit, http://www.geostoryteller.org/mobile.php?usePortal=soundscape (accessed 23 January 2017).

Moreno, Louis. 2014. 'The Sound of Detroit: Notes, Tones, and Rhythms from Underground'. In *The Acoustic City*, edited by Matthew Gandy and B. J. Nilsen. Berlin: Jovis, pp. 98–107.

Mullins, Paul. 2014. 'The Ruins of Music', *Archaeology and Material Culture* blog, 16 August. https://paulmullins.wordpress.com/?s=popular+music (accessed 28 July 2016).

Novy, Johannes and Claire Colomb. 2013. 'Struggling for the Right to the (Creative) City in Berlin and Hamburg: New Urban Social Movements, New "Spaces of Hope"?', *International Journal of Urban and Regional Research*, 37(5): 1816–38.

O'Keeffe, Tadhg. 2013. 'Performance, Materiality, and Heritage: What Does an Archaeology of Popular Music Look Like?', *Journal of Popular Music Studies*, 25(1): 91–113.

Ouzonian, Gascia. 2013. 'Recomposing the City: A Survey of Recent Sound Art in Belfast', *Leonardo Music Journal*, 23: 47–54.

Owens, Keith. 2015. '13 Ways Detroit can Assert Itself as a Music Capital', *Model D Media*, 17 March. http://modeldmedia.com/features/detroitmusiccapital031715.aspx (accessed 28 July 2016).

Parkman, E. Breck. 2014. 'A Hippie Discography: Vinyl Records from a Sixties Commune', *World Archaeology*, 46(3): 431–47.

Penrose, Sefryn. 2007. *Images of Change: An Archaeology of England's Contemporary Landscape*. London: English Heritage.

Roberts, Les. 2014. 'Marketing Musicscapes, or the Political Economy of Contagious Music', *Tourist Studies*, 14(1): 10–29.

Ryzewski, Krysta. 2012. 'Multiply Situated Strategies? Multi-Sited Ethnography and Archeology', *Journal of Archaeological Method and Theory*, 19(2): 241–68.

Ryzewski, Krysta. 2014. 'Interview on RecordDET'. Podcast Interview, Detroit Sound Conservancy, 17 November. http://detroitsoundconservancy.org/artifact/krysta-ryzewski/ (accessed 28 July 2016).

Ryzewski, Krysta. 2016a. 'Reclaiming Detroit: Decolonizing Archaeology in the Post-Industrial City'. *Savage Minds*, blog post, 5 July. http://savageminds.org/2016/07/05/reclaiming-detroit-decolonizing-archaeology-in-the-postindustrial-city/ (accessed 28 July 2016).

Ryzewski, Krysta (ed.). 2016b. *The Grande Ballroom Archaeological Survey Report*. Unpublished report submitted to the Friends of the Grande Ballroom and Preservation Detroit. On file with the Wayne State University G.L. Grosscup Museum of Anthropology.

Schofield, John. 2014a. 'Characterizing the Cold War: Music and Memories of Berlin, 1960–1989'. In *Sounds and the City: Popular Music, Place and Globalization*, edited by Brett Lashua, Karl Spracklen, and Stephen Wagg, London: Palgrave Macmillan, pp. 273–84.

Schofield, John. 2014b. 'The Archaeology of Sound and Music', *World Archaeology*, 46(3): 289–91.

Sicko, Dan. 2010. *Techno Rebels: The Renegades of Electronic Funk*. 2nd edn. New York: Painted Turtle.

Sugrue, Thomas J. 2014. *The Origins of the Urban Crisis: Race and Inequality in Postwar Detroit*. 3rd edn. Princeton: Princeton University Press.

UNESCO. 2011. *Recommendation on the Historic Urban Landscape*. Paris: UNESCO.

UNESCO. 2013. Creative Economy Report. Special Edition: Widening Local Development Pathways. Paris: UNESCO.

Section II

Ruination

4

Embers from the House of Blazes

Fragments, Relics, Ruins of Chicago

Rebecca S. Graff

Fragments imply a former whole, and ruins invoke a material landscape once cared for and conserved, now neglected. What meaning is conveyed when fragments of formerly whole structures—ruined or plundered as 'relics'—are incorporated into new ones, devoid of prior context? Does an aesthetic appreciation for *in situ* ruins also relate to interest in their fragments? This tradition of, and fascination with, reusing and recontextualizing fragments of ruined structures spans the broad sweep of time from antiquity to the present day (see also Shanahan and Shanahan, Chapter 5). Rome's Arch of Constantine (erected 315 CE) incorporated fragments from the arches of Hadrian and Marcus Aurelius, visually and materially connecting their collective glory to the new reign. Such reuse is found plentifully in indirect gestures, such as the Beaux-Arts municipal buildings of the United States that draw stylistic influences from classical antiquity, as reimagined in the Italian Renaissance and incorporated into the nineteenth-century architectural canon. Still other examples of direct reuse of fragments, such as architectural fragments from New York's World Trade Center that have been incorporated into myriad 9/11 monuments, are often a way to commemorate the tragic circumstances that created such ruins, reminding us how the materiality of age, added by narrative and even literal labels, provides a space for nostalgic reminiscence or communion with an event that might be personally distant, though emotionally compelling just the same (see White and Seidenberg, Chapter 1, for discussion of a similar phenomenon in Berlin).

Inspired by the increasing impact of contemporary archaeology on considerations of materiality, temporality, and erasure within archaeologically produced 'present pasts' (see Harrison et al. 2014), this essay focuses on two cases of creative reuse of fragmentary architectural and building materials in Chicago, one still extant, and the other no longer even a ruin. The first case, once made of 'ruins', has been demolished and, more significantly, erased: the Relic House, built in 1872 from 'leavings' of the 1871 Chicago Fire. Serving as a saloon, salon, and speakeasy until its demolition in 1929, the Relic House drew guests who wished to commune with the 'ruins' of the tragic fire in a space mediated by recreational consumption and novelty. One of these uses included a venue for the bohemian Dill Pickle Club, whose founder renamed the structure the 'House of Blazes', evoking its fabrication from Fire debris. Whilst the final ruination of the Relic House may have been motivated by the loss of business mandated by National Prohibition (1920–33), the reasons for its erasure from contemporary memory remain as yet unexamined (see Mullins, Chapter 12, for discussion of communal forgetting in Indianapolis).

The second case, the Chicago Tribune Tower, is a 1925 building on Chicago's 'Magnificent Mile'. Its façade is peppered with architectural fragments of buildings and locations tacitly portrayed to represent a Western view of the important symbols of 'cultural heritage'. *Chicago Tribune* correspondents opportunistically collected many of these since World War I in a manner that would raise ethical and legal questions today. Still other 'Famous Stones' are from important sites in forty-nine of the fifty United States, and include natural elements, such as a rock from Wyoming's Yellowstone Park, in addition to cultural ones, though without explanation or apparent hierarchical ordering for these different commemorative forms. In 1999 the Tribune Tower acquired a piece of moon rock collected from the 1971 Apollo 15 expedition, thereby extending its collection's domain to outer space. I have argued elsewhere (Graff 2001) that the spatially compact distribution of these stones encourages would-be travellers to interface with the whole world in the space of a block. Furthermore, the 'Famous Stones' allow those who view them to locate Chicago within a narrative of ancient and modern human accomplishments.

Using these two case studies, this chapter grapples with a series of questions: what is the relationship between the creative reuse of architectural fragments and the social memories of those who view them? Under what circumstances do some narratives of civic identity become part of 'authorised heritage discourse' (Smith 2006) and written into the built environment through the reuse of fragments? How might a contemporary archaeology of urbanity engage with such reuse—in Chicago and elsewhere—and what can it offer in terms of its own narrative? Finally, is it in these seemingly unrelated fragment- and ruin-laden narratives that a coherent narrative whole can be found?

4.1 FROM CITY TO RUIN: THE 1871 CHICAGO FIRE

One of the most iconic and reproduced photographs depicting the devastation of the 1871 Chicago Fire shows an old woman, her shawl-wrapped figure stark against a ravaged landscape. To her right sits a younger woman, looking at the fire's results from a curb; to her left, a group of nine men congregate steps away from the Chicago Water Tower and Pumping Station, two of a handful of structures that survived destruction in the Burnt District (Figure 4.1). The picture emphasizes that little seems to remain of the once vibrant and thriving city: it has become a ruin.

On the evening of 8 October 1871, a fire that started south-west of the downtown quickly raged through the city, even jumping the South Branch of the Chicago River. By the morning of the 10th, over four square miles of the city were burnt, leaving 100,000 people homeless, 300 dead, and costing its citizens upwards of $150,000,000 in destroyed property (Goodsell 1871; Goodspeed 1871) The Chicago fire had two long-term impacts: one, it effectively razed most of the downtown area, leaving a clean slate for future architects tasked with stricter building codes (on anticipating the effects of capitalistic 'creative destruction' on material heritage; see Penrose, Chapter 8, and Schumpeter 1942); and two, it became a source for comparison between the enormity and the tragedy of the Chicago fire and conflagrations with ancient and modern precedents. 'Boosters' (promoters; often leading

Figure 4.1. Chicago Water Tower and Pumping Station, after the Fire; from a Stereograph, 1871. Chicago History Museum (ICHI-13918).

businesspeople) of the city compared Chicago's fire to those of the distant—Babylon, Troy, Rome—and the more recent past—London of 1666 and Moscow of 1812. They also made analogies with fires of established east coast cities, such as New York (1835) and Philadelphia (1850). Their conclusions as disseminated in the official post-Fire narrative of, and identity for, Chicago seemed to be that the city had the potential to be as important and as great a city as any others in the history of humankind, and could thus be 'resurrected' to join their ranks.

Joseph Medill, editor of the *Chicago Tribune*, adopted this grandiose position in the first post-fire *Tribune* edition in an editorial titled, 'Cheer Up': 'In the midst of a calamity without parallel in the world's history, looking upon the ashes of thirty years' accumulations, the people of this once beautiful city have resolved that CHICAGO SHALL RISE AGAIN' (1871: 2). The fire became a generative event, with the city depicted as a phoenix rising from its ashes. One anecdote from the many volumes recollecting the fire claims that the re-building process started almost immediately: 'On the Monday morning of the fire...a man was observed carefully examining the bricks of the ruins of the Reynolds' Block, picking them up carefully and "feeling" them. An observer asked him to explain his conduct, he replied: "I was just seeing if they were cool enough to build with again!"' (Sheahan 1871: 263).

Rubble from the ruined buildings was deposited along the lakeshore, transforming the city by extending the sought-after lakefront ever eastward. Before the fire, the downtown's easternmost street was Michigan Avenue, not far from the Lake Michigan shore. After the Fire and subsequent construction, valuable square miles of land were added, which now host some of the most visited and iconic parts of the city—Grant Park, the Museum Campus, and a range of expensive apartment blocks. Rubble made an excellent building material, as it has been reused in centuries past; it was used to conspicuously fashion the Relic House, the first subject of this chapter. Whilst this structure is no longer extant, I argue it can still be considered part of an archaeology of the contemporary.

Following Nancy Munn's insights on the 'becoming-past-of-places' in nineteenth-century New York, where she argues a sense of 'dissolution of place' fomented by modernity's rapid currents is mediated by space, time, and memory (2004: 4), the ultimate disappearance of the Relic House from the Chicago cityscape is itself a subject of archaeological inquiry. Contemporary archaeology allows for such investigations by 'presenc[ing] absences...by constituting an archaeological record of sorts' (Buchli quoted in González-Ruibal et al. 2014: 273): creating a distinctly spatiotemporal experience of place through a focus on materiality. Although the current materiality of the Relic House is composed of newspaper clippings, photographs, postcards, and volumes of personal reminiscences held in archives, this documentary record produces what might be termed an archival archaeology of the contemporary.

The interplay between text and artefact that is foundational to historical archaeology (see Beaudry 1988a) promises illumination for disappeared materialities; the 'notions arising from a material perspective on the past dictated by the nature of archaeological evidence' (Beaudry 1988b: 1–2) can also be applied to the vanished, through the conception of the document as material culture as well as text. Thus an archaeology of the Relic House elevates the vanished, the ruin, the fragment, the rubble, and moves them from the hidden substrate into the visible and featured surface.

4.2 RELIC HOUSE

A row of nondescript bushes flank the rear plaza of the Chicago History Museum (formerly the Chicago Historical Society, founded in 1856 by Chicago's most prominent entrepreneurs), marking the place where the institution's space terminates into the landscape of Lincoln Park. The rear of the museum is not particularly interesting in an architectural sense, and the plain landscaping reinforces the idea that the important part of the structure is both inside—in terms of exhibits—and in front—in terms of its official entrance and façade on North Clark Street.

Within a clearing in the bushes, lie unmarked chunks of what appear to be formerly molten masses of metal. The foliage is pruned just enough to allow the informed seeker the ability to see the objects hidden within the leaves *if* they know where to look. Knowing what these objects are is a different issue: no signage or other marker alerts the viewer to their provenance. Many people, myself included, learned of these mysterious artefacts by word of mouth. In fact, with the exception of the occasional segment on public television, there is little mention or explanation of what these items are: reconstituted objects created by the 1871 Chicago Fire.

The Chicago Historical Society acquired these pieces of fire-altered iron, stone, and brick in 1921 as part of a large donation by Chicago candy manufacturer, Charles Frederick Gunther (1837–1920) (Chicago Park District 2010). Gunther, a former director of the Chicago Historical Society, made his fortune from his popular caramel candies, and used it to purchase art and historic materials, especially those relating to the American Civil War (Wolf 2012). Perhaps because his own business was destroyed in the 1871 Fire (Journal of the Illinois State Historical Society 1920), Gunther also extended his collecting interests to fire materials. In 1890 the estimated twenty-ton chunk of fire debris, eventually owned and donated by Gunther, was uncovered during excavations for the footings of the Masonic Temple at State and Randolph, along with a melted pair of steel scissors and part of a silver watch (*Chicago Tribune* 1890: 8).

Why these fragments are so hard to visually locate today—'buried in the shrubbery on the east side of the museum' (Chicago Park District 2010)—is not made clear by their presumptive caretaker, the Chicago History Museum.

Although currently hidden, the Chicago History Museum fragments were intentionally preserved for some time after the Fire. Likewise, the Relic House was created to display and preserve the remnants of the 1871 Chicago Fire: to remember, to fascinate, and, at a base level, to serve as construction material that purposely maintains a material connection to the initial event. In 1872 a man only recorded as 'Rettig' constructed a cottage-sized structure from 'a melted mixture of stone, iron and other metals' at the corner of North Park Avenue and Central Street (*Chicago Tribune* 1890: 8, see also Flinn 1893: 401). Further accounts state that the structure had walls made from melted globules of metal, masonry, sewing machines, and china doll parts, with an interior decorated with pre-1871-style furnishings (Weis 1906; *Chicago Tribune* 1929a: 2). A brief mention in a 1920 obituary of one Joseph Wallace, an undertaker, even claims that the Relic House was used as a temporary mortuary for the care of Fire dead, although this seems at odds with the purported timeline of its construction (*Chicago Tribune* 1920d). An 1878 advertising card (Figure 4.2) shows the Relic House surrounded by streetcars, pedestrians, and prancing horses, and it lists Hermann Klanowsky as proprietor. Klanowsky was the maternal grandfather of actress Gloria Swanson, whose father supposedly took over the establishment in the early twentieth century (*Chicago Tribune* 1929a: 2).

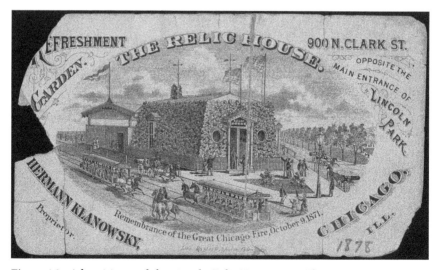

Figure 4.2. Advertising card showing the Relic House, 1878. Chicago History Museum (ICHI-63841).

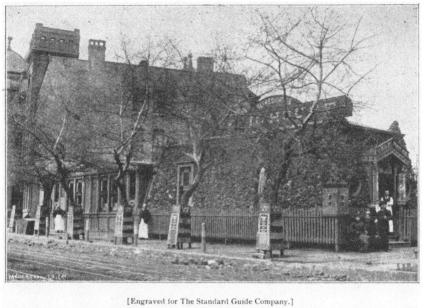

[Engraved for The Standard Guide Company.]
THE RELIC HOUSE—NEAR LINCOLN PARK.
[See " Relic House."]

Figure 4.3. Relic House, 1893. From Flinn 1893: n.p.

A popular and often reprinted account (*Chicago Tribune* 1890: 8) claims that around 1882, Phillip Vinter (or Winter, see Weis 1906) took over the Relic House and moved it to North Park Avenue (now Lincoln Park West) and Clark Street (specifically 900 N. Clark, changed after the 1909 street renumbering to 2037 N. Clark). However, an Albert Rettig—likely the same Rettig who built the Relic House in 1872—is listed as a saloonkeeper living at 900 N. Clark in the 1880 Census, casting doubt on the Vinter attribution (United States Census 1880).[1]

William Lindemann bought the Relic House sometime before 1890 and established a 'refreshment parlor' in the saloon (*Chicago Tribune* 1890: 8; Flinn 1893: 402; see Figure 4.3). By 1890 its importance had risen to a point that a *Chicago Tribune* editorial called for the entire structure to be temporarily moved to Jackson Park to display the city's history, specifically the

---

[1] Albert Rettig, saloonkeeper, is first found at 774 Franklin Street in 1875 (Chicago Directory Company 1875: 830) and then at the Relic House site of 900 N. Clark with a home at 948 N. Clark in 1880 (Chicago Directory Company 1880: 933). By 1885, Albert Rettig, saloonkeeper, has moved to 976 Clybourn Avenue (Chicago Directory Company 1885: 1152; now 2511 N. Clybourn Ave, see Chicago Directory Company 1909), either ending his time at the structure he created and the saloon he founded, or merely moving on to another saloon in another part of the city.

'fantastic freaks of the flames' from the 1871 Fire, to tourists at the 1893 World's Columbian Exposition (*Chicago Tribune* 1890: 8). Such an exhibit was a fit medium to position the fair planners' narrative of the Chicago's rebirth from flame (see Graff 2001). Lindemann agreed: 'It would make a good American curiosity', but only if he was paid enough for his efforts (*Chicago Tribune* 1890: 8). This plan did not come to fruition, nor did Lindemann's proposed six-storey revamp of the Relic House of 1896 (*Chicago Tribune* 1896: 38). Lindemann purportedly continued to add 'relics' to his establishment as new construction projects continued to unearth them, although precisely what these items may have been has not been located in documentation.[2]

The Relic House served as a saloon into the twentieth century, and a speakeasy during National Prohibition (1920–33), and its ownership continued to change hands during this period. By 1906 John Weis had become the proprietor, spending time and money to improve his establishment. With 'the most tempting dishes... served in real German style' in a setting newly decorated with 'stuffed moose and deer heads, stuffed sharks, engravings of German arts, and a large oil painting of the Chicago Fire', Weis encouraged visitors to his 'quaint monument and rustic resort' (Weis 1906: 12, 13, 15).[3] In 1914 an advertisement shows it as one of the seven saloons in Chicago to have Munich's St Benno Bier on tap (*Chicago Tribune* 1914: 14). Its location, directly across from Lincoln Park, made it a prime spot 'for thirsty tourists travelling the Clark street cable cars' (*Chicago Tribune* 1928a: 31).

During National Prohibition the space continued to serve alcohol as a speakeasy, as did many other Chicago saloons (see Graff 2013). In 1922 the *Tribune* ran the impish headline: 'Relic House Shelter for Relics of Pre-'19 Period', recounting the raid on the establishment by federal prohibition agents (*Chicago Tribune* 1922: 9). The Relic House 'served for many years as an establishment for washing dust from parched throats' until '[t]he stern Mr. Volstead ended this pleasant process' (*Chicago Tribune* 1928b: B1). The space was then turned into a restaurant (*Chicago Tribune* 1929a), though it had served food from *c*.1900 as a 'Familien Lokal', or family-style German restaurant, as well as during its time under the auspices of Weis (Clark 1954: E2; Weis 1906).

The Dill Pickle Club added a bohemian chapter to the Relic House story. The club, started in 1914 as a cultural centre by Archibald 'Jack' Jones, an organizer for the Industrial Workers of the World, initially was located at 859 N. State Street in Tooker Alley (Newberry Library 2009). In 1920, having been

[2] William Lindemann is listed at the Relic House site in the 1892 and 1900 directories, though not in the 1910 edition (Chicago Directory Company 1892: 916, 1900: 1160, 1910: 806).
[3] John Weis is still listed as proprietor in 1910 at the newly renumbered 2037 N. Clark site (Chicago Directory Company 1910: 1101, 1386).

kicked out of their previous address, anarchist Dr Ben L. Reitman arranged for the Club to meet at the Relic House for the first of many poetry nights. The Club members renamed their venue the 'House of Blazes', reaffirming its link to the 1871 Fire (*Chicago Tribune* 1920a: 17, 1920b: 4). Considered an offshoot of the Dill Pickle Club proper, Reitman leased it for two years (*Chicago Tribune* 1920c: A5). Other artistic uses for the Relic House include as a home for Meyer Levin's experimental Marionette Theatre in 1926 (Solomon 1983).

In the years after the Fire, there were many collections made of debris and souvenirs besides that which formed the Relic House, including the remnants now in the grounds of the Chicago History Museum. Though not 'relics' in the religious sense, the items were visited by pilgrims who wanted to commune with the lasting, material evidence of a horrific and constitutive event in Chicago history. A fountain created from Fire architectural fragments was built in the yard of W. M. Scudder on North Michigan Avenue, formerly 674 Lincoln Parkway (*Chicago Daily News* 1911). The Chicago Historical Society—itself a victim of the fire with the loss of its building on Ontario and Dearborn—received collections of melted forks, movable type, marbles, jews harps, thimbles, china dolls, coffee, and a piece of the Old Courthouse Bell (*Chicago Tribune* 1890: 8; see also Chicago History Museum and Northwestern University 2011). Many of these items came from former Burnt District business owners, and were representations of the stock lost to the fire. A 1933 report titled 'Relics of the Chicago Fire' by Laura Kendall Thomas traced the removal and relocation of several limestone urns from their original home atop the Chicago Court House to their dispersal around post-Fire Chicago (Thomas 1933).

With all of the public interest and popularity of the site, it might seem strange that the Relic House was demolished only fifty-seven years after it was built. Like the landmarks that fell to the Chicago Fire, the Relic House would also be removed from the city streetscape, although intentionally, and for capital profit. In 1929 the structure was razed so that a new, 210-unit apartment building with mechanical refrigeration and other modern appliances could be constructed (*Chicago Tribune* 1928b: B1, 1929b: B1). At the time of its sale there was a sense that an important symbol was about to disappear for good, as the developer of the property, Peter F. Reynolds, was given the moniker based on the upcoming transaction: 'Chicago['s] greatest effacer of landmarks' (*Chicago Tribune* 1928b: B1). Today, Reynolds' apartment building still sits at 2000 Lincoln Park West.

In the same manner that the hidden relics of the Chicago Fire persist without interpretation behind the Chicago History Museum just a few blocks away, no signage marks the Relic House site. In Chicago an absence of memorials for formative events and sites is not uncommon; the 1893 World's Columbian Exposition site of Jackson Park, once host to 27 million people and still invoked by politicians, history buffs, and locals, likewise has no signage announcing its former significance. Following Munn, although 'the power of presencing the past was problematized in the spatiotemporal disorders of vanishing places' (2004: 13) like the Fair and the Relic House sites, it is the presence of social memory and a documentary record—both still mediated by materiality—that craft narratives. Such erasure and lack of material commemoration lies in stark contrast to the Chicago Tribune Tower's decidedly non-local 'Famous Stones', whose physical labelling is more important than the material fragments themselves in telling a particular tale of Chicago.

4.3 THE CHICAGO TRIBUNE TOWER'S 'FAMOUS STONES'

Walk down North Michigan Avenue on a warm summer day and be prepared to navigate people stopped along the substantial Chicago Tribune Tower. These tourists are looking intently at the wall of the building. A closer inspection reveals fragments of masonry, stone, and brick, labelled with chiselled letters that reveal purported origins like 'MOSQUE OF SULEIMAN THE MAGNIFICENT 1557 ISTANBUL, TURKEY' or 'STABIAN BATHS POMPEII'. Some will pose for a quick snapshot in front of one or another fragment, whilst others will touch the stones as they momentarily commune with a temporally and geographically distant place or civilization.

Construction of the Chicago Tribune Tower finished in 1925, three years after an international competition that attracted many of the world's greatest architects. Nowhere in the winning design or in any of the other entries was there any mention of incorporating architectural fragments into the façade of the Tower. Yet today, the most visible and celebrated features of the Tribune Tower are the almost 150 'Famous Stones': architectural fragments of famous buildings, from a collection begun by the *Tribune*'s past editor, Robert McCormick.

Robert Rutherford McCormick, Jr (1880–1955), was born in Chicago to parents Robert Sanderson McCormick, Sr, the nephew of mechanical reaper inventor Cyrus McCormick, and Katherine Medill McCormick, daughter of Joseph Medill, the editor of the *Chicago Tribune* from 1855 to 1899. McCormick's middle name was changed by his mother from Sanderson to 'Rutherford', the name of a descendent he shared with Sir Walter Scott, in order to evoke a sense of high-class European heritage. This name-change was but the first evidence of a European borrowing and invented connection associated with McCormick. His wealthy and peripatetic childhood, which included several years in London where his father served as a diplomat, may well be seen as a starting point for his fascination with the architecture of the world (Smith 1997).

McCormick eventually joined the family business, becoming acting president of the *Tribune* in 1911 and co-editor along with his cousin Joseph Medill Patterson in 1913. In 1915 McCormick travelled to Europe as a war correspondent. McCormick was captivated by his experiences at the front lines of the Western Front, especially the American-led triumph at Cantigny—for which he would name his Wheaton, Illinois, estate—and set up one of the first bureaus of foreign correspondents for the *Tribune* at the War's conclusion. Most significantly, it was McCormick's experience in World War I France, in the shelled town of Arras, which led him to initiate his 'Famous Stone' collection.

There are differing accounts of the acquisition process of the 'Famous Stones'. A pamphlet printed by the *Tribune* and available in the Tribune Tower lobby reads: '[t]he Colonel had a collection of stones that he had picked up during his travels. Chicago Tribune correspondents supplemented the collection with stones obtained during their overseas assignments' (Chicago Tribune Company 1999: n.p.). According to the Tribune's architecture critic, Blair Kamin, the first stone's provenance is cited as Ypres, Belgium, and it was collected after German shelling damaged a medieval cathedral (Kamin and Fila 2000: 17). Further stones were coerced from his corps of foreign correspondents, who were told to add to the collection (Gies 1979: 1; Kamin and Fila 2000). Today, fragments from over thirty countries, as well as almost every state in the Union, decorate the façade.

4.3.1 The Chicago Tribune Tower Architectural Competition: A Setting for the Stones

The Chicago Tribune Tower's flying buttresses and other Gothic Revival touches locate it within a spatiotemporal aesthetic that informs the collection of stones. Although the first architectural fragments were collected before the construction of the Tribune Tower, the stones were not publicly shown until after the new building was completed. After a worldwide design competition, the structure opened in 1925. The Tribune Tower Competition, like the 'Famous Stones', reflects a particular worldview regarding older, vaunted, and European-inspired architectural forms and their concomitant notions of cultural legitimacy, as well as the desire, held by McCormick and other businessmen, to transform Chicago into a great, international city.

Founded in 1847, the *Chicago Tribune*'s headquarters on Dearborn and Madison Streets served the paper until the beginning of the twentieth century. Partly to draw more publicity for the *Tribune*, a design competition was announced for its new headquarters on 10 June 1922. Coinciding with the seventy-fifth anniversary of the paper, the competition drew entries by architects competing for a grand prize of $50,000. The competition ran for three months, and a total of 263 entries were submitted from twenty-three different countries. Eventually, the neo-Gothic design of John Mead Howells and Raymond Hood (a graduate of the Paris École des Beaux-Arts) won.

During the competition, the *Tribune* ran a series of rotogravure pictures of structures from around the world, including the Roman Pantheon, Florence's Il Duomo, the British Houses of Parliament, and New York's Woolworth Building. Readers of the paper were asked to submit their opinions on these buildings, with the idea that this feedback would be given to the competition judges. The rotogravures encouraged the 'traditional' style that the judges of the competition desired (Stamper 1991). When looking at, for example, the rotogravure of the Pantheon, the glory of Rome would be evoked for the reader at the same time they were being told that the new Tribune Tower would encompass this tradition in an even grander, and perhaps more 'American', manner. Six buildings from New York were included to show the beautiful architecture of that city and to spark an interest in the readers in creating a building better than anything the east coast had known. The rotogravures served as a sort of propaganda, sparking the competitive desire of Chicagoans to out-design the world.

Howells and Hood's design won over more modern counterparts because it embodied a sense of European architectural style, and more importantly, a 'traditional' grandeur (see Solomonson 2001). Taking inspiration from the Butter Tower of the Rouen Cathedral, the Gothic building with its intricate traceries and decorative flying buttresses brought the Old World to the New World of Michigan Avenue. The façade and the interior contain stained-glass windows, gargoyles, and grotesques. Louis Sullivan criticized the Howells and Hood design: '[c]onfronted by the limpid eye of analysis, the first prize trembles and falls, self-confessed, crumbling to the ground. Visibly it is not architecture' (Sullivan 1988: 230). He claimed that some romantic sentiment or emotional necessity in the judges or the people of Chicago caused them to embrace the backwards-looking Tribune Tower.

In 1957, two years after he died, a brick from Robert McCormick's child-hood home was placed in the Tribune's façade as a tribute to the man that inspired both the building and its collection. In placing the collection of 'Famous Stones' on the façade of a nascent Chicago landmark, McCormick suggested that the great achievements of the world's heritage (and, metonymically, the world itself) were encapsulated in both the Tribune Tower and the city of Chicago that surrounded it. Today, the Tribune Company continues to collect specimens for the façade. The collection that McCormick started continues to grow. In 2002 a ribbon of metal from the ruins of New York's World Trade Center found a site of honour on the façade of the Tribune Tower, adjacent to a piece from the mosque of the sixteenth-century Ottoman Ruler Suleiman the Magnificent (Figure 4.4).

Figure 4.4. Façade of Chicago Tribune Tower. Photo by Rebecca S. Graff.

The similarity of mundane objects—salvaged then enmeshed together—in the Relic House and the Chicago Tribune Tower speak to the vast literature on collections and collecting, and how meaning is made through these materials. In her volume on collecting in the European, museological tradition, Susan Pearce defines a collection as 'a group of objects, brought together with intention and sharing a common identity of some kind, which is regarded by its owner as, in some sense, special or set apart' (1995: 159). The materials that made up the Relic House and the Tribune Tower's Famous Stones are these sorts of collections, and both share the fact that, over the years, other people have added materials to the assemblage. To this sense of collectivity, add 'the comfort of things': Daniel Miller's ethnography of thirty London households and the objects they hold dear—including collections of toys from McDonalds Happy Meals, stamps, Beatles memorabilia—explored the way that 'things' connect us to each other, and to ourselves (Miller 2008). For the Relic House and the Tribune Tower, the collections found in their walls each offered a particular collector's vision of Chicago, connecting individuals united by tragedy (the Fire) or by a business-oriented sense of civic worth (the *Chicago Tribune*). It is not the materials themselves, or the individual collectors who gathered them, that concerns the final section of this chapter, but the way that narratives of civic identity are materialized by engaging with these collections.

4.4 FRAGMENTS OF MEMORIES, COLLECTIONS OF RUINS

'Whose memories become history?' asks David Hurst Thomas in the introduction to his work on the Kennewick Man controversy, a case where the corporeal and material remains of a Native American ancestor became a fraught, international controversy over the right to assert, deny, or appropriate Native American identities (Korsmo 1999: 131 in Thomas 2000: xxiv). To this I answer: the memories that those with structural power make material. They manifest as maintained structures, ruins, monuments, or fragments. They exert commemorative force, often validating present practices (see Shanahan and Shanahan, Chapter 5, for a similar interpretation of Melbourne's parkscapes). As Smith (2006: 4) argues, such authorized heritage discourse 'works to naturalize a range of assumptions about the nature and meaning of heritage': meanings used by those in power or with institutional authority to solidify their claims. Yet however strong the dominant narrative is, there is always potential for other narratives—including counter-narratives—to coalesce around contentious events and sites through continuing re-engagement with materials. A large literature focusing on memory and the politics of heritage provides insight into the meaning and importance of alternate commemorations; for example, how contemporary union workers continue to agitate around the memory of Colorado's Ludlow Massacre Site (Warner 2003).

In the cases thus examined, it is clear how a foundational moment in Chicago history (the 1871 Fire) and an early twentieth-century view of Chicago's global future (the Tribune Tower and its 'Famous Stones') were recontextualized and transformed by the collection and display of ruins, relics, and fragments. The collection and prominent display of the ruins from the Chicago Fire in the Relic House, and the clearly labelled and displayed 'Famous Stones' of the Tribune Tower both attempted to muster a collective memory, selecting particularly evocative temporal and spatial moments to form a narrative of Chicago's exceptionalism.

Yet only one collection continues to be officially venerated, advertised, and protected, indicating a profound disparity among instances of fragment reuse. A vision of Chicago and its past is materialized—and thereby served—by allowing some features of the built environment, like the Relic House, to disappear from material commemoration. The Tribune Tower's collection of random architectural fragments evoke not a concrete event, like the Relic House did with the Chicago Fire, but an imagined narrative of Chicago's place on the global stage in the years after World War I. Nevertheless, it remains a major stopping point on one of the most heavily traversed intersections in Chicago, and as such can more directly imply an identity and a narrative for Chicago. Moreover, collectors' links to institutional power are crucial— consider Rettig vs McCormick—but so too are uses of fragments that do not seem to complicate or make light of official narratives and identities, though what is 'official' or even desirous does change over time. The vernacular Relic House combined local fragments of old Chicago in a carnivalesque jumble that promoted communion but perhaps not reverence; though such an interaction with a traumatic event seemed to be suitable if not emotionally restorative for many years after the Fire, as indicated by the popularity of the venue. By contrast, the official, École des Beaux-Arts-influenced Tribune Tower curates a quasi-museological collection of global 'Famous Stones' to invite edification, admiration, even awe, even though the motivation for the collection was to imagine Chicago's future in a particular manner. The current disparity between the two structures and their relics—though noting their temporal difference—deserves to be investigated using the toolkit and vision of an archaeology of the present.

4.4.1 Spolia and the Archaeology of the Present

How can one compare the architectural fragments that grace the Tribune Tower to the 1871 Fire remnants that composed the Relic House? They are seemingly dissimilar, with 'Famous Stones' as architectural fragments being constituted quite differently than the Fire debris. The Relic House fragments were reconstituted as a building in a spatially proximate location to their original contexts, whilst the 'Famous Stones' were removed from architectural contexts the world over and placed in one installation. Yet the materials that formed the Relic House and the 'Famous Stones' of Tribune Tower both draw their evocative power from being *outside of* and *displaced from* their former context, temporal and spatial distances notwithstanding, and the new context—the whole made of formerly unrelated fragments—that emerges where their new meaning is made.

An interesting false opposition between (art) historical and archaeological approaches to artefacts removed from original contexts (referred to as *spolia*) provides a starting point for connecting the Relic House and the Tribune Tower:

> To begin, these disciplines direct their gazes in different directions. For the archaeologist, the *spolium*[4] is a piece that was *removed* from Antiquity, whereas

---

[4] Scholars have long noted that the reuse of architectural fragments in structures like the Tribune Tower can aid in linking or appropriating ancient ideas and ideals for contemporary purposes. The term 'spolia', coined by historian Arnold Esch in 1969, primarily refers to 'reused architectural components and sculptures from Greco-Roman antiquity' (Kinney 2011: 1). Chiefly used by art historians, the term carries with it the sense of violation or violence that created the conditions for the physical transfer of an object, in this case, of ancient Roman military mementos (*spolia opima*) or 'spoils'. In characterizing the contemporary preoccupation with the 'cult' of popular heritage—found in Elvis memorabilia, Stonehenge, and even

for the historian and the art historian...the same piece was *received* from
Antiquity. This leads to diverse methods and ways of posing the question. The
archaeologist is inclined to bring the *spolium* back to its original home, as it were,
and once more to complete the ancient monument that was 'damaged' through
spoliation. Art historians and historians, on the other hand, take an interest just
in the new contexts and ask in what sense the use of *spolia* was actually the
'appropriation' of Antiquity, or simple recycling, or something else altogether.

(Esch 2011: 14, emphasis in original)

The author calls for a multidisciplinary view to overcome what he sees as a
broad disciplinary divide. Perhaps unfair to both the classical archaeologists
that serve as his interlocutors, as well as to archaeologists in general who are
aware that we are always ontologically wrestling with the past in the present,
the work of the contemporary archaeologist is here summoned. Esch writes,
'When reused, the treasure administered by classical archaeology falls under
the aegis of others: historians and art historians' (2011: 14). Rather than
abandon the insights of archaeology, and emphasize the need to return or
repatriate these objects, contemporary archaeology purposely engages with
the recontextualization made by the degradation, conflation, and reclamation
of the old. It does so by participating in the merging of 'archaeology *in* the
modern world with the archaeology *of* the modern world' (Holtorf and Piccini
2011: 16; see Buchli and Lucas 2001), unabashedly probing the meaningful
recontextualizations of materials, rather than privileging an often impossible
relocation to their origins.

The introduction to the volume on *spolia* where Esch essentializes 'the'
archaeological standpoint in regard to context suggests that the current
academic interest in architectural fragments coincides with their 'post-
modern' characteristics: 'fragmentation, historicism, memory, authenticity,
authorship, and appropriation, to name only a few' (Kinney 2011: 3). Elsewhere I have argued (Graff 2011) that Shannon Dawdy's call to 'willfully
collaps[e]' archaeological and ethnographic timescales and related division
of labour—her Walter Benjaminian 'Clockpunk' archaeological turn—allows
the archaeologist an alternative to furthering modernity's imagined rupture
(Dawdy 2010: 762). If the emphasis remains on tracing original contexts of the
material world without, or instead of, the thoughtful consideration of new
contexts produced by reuse of old materials, we continue to reify a rupture
between past and present that can blind us to how various temporal contexts
are entangled. Archaeologists in general, as well as contemporary archaeologists explicitly, are always working in the present, both materially and temporally. To understand which vision of Chicago and its past is materialized by
erasure or recontextualization, the strategies of contemporary archaeology call

---

Disneyland—David Lowenthal (1998) similarly used the term 'spoils of history' to draw attention to the darker sides of the heritage industry.

the seeker—whether looking behind the unlabelled Chicago History Museum shrubbery or at the stones of the Tribune Tower—to refrain from focusing so closely on original contexts that the current contexts are eclipsed.

4.5 CONCLUSION

Whose ruins become history? If the ruins are erased or fragmented, how do we remember them? If their fragments are reincorporated or recontextualized, how do we understand them? We do not know definitively the first name of the man who built the Relic House, and why he chose to construct it so soon after the tragedy of 1871. This small businessman, Rettig, created a profitable watering hole where a quality beer or poem could be consumed. Contrast this with the Chicago Tribune Tower, constructed by the scion of two leading families in Chicago, after an international audience vied for the chance to design it. Its towering structure envelops the leading newspaper of a major city in neo-Gothic ornament that adheres to a strict European canon. The 'Famous Stones', taken from their original contexts, create a sidewalk museum that, piece by piece, tells the story of the history of civilization.

In the absence of remaining Fire ruins as the people rushed to rebuild, the Relic House provided a kitschy place for people to sit in close proximity with the material dimensions of the tragedy. The Chicago Tribune Tower reflects an Old World architectural style, presenting a collection of disparate fragments as a coherent whole. Rather than an object from the 1871 Chicago Fire, a ribbon of twisted metal from the World Trade Center embedded in the Tribune's walls speaks to the lasting materiality of memory via ruin. In these new contexts made with fragment- and ruin-laden structure a narrative whole can be found, but only if the meanings in the present are not made subordinate to the meanings in the past.

ACKNOWLEDGEMENTS

Thanks to Laura McAtackney and Krysta Ryzewski for developing the Archaeologies of the Present workshop and inviting me to participate, and to the Wenner-Gren Foundation and Wayne State University for making it possible. Special thanks to the Wayne State graduate students, especially Kimberly Shay, for introducing Detroit to us, and to Krysta for sharing her knowledge of Chicago's sister city. Laura and Krysta's editorial expertise was very welcome in preparing this chapter, as were comments from anonymous reviewers. Ryan J. Cook provided keen insights in the final stages of writing, and I thank him and Alexander Cook for accompanying me in my explorations of Chicago and Detroit.

REFERENCES

Beaudry, Mary. C. (ed.). 1988a. *Documentary Archaeology in the New World.* Cambridge: Cambridge University Press.

Beaudry, Mary C. 1988b. Introduction. In *Documentary Archaeology in the New World,* edited by Mary C. Beaudry. Cambridge: Cambridge University Press, pp. 1–4.

Buchli, Victor, and Gavin Lucas (eds). 2001. *Archaeologies of the Contemporary Past.* London: Routledge.

Chicago Daily News. 1911. DN-0057047, Chicago Daily News negatives collection. Chicago: Chicago History Museum.

Chicago Directory Company. 1875. *The Lakeside Annual Directory of the City of Chicago.* Chicago: Chicago Directory Company.

Chicago Directory Company. 1880. *The Lakeside Annual Directory of the City of Chicago.* Chicago: Chicago Directory Company.

Chicago Directory Company. 1885. *The Lakeside Annual Directory of the City of Chicago.* Chicago: Chicago Directory Company.

Chicago Directory Company. 1892. *The Lakeside Annual Directory of the City of Chicago.* Chicago: Chicago Directory Company.

Chicago Directory Company. 1900. *The Lakeside Annual Directory of the City of Chicago.* Chicago: Chicago Directory Company.

Chicago Directory Company. 1909. *Plan of Re-numbering, City of Chicago.* Chicago: Chicago Directory Company.

Chicago Directory Company. 1910. *The Lakeside Annual Directory of the City of Chicago.* Chicago: Chicago Directory Company.

Chicago History Museum and Northwestern University. 2011. *Souvenirs.* The Great Chicago Fire and the Web of Memory. http://www.greatchicagofire.org/souvenirs (accessed 11 June 2014).

Chicago Park District. 2010. *Chicago Fire Relic.* http://www.chicagoparkdistrict.com/parks/lincoln-park/chicago-fire-relic/ (accessed 12 January 2017).

Chicago Tribune. 1890. Relics of the Fire. 28 December: 8.

Chicago Tribune. 1896. Among Architects and Builders. 13 September: 38.

Chicago Tribune. 1914. Display Ad: St. Benno's Bier. 12 March: 14.

Chicago Tribune. 1920a. Verse Flows as Beer Once Did in Relic House. 3 May: 17.

Chicago Tribune. 1920b. Famed Chicago Relic House is Now Poet's Lair. 4 May: 4.

Chicago Tribune. 1920c. Famous Old Halfway House Sold. 8 August: A5.

Chicago Tribune. 1920d. Obituary, Joseph Wallman. 29 November: 21.

Chicago Tribune. 1922. Relic House Shelter for Relics of Pre-'19 Period. 4 June: 9.

Chicago Tribune. 1928a. Relic House to Make Way for New Building. 23 May: 31.

Chicago Tribune. 1928b. Relic House to Disappear on January 1. 3 September: B1.

Chicago Tribune. 1929a. Raze Old Relic House, Built of Fire's Salvage. 28 February: 2.

Chicago Tribune. 1929b. Huge Apartment Building Replacing Relic House. 10 March: B1.

Chicago Tribune Company. 1999. *Tribune Tower: Famous Stones.* [Pamphlet] Chicago: Tribune Company Publications.

Clark, Herma. 1954. 'When Chicago Was Young', *Chicago Tribune,* 21 February: E2.

Dawdy, Shannon. 2010. 'Clockpunk Anthropology and the Ruins of Modernity', *Current Anthropology*, 51(6): 761–93.

Esch, Arnold. 1969. 'Spolien. Zur Wiederverwendung antiker Baustücke und Skulpturen im mittelalterlichen Italien', *Archiv für Kulturgeschichte*, 51(1): 1–64.

Esch, Arnold. 2011. 'On the Reuse of Antiquity: The Perspectives of the Archaeologist and of the Historian'. In *Reuse Value: Spolia and Appropriation in Art and Architecture from Constantine to Sherrie Levine*, edited by R. Brilliant and D. Kinney (B. Anderson, trans), Farnham: Ashgate, pp. 13–32.

Flinn, John J. 1893. *Chicago, the Marvelous City of the West: A History, An Encyclopedia, and a Guide*. 2nd edn. Chicago: Flinn and Sheppard.

Gies, Joseph. 1979. *The Colonel of Chicago*. New York: E. P. Dutton.

González-Ruibal, Alfredo, Rodney Harrison, Cornelius Holtorf, and Laurie Wilkie. 2014. 'Archaeologies of Archaeologies of the Contemporary Past: An Interview with Victor Buchli and Gavin Lucas', *Journal of Contemporary Archaeology*, 1(2): 265–76.

Goodsell, James H. 1871. *The Chicago fire and the fire insurance companies. An exhibit of the capital, assets, and losses of the companies, together with a graphic account of the great disaster, accompanied by maps of Chicago showing the burned district.* New York: J. H. and C. M. Goodsell.

Goodspeed, Edgar J. 1871. *History of the Great Fires in Chicago and the West*. Chicago: H. S. Goodspeed.

Graff, Rebecca S. 2001. *The Chicago Tribune Tower: The Consumption of Architecture and the Evocation of a Created Past*. MA Thesis, Department of Anthropology, University of Chicago.

Graff, Rebecca S. 2011. *The Vanishing City: Time, Tourism, and the Archaeology of Event at Chicago's 1893 World's Columbian Exposition*. PhD Dissertation, Department of Anthropology, University of Chicago.

Graff, Rebecca S. 2013. Remembrances of Beers Past: Chicago and the Relics of Prohibition. Unpublished paper given at the Theoretical Archaeology Group Meetings, Chicago, Illinois.

Harrison, Rodney, Laurie Wilkie, Alfredo González-Ruibal, and Cornelius Holtorf. 2014. Editorial. *Journal of Contemporary Archaeology*, 1(1): 1–6.

Holtorf, Cornelius and Angela Piccini (eds). 2011. *Contemporary Archaeologies: Excavating Now*. 2nd edn. Frankfurt: Peter Lang.

Journal of the Illinois State Historical Society. 1920. 'Obituary of Charles F. Gunther, 1837–1920', *Journal of the Illinois State Historical Society*, 13(1): 141–2.

Kamin, Blair and Bob Fila. 2000. *Tribune Tower: American Landmark: History, Architecture, and Design*. Chicago: Tribune Co.

Kinney, Dale. 2011. Introduction. In *Reuse Value: Spolia and Appropriation in Art and Architecture from Constantine to Sherrie Levine*, edited by R. Brilliant and D. Kinney, Farnham: Ashgate, pp. 1–11.

Korsmo, Fae L. 1999. 'Claiming Memory in British Columbia: Aboriginal Rights and the State'. In Contemporary Native American Political Issues, edited by Troy R. Johnson, Walnut Creek: AltaMira Press, pp. 119–34.

Lowenthal, David. 1998. *The Heritage Crusade and the Spoils of History*. Cambridge: Cambridge University Press.

Medill, Joseph. 1871. 'Cheer Up', *Chicago Tribune*, 11 October: 2.

Miller, Daniel. 2008. *The Comfort of Things*. London: Polity.

Munn, N. D. 2004. 'The "Becoming-Past" of Places: Spacetime and Memory in 19th-Century, Pre-Civil War New York', *Suomen Antropolgi/Journal of the Finnish Anthropological Society*, 29(1): 2–19.

Newberry Library. 2009. 'The World of the Dill Pickle Club'. In *From Frontier to Heartland: Making History in Central North America*. http://publications. newberry.org/frontiertoheartland/exhibits/show/perspectives/dillpickle (accessed 17 June 2014).

Pearce, Susan. 1995. *On Collecting: An Investigation into Collecting in the European Tradition*. London: Routledge Press.

Schumpeter, Joseph A. 1942. *Capitalism, Socialism, and Democracy*. New York: Harper and Brothers.

Sheahan, James W. 1871. *The Great Conflagration*. Philadelphia: Union Publishing Company.

Smith, Laurajane. 2006. *Uses of Heritage*. London: Routledge.

Smith, Richard Norton. 1997. *The Colonel of Chicago: The Life and Legend of Robert R. McCormick*. Boston: Houghton Mifflin Company.

Solomon, Alisa. 1983. 'The Marionette Theatre of Meyer Levin', *Performing Arts Journal*, 7(3): 103–8.

Solomonson, Katherine. 2001. *The Chicago Tribune Tower Competition: Skyscraper Design and Cultural Change in the 1920s*. Cambridge: Cambridge University Press.

Stamper, John W. 1991. *Chicago's North Michigan Avenue: Planning and Development, 1900–1930*. Chicago: University of Chicago Press.

Sullivan, Louis. 1988. 'The Chicago Tribune Tower Competition'. In *The Public Papers*, edited by R. Twombly, Chicago: University of Chicago Press, pp. 223–33.

Thomas, David Hurst. 2000. *Skull Wars: Kennewick Man, Archaeology, and the Battle for Native Identity*. New York: Basic Books.

Thomas, Laura Allen. 1933. *Relics of the Chicago Fire*. Manuscript, F38BD T36. Chicago History Museum, Chicago, Illinois.

United States Census Bureau. 1880. *Tenth Census of the United States, 1880* (NARA microfilm publication T9, 1,454 rlls). Records of the Bureau of the Census, Record Group 29. National Archives, Washington, DC.

Warner, Mark. 2003. 'The Ludlow Massacre: Class, Warfare, and Historical Memory in Southern Colorado', *Historical Archaeology*, 37(3): 66–80.

Weis, John. 1906. *A Landmark of the Chicago Fire, The Relic House, 1871–1906*. Pamphlet, ICHi-63842. Chicago: Chicago History Museum.

Wolf, Wayne L. 2012. 'Charles F. Gunther: An Illinois Yankee Trapped into Working for the Confederacy', *Journal of the Illinois State Historical Society*, 105(2–3): 225–36.

5

Commemorating Melbourne's Past

Constructing and Contesting Space, Time, and Public Memory in Contemporary Parkscapes

Madeline Shanahan and Brian Shanahan

Melbourne's urban parkscapes contain a range of memorials, monuments, and features, all of which have a role in the creation, performance, and reiteration of public memory and contemporary identity. These include a collection of sites and objects that originated in Australia's pre-colonial and colonial past, but which were recontextualized and memorialized in the twentieth or twenty-first centuries. Despite the earlier origins of the material and remains incorporated at these sites, their subsequent recontextualization can tell us a great deal about the changing values and identities of the city's communities over time. Thus, in this chapter we will argue that Melbourne's urban parks have been used as places for reflection on the foundation stories of the city, and that through this engagement contemporary identities are reinforced, contested, and negotiated. Considerable attention has been paid previously to sites such as the Shrine of Remembrance, which commemorate Australia's involvement in the World Wars, but in this chapter we will examine the practice and process of memorializing older material (see also Graff, Chapter 4, for examples of long-term memorial practices in Chicago). We are interested in what each site tells us about contemporary Melbourne's changing relationship with its colonial and pre-colonial past, and the current nature of its post-colonial discourse.

5.1 TERMINOLOGY

The terms 'memorial', 'memorialization', and 'monument' will appear through-out this chapter. We use 'memorial' to refer to an object erected or modified to commemorate an individual, organization, or event. This adheres to the literal definition ('memorial' 1, *OED Online*), but is also the way in which the term is used by local park and heritage authorities (City of Melbourne 2003: 1). By extension, 'memorialization' refers to the process by which something or someone is memorialized, or, as is more relevant to this chapter, the process through which an object or site becomes a memorial. We use the term 'monument' to refer more specifically to architectural or archaeological sites, which are commonly defined by their large or physically imposing presence (see Carver 1996). These may also have a memorial function, but they are not inherently defined by their commemorative value (Cooper et al. 2005: 240; Carman 2002: 46–7).

'Relic' is another term that will appear throughout this chapter, in relation to the non-Aboriginal sites discussed (see Graff, Chapter 4, for discussion of the 'Relic House' in Chicago; refer to Smith 2000: 112–13 for a discussion of the problematic use of the term 'relic' in relation to Aboriginal heritage). In the broadest sense, a 'relic' can be defined as 'an object vested with interest because of it age or historical associations' ('relic' 4.b, *OED Online*). This definition follows David Lowenthal's use of 'relic' as a term for any material object associated with the past. He argues that relics, alongside memory and history, are one of the ways in which we encounter and attempt to understand the past. Most importantly, their materiality is central to our ability to intimately engage with, experience and ultimately 'believe' in the past (Lowenthal 2015: 383–410). The tangible nature of relics also connects to the more precise Christian definition, as either the physical remains of a religious figure, or as an object sanctified by contact with that person ('relic' 1.a, *OED Online*; Azaryahu 1993: 88). We will argue that some of the non-Aboriginal sites we discuss here also adhere to this more precise definition of the term 'relic', albeit in a secular, modern translation of that concept. Finally, the term relic can also be used to describe the remnant or residue *of* a nation or people ('relic' 2.a, *OED Online*). In this sense, it is related to the concept of a 'ruin', which has been a persistent theme in contemporary archaeology (see González-Ruibal, Chapter 7, for a broad discussion of ruins within and beyond the 'Global North'). Contemporary archaeologists are increasingly addressing how ruins are conceived of and how they are assigned cultural value in the present (Olsen and Pétursdóttir 2014). We will pursue these areas of inquiry, considering some of the ways in which such assignations of value diverge between groups within the city.

5.2 PARKS

From the late eighteenth century onwards park design became both more accessible to the public and increasingly didactic. Scholars of parks have focused on the ideological underpinnings of these landscapes, arguing that their development was connected to concerns surrounding public health, industrialization, and urbanization (Brück 2013; Taylor 1995; Jordan 1994). Parks were central to the process of improvement, and were seen by middle- and upper-class reformers as a remedy for the physical, moral, and spiritual condition of the poor. The layout and planning of parks also forced the visitor into a bodily discipline which reinforced dominant ideologies relating to class, gender, and even imperialism (Brück 2013). As public spaces they were also contested; a point of critical relevance here. Joanna Brück has argued that Victorian and Edwardian parks were 'ideologically charged' spaces in which imperialist and class-based narratives were constructed, but they were also spaces of resistance in which these could be publicly contested (Brück 2013). In this chapter we explore the way in which these same spaces have been used more recently to both construct and challenge narratives relating to Melbourne's past, and particularly its colonial history.

Within public parks the erection of memorials and monuments is meaningful. Jonathon Porter argues that monuments are always didactic to some degree, as they instruct the viewer on how the past should be understood, and actively construct memory and identity (2009: 65). On this basis, monuments and memorials can tell us a great deal about a contemporary society, and may reveal less about the history that they commemorate, than they do about the era in which they are created. At such sites, the past is used to create meaning in the present. This is not a linear process though. Laurajane Smith has argued that identity is not simply produced at heritage places, but is actively and cyclically recreated and renegotiated as audiences encounter, reinterpret, remember, forget, and reassess the meanings of the past, in light of the present (Smith 2006: 44–5; see also Ernsten, Chapter 10, for an example of this process in Cape Town). Thus, performance plays a central role in the production of meaning and identity at heritage sites (for a discussion of this process in museum contexts, see Smith 2015: 479). Paul Shackel also highlights the use of the past to create meaning in the present, and emphasizes the point that public memory changes as contemporary political and social conditions change (Shackel 2001).

5.3 A BRIEF HISTORY OF MELBOURNE

Prior to European colonization, the area that is now the City of Melbourne was the territory of the Woiwurrung, whose contemporary descendants are the Wurundjeri people. Their neighbours to the south, the Boonwurrung, also had interests in the wider region. After the 1788 colonization of New South Wales, attempts were made to settle in the Melbourne region in the early nineteenth century. The first permanent European settlement did not begin until 1835, when pastoralists known as the Port Phillip Association arrived from Van Diemen's Land. The New South Wales government, concerned by the prospect of a private colony, annulled the 'treaty' the pastoralists had signed with the Aboriginal owners of the land, and commenced the foundation of a new town under their control. In 1837 Governor Sir Richard Bourke named the new settlement Melbourne, and gave the instructions for a town to be established on a grid, which was laid out by the Assistant Surveyor General Robert Hoddle. Rapid growth and development followed this, bringing about the systematic and brutal dispossession of the region's Aboriginal owners. In 1851 the Port Phillip District separated from New South Wales and became the colony of Victoria (Whitehead 2015: 3). In that same year the discovery of gold began to transform Melbourne further, as migrants flooded in from around the world. By the 1880s gold and agricultural commodities made Melbourne one of the richest cities in the world. This pace of development led to large-scale building programmes and rapid expansion, and it is within this context that Melbourne's parks emerged. Colonists believed that Melbourne was destined for greatness and so from the outset they set aside land for recreation and display, which came to have a central role in the life of the city (Whitehead 2015: 1–2; Nankervis 1998: 162–3).

5.4 CASE STUDY MEMORIALS IN MELBOURNE'S PARKS

This section addresses our selection of four of Melbourne's parkland memorials, all of which derive from earlier colonial and pre-colonial material and remains. As Figure 5.1 demonstrates, these are all located very close to the Melbourne CBD, in some of the city's most celebrated parks and gardens. These spaces are central to life and leisure within Melbourne and are regularly visited by a range of city-goers. As important sites all of the memorials we discuss have been written about previously to some extent, but the connections between them, and the role that they play in the contemporary building of public memory and identity, have not been addressed. We will discuss them in the chronological sequence of their memorialization, in order to demonstrate how the changing socio-political climate has altered Melbournians' relationship with the past, and influenced the ever-developing post-colonial discourse of the city.

By examining them in relation to one another, but also to the city and its communities in the present, our discussion positions this collection of memorials as a type of 'surface assemblage', as defined by Rodney Harrison (2011). A 'surface assemblage' might contain a mix of artefacts from a number of periods, but it arises out of the enduring relationships between the past and

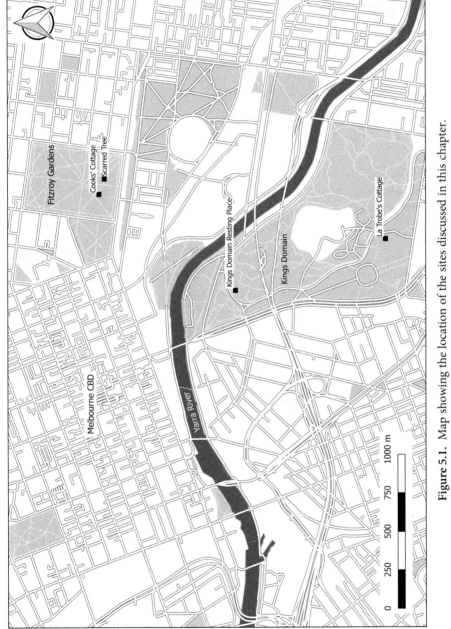

Figure 5.1. Map showing the location of the sites discussed in this chapter.

present, and between contemporary observers and actors in the past (Harrison 2011: 155). Harrison's discussion of 'surface surveys' is also useful. Surfaces consist of the present, but also all 'physical and imagined pasts' (Harrison 2011: 154). Therefore, contemporary Melbourne's fabric, identity, culture, and communities are based upon, but are also in constant tension and negotiation with, their past. Through an engagement with that past (by memorializing, curating, visiting, vandalizing, and repairing its remains, relics, and ruins), its meanings and the identities of the city's communities are in a constant state of formation, revaluation and reconstruction.

5.4.1 Cooks' Cottage, Fitzroy Gardens

One of the most famous and thoroughly researched examples of the recontexualization of an older structure in Melbourne is Cooks' Cottage, in the Fitzroy Gardens (Colour plate 6, bottom) (Young 2011; Young 2008; McCubbin 2000: 118–37; McCubbin 1999; Healy 1997: 11–72; Gill 1934). Originally located in Great Ayton, Middlesborough, in England, it was purchased by the Melbourne businessman Russell Grimwade in order to commemorate the 1934 Centenary celebrations of European settlement. Despite being advertised by the auctioneers at the time as 'the home of Captain Cook's early days', the cottage was actually the home of his parents, Grace and James Cook. A lintel over the doorway inscribed with their initials suggests that Cook's parents built the house in 1755, ten years after he had left home. This means that it is highly unlikely that Captain Cook ever lived in the cottage, but he may have visited in his periods of leave (Young 2008: 1). Despite this, at the time of its purchase those involved went to considerable lengths to prove that he had in fact lived there (McCubbin 1999: 38–69). The dubious connections to Captain Cook were not the only problematic element of the cottage's role in commemorating Melbourne's centenary. There was also the inconvenient fact that Cook had never visited what would eventually become Victoria. In answer to critics who pointed this out, the cottage's sponsors argued that as he first sighted Australia in 1770 at Point Hicks, Victoria's extreme south-eastern point, their claim to the national hero was legitimate (Gill 1934: 25).

In December 1933, following much public debate over the selection of an ideal location for the cottage, Grimwade requested that it be placed in Fitzroy Gardens. In response to Grimwade's orders painstaking effort was put into ensuring that it was dismantled and rebuilt as it originally stood in 1755. Additional materials required for its reconstruction were imported from England, and even the ivy attached to the cottage was transported. Furniture and objects were carefully selected to represent the period from 1700 to 1750 (McCubbin 1999: 40–2). Objects associated with Cook were also sourced, as it was believed that through his touch they could have absorbed something of his 'spirit'. Linda Young has explored the role of Cook's touch in the project, developing James Frazer's concept of 'contagious magic'. She argues that without that physical connection to the man the building would be rendered meaningless (Young 2008).

The desire to implant Cook into Melbourne park space reflects a number of motivations. The most obvious is because he personified the Empire, and is the protagonist of a grand colonial narrative (Healy 1997: 18–19). His mythology depicts him as a brave British man of humble origins who circumnavigated the Globe, claimed continents, and eventually made the ultimate sacrifice; becoming an imperial martyr (McCubbin 1999: 37). The role of the cottage as a relic is very clear here, as it derives its meaning from the physical connection to the man himself. The narrative of Cook the imperial hero is also mirrored in the life cycle of the cottage; a humble English dwelling transported across the Globe and memorialized, transcending its origins and itself becoming part of the mythology. Its importance to imperial narratives is also demonstrated by the fact that the vendor of the cottage only consented to its removal from the site on the basis that it did not leave the British Empire (Young 2011: 151).

As with all relics, the original context of the building is central to its meaning. Grimwade wrote that part of his intention in bringing the cottage to Melbourne 'was to introduce some solid reminder of the old world to this young country…and to endeavour to foster national traditions that must necessarily be absent in so young a country as our own' (cited in McCubbin 1999: 39; Healy 1997: 35). McCubbin explains that Grimwade was troubled by the nation's youthfulness and modernity, and especially the tenuousness of 'the bonds of kinship that are the fundamental links of Empire' (cited in McCubbin 2000: 126). Thus, it is not just the connection to Cook the man that is important, but also the perceived Britishness of the building. This Britishness was emphasized in the choice of its location in the Fitzroy Gardens, the alien landscaping and planting of which reinforced the connection the 'Mother Country' (McCubbin 1999: 40). Like the connection to Captain Cook, the recontextualized situation and landscape surrounding the cottage was the invention of a (post-)colonial imagining of that 'green and pleasant land'.

We argue that time is also central to the meaning of Cooks' Cottage. Its rebuilding demonstrates that the elite classes were not simply content with commemorating the centenary of their forefathers colonization of space, but felt compelled to colonize time as well (an issue also explored in Cape Town by Ernsten, Chapter 10). Marketing itself as the 'oldest building in Australia', it explicitly links to a period eighty years before Victoria's colonization. In this sense, it is an attempt to create a rootedness for British occupation that is a fiction; colonizing the pre-colonial Australian past, reaching deeper and deeper into time. As we will see in the discussion of the Fitzroy Gardens scarred tree (§5.4.4), Aboriginal sites have the power to challenge this fiction, reasserting the presence of Aboriginal people in both the past and present.

The mythology has also been challenged at the site itself through acts of vandalism. Chris Healy highlights Aboriginal conceptualizations of Cook, writing that his name 'has been used by Aboriginal people as a means of accounting for certain kinds of change and as a metaphor for ethical dilemmas' (Healy 1997: 15). Just as he became a symbol of Empire for British-Australians, Cook has become the personification of dispossession for many Aboriginal people. As such, the cottage became a focus for protests from the 1970s on, as the Aboriginal Rights Movement gained momentum. In 1970, on the bicentenary of Cook's taking possession of the continent in 1770, Aboriginal people held a protest and an all-night vigil, denouncing Cook as an invader (Nicoll 2011: 17).

Since then protests have continued, particularly around commemorations of significant colonial events, such as Australia Day, which marks the British First Fleet's landing in Sydney on 26 January 1788. The materiality of the site has made it a target for protestors. The cottage was vandalized two days before Australia Day in 2014. A window was smashed, paint bombs were thrown on the roof, and profanities and anti-Australia Day slogans such as '26th Jan Australia's Shame!!!' were graffitied on the walls (Zielinski 2014). Staff at the cottage attempted to hide the graffiti as quickly as possible, covering it with a large painting of Cook's ship, HMS Endeavour (O'Shea and Sears 2014). The immediate covering of the graffiti with an image of HMS Endeavour, which is itself ideologically encoded, is telling. These dissenting narratives needed to be quickly hidden from the view of curious tourists and happy Australia Day revellers, with nothing less than the ultimate symbol of Britain's imperial expansion. This was also not the first time the cottage had been vandalized. In 2013 it was vandalized twice. Anarchist protesters threw paint on the Cottage, and painted the slogan 'Cappy Cook was a crook killer liar thief' across it. On the Anarchist News website protesters described it as an 'absurd shrine to genocide' and wrote that 'the monuments and museums that fill this dead city only enrage us' (Zielinski 2014). Thus, the cottage plays a central role in contemporary Melbourne's post-colonial discourse. It was originally brought to the city to commemorate the start of the colonial project and it has since become a site at which objections to dispossession can find a material expression. Just as the figure of Cook has become the personification of colonization for many Aboriginal people, the cottage itself has become an icon of that injustice, and so it plays an active role in the performance of contemporary debates relating to Melbourne's past.

5.4.2 La Trobe's Cottage

In contrast to Cooks' Cottage, La Trobe's Cottage (Figure 5.2) has a more authentic connection to Victorian history. Charles La Trobe was appointed

Figure 5.2. La Trobe's Cottage, Melbourne. Photo by Brian Shanahan.

Superintendent of the Port Philip District in 1839. In 1851 he became the first Lieutenant-Governor of the newly separated colony of Victoria, and is remembered as the man under whose stewardship Melbourne developed into a global city. Upon his arrival La Trobe encountered a new settlement with no suitable Superintendent's residence. In response, and at his own expense, he had two prefabricated homes shipped from Manning of London. The first was a modest dwelling that he intended to replace with a more imposing successor. He erected the small simple cottage on government land as a temporary arrangement until he could establish himself, but after successfully bidding for the block at open auction it became his permanent residence and was soon extended and surrounded by outbuildings and landscape features (Lewis 2010: 6; Barnes 2007: 45). The estate was located in an area to the east of the new town and he named it Jolimont, in reference to his wife's home. Even after the larger prefabricated house arrived La Trobe continued to reside at the 'portable cottage', and so, while not officially a government house, it took on greater significance than originally intended.

Jolimont had a relatively short life as the residence of a major colonial figure. La Trobe departed for London in 1854 and the entire estate was either leased or sold in parcels (Lewis 2010: 7, 9). By 1888 Jolimont was described as being 'overshadowed by a huge brick store in the centre of the square of buildings' (*The Australasian Sketcher with Pen and Pencil* 1888). The idyllic and romantic scene recorded in earlier paintings and drawings was no more. From the late nineteenth century onwards La Trobe's cottage succumbed to the advancing and modernizing city. It decayed, almost forgotten, and became a ruin as the city expanded around it. The site was threatened in 1919 by plans to extend the adjacent factory, although representations by the Early Pioneers' Association halted that threat (*The Leader* 1914). One correspondent, discussing the state of the cottage, 'lying in obscurity and neglect' in 1930, suggested that 'this interesting relic be rescued before too late' and re-erected in a public park or museum (*The Argus* 1930: 15). The cottage was under threat again in 1942 when *The Argus* newspaper noted that 'Jolimont, is to be demolished, and Melbourne will thus lose one of its most interesting relics' (*The Argus* 1942). The Bedggood family who owned the land intended to construct an air raid shelter there for their employees who worked in the adjacent boot factory. Nonetheless, some parts of the cottage were retained on the site because in 1956 Horace Bedggood promised that the cottage would be in the best possible condition in the lead-up to the Melbourne Olympic Games. Defending its sorry condition, he stated, 'We have left the building there as an antique for people to see, and naturally it looks like an antique' (*The Argus* 1956). The use of the terms like 'antique' in several correspondences at this time is striking, and evokes a sense of fading antiquity within what was actually a young and modern city.

In 1963–4 the cottage was finally moved to the Royal Botanic Gardens (Lewis 1994: 70). It was carefully reconstructed to evoke the experience of the residence in the 1840s, but in reality, very little of the original house remained (Lewis 2010: 7). Like Cooks' Cottage, it was also furnished with objects from the La Trobe household through which visitors could engage with the appearance of an 'authentic' experience (Botham 2010: 12). Unlike Cooks' Cottage though, it was not left to rest in peace. In 1998 it was moved a second time to its current location, to make way for the Ian Potter Foundation Children's Garden. One issue raised by heritage consultants prior to its second relocation was that despite inaccuracies having been identified in the 1960s reconstruction, these should not be altered because that original conservation project had become significant in its own right (Botham 2010: 14). The building, as re-erected for the second time, embodies a variety of tensions. Although it contains some original fabric it is largely a speculative reconstruction and therefore reflects a contemporary desire to enshrine a decaying artefact of an idealized past. It also represents a yearning for a tactile and immersive connection to the disappearing architectural fabric of earliest years of the City of Melbourne. In reality, the most authentic aspect of the modern cottage is its reflection of early pioneering conservation practices. The act of deconstruction, removal, and reconstruction has created new meanings and has unintentionally revealed new insights into the old fabric. For example, the second move revealed that the dining room is the oldest identified example in the world of the light industrialized framing techniques that became the mainstay of Australian housing stock (Lewis 2010: 12).

In contemporary Melbourne there has been a renewed interest in celebrating La Trobe's legacy, and this finds a material expression at the cottage.

In 2001 the C J La Trobe Society was founded, followed in 2009 by The Friends of La Trobe's Cottage. This latter group is dedicated to ensuring the maintenance and presentation of the building and its gardens. In 2010 they compiled a development proposal in response to the perceived under-appreciation of the man and his former residence. This demonstrates an anxiety over whether or not the future of this not-quite-loved-enough building is entirely secure. Within these debates over the heritage management of the building and its surrounds we see tensions relating to the meaning of the house to contemporary Melbourne, and anxieties for the future of this twice moved relic.

The presentation of both cottages discussed here focus on their period of foundation. Their contemporary survivals reflect conservation practices at the time of their reconstructions, but also indicate what the value of the buildings was perceived to be. Their geneses were moments deemed worthy of commemoration, and so the presentation of the houses was fossilized in that moment. In the case of Cooks' Cottage, this was the humble British origins of the imperial martyr, and while mostly acknowledged to be fictitious, is relatively straightforward. The meanings behind La Trobe's Cottage are perhaps more complex. La Trobe became a cypher for the settlement of Melbourne and by extension the newly emerged colony and later State of Victoria. However, his cottage was a private residence rather than a government house. Transforming this private dwelling into a shrine to Victorian statehood therefore involves conceptual leaps of identity and representation. Using such a building to commemorate the origins of the colony requires an idealized evocation of the place as it might have been when La Trobe and his family first lived there, again highlighting the act of foundation, as opposed to the gradual accretion of buildings that represented the actual life cycle of the estate. Whereas the tenuous connection to Cook has allowed the post-colonial imagination to run wild, curation of La Trobe's Cottage is bound to, but also frustrated by, how best to accommodate reality. Two relocations against the backdrop of evolving conservation practice and a continuing maturation of Victorian identity means that, to some extent, the meanings and contemporary purpose of La Trobe's cottage are still being decided. It is a work in process.

The fact that these two worthy individuals are male is also central to the narratives represented by these memorialized moments. This focus on men is in no way uncommon at colonial heritage sites; the 'founding father' phenomenon has been written about previously (Smith 2008; Aitchison 1999). Class and race are central too. Such memorials provide an account of the past that is fundamentally an 'elite-Anglo-masculine' one (Smith 2008: 159). These worthy individuals are commemorated in prime public spaces, setting out the hierarchical structure of gender, class and race in the city's history, but also in the contemporary experience of these places (McCubbin 1999: 42). Indeed, it has become so normalized in Western society to associate memorials with elite white men, to the exclusion of women, ethnic minorities, and the working classes, that commenting on it seems almost a truism. However, as we will see in §§5.5.3 and 5.5.4, the memorials created by Aboriginal people within the City of Melbourne do not adopt class, gendered, and individualistic values in this way, and demonstrate a distinctly different way of valuing and commemorating the past.

Despite the clear value placed upon the houses associated with these men, it is important to see that their status as relics also represents a loss of significance in other ways. Memorialization may highlight the value placed upon certain narratives that a site or object is deemed to represent, but the fact that they had become relics also demonstrates that in other ways they were no longer actively relevant. La Trobe's cottage had become a ruin, and while money was spent moving and conserving it, it was not seen as so precious that Melbournians felt it necessary to respect its original site. Its removal was partly due to the fact that the redevelopment of Jolimont was seen as lucrative. Mid-twentieth century Melbournians may have valued it enough to prevent its total destruction, but not so much that they wanted to conserve it *in situ*. Likewise, the vendor of Cooks' Cottage wanted it to remain in the Empire, but still saw fit to have is disassembled for a cash incentive. This demonstrates an interesting paradox inherent in our relationships with ruins, in which abandonment and value are placed in tension with one another. To interrogate this we need to probe how ruins are formed and conceived of, but also how, when and, critically, why we assign cultural value to them (Olsen and Pétursdóttir 2014).

5.4.3 The Kings Domain Resting Place

The Kings Domain Resting Place is an Aboriginal site and as such both its nature and meaning vary in some key ways from previous examples. While its location, signposting, and plaque mark it as a memorial in the European tradition (Glendinning 2003), it has additional layers of culturally specific meaning. In 1985, following legal action taken by the Koorie Heritage Trust, the skeletal remains of thirty-eight individuals held by the Melbourne Museum were returned to the Aboriginal people of Victoria. As the identities and tribal affiliations of the individuals were unknown they could not be repatriated on Country,[1] so a group of Aboriginal people led by Gunditjmara Elder Jim Berg applied to have them reburied in the City of Melbourne's gardens. The site they selected was on the side of a hill in Linlithgow Avenue, in the Kings Domain. On the day of the reburial Aboriginal people from across Victoria gathered at the Museum. A traditional smoking ceremony took place and then the remains of each individual were wrapped in cloth and bark. They

---

[1] The word 'Country' in Aboriginal English is used by Aboriginal people to refer to the land they belong to and their place of Dreaming.

were then carried from the museum through the city to the Kings Domain, accompanied by 200 people. When they arrived at the Resting Place each parcel was carefully placed in the ground with a wreath of native plants before being buried and covered with a large boulder from the You Yangs Regional Park which marks the site (Faulkhead and Berg 2010: 22–6). For cultural sensitivity reasons we have not included an image of the site itself, but a plaque on the boulder carries an image of the Aboriginal flag and the following inscription:

> This is the resting place for the skeletal remains of 38 Aboriginal people. They are the representatives of the following tribes of Victoria.
>
> BIDAWAL BRABIRALUNG BRAIKAULUNG BRATULUNG BUNGJAN-DITJ BUNJILKRAURA BUNRNG DILILAMATANG DUDUROA GUN-DITJMARA JAADWA JAARA JAITMATHANG JARIJARI JUPAGALK KATUBAMUT KIRRAE KOLAKNGAT KRAUATUNGALUNG KURNAI KURUNG KWATKWAT LATJILATJI MARDITJALI MINJAMBUTA NGURELBAN PANGERANG TATITATI TATUNGALUNG TAUNGUR-ONG TJAPWURUNG WAMBAWAMBA WATIWATI WATHAURUNG WARKAWARKA WATJOBALUK WURUNDJERI YORTAYORTA
>
> Rise from this Grave Release your anger and pain
> As you soar with the winds
> Back to your homelands
> There find peace with our Spiritual Mother The Land
> Before drifting off into the Dreamtime

Since the reburial the Resting Place has been declared a significant Aboriginal site. Its establishment was also a major milestone in the ongoing struggle for the repatriation of human remains and cultural material by Aboriginal Victorians (Broome 2005: 376–9).

The significance of the Resting Place is best described in the words of the Aboriginal people involved. In their book, *Power and the Passion: Our Ancestors Return Home*, Jim Berg and Shannon Faulkhead, a scholar and Aboriginal woman, record the memories and perspectives of the people who participated in the reburial. A number of themes emerge, but one repeated by multiple people was the importance of the ceremony associated with the site. Berg explains that:

> This ceremony was more than just a reburial. It was also a celebration of reclamation of Koorie control and ownership of culture. For some participants the reburial was one of the first contemporary ceremonies. Bringing them home.
>
> (Faulkhead and Berg 2010: 33)

Berg's quote highlights the importance of the ceremony, and the multiple layers of meaning to the participants; it both honoured the Ancestors and fulfilled traditional customs, but it was also political, demonstrating the reclamation of control and culture.

The interweaving of past and present, and the stark contrast between traditional ceremony and urban space was also highlighted, as we see in this quote by Wayne Thorpe:

> Another thing that stood out was the number of people carrying the parcels. The human remains wrapped in paper bark. That was significant. I thought, well I've never seen that before. Living in a city you don't see many traditional things at all, so when you do, it sticks in your mind and that experience did. That was a traditional way of burial for our people, they would wrap up the body in stringy bark. There is significance with the ti-tree bark. The ti-tree are known as the warrior trees that take up the frontline of the recently cleared areas to protect the bush. These trees are the warriors of the bush as were the Skeletal Remains.
>
> (Wayne Thorp cited in Faulkhead and Berg 2010: 46–7)

The importance placed upon the traditional ceremony here highlights a key difference in the use of material from the past by Aboriginal people in the process of memorialization. The Aboriginal people interviewed by Berg and Faulkhead focus more on the significance of the ceremony, on their duty of care to their Ancestors and on the continuity of their culture. For European Australians memorialization is fundamentally material-based (see also McAtackney, Chapter 9, for a case study of material-focused memorialization in Northern Ireland). For the communities involved in the establishment of the Resting Place, while the human remains are sacred, the performative act is also central. In this sense, the Resting Place is underpinned by a crucial element of intangible cultural heritage, as defined by UNESCO in the 2003 *Convention for the Safeguarding of Intangible Cultural Heritage*. Its meaning and value stems not just from the importance of the human remains, but also from the practices, knowledge, and performance that was a part of its creation. The importance of these intangible aspects means that Aboriginal experiences of the site are fundamentally different. For a non-Aboriginal visitor to the Resting Place it is a memorial, but for Aboriginal people who are a part of the communities who participated that day, the site is commemorative and connected to knowledge, performance, and culture. This means that it has a layer of meaning that is not accessible to non-Aboriginal visitors, but which is critically important to its custodians. The memorial functions on multiple levels; it simultaneously obeys European material conventions related to memory and displays modern historical consciousness (Glendinning 2003), but the importance of the ceremony, knowledge, and ritual mean that it is fundamentally different to the other sites discussed thus far.

Another theme raised repeatedly by the Aboriginal people interviewed by Berg and Faulkhead is the significance of the location of the site. Some argued that it was far too public, while for others, the central nature of the site was part of its meaning (see Figure 5.1). This prime location in the middle of a much frequented park means that it has the potential to educate the general public about Aboriginal people's ownership of the land, and the crimes committed against their Ancestors in the process of colonization (Faulkhead and Berg 2010: 35, 40). The selection of the particular site, opposite an imposing statue of Queen Victoria is also meaningful; it is a counterpoint, a statement of ownership and a reminder of Aboriginal people's past, present, and future in this land. Faulkhead explains that it was 'as if our Ancestors were reclaiming land belonging to the King, if only in name, and watching over Queen Victoria, and consequently all the land that was named after her— Victoria' (Faulkhead and Berg 2010: 34–5). This location also made the memorial a suitable protest site during the 2006 Commonwealth Games. A group called 'Black GST (Genocide, Sovereignty, Treaty)' established 'Camp Sovereignty' and lit a fire there during what they called the 'Stolen-wealth Games' (Kleinman 2006: 13). The flames were eventually forcibly extinguished by authorities. This wrestling for control over the space surrounding the Resting Place demonstrates that it continues to play a central role in Melbourne's ongoing post-colonial discourse. Despite an increasingly visible Aboriginal presence being permitted within Melbourne's public spaces, events such as those during the 2006 'Stolenwealth Games' demonstrate that tensions surrounding Aboriginal assertions to land within the City of Melbourne are still far from over. Debates surrounding public space and monuments are just one component of the ongoing journey towards social justice, but they are powerful arenas in which the battle to create and control the collective memory is fought (Shackel 2001: 665).

5.4.4 The Fitzroy Gardens Scarred Tree

Not far from Cooks' Cottage in the Fitzroy Gardens is another important, although very different, type of memorialized Aboriginal site, the Fitzroy Gardens Scarred Tree (Figure 5.3). While we would not normally define a living scarred tree as a memorial, this example had been long dead when it collapsed in November 1998. Restoration work was subsequently undertaken by Aboriginal Affairs Victoria, and in 2002 its truncated and capped stump showing the original scar was re-erected with a plaque at its original location, meaning that it has transitioned from its natural form into a memorial.

Scarred trees are not unique to Australia, but they are highly significant sites here both from an archaeological and cultural perspective. They are trees which had bark removed by Aboriginal people to make canoes, shelters, shields, containers, baby carriers, and other items. The removal of the bark results in an exposed panel of wood known as a 'dry face'. Fresh tissue known as 'overgrowth' then grows in from the sides, resulting in the scar feature, which varies in size and shape depending on the nature and age of the original damage, the species of the tree and other environmental factors (Long 2003: 3–6). As the

Figure 5.3. The Fitzroy Gardens Scarred Tree, Melbourne. Photo by Brian Shanahan.

scar ages the dry face will become weathered, and tool marks where the bark was originally cut are sometimes preserved. Some Victorian scarred trees date to the pre-colonial period, while others were made after colonization and demonstrate the continuity of Aboriginal culture and land use (Long 2003: 10). The large oval scar on the Fitzroy Garden Scarred Tree may indicate that the bark was used for a shelter and probably predates British colonialization (Eidelson 2014: 28).

Like the Resting Place, the Scarred Tree exhibits aspects of intangible cultural heritage that are inaccessible to non-Aboriginal visitors. It has been argued elsewhere that scarred trees represent the Wurundjeri's relationship to their Ancestors, and as such, they have a pedagogical role. They indicate to them how their Ancestors managed to harvest resources whilst simultaneously showing respect to the life of the tree. This contains broader lessons in managing Country sustainably, using the knowledge handed to their Ancestors by their creator, Bunjil (Griffin et al. 2013). To non-Aboriginal observers the site provides a testament to the ancient and enduring presence of Aboriginal people, and is a surviving remnant of the pre-colonial native landscape, but the engagement stops there. Only Wurundjeri people are entitled to share in the multifaceted, culturally and spiritually rooted, and intangible meanings of the tree.

The conversion of this dead tree into a memorial through preservation and the addition of a plaque in the early years of the twenty-first century is reflective of contemporary post-colonial practice. The erection of the Scarred Tree and the establishment of the Resting Place represent the growing strength of the Aboriginal community, the slow but increasing recognition of them by non-Aboriginal Australians, and ultimately, the momentum of the Reconciliation movement. In restoring and resituating the tree the Wurundjeri's traditional ownership of the land was reinforced, in a visible and public way. However, while its re-erection can be seen as an attempt to have Melbourne's Aboriginal past recognized, its location in the Fitzroy Gardens, just near Cooks' Cottage also makes for a strikingly disjointed scene. The landscape around the tree has been fundamentally colonized; European plants, green lawn and pathways form the shape of the Union Flag, and the dominant feature is the idyllic English cottage. By contrast the tree is stark in its truncation. Its memorialization reminds us of the continual presence of the Wurundjeri in this land, but as a leafless stump, its death cannot be ignored. Nor can the Anglicized surroundings complete with ornamental gardens, European vistas, eighteenth-century cottage, and even a model Tudor Village. The dead tree's presence within the colonized urbanized landscape is poignant, and to European eyes, one cannot help but be struck by the sense of loss and displacement. However, despite the loss inherent in the scene, the Scarred Tree also makes a powerful contrast to the fabricated historical mirage of Cooks' Cottage. The enduring scar on the tree connects it to the Aboriginal communities of both the past and present very tangibly. The tree is clearly an authentic material witness to Melbourne's past, demonstrating land and resource use pre-dating the planned European gardens and their high-rise backdrop. It is also a challenge or counterpoint to Cooks' Cottage. The authenticity of that problematic monument to an Imperial martyr, which reaches further and further back in time is challenged by this tree with is undeniable connection to its place and its past.

5.5 CONCLUSION

As designed landscapes, parks are ideologically charged spaces (Brück 2013). From the late eighteenth century on they became highly encoded; underpinned by class, gendered, and imperialist narratives. Importantly though, parks have also always been contested landscapes; public spaces in which these ideologies could be visibly challenged. These discourses have played out in Melbourne's nineteenth-century parkscapes, which reflected the aspirations of the elite of a new-born city, to present day. From the outset they were places used to commemorate people and events, and to communicate colonial, national, and state narratives, which continue to evolve, be disrupted, and contested.

The recontextualization and memorialization of material from Melbourne's past demonstrates that an ongoing debate about Australia's history and its place in the present has found a material expression within the city's parks. In this paper we have selected four of these materializations for a detailed reading. Each of these derives from an earlier time, but each was memorialized in the twentieth or early twenty-first centuries; an act which tells us a great deal about Melbournians' changing relationship with that past. Early memorializations focused on the commemorative monuments to elite British men; the founding fathers and heroes of Empire. The reconstructions of these two houses also occurred at key moments in the early to mid-twentieth century when there was a desire (or anxiety) to highlight connections to these imperial and colonial narratives. The Resting Place and Scarred Tree demonstrate the growing strength of Aboriginal Victorian communities and the slow but nonetheless increasing acknowledgement of them by wider society from the late twentieth century to the present. The granting of small public spaces is far from adequate and reconciliation is still a distant dream, but it is true to say that the establishment of such memorials would have been unlikely at the time that Cooks' Cottage was built. This chronology indicates the changing socio-political climate of Melbourne from the 1930s to the present, demonstrating how the maturation of the city's post-colonial discourse was expressed through its relationship with material and remains from its past in public spaces.

In this chapter we have also attempted to identify how these memorials indicate divergences between the ways different segments of Melbourne's community have memorialized material from the past. In the case of the non-Aboriginal, or more specifically, the British-Australian sites, tangible physical connections to important elite men and moments in time are highlighted in order to reinforce the significance of those narratives. In this sense they rely on the power of 'relic magic' and derive their meanings from their connection to individuals deemed worthy of remembering and celebrating in the past. This is markedly different at the Aboriginal sites. Not only are these gender-neutral and focus on collective rather than individualistic identities, they also have layers of intangible cultural heritage which are only accessible to their custodians and in no way 'relic' (Smith 2000: 112–13). The tangible physical connection to Australia's past and what that says about the rights of its Indigenous communities are evident to all viewers, but only Aboriginal people can engage with the memorials in the additional culturally and spiritually rooted ways which are pivotal to their contemporary experience, culture, activism, and performance.

The sites discussed here demonstrate the role that memorialized material and remains from the city's past plays in the construction and contestation of public memory over time and in the present. Such memorials are used to construct and legitimize official narratives about the past, but they can also be used to challenge those narratives (Shackel 2001). This can be done through the erection of examples that tell a counter-narrative, such as the Resting Place and the Scarred Tree, but also through acts of vandalism, as we have seen at Cooks' Cottage. Just as memorials can be used to mask or naturalize inequalities, those same injustices can also be challenged through the public forum of parkscapes and their commemorative material culture.

ACKNOWLEDGEMENTS

We would like to thank to Laura McAtackney and Krysta Ryzewski for their help in preparing and editing this chapter. Their expertise, feedback, and guidance were invaluable throughout the process.

REFERENCES

Aitchison, Cara. 1999. 'Heritage and Nationalism: Gender and the Performance of Power'. In *Leisure/Tourism Geographies: Practices and Geographical Knowledge*, edited by D. Crouch, London: Routledge, pp. 59–73.

Azaryahu, Maoz. 1993. 'From Remains to Relics: Authentic Monuments in the Israeli Landscape', *History and Memory*, 5(2): 82–103.

Barnes, John. 2007. 'C. J. La Trobe "A letter from Jolimont en Murs", to Charlotte La Trobe, 2 March 1840', *La Trobe Journal*, 80: 45–51.

Botham, John. 2010. *La Trobe's Cottage Development Proposal: Report prepared for National Trust of Australia (Victoria)*. Melbourne: Friends of La Trobe Cottage.

Broome, Richard. 2005. *Aboriginal Victorians: a history since 1800*. Crows Nest: Allen & Unwin.

Brück, Joanna. 2013. 'Landscapes of Desire: Parks, Colonialism and Identity in Victorian and Edwardian Ireland', *International Journal of Historical Archaeology*, 17(1): 196–223.

Carman, John. 2002. *Archaeology and Heritage: An Introduction*. New York: The Continuum Publishing Group.

Carver, Martin. 1996. 'On archaeological value', *Antiquity*, 70(267): 45–56.

City of Melbourne. 2003. *Policy for Monuments and Memorials in the City of Melbourne's Parklands*. Melbourne: City of Melbourne.

Cooper, Malcolm A., Antony Firth, John Carman, and David Wheatley (eds). 2005. *Managing Archaeology*. London: Routledge/Taylor and Francis.

Eidelson, Meyer. 2014. *Melbourne Dreaming: a guide to important places of the past and present*. Canberra: Aboriginal Studies Press.

Faulkhead, Shannon and Jim Berg. 2010. *Power and the Passion: our Ancestors Return Home*. Melbourne: Koorie Heritage Trust Inc.

Gill, Hermon. 1934. *Captain Cook's Cottage*. Melbourne: Lothian.

Glendinning, Miles. 2003. 'The Conservation Movement: A Cult of the Modern Age', *Transactions of the Royal Historical Society*, 13: 359–76.

Griffin, Darren, Delta Lucille Freedman, Bill Nicholson, Jnr, Fiona McConachie, and Alexander Parmington. 2013. 'The *Koorong* Project: experimental archaeology and Wurundjeri continuation of cultural practice'. In *Excavations, Surveys and Heritage Management in Victoria, Vol. 2*, Melbourne: the authors, pp. 59–66.

Harrison, Rodney. 2011. 'Surface assemblages. Towards an archaerology *in* and *of* the present', *Archaeological Dialogues*, 18(2): 141–61.

Healy, Chris. 1997. *From the Ruins of Colonialism: History as Social Memory*. Cambridge: Cambridge University Press.

Jordan, Harriet. 1994. 'Public Parks, 1885–1914', *Garden History*, 22(1): 85–113.

Kleinman, Rachel. 2006. 'Protesters won't leave park until demands met', *The Age*, 10 May: 13.

Lewis, Miles. 1994. *La Trobe's Cottage Conservation Analysis*. Melbourne: National Trust of Australia (Victoria).

Lewis, Miles. 2010. 'Jolimont in Context', *La Trobeana: Journal of the CJ La Trobe Society*, 9(1): 2–12.

Long, Andrew. 2003. *Scarred Trees: an identification and recording manual*. Melbourne: Aboriginal Affairs Victoria.

Lowenthal, David. 2015 [1985]. *The Past is a Foreign Country-Revisited*. Cambridge: Cambridge University Press.

McCubbin, Maryanne. 1999. 'Cooked to Perfection: Cooks' Cottage and the Exemplary Historical Figure', *The Journal of Popular Culture*, 33(1): 35–48.

McCubbin, Maryanne. 2000. 'Object Lessons: public history in Melbourne 1887–1935', MA Research Thesis, University of Melbourne.

Nankervis, Max. 1998. 'Our urban parks: Suitable pieces of real estate?', *Journal of Australian Studies*, 22(57): 162–71.

Nicoll, Fiona. 2011. 'Notes of Captain Cook's Gambling Habit: Settling Accounts of White Possession', *Critical Race and Whiteness Studies*, 7(2): 1–23.

O'Shea, Bernard and Richard Sears. 2014. 'Captain Cook's Cottage defaced by vandals in anti-Australia Day protest', *The Daily Mail*, 24 January.

Oxford English Dictionary Online, http://www.oed.com/ (accessed 3 January 2016).

Olsen, Bjørnar and Þóra Pétursdóttir (eds). 2014. *Ruin memories: Materialities, Aesthetics and the Archaeology of the Recent Past*. Abingdon: Taylor and Francis.

Porter, Jonathan. 2009. '"The Past is Present": The Construction of Macau's Historical Legacy', *History and Memory*, 21(1): 63–100.

Shackel, Paul. 2001. 'Public Memory and the Search for Power in American Historical Archaeology', *American Anthropologist*, 103(3): 655–70.

Smith, Laurajane. 2000. 'A history of Aboriginal heritage legislation in south-eastern Australia', *Australian Archaeology*, 50: 109–18.

Smith, Laurajane. 2006. *Uses of Heritage*. London: Routledge.

Smith, Laurajane. 2008. 'Heritage, Gender and Identity'. In *The Ashgate Research Companion to Heritage and Identity*, edited by Brian Graham and Peter Howard, Aldershot: Ashgate Publishing, pp. 159–78.

Smith, Laurajane. 2015. 'Theorizing Museum and Heritage Visiting'. In *The International Handbooks of Museum Studies: Museum Theory*, edited by Kylie Message and Andrea Witcomb, Chichester: Wiley-Blackwell, pp. 459–84.

Taylor, Hilary A. 1995. 'Urban public parks, 1840–1900: Design and meaning', *Garden History*, 23(2): 201–21.

The Argus. 1930. 'Governor La Trobe's Residence', 10 July: 15.

The Argus. 1942. 'LaTrobe cottage is to go', 10 March.

The Argus. 1956. 'Cottage is an antique', 27 September.

The Australasian Sketcher with Pen and Pencil. 1888. 'Victoria Past and Present: the special supplement', 1 November.

The Leader. 1914. 'The earliest government house'. 28 March.

Whitehead, Georgina. 2015 [1997]. *Civilising the city: A history of Melbourne's public gardens.* Melbourne: State Library of Victoria.

Young, Linda. 2008. 'The Contagious Magic of James Cook in Captain-Cook's Cottage', *reCollections*, 3(2): 1–18.

Young, Linda. 2011. 'Magic Objects/Modern Objects'. In *The Thing About Museums.* Abingdon: Routledge.

Zielinski, Caroline. 2014. 'Vandals Target Captains Cook's Cottage in Fitzroy Gardens', *The Age*, 24 January.

6

Ruined by the Thirst for Urban Prosperity

Contemporary Archaeology of City Water Systems

April M. Beisaw

City residents expect pressurized water to flow from kitchen, bath, and laundry room taps. Access to clean water is a contemporary human necessity, but is it a human right? City water is not *free*—creating and maintaining urban water systems is a complex engineering process that requires political power; land and labour are necessary to obtain and store water, operate pumping stations, maintain plants for filtration and wastewater treatment, and build out the subsurface pipe network. After initial construction costs have been paid, the efficiency of an entire water system dictates the costs of residential flow. Some cities, like Detroit, have an adjacent freshwater source, in this case the Detroit River, whose water can be pumped, treated, and distributed to residents rather efficiently. Other cities, like New York, have to acquire water from distant sources. Built on an island surrounded by salt water, New York City had to wield significant political power to construct new water sources and transport water from up to 125 miles away. Access to this water allowed the urban development of Manhattan Island while selectively destroying rural communities.

New York City began building reservoirs in 1776; today there are nineteen reservoirs and three controlled lakes that hold 550 billion gallons of water. Official statistics on the rural communities sacrificed for this water are only available for the six reservoirs put into service between 1915 and 1955: the Ashokan (1915), Kensico (1915), Schoharie (1926), Roundout (1950), Neversink (1954), and Pepacton (1955) reservoirs. Their construction submerged a total of seventeen villages, and displaced 4,464 living from their land and 8,093 from their graves (BWS 1950: 35, 76). Those whose lands were not taken were left to reconstruct their lives without their long-time neighbours, the fertile valleys they lived in, and the roads, railroads, and unobstructed water ways that once tied communities together and facilitated economic activity. Some residents were unable to adjust and abandoned their lands. A city land acquisition programme is currently purchasing up to an additional 355,000 acres in their watersheds. The goal is to meet pollution control requirements set by the Environmental Protection Agency.

Archaeological survey of New York City-owned lands in the Croton and Catskill watersheds has documented the structural and artefactual remains of those who were left behind after reservoir creation. Together, these data reveal a 150-year legacy of rural ruination and displacement. Ruination is a political project that lays waste to certain peoples and places, often in the name of humanitarian work (Stoler 2008). When political power forces population removals, the ruins of homes and businesses often persist within newly created zones of uninhabitable space. Presently, New York City authorities use small metal signs and fencing to demarcate their watershed lands; some of these lands are designated as public access lands, others are open to public recreation by permit only, and some are entirely closed off. Such government strategies for managing uninhabited space are a common feature of landscapes of ruination (cf. Stoler 2013). In this context the ruins of communities displaced by watershed construction may be read as political symbols that draw on the past, make claims on the future, and haunt the present (Stoler 2008: 201). When rural ruins on abandoned city-owned lands are juxtaposed with that the urban development that they served, the cumulative costs of modernization are revealed (Rao 2013: 291).

This contemporary archaeology study of New York City's watersheds provides a means of addressing cultural and historical amnesia (González-Ruibal 2013) that allows urban residents to devalue city water in the monetary sense. The city of Detroit, a present-day comparative case study, is currently in a water crisis. There, a decade of declining population has caused water prices to skyrocket. The problem is not only perpetuated by fewer residents and businesses to share the costs of water distribution, but also by an ageing water system in need of repairs. Residents who remain in areas with otherwise high abandonment stress the system the most and contribute to driving up prices city-wide. Their continued occupation of sparsely inhabited areas reduces the efficiency of the entire urban water system. By historicizing and reframing the issue of water systems, it is apparent that city water management strategies often encourage the ruination of some landscapes and communities to enable the revitalization of others. The lessons for cities like Detroit that are inherent in New York City's watershed ruins are that: 1) places rich in water are inhabited places; 2) pollution of water in densely settled places is inevitable; and 3) when water needs arise, those lower on the socio-economic spectrum are more likely to be targeted for displacement. An archaeological approach to documenting the ruins of water management practices highlights these connections and encourages new dialogues about water rights, needs, and costs.

This chapter describes the evolution of New York City's water system as it progressed from the tapping of a natural source on the island of Manhattan to the construction of an expansive system of reservoirs, lakes, and aqueducts, extending up to 125 miles away from the city. The results of archaeological pedestrian survey on city-owned lands around two distant water sources, the Ashokan and Boyds Corners (1873) reservoirs, are then provided as a way of assessing the long-term cultural costs of watershed creation and maintenance. The physical ruins documented by archaeological survey are then compared to the imagined ones that local residents claim to see within reservoirs during droughts. Based on engineering reports, any remains present in the reservoirs are more likely by-products of the reservoir construction process than ruins of abandoned towns. The existing disparity between imagined and documented ruins is an example of how lingering resentment among displaced communities and their descendants complicates water politics. Lastly, the potential for an archaeology of Detroit's water system, through a focus on Water Works Park, is presented as a brief postscript to the New York City watershed case study. Drawing from the lessons learned in New York City, the Detroit example serves to illustrate the extent of water management issues facing contemporary, post-industrial cities and call attention to the economic, environmental, and social costs of the city's water and its associated ruins.

6.1 RUINED FOR WATER: A SHORT HISTORY OF NEW YORK AND ITS WATER SUPPLY

The city of New York began on the southern tip of Manhattan Island in the seventeenth century. Many of those who helped build the city were so economically marginalized by it that they lived and were buried outside of the city limits (Yamin 2001), a boundary once marked by a palisade at Wall Street (Figure 6.1). The south side of Wall Street was home to prosperous urban settlements, while the north side contained rural neighbourhoods of African and European labourers, poorhouses, and the city's main water source, the Collect Pond. As populations on both sides grew, the Collect Pond became polluted with residential and commercial waste. Around the pond, privies emptied onto the streets and animals roamed freely. Nearby industries, like beer breweries, siphoned off large amounts of fresh water from the pond's sources (Koeppel 2000: 13–15). The pond could not cleanse itself. The city's water became so contaminated that residents drank only boiled or bottled water. All of this occurred before the year 1776.

Figure 6.1. Maerschalck's early plan of New York City (1755) showing the Collect Pond's rural location. Wikicommons.

An early solution to the city's water problem was to construct a reservoir to hold water pumped from the Collect Pond's underground sources. This strategy provided cleaner water than the pond itself but it was still a polluted and insufficient supply. By the early nineteeth century the city was growing quickly, fed by a flood of immigrants eager to benefit from the Industrial Revolution. The palisade wall was removed and the urban–rural divide was pushed further from Manhattan's southern tip (Wall 2001). Pollution increased around the Collect Pond and by the mid-nineteenth century it was linked to residents' poor health. Cholera, a water-borne illness, claimed 3,500 lives during an 1832 epidemic (Koeppel 2000: 146) and two-thirds of those deaths came from neighbourhoods in the vicinity of the Collect Pond (*New York Times* 1874). The Collect Pond Reservoir also could not provide pressurized water to fight city fires. The Great Fire of 1835 destroyed 52 acres. Unable to douse the flames, buildings in the fire's path were intentionally destroyed to create a firebreak. Construction of a clean and pressurized water source became an integral part of the city's rebuilding effort.

In 1837 construction of the Croton Dam began in a rural area of New York, 45 miles to the north of Manhattan Island. This project created the first off-island reservoir for New York City and it marked the first time the city claimed land outside of its borders. The Croton Dam gathered water that was gravity-fed through a new aqueduct into a new Manhattan Island reservoir. Official tallies of those displaced by construction of the dam, aqueduct, and receiving reservoir do not seem to exist. Indirect references to displaced residents can be found in some histories of Manhattan's Central Park, which was built around the new receiving reservoir (Rozenweig and Blackmar 1992). The rural Manhattan neighbourhood of York Hill was demolished for the receiving reservoir and the adjacent community of Seneca Village was taken for the construction of Central Park. Both were communities of immigrants and free Africans that had grown after New York's emancipation declaration of 1827 (Wall et al. 2008).

The lack of official records documenting the people who were displaced by the Croton water system understandably fuels the cultural and historical amnesia related to its cultural costs. However, the amnesia that surrounds Central Park is less explicable. While many official histories of Central Park portray its landscape as previously uninhabited (Hecksher 2008), others contain details on the propaganda used to justify the destruction of the area's working-class communities. Some powerful landowners saw Central Park as a way of clearing low-income people and their associated trades from the city landscape (Rozenweig and Blackmar 1992: 63–4). The creation of the Park displaced approximately 1,600 African, Irish, and German inhabitants, 10 per cent of whom ran small businesses in the area. Like other public works projects, the construction of Central Park is often remembered in a positive light, a perspective that frames the destruction and ruination that the process caused as necessary sacrifices.

The sacrifices by the residents of York Hill, Seneca Village, and Croton were forgotten soon after clean and pressurized water began to flow onto Manhattan. Despite the vast spaces reappropriated to accommodate the city's water supply, the new water availability only served to increase local demand. Between 1842 and 1894 consumption of water in New York City expanded from 12 million to 183 million gallons per day (Finnegan 1996: 595). The Croton Dam and Reservoir's flow of 20 million gallons per day was no longer an inexhaustible water supply. A series of new rural reservoirs and aqueducts were planned and built, with construction of each new phase starting as soon as the previous one ended. Recognizing the need for a major reservoir the city began plans to create the Ashokan, a 128 billion-gallon behemoth located over 85 miles north-west of Manhattan. Construction of the reservoir required the destruction of at least seven rural communities in order to provide the water that would ensure New York City's prosperity.

The legal battles involving those whose land was seized for the Ashokan Reservoir by eminent domain are the subject of many books and articles. But the stories of those who were left to live in the dramatically altered landscapes of the Ashokan region are largely untold. Clearing communities from landscapes often creates personal and collective grief, defeat, and outrage (Smith 2008: 18). In the Ashokan case a disconnection from community heritage occurred when ten churches and thirty-two cemeteries were demolished. The Crispell homestead, celebrated on a *c.*1900 postcard as the oldest home in the valley, was also lost during the demolition process. Johannis Crispell was a community leader in 1737 and the Crispell family name appears at least forty-eight times in the 1880 history of Ulster County (Sylvester 1880).

Once completed, the Ashokan Reservoir was celebrated for its 'natural beauty'. In the 100 years since its waters began flowing to Manhattan, many properties surrounding the reservoir have been vacated by former residents and then acquired by New York City to prevent development that could introduce pollution to the reservoir. What was once a well-developed agricultural valley of rolling meadows and hay fields has become a sparsely inhabited forest bordering the watershed lake. The cleared cultural landscape is now re-associated with nature and wilderness, such transitions have been shown to increase negative feelings of those who experienced the clearance (Guernsey 2008: 115–16). While their grief must be acknowledged, this research seeks to move away from the dominant narrative of the city's water battles, one that Finnegan classifies as 'the history of the struggle between property rights and public health protection, urban sophistication and rural simplicity, water consumers versus watershed residents, and the now centuries old political struggle between upstate [mainly rural] and downstate [mainly urban and suburban]' (1996: 585–6).

Anthropological studies of water conflict have successfully articulated related hardships, injustices, and inhumane conditions within various cultural contexts, but they have not been able to impact public policy (Treitler and Midgett 2007: 141). An archaeological study's tangible material evidence can show evidence of how environmental engineering produces unexpected ripple effects. The city watersheds contain ruins that document over 100 years of successes and failures. Mapping the ruins associated with watershed-related displacement reveals some general conditions, such as topographic slope and distance to infrastructure, which likely influenced abandonment. But there is a disconnect regarding how these vacant lands are treated—cordoned off as environmental resources and recreation areas by the city but treated as extensions of private property or trash dump sites by locals. While vacancy has created woodlands where none existed for generations, these spaces are not celebrated *natural* places (also see González-Ruibal, Chapter 7). These lands are also not celebrated *cultural* places, as the visible ruins here are ignored by local residents who subscribe to legends of submerged ruins within the reservoir itself. By refocusing attention away from the reservoir and towards the tangible, physical ruins that remain, the city may be able to increase local stewardship of their watershed lands while reminding all city water consumers about the sacrifices rural residents make to provide that water.

6.2 CONTEMPORARY ARCHAEOLOGY OF DISTANT CITY LANDS

A city's ruins are not necessarily problems to be solved or sites to be restored, but they are always containers of involuntary mementos ripe for remembering (González-Ruibal 2014; see Russell, Chapter 2). Ruins hold stories about those who have left while revealing responses to their absence by those left behind (Dawdy 2010). Recent ruins can reveal a diversity of past and current viewpoints just by examining exposed surface deposits (González-Ruibal 2013). For this project, city owned lands around the Croton's Boyds Corners Reservoir and the Catskill's Ashokan Reservoir were surveyed by archaeologists using only hand-held global positioning (GPS) units to document the locations of building foundations, stone walls, artefact scatters, a mill, a stone quarry, and one cemetery in the woods. Each find was photographed and described but otherwise left *in situ*. No artefacts were collected and no soil was excavated and therefore no excavation permits were needed (all team members had valid hiking permits.) Such surface survey and documentation of ruins allows archaeologists to witness abandonment, manifest the desire that things could have happened differently, and share the responsibility of knowledge about the displaced communities and their histories with others (González-Ruibal 2014).

6.2.1 Croton System History and Archaeology

Before being dammed by New York City in 1837, the Croton River provided fish for food, power for mills, and water for residents and farms, while linking together many rural communities (Tompkins 2000). Construction of the dam did more than change the course of the river, it raised the waterline by forty feet, flooding prime farmland, pastures, and orchards. Once the rural landscape was transformed, the population around Croton Lake grew. Approximately 2,000 homes with 20,000 people and 12,000 domestic animals inhabited the area in 1888. By 1896 the Croton was 'much polluted by manufacturing wastes, the drainage from manure-heaps, pigsties, etc.' and the city was given the power to condemn 'all property adjacent to any stream, pond, or reservoir, used for the city's water-supply' (Wegmann 1896: 190). Over the next one hundred years the Croton watershed would grow to include fourteen reservoirs, the northernmost of these, the Boyds Corners Reservoir, was completed in 1873. Archaeological investigation of three city-owned properties around Boyds Corners (Boyds Corners North, Horse Pound Road, and Richardsville) documented a cemetery and several extensive networks of stone walls created for both cropland and livestock management, and two building foundations, a mill and a late nineteenth- to early twentieth-century residence.

At the Boyds Corners North survey unit, the archaeological team hiked over a mile into the woods to document a cemetery of twelve gravestones, which had been cut off from road access by the removal of a bridge (Colour plate 7, bottom middle), presumably after the city obtained the property. The oldest headstone in the cemetery dates to 1849; a date after water started flowing from Croton into New York City. The most recent headstone, of Elsie J. Lee Robinson, dates to 1924; more than fifty years after the Boyds reservoir was built. Elsie, wife of Nelson R. Robinson, would have witnessed these changes, as she lived from 1860 to 1924 (Colour plate 7, bottom left). Nelson is buried with Elsie but only his birth date (1865) is inscribed on the headstone. Many of the eleven other headstones belong to Elsie and Nelson's relatives, members of the Robinson and Lee families. These families did not immediately abandon the region when the Boyds reservoir was constructed, but genealogy confirms that within two generations they had relocated.

At the city's Horse Pound Road unit, the survey team followed the remnants of the unpaved Washington Road into the woods and across a dry brook, where they documented the ruins of a large mill, whose foundation measures 3,876 square feet (Colour plate 7, top left). Near the mill were the remnants of two rakes of the type once used for the management of hay. On both sides of Washington Road were networks of stone walls, some with remnant posts and fragments of barbed wire, indicating the boundaries of an animal pasture. Diversion of water into city reservoirs may explain why the waterway that once powered the mill is now completely dry. The loss of such waterways would have made it difficult to keep livestock on these lands.

Despite its large area, the Richardsville survey unit contained few ruins; only the foundation of a late nineteenth- to early twentieth-century residence and a minor network of stone walls were located. Although construction of the Boyds Corners Reservoir pushed the town of Richardsville westward towards this unit, post-reservoir construction was minimal. The sloped topography of the Richardsville land certainly restricted its use value. The city allows both hunting and hiking on this land and the property is extensively used by hunters, who have installed hunting blinds and perches. One area of the survey unit appears to have recently been mined for topsoil, and another contains a trail built completely out of old phone books. This trail leads directly to a private residence. Everything about the Richardsville unit suggests that locals treat this property as their land, not public land owned by the city.

6.2.2 Catskill System History and Archaeology

Once construction of the Croton watershed was completed in 1905, the city turned to the Catskill Mountains, approximately 100 miles north-west of the city, to build their next reservoir. This Catskill valley was not only an inhabited landscape, it was also a tourist destination for city residents. Construction of the Ashokan Reservoir began in 1907 by damming the Esopus Creek. Approximately 12,000 acres of land containing boarding houses, farm houses, mills, churches, shops, railroad stations, and post offices were cleared (Stradling 2007: 167). Due to the scale of this project, the local community was enlisted in the process of their own ruination. Residents were paid to burn down their own houses and dig up their own ancestors. In return they were given half of their land's assessed value and had to file claims to determine what, if any, additional compensation they would receive (Stradling 2007: 167). Archaeological survey of city-owned properties outside of the original reservoir take-line (the continuous land area taken by the city by eminent domain) revealed networks of stone walls similar to those found around Boyds Corners Reservoir in the Croton watershed. The main difference between the two regions is that in the Catskills there are no cemeteries or mills in the woods, yet there are the ruins of many residences and barns, as well as ruins of the reservoir construction itself, including the Yale stone quarry. Another difference is that archaeological survey of each city-owned Ashokan property reveals a different story of resilience and abandonment, depending on the property's topographic slope and distance to reconstructed roads and railroads.

Archaeological remains recorded within the city's Black Road recreational unit on the north side of the reservoir clearly reveals short-lived attempts at economic diversification. While the foundations of two residences (Colour plate 7, bottom

1. Wolfgang Ganter's studio 'outside space', Berlin. Top: Ladder to storage area, plastic sheeting curtain that divides the space, table-saw used for framemaking, and dust. Bottom: Supplies used for framing and cleaning. Photos by Steven Seidenberg.

2. Wolfgang Ganter's studio 'inside space' showing light table used for injecting slides with bacteria, Berlin. Photo by Steven Seidenberg.

3. Top: Elmgreen & Dragset studio, Berlin, a renovated water pumping station in Neukölln. Photo by Steven Seidenberg. Bottom: Interior of Elmgreen & Dragset studio. View of main floor and mezzanine with staging area for exhibition below. The summer working space for staff is visible on the left side. Photo by Steven Seidenberg.

4. Top: Installation view of *An Innocent City*, Istanbul. July 2014. Photo by Ian Alden Russell. Bottom: Installation view of objects borrowed from the local community from *An Innocent City*. July 2014. Photo by Ian Alden Russell.

5. Top: Postcards with stories written on them left by visitors to *An Innocent City*, Istanbul. July 2014. Photo by Ian Alden Russell. Bottom: Interior of the former Michigan Theatre, Detroit, built on the site of Henry Ford's first garage, and current home to a car park. Wikicommons, 2011.

6. Top: The remains of the Grande Ballroom, Detroit. The Ballroom is currently slated for demolition. Wikicommons, 2012. Bottom: Cooks' Cottage, the Fitzroy Gardens, Melbourne, Australia. Photo by Brian Shanahan.

7. Ruins associated with the Boyds Corners Reservoir (New York) include a mill adjacent to a now dry waterway (top left), and a cemetery located in secondary growth forest (bottom left). Ruins associated with the Ashokan Reservoir include very large stone walls constructed to clear the landscape for livestock (top right) and house foundations (bottom right). Photos by A. M. Beisaw and students.

8. Top: Abandoned nineteenth-century houses in the historic centre of Belém do Pará, Brazil. Photo by Alfredo González-Ruibal, 2008. Bottom: An illegal settlement of landless peasants inside an Awá reservation, Maranhão. Photo by Alfredo González-Ruibal, 2006.

9. Top: A street with ruins of early twentieth-century buildings in Rio Grande, Brazil. Bottom: A decaying art nouveau house in Rio Grande, partly occupied by a shop. Photos by Alfredo González-Ruibal, 2013.

10. Top: West India Quay, Docklands, London. Photo by Sefryn Penrose. Bottom: The Titanic Museum, East Belfast, Northern Ireland. Photo by Laura McAtackney, 2016.

11. Top: 'Ulster's Past Defenders' mural referencing the UDR and USC on Lower Newtownards Road, Belfast, Northern Ireland. Photo by Laura McAtackney, 2013. Bottom: Ulster's Present Day Defenders' adjacent mural referencing the UDA on Lower Newtownards Road. Photo by Laura McAtackney, 2013.

12. 'Waiting for Rain' by Jazzart Dance Theatre, choreographed by Jacqueline Manyaapelo. GIPCA's 'Land' project, 21 November 2013, Cape Town, South Africa. Photo by Ashley Walters, © GIPCA.

13. Top: A pair of shoes and a bottle. District Six, Cape Town, 2013. Photo by Sara C. F. de Gouveia. Bottom: 'Where worlds collide'. District Six, Cape Town, 2014. Photo by Dirk-Jan Visser.

14. Top: The grassy 'jungle' adjacent to the Davidson Street Bridge Encampment, Indianapolis, Indiana. Photo by C. Singleton. Bottom: The back porch lounging area of an individual's private campsite. The guest bed is located directly under the 'No Trespassing' sign. Photo by C. Singleton.

15. Richard's home structured from a shopping cart, Davidson Street Bridge Encampment, Indianapolis, Indiana. Photo by C. Singleton.

16. German troops based in Oulu, Finland left this monument in 1942. Photo by Timo Ylimaunu.

right) and two barns were identified, none of these structures appear on historic maps. The fact that residents once invested considerable time in managing this property is indicated by the massive stone walls constructed from relatively small stones (Colour plate 7, top right). Collection of these stones cleared the adjacent hay fields, animal pasture, and animal pens. An expansive network of stone walls includes a few high-walled animal pens, complete with stone features for collecting and retaining water. A dry creek bed suggests that water availability may have been a recurring problem in the immediate area. Closer to the residential foundations, the stone walls are more decorative, well-made short wall segments separating residences, and a few garden plants still survive. Near the residences, rusted pails adjacent to maple trees attest to the syrup harvesting that also once took place on the property.

On the south side of the Ashokan Reservoir the ruins of the South Mountain property tell a very different story, one of perseverance. Here there are fewer stone walls and building foundations and much more decorative landscaping; rose bushes and daffodils still bloom. Separate foundations of a house and barn sit high atop the steep slope overlooking the reservoir below. The lower slopes were used as hay fields and the stone walls around those fields are more decorative than functional (functional stone walls are associated with the need to clear land of rocky obstructions and decorative walls are associated with landscaping). Historic maps confirm what pedestrian survey found: that this house was the only domestic structure to exist on this property for over one hundred years. The residents neither benefited from nor were severely impacted by the reservoir construction.

A comparison between the Black Road and South Mountain landscape features illustrate how subtle the differences in the form of ruins can be to the naked eye. Central to Stoler's concept of ruination is the recognition of how human potential can become bound to or bounded by the degraded environments they are left to live in after a government project has altered their landscape. Individuals extricate themselves from the colonial order of things at an uneven pace (Stoler 2008: 193). Some, like those at Black Road, engage in creative and sometimes costly measures in an attempt to improve their lot. Others, like those at South Mountain, continue on to the best of their abilities. Once the flat and fertile farmland was submerged by the reservoir, the economy of the region shifted. Those who previously farmed the flatlands could not continue as farmers in the area because the higher elevation land that remained was not suitable for agriculture. Clearing the rocky soil in the higher elevations required a great deal of effort, and without sufficient clearing plant yields would be low and livestock movement difficult.

On the south side of the reservoir, not far from the dam that created the Ashokan Reservoir is the Acorn Hill recreation unit. Here the ruins of the Yale Quarry remain within what is now dense forest. Around the quarried cliff face are piles of discarded waste. One pile contains light bulbs, beer cans, gas cans, shoe soles, and American stoneware. Further away, along an abandoned road, is the tub of an electric washing machine. It is surrounded by fragments of perfume bottles, liquor bottles, eye ointments, plates, mason jars, and clam shells. Further downslope, towards the reservoir, are rusted 55-gallon drums adjacent to a discontinued railroad bed. These are just some of the numerous artefact scatters documented within the Acorn Hill unit. Ordinarily these artefacts would warrant focused archaeological attention but they seem minor when compared to the monumental architecture and debris from the quarry operation itself. Piles of waste stone, footings for winches, and a passageway for railroad cars receiving crushed stone dwarf the artefact scatters. On the flatlands closest to the reservoir, a few minor stone walls are all that remain of the previous agricultural activities. While no building foundations were located within the Acorn Hill unit, two are visible just across the roadway that separates the unit from the city-owned land that encircles the reservoir. This land is not open to hikers and therefore could not be surveyed.

Although Acorn Hill contains spectacular ruins and discontinued roads that should attract nature hiking and historical tourism, it appears to receive few visitors. The lack of an adjacent parking area and the dense growth within the unit are the likely deterrents. Also, there are no interpretive signs or other sources informing visitors about the existence and historical importance of the ruins. In the absence of official information one would expect local legends to thrive, yet residents seem unaware of the area's historical remains. In contrast, legends about the ruins of villages submerged by reservoir waters are pervasive. Archaeologists working in the region are frequently asked about them, despite the fact that reservoir construction reports suggest the submerged villages do not exist at the bottom of the reservoir.

6.3 GHOSTLY RUINS AND A LEGACY OF CONFLICT

The villages allegedly *submerged* by the Ashokan Reservoir were more likely erased when city crews scoured the valley floor before the reservoir was filled. Official reports describe the removal of everything, including buildings and tree roots from the village landscape during the construction process. Yet even today, those who live and work around the reservoir claim that they can see village ruins whenever water levels drop. An officer with the city's Department of Environmental Protection, which polices the watershed and enforces city rules regarding land use, provided an interpretation of one ruin to a reporter, 'We think it was a bar or church' (Foderaro 2002). According to a regional magazine, some residents believe that church steeples and chimneys occasionally poke out of the water (Loftin 2008). For those without familial connections to the lost towns, this mythology may stem from the somewhat misleading signs the city erected along reservoir banks. The signs declare specific places as the 'former site of' but these signs are actually far from the past town centres (Figure 6.2). No signage exists to describe the process of demolition and excavation that created a deep basin where the undulating valley once existed. For those with familial connections, continuing the mythology of submerged towns may help them remember their lost communities.

A case study from southern India provides further comparative insight into how submerged towns are remembered. Srisailam, a mega dam, submerged 100 villages, displacing more than 150,000 people. In the dry season some portions of these villages do reappear and 'haunt those who once lived there' (Stoler 2013: 21). Many left the region because they no longer had homes, livelihoods, or the will to carry on (Rao 2013: 288). For those who remained, the ruins are constant reminders of what was lost, even when they are invisible below the dam waters. Resentment in the Srisilam region is focused on ancient temples that were relocated and preserved, with the help of archaeologists. Locals are angry that their government chose to save the distant past, but sacrificed the present for the future. 'Unmoored, without land, water, and livelihoods' the residents use both submerged and visible ruins to describe their relationship to development and destruction (Rao 2013).

In November 2016 a drought reduced the water levels to 57 per cent of capacity. Visual survey along the dam's recreational walkway revealed no more than a construction crane's footings. Still, the ghostly presence of the former towns cannot be denied. Meanwhile, the ruins that do exist and are readily visible on city-owned lands around the reservoir are largely ignored. Because the city has been slowly acquiring lands in the vicinity of the reservoir as they become available, there is no sudden and dramatic disaster narrative to capture the public's attention. Their lack of awareness of the ruins that do exist goes hand-in-hand with a lack of stewardship for the lands they occupy as environmentally sensitive places. One city-owned Boyds Corners recreation unit, Richardsville, is being mined for topsoil and has a trailway constructed out of telephone books leading to a private residence. On one city-owned Ashokan recreation unit, Piney Point, a wetland is being used as a dump site for landscaping equipment. Near by a small environmental-monitoring station (a PVC pipe and an electronic box) emerge from the ground. Other recreational units have older dumps, several of which include the remains of automobiles.

6.4 URBAN WATER DEMANDS AND RURAL RUINATION

Archaeological methods can never fully document the ruination that New York City reservoirs brought to their watersheds. Together, construction of nineteen reservoirs and three controlled lakes within these watersheds

Figure 6.2. Sign erected by New York City that suggest the presence of ruins below the waterline. Photo by A. M. Beisaw and students.

spanned almost 150 years and impacted countless residents. Ruination continues as the city is actively acquiring thousands of additional acres to curb pollution. Archaeological survey of acquired lands reveals the presence of standing ruins surrounded by secondary growth forest. Each ruin may be connected with individuals and families who made their own choices about how to respond to the city's displacement efforts (for a comparison of curated 'ruin' homes see Shanahan and Shanahan, Chapter 5). When considered together, these ruins reveal how watershed creation and maintenance changed the cultural trajectory of entire regions. Juxtaposing the mundane, a house foundation or stone wall, and the monumental, a dam or reservoir, reveals the unquestioned privilege (Mullins 2013) among those who created and maintained New York City's urban water system (see Mullins, Chapter 12, for discussion of privileging in Indianapolis).

Contemporary archaeology of urban water systems emphasizes the fact that that there is nothing natural about city water; there are high cultural and economic costs to harvesting and transporting water to every urban tap, often involving processes wrought with political inequalities and contentious episodes of displacement. In New York, some rural communities have been forced to sacrifice their homes, businesses, and infrastructure to ensure distant urban prosperity. In Detroit efforts to rebuild urban prosperity may require similar sacrifices by residents living within sparsely inhabited areas of the once densely populated city. Pumping water to them, through aged and inefficient infrastructure, ensures that water costs will remain unacceptably high.

6.5 POSTSCRIPT: JUXTAPOSING DETROIT'S WATER CRISIS WITH ITS WATER HISTORY

In the last decade, Detroit water rates have increased by 119 per cent, mainly because consumption decreased by 26 per cent. The Detroit Water and Sewage Department links this decline to the loss of 400,000 jobs, the relocation of 300,000 people away from the city water system, and the construction of new and more efficient urban buildings (DWSD 2012). Many low income residents and those who live in older and less efficient buildings cannot afford the higher water costs. In response, the city began cutting off water supplies to these residents in mid-2014 (Guilien 2014). While critics are labelling the water shutoffs a violation of human rights (Associated Press 2014), the city is strapped for funds to maintain and repair its deteriorating water infrastructure.

Detroit's earliest water system was the Detroit Water Works, a for-profit business that operated between 1827 and 1835 (Daisy n.d.). Profits were meagre enough that the city government had to purchase the water works to ensure the city's survival and future growth. As the water supply stabilized and expanded so did Detroit. A new pumping station was built on the then outskirts of Detroit in 1854 and again on the new outskirts of the city in 1877. Water output grew from 540 million gallons in 1855 to almost 2 trillion gallons in 1870 (Daisy n.d.: 8). A new water works was needed and one that would be able to grow with the city.

In 1879 Detroit's Water Works Park opened. The park functioned as much more than a utility facility. Much of the engineering was housed in a grand building and an adjacent 185-foot tall tower that pressurized the water flow. The surrounding fifty-six acres was designed as an urban park with the political and financial support of Chauncey Hurlburt, president of the Board of Water Commissioners (Figure 6.3a). By 1900 the park was a major tourist attraction with facilities for water recreation, including boating, fishing, wading, but also a library, tennis courts, and a baseball diamond. As a public leisure space, Water Works Park connected city residents to their water source. This idyllic version of the park was short lived.

Pollution from Detroit's growing population required construction of a wastewater treatment plant, which destroyed portions of the park in the early 1920s (Daisy n.d.: 13). Wartime fears of intentional contamination (or destruction) also closed what remained of the park during World Wars I and II, and the Korean War. The wading lagoon was condemned in 1960 and the pressurizing tower was dismantled in 1962. Two layers of fencing, decorated only with 'No Trespassing' signs, now surround the site of what was once Water Works Park (Figure 6.3b).

In the present water crisis, some residents call for Detroit water to be free while others suggest that water management should be run as a private enterprise. The high cost of urban water is why it became a Detroit government

Figure 6.3. The Hurlburt Gate entrance to Detroit's Water Works Park (a) *c*.1910 and (b) January of 2015. Photo by A. M. Beisaw.

responsibility 200 years ago, even before costly pollution filtration was a necessity. Many Detroiters are unaware of Water Works Park's history and its past functions. Its ruins provide an opportunity for archaeologists, heritage practitioners, and planners to reconnect Detroit's residents to their water system. The park offers a tangible mechanism for reviving cultural memory that also historicizes the current crisis, and situates it within the broader context of water management histories for other urban areas.

REFERENCES

Associated Press. 2014. 'Groups Discuss Detroit Water Shutoffs with UN Experts', 19 October. *Detroit Free Press*. http://www.freep.com/story/news/local/michigan/detroit/2014/10/19/detroit-water-shutoffs-united-nations/17585855/ (accessed 23 January 2017).

Board of Water Supply, New York. 1950. *The Water Supply of the City of New York: A Volume Descriptive of its Sources, Storage Reservoirs, and Transportation with Certain Construction Features of the Catskill, Delaware and Interconnected Water Supply Systems*. New York: Reproduction Section, Board of Water Supply.

Daisy, Michael (ed.). n.d. *Detroit Water and Sewage Department: The First 300 Years*. Detroit: Detroit Water and Sewage Department. Available at http://dwsd.org/downloads_n/about_dwsd/history/complete_history.pdf (accessed 23 January 2017).

Dawdy, Shannon Lee. 2010. 'Clockpunk Anthropology and the Ruins of Modernity', *Current Anthropology*, 51(6): 761–93.

(DWSD) Detroit Water and Sewage Department. 2012. *Putting Rate Increases Into Perspective. Wholesale Customer Outreach Technical Advisory Committee*. http://www.ycua.org/PDFs/PuttingRateIncreasesIntoPerspective.pdf (accessed 23 January 2017).

Finnegan, Michael C. 1996. 'New York City's Watershed Agreement: A Lesson in Sharing Responsibility', *Pace Environmental Law Review*, 14(2): 577–644.

Foderaro, Lisa W. 2002. '"Watery Graves" Was No Figure of Speech; A Receding City Reservoir Reveals a Turbulent Past', 14 May, *New York Times*. http://www.nytimes.com/2002/05/14/nyregion/watery-graves-was-no-figure-speech-receding-city-reservoir-reveals-turbulent.html (accessed 23 January 2017).

González-Ruibal, Alfredo. 2013. 'Reclaiming Archaeology'. In *Reclaiming Archaeology: Beyond the Tropes of Modernity*, edited by Alfredo González-Ruibal, London: Routledge, pp. 1–30.

González-Ruibal, Alfredo. 2014. 'Returning to Where We Have Never Been: Excavating the Ruins of Modernity'. In *Ruin Memories: Materialities, Aesthetics and the Archaeology of the Recent Past*, edited by Bjørnar Olsen and Þóra Pétursdóttir, London: Routledge, pp. 367–89.

Guernsey, Brenda. 2008. 'Constructing the Wilderness and Clearing the Landscape: A Legacy of Colonialism in Northern British Columbia'. In *Landscapes of Clearance: Archaeological and Anthropological Approaches*, edited by Angèle Smith and Amy Gazin-Schwartz, Walnut Creek: Left Coast Press, pp. 112–24.

Guillen, Joe. 2014. 'Detroit City Approves 8.7% Water Rate Increase', *Detroit Free Press*, 17 June.

Hecksher, Morrison H. 2008. *Creating Central Park*. New Haven: Yale University Press.

Koeppel, Gerard T. 2000. *Water for Gotham: A History*. Princeton: Princeton University Press.

Loftin, A. J. 2008. 'The Creation of the Ashokan Reservoir Changed the Catskills Forever', *Hudson Valley Magazine*, August, http://www.hvmag.com/Hudson-Valley-Magazine/August-2008/History-The-Ashokan-Reservoir/ (accessed 23 January 2017).

Mullins, Paul. 2013. 'Race and Prosaic Materiality: The Archaeology of Contemporary Urban Space and the Invisible Colour Line'. In *The Oxford Handbook of the Archaeology of the Contemporary World*, edited by Paul Graves-Brown, Rodney Harrison, and Angela Piccini, Oxford: Oxford University Press, pp. 508–21.

New York Times. 1874. 'General Viele's Health Map', 9 April: p. 5.

Rao, Vyjayanthi. 2013. 'The Future in Ruins'. In *Imperial Debris: On Ruins and Ruination*, edited by Ann Laura Stoler, Durham: Duke University Press, pp. 287–322.

Rosenzweig, Roy and Elizabeth Blackmar. 1992. *The Park and The People: A History of Central Park*. Ithaca: Cornell University Press.

Smith, Angèle. 2008. 'Landscapes of Clearance: Archaeological and Anthropological Perspectives'. In *Landscapes of Clearance: Archaeological and Anthropological Approaches*, edited by Angèle Smith and Amy Gazin-Schwartz, Walnut Creek: Left Coast Press, pp. 13–24.

Stoler, Ann Laura. 2008. 'Imperial Debris: Reflections on Ruins and Ruination', *Cultural Anthropology*, 23(2): 191–219.

Stoler, Ann Laura. 2013. 'Introduction "The Rot Remains": From Ruins to Ruination'. In *Imperial Debris: On Ruins and Ruination*, edited by Ann Laura Stoler, Durham: Duke University Press, pp. 1–38.

Stradling, David. 2007. *Making Mountains: New York City and the Catskills*. Seattle: University of Washington Press.

Sylvester, Nathaniel Bartlett. 1880. *History of Ulster County, New York with Illustrations and Biographical Sketches of its Prominent Men and Pioneers*. Philadelphia: Everts and Peck.

Tompkins, Christopher R. 2000. *The Croton Dams and Aqueduct: Images of America*. Charleston: Arcadia Publishing.

Treitler, Inga and Douglas Midgett. 2007. 'It's About Water—Anthropological Perspectives on Water and Policy', *Human Organization*, 66(2): 140–9.

Wall, Diana diZerega. 2001. 'Afterword: Becoming New York: The Five Points Neighborhood', *Historical Archaeology*, 35(3): 133–5.

Wall, Diana diZerega, Nan A. Rotschild, and Cynthia Copeland. 2008. 'Seneca Village and Little Africa: Two African American Communities in Antebellum New York City', *Historical Archaeology*, 42(1): 97–107.

Wegmann, Edward. 1896. *The Water Supply of the City of New York, 1658–1895*. New York: John Wiley and Sons.

Yamin, Rebecca. 2001. 'From Tanning to Tea: The Evolution of a Neighborhood', *Historical Archaeology*, 35(3): 6–15.

7

Ruins of the South

Alfredo González-Ruibal

The ruins of modernity are inevitably the ruins of the North. Actual or imagined ruined cities (the real Detroit or a post-apocalyptic London) are always Euro-American industrial or post-industrial metropolises (Vergara 1999; Woodward 2002; Edensor 2005; Jorgensen and Keenan 2012). These ruins are receiving growing attention by researchers, who often see them as metaphors of a diverse kind—including of our cultural anxieties and fears, of colonialism, capitalism, of the end of master narratives (Hell and Schönle 2010; Dillon 2011; Stoler 2013). They are also scrutinized by cultural heritage managers and politicians who try to transform them into spaces of memory, of leisure and consumption, or both. The post-industrial ruins of the South have received much less attention in recent debates on ruination, decay, recovery, and gentrification, although there are a few significant exceptions, most notably the work of Gordillo (2009, 2014) in Argentina and also Rodríguez Torrent et al. (2011, 2012) and Vilches (et al. 2008, 2011) in Chile.

This is due to several reasons: one of them is the fact that southern urbanization and industrialization are usually perceived as a recent process. They are too young to have generated ruins: after all, none of the diverse southern 'miracles' of which economists speak (South-east Asian, Brazilian, African, and so on) dates from before the 1960s. It is well known that when companies do outsourcing, it is the so-called emerging economies that benefit from it: new factories for the South, new ruins for the North. Another reason is that the long-term process of modernity is still very much associated with Euro-American history. The rest of the globe is seen as having a later, incomplete, or surrogate modernity, as post-colonial historians have abundantly criticized (Chakrabarty 2000). In addition, the cultural and political conditions of the North have enabled the emergence of popular engagements with ruins, such as urban exploring or video games, that have made their processes of metropolitan ruination more conspicuous at a global level (Garrett 2013; Pétursdóttir and Olsen 2014: 4). Finally, it is also probably relevant here that urban decay in the North is strongly associated with the decadence of the middle classes (Gordillo 2014: 254): the imagery of ruins is populated by bourgeois houses, factories, and skyscrapers. This is perhaps what makes it so fascinating for scholars and artists: they come from the same social background as the people who once lived and worked in those abandoned neighbourhoods. When one thinks of urban abjection in the South, instead, it is not once-thriving bourgeois cities now ruined that come to mind, but immense shanty towns that have never seen better times.

The South, however, has its modern, post-industrial ruins as well. And they are neither a later nor an imperfect version of those in the North. Quite the opposite: they antedate the post-industrial ruins of Europe and the United States, sometimes by a hundred years. As with other disasters (most notably genocides), events happening in the South often foreshadowed those that were about to happen in the 'developed' world. While the industrialization of the South came later than that of the North, it can be argued that large-scale deindustrialization was first experienced in places like the Chilean desert or the Brazilian rainforest, rather than in the early industrialized regions of Europe. In South America, many large metropolises witnessed a phase of collapse during the first third of the twentieth century, due to the cycles of boom and bust of global capitalism and, in particular, the end of the first phase of globalization in 1914. However, with exceptions such as Buenos Aires and some mining towns in Chile, these recent South American ruins have been scarcely studied, reclaimed, or gentrified. Conservation efforts have focused mostly on older buildings from the nineteenth century and the colonial period. The early post-industrial ruins of South America are an excellent material to reflect critically on ruination, other modernities, the global logic of capitalism (see Penrose, Chapter 8, for a British comparative), and the work of coloniality, both in the region and elsewhere. In this chapter, I will focus on one of the countries that have generated more and more fascinating ruins of modernity: Brazil.

7.1 RUINS OF BRAZIL

Brazil is a country in ruins and obsessed with its own ruination. In that, Brazilians are ahead of time: Gitahy and Hardman (1997: 86) argue that the experience of precariousness and instability that has characterized the life of Brazilians for centuries is typical of post-modernity. It might seem surprising to present the country and its peoples in this way; a young, powerful, and creative nation, which one would associate more readily with euphoria than melancholia.

It is also one of the BRICS, the five 'emerging' economies characterized by extraordinary fast rates of GDP growth. Yet the truth is that the idea of decay has been prominent in the Brazilian imaginary since at least the eighteenth century, even before the cities had had the time to develop and become entropic monsters, amorphous cannibals that eat away the country and are eaten in turn by rain, heat, vegetation, and themselves. Brazil is a country of ruins: of indigenous civilizations that are now exposed through another process of ruination: the destruction of the rainforest (Heckenberger and Neves 2009); of colonial forts, towns, and missions; of conservative modernism at the turn of the twentieth century; of modernist-authoritarian fantasies in the 1930s–40s and modernist-futurist fantasies of the 1960s (Jaguaribe 1999); ruins of the present-day favelas, where construction and destruction are so deeply enmeshed that they are impossible to disentangle.

Many authors have written about Brazil through the tropes of decay and ruination. They include classic writers, such as Euclides da Cunha (Hardman 1996). Euclides was a witness in the late nineteenth century of the instant production of an epochal ruin: the devastation of the town of Canudos and the massacre of its inhabitants by the army of the young Brazilian Republic (1896–7). They had dared to challenge the modern state following a messianic leader who rejected the new regime and its ideological foundations. Canudos was laid to waste and its ruins forgotten until archaeologists excavated them at the beginning of the twenty-first century (Zanettini 2003), shortly before they were swallowed by progress in the shape of a reservoir: a city destroyed twice by modernity. During the first third of the twentieth century, intellectuals in north-eastern Brazil were comparing the fresh ruins of abandoned towns with Pompeii and Rome (Pflueger 2008). Similar tropes can be found in the literature of the United States (Yablon 2010), which proves that young nations in the Americas were going through similar anxieties. In fact, the large majority of discussions on ruination in Brazil (by art historians and literary critics) concentrate on metaphoric ruins or at least metaphoric visions of real ruins (Hardman 1993, 1996; Jaguaribe 1999; Cury 2003; Pressler 2012). In real or imagined derelict buildings, writers see the life of individuals or of the nation as on a distorted mirror.

The study of urban decadence in Brazil has been associated with two dominant themes: oblivion and concealment (Gitahy and Hardman 1997; Hardman 2004; Elmir 2004; Eckert and Rocha 2005). Erasure is the forgotten twin of modernization. Decay and the destruction of memories are associated with the indigenous peoples, the impoverished proletarians, landless masses, and urban underclasses. Their existence is covered in thick layers of glittering progress, often disguised as modernist architecture (Jaguaribe 1999)—a move that was lavishly used during the 2014 FIFA World Cup hosted by Brazil. In this context, ruins work as a purulent wound in the urban fabric that poisons the monuments of progress and exposes its falseness. A similar concern with the erasure of the other Brazil is also found among archaeologists, who have devoted their efforts to reveal the repressed memories of slaves, indigenous peoples, and the poor through their material traces (Funari 2002; Zanettini 2003; Ferreira 2009). The destruction of experience and of memories has been considered a characteristic of late modernity (Olivier 2008): the age that erases the past in exchange for an uncertain future. The fact that countries like Brazil fit this supermodern pattern a hundred years in advance is not surprising. The economic, political, and social model that developed in the country since the late nineteenth century had nothing of the archaic: it was truly futuristic. We can see our future in their past. This time it is not our prehistory reflected on the indigenous populations of South America that we should be seeking, but our post-history.

Between 1751 and 1759 captain general Francisco Xavier de Mendonça Furtado wrote several letters to his half-brother Sebastião José de Carvalho e Melo, Marquis of Pombal, secretary of Overseas Affairs in Portugal (Pressler 2012). Captain General Furtado was on an official tour, travelling the Amazon basin, a wild territory—depopulated, raped, and enslaved. At that time, the Amazon was a river like the Congo would be 150 years later: an immense colonial, uncolonized land, subjected to a tiny European country through isolated outposts. These were forts in the middle of the forest with half-a-dozen Europeans, twenty at most, surrounded by millions of square kilometres of old-growth forest.

Furtado's letters are a litany of ruins. When he arrives at Belém do Pará, on the mouth of the Amazon, he writes: 'Here, there is no fortress without ruin, the few military officers that are left are all broken, old and ignorant (*estropiados, velhos e ignorantes*)'. And he continues: 'This State is in the last ruin' (*Este Estado está na última ruína*), 'all the Fortresses were ruined and almost all the Populations lost' (*as Fortalezas estavam arruinadas e quase todas as Povoações perdidas*). Furtado's travel was meant to be a turning point, between the predatory political economy of the sixteenth and seventeenth centuries and the productive, developmental system of the Age of Reason; the latter an Age whose light would penetrate the forest and liberate the Indians (from abuse and superstition). Progress would be achieved through the construction of a civil space, the establishment of cities endowed with an urban rationality, and the erection of monuments representing the State (Coelho 2005, cited in Pressler 2012: 361). The reality of the next two hundred years would be very different.

7.2 RUINS OF THE CITY

Lévi-Strauss (1955: 106) famously wrote that the Americas are like a country that has passed from barbarism to decadence without ever knowing civilization. The traces of civilization in Brazil appeared to the anthropologist as outdated kitsch. 'The tropics are less exotic than old-fashioned. It is not the vegetation that attests to it, but minor architectural details and the suggestion of a way of life that convinces one that, rather than having crossed vast spaces, he has gone back imperceptibly in time' (Lévi-Strauss 1955: 96). Interestingly, for Lévi-Strauss the impression of time-travelling was not caused by the encounter of the primeval forests or the indigenous inhabitants of South America, but by the *fin-de-siècle* architecture that prevailed in Brazilian cities.

This anachronistic environment, of whose early decline Lévi-Strauss was witness in the 1930s, was the byproduct of the 'conservative modernization' of the late nineteenth century (Gorelik 2003), which in turn was made possible by the expansionist cycles of capitalism and the first wave of globalization. One of these cycles was the rubber boom (1879–1912), which is by far the most famous. It has left the most enduring and powerful images of ruination. They all develop one main trope: the clash of technology and primordial nature. Thus we have ships climbing mountains (Herzog 1982), plantations gone wild (Grandin 2009), overgrown railways in the forest (Hardman 1988). The destruction of the forest and its inhabitants had as its counterpart the development of luxurious cities: Manaus, of course (Dias 1999), but also Belém and Santarém. In the surroundings of Manaus, there are ruins of *fazendas* (farms) and *hospedarias* (hostels) for immigrants. One is Paricatuba. It was built in 1898 for the many foreigners that were coming to the Amazonia, attracted by the easy money of the rubber boom (Duarte 2009: 248). Parica-tuba ended its days, most appropriately, as a leper colony. It brings to mind Fushía, the character from *La Casa Verde* by Mario Vargas Llosa (1966), a novel, among other things, about the rubber boom in the Peruvian Amazon. Fushía is a small predator of the forest, a fugitive from Brazil who enters the rubber trade as a smuggler. He befriends the Indians, then alienates the Indians, he becomes mad and isolated. He catches an unnamed illness and gradually rots. He ends his days in an abandoned leper colony. Bodies and buildings succumb to the same fate.

The end of the boom was sudden: 'Overnight, luxury, ostentation, squan-dering and opulence came to an end. They were based on the work of the *caboclo seringueiro* (mixed-race rubber tapper), which was tantamount to slavery' (de Figueiredo 2001: 273). The opera house of Manaus has become a symbol of the folly of those years, also the Theatro da Paz in Belém, founded in 1878. These are just the most conspicuous buildings of the rubber era and are still looked after. But Manaus and Belém are full of ruinous art nouveau buildings that have fared much less well.

In Belém, one of the rubber capitals, ruination affects the entire historical city. Some efforts at rejuvenating the area (including repainting façades) had a limited success when I visited the place in 2008. From afar, the old town looks picturesque. When my companion and I tried to access the streets in the evening, we were discouraged by a group of neighbours: *Tem muito ladrão,* 'there are many thieves'. The next day we tried again during the morning and we understood. Behind the first row of colourful buildings there exists a ghost town full of derelict houses (Colour plate 8, top). Almost no buildings were inhabited. Even the large baroque church in the main plaza was abandoned, with the painting peeling off and vegetation growing in the cracks. The historic centre would have looked spectral anywhere, but it was more so in Brazil, where cities are always crammed, full of traffic, and noisy. The colonial fort and church near the river had been beautifully restored and become a tourist attraction. The rest of the town lay in silence. The atmosphere of ruination seems to have infected the new city as well. Lévi-Strauss had the feeling of being in a *démodé* environment in Rio, surrounded by art nouveau houses. In the new Belém I had the same impression with the high-rises of the 1950s and 1960s. The tropical weather does not suit them well: they are grey, dirty, and with the paint peeling off. They look like tall ruins towering over the smaller ruins of the turn of the century, of the rubber boom.

Rubber was not the only product that created a mirage of development. From the 1830s, coffee was another, especially in the São Paulo arca. In Maranhão state, in the north-east, it was the economic cycles of cotton and sugar that created and destroyed cities (Pflueger 2007: 6). Further south it was salted meat (*charque*) and hides. During the nineteenth century, the elite of Pelotas in Rio Grande do Sul became extremely rich producing jerked beef for export. Likewise, the neighbouring Rio Grande witnessed a period of prosperity commercializing the *charque* through its harbour. Until the abolition of slavery (1888), the factories were manned by African slaves, who worked in appalling conditions (Gutiérrez 2001): the life expectancy was less than five years. Pelotas still had almost 6,000 registered slaves in 1884 (Vargas 2011: 14). Nevertheless, the end of slavery was not the end of the business. Decline came when salted meat was gradually replaced by corned beef and, from the beginning of the twentieth century, by frozen meat. As in the plantation economies of the American South or the Antilles, the landscape of Pelotas until the late nineteenth century was characterized by refined mansions and an architecture of horror: the barracks and work spaces of the slaves (da Rosa 2011; see Ernsten, Chapter 10, for an exploration of the material remnants of racialized inequality in Cape Town).

After slavery, the Pelotas of the Belle Époque saw the erection of grand mansions in the centre of the city (the same slave owners still rich) and monumental theatres, churches, a market, and a library (Figure 7.1). Outside the city, there was a less glamorous landscape of workers' houses and factories and ruined *charqueadas* where the slaves once toiled (Figure 7.2). Some *charqueadas* have been restored as heritage sites or as luxurious hotels, where history is sanitized. The *charqueada* de São João boasts classical statues, in porcelain not marble, mostly broken or worn. One represents Minerva, the Goddess of Wisdom, only that the sign is misspelt: 'Minerba'. By the 1930s, the

Figure 7.1. The derelict Bank of Brazil in Pelotas (1926–8). Photo by Alfredo González-Ruibal, 2013.

splendour of Pelotas vanished. Many mansions were abandoned and today are derelict or in ruins, some looted, stripped of their classical statues and bronze fixtures. Decay, but not ruination, came to the workers' houses, because there is always a steady supply of subalterns to occupy them (slaves, industrial workers, post workers). Now some houses are inhabited by homeless people from the countryside (*invassores*) and crack-addicts (see Singleton, Chapter 11, for a comparative in Indianapolis). The town is presided by a spectral tower block, recently constructed but never finished, not yet inhabited, already in ruins.

The fate of Rio Grande was tied to Pelotas. The local bourgeoisie built palaces, houses, and hotels (a Hotel Paris, of course). They also built a large neo-Gothic church that would fit well in Britain, a library, and a casino. They replicated the styles fashionable in Europe at that time (historicism, Beaux Arts, art nouveau). The casino was a few kilometres away from the city in a resort for the city rich. They connected city and resort with a railway, today abandoned: the useless station, in typical Central European style, is a vestige of the first wave of globalization. People now have to take buses along a congested road: it can take much more time to reach the Casino neighbourhood now

Figure 7.2. An abandoned nineteenth-century *charqueada* in Pelotas. The place is now under excavation by Lúcio Menezes Ferreira (Universade Federal de Pelotas). Photo by Alfredo González-Ruibal, 2013.

than it did in the early twentieth century. In Rio Grande itself, a large part of the Belle Époque downtown is in ruins (Colour plate 9, top). Hundreds of late nineteenth- and early twentieth-century buildings are abandoned or reused by low-income families or as small shops. It is like the revenge of the underdog: elaborate art nouveau cornices in stucco broken by gaudy signs advertising cheap shoes or popular music (Colour plate 9, bottom). The early twentieth-century factories and workers' quarters are also in ruins, a testimony of an industrial past now remote, almost unbelievable.

By definition, cities are the pillar of civilization. The word city comes from the Latin *civitas*. Yet cities in Brazil were the product of what is usually associated with savagery, not civilization. They adopted the external trappings of the civilized and some of the elements of modernity: its concern with hygiene, order, and division (de Sousa 2009; Santos Júnior 2010). They were intended to be devices of modernization (Gorelik 2003: 14), but ended as modernist cities without modernity (Guillén 2004): in 1890, 80 per cent of the inhabitants of Manaus were illiterate (de Figueiredo 2001: 275). Boom cities were mostly based on an extractive economy, sustained by slaves first and labourers working as slaves later. In the last instance, the modern economy of Brazil is an economy of predation: suck all resources from the land and move on. You can still do that in a country the size of a continent—for a while. The boom and bust cycles of capitalism burn down cities; cities burn down the forest.

7.3 RUINS OF THE FOREST

In 1929, the same year that was to ruin the cities of Rio Grande and Belém, already half-ruined, Ford Motor Company acquired 76,000 acres of land in the Amazon forest and began to transform the wilderness into an ordered space of production. The idea was to export the contemporary industrial model that had succeeded in the United States to Brazil (Barkermeyer and Figge 2011). They failed miserably. But before they failed, they created an enormous scar, of the kind we have grown used to see in satellite images (a bald patch in the middle of a receding forest), and a company town, with its houses, schools, hospital, shops, and other facilities (including a golf course). The clearing was opened in 'presumably unowned land' (Russell 1942: 125), which is to presume too much. The land might not have been the property of anybody at the time according to capitalist notions of property, but it was originally inhabited by the Tapajós Indians who were mostly exterminated during the seventeenth century; in another cycle of capitalist predation.

There are many factors behind the failure of Fordlândia: the lack of local workers, pests, the soil, and the terrain (Russell 1942). Authors have seen in the enterprise a typical ruin of modernity: the high-modern tendency to design grand, abstract plans of development from an office without taking reality into account (Scott 1998). Interestingly, this is the fate that affected another offshoot of Detroit as well: the DeLorean factory that was established in Belfast, without proper planning and local knowledge, had a similar fate to Ford's dreams in the forest. The problem with Fordlândia is that it failed to respect the forest. Koepnick (1993: 134) argues in his discussion of Gianbattista Vico on the origin of civilization that, for the philosopher, to be civilized is not just to create a clearing (the foundational act of civilization), but also to respect the otherness of the forest. In the modern attitude against nature, Vico identifies the roots of a new form of barbarism that will foster violence and turn history into nature again. His ideas came to be true in Fordlândia.

But the failure to reap benefits cannot be attributed only to bad planning and modern hubris. This would mean that the scheme, had it been well planned (taking into account local knowledge, communities, and environment), would have succeeded (Barkermeyer and Figge 2011). In retrospect, it is obvious that the Ford executives failed to understand the essence of the modern economy in Amazonia. It is predation, not production, which makes one rich—at least for a while. It is not order, but disorder. There has been a lot of discussion on why the immense revenues that came to the Amazon region during the late nineteenth and early twentieth centuries failed to create a sustained industrial development, similar to that of the North (Weinstein 1983; Coomes and Barham 1994). But everything boils down to this: wild rubber extraction was too successful. Predation was much more profitable than production could ever be: it yielded fast returns with minimal investment and no infrastructure. It produces fast ruins, too: ephemeral cities of concrete and plaster, post-industrial cities without industry consumed in a festival of consumption. And the ruins of the forest.

The ruins of Fordlândia and its company town have proved to be attractive (Grandin 2009), as any other modern ruin eaten away by nature (Simmel 1959: 260). Jaguaribe (1999: 299) speaks of the derelict modernist buildings in Brazil as engaging in a 'dialogue between modernity and history further dramatized by the encroachment of natural tropical vegetation upon the cultural buildings of functionalist architecture'. But I see no dialogue here: it is a violent discussion at best. The landscape tropes of the North do not necessarily fit in the South. In looking at derelict towns and their decaying buildings, we forget the other ruins: those of the forest. Unlike crumbling cities and factories, they are ugly. They do not elicit feelings of melancholia or lend themselves to romantic daydreaming (Gordillo 2014: 45–9).

It is again Lévi-Strauss who writes perceptively of the devastated forest as a ruin. It can be argued that the ruination of nature is not different from Europe— this is what many Brazilians say today. In a sense, they are right. The landscape of Europe is an ecological catastrophe of sorts. The difference lies in temporality. The Brazilian landscape is a materialization of the accelerated time of super-modernity. 'An attentive reciprocity has never been established between man and the soil', writes Lévi-Strauss (1955: 103), a reciprocity 'which in the Old World founded a millennial intimacy, through which they have both shaped each other. Here, the soil has been raped and destroyed. An agriculture of predation has taken over the available richness and gone elsewhere, after having snatched some profit.' Of course, the 'millennial intimacy' with the land did exist in the Americas before the European colonial expansion, but it was soon annihilated. Meaningfully, the anthropologist resorts to archaeological tropes: 'the territory crossed by the road from Santos to São Paulo...seems like an archaeological site devoted to a defunct agriculture' (Lévi-Strauss 1955: 104). The colonizer leaves behind 'a wounded landscape, all muddled with vestiges' (Lévi-Strauss 1955: 105).

Between 2005 and 2008 I had the opportunity to participate in an ethno-archaeological project in the forests of Maranhão, working with the Awá Indians, one of the last remaining groups of hunter-gatherers in South America (Hernando and Coelho 2013). My perception of the landscape was similar to that of Lévi-Strauss seventy years before. The same impression of fast ruin-ation; fast urbanization; fast deforestation. An ancient world being shattered in just a few years and a new, dismal one created in its stead (Colour plate 8, bottom). Driving towards the remaining forests, one crosses vast expanses of pasture lands and *cocais* (palm tree groves): these are the ruins of the forest. One of the drivers who takes us to the border town of São João do Carú comments that in the 1970s this was all thick, primeval forest. He remembers people coming here to hunt *onça* (jaguar). Around that time, or even later, some Awás were still roaming the forests and hunting monkeys and peccaries with their bows and arrows. Some of them did it until it was too late. They were discovered by peasants hunting in a forest that was no longer a forest but a ruin. They were taken to the reservation where they live today: like an ancient church that has been preserved in the middle of a new city, all skyscrapers of glass and concrete. To talk about the ruins of the forest is not mere metaphor. We live in cities, the Awá live in the forest. For us the end of the city is the apocalypse, the end of the forest is the apocalypse for the Awá.

The forest of the Awá started being turned into a ruin in the 1970s. Destruction has never stopped. Current satellite photographs show the enormous devastation that the tree cover has undergone since 2008, the last year we visited the reservation: half or so of the legally protected forested area has disappeared in six years. It is precious wood and pastures that destroy trees here. In the Mato Grosso it is soya, which is exported through Rio Grande, still a capital of predation (a rich man from Rio Grande owned one of the illegal ranches inside the Awá lands, 4,000 kilometres away). The first time I went to Brazil, there was a local cell phone company, called Amazônia Celular, whose slogan was 'All fast. All evolves. Evolution is with you' (*Tudo rápido. Tudo evolui. A evolução com você*). The first thing is true: everything fast. The others are not. Things do not evolve: a rubber tapper from 1905 would find himself very much at home in the ruinous forests of Maranhão in 2005. The same landscape of devastation, the same political economy of predation. Today ephemeral cities of glass and reinforced concrete emerge out of the ruins of the forest, as cities of stucco and porcelain emerged out of the felled trees of the rubber boom.

7.4 DISCUSSION: RUINS OF THE SOUTH/RUINS OF THE NORTH

How modern ruins are appraised is not an irrelevant matter. There is nothing innocent about a ruin—of a forest or a city. However, a large part of the discussion on the ambivalence of recent ruins has focused on the contrast between the appealing picturesque and the threat of nature, processes of entropy, the inevitable passing of time and so on (Augé 2003; Jorgensen and Keenan 2012; see Penrose, Chapter 8, for a Global North counterpoint). This owes much to the Romantic experience of the ruin in northern Europe (Woodward 2002), which is highly selective: abbeys, castles, and Roman buildings figure prominently in this antiquarian imagination (see Shanks 2012). This imagination eschews the ruins of famine, pests, or poverty, which have always abounded in European landscapes. Ruins in Europe have been represented as positive: ancient vestiges stand for the beauty of old civilization and glorious ancestors; modern ones are material proof of technical ingenuity and economic development, superseded by a cleaner economy and a better society. The ruins of factories tell a tale of progress: from heavy to light modernity (Bauman 2000, 113–18). With the ruins of the North, we can play, be creative, imagine other futures, reclaim their humble materiality from unjust oblivion (Edensor 2005; Woodward 2002; Pétursdóttir 2013; Hudson 2014). We can do that where the otherness of the ruin is under control, not threatening. This is similar to what happens with wilderness in Europe. European forests are no longer perceived as a menace to civilization and in fact they are usually protected as national parks which we can visit *as if* they were wild; in the same way, ruins—even post-industrial ruins—are bounded preserves of otherness that we can explore as adventurers who know that they run no real risk.

The ruins of the South are quite different (see also Chapter 10, this volume, for discussion of the contemporary remnants of colonialism in South Africa). That is the South conceived not only as a geographical concept, but as a political one (I would call it Third World, if the word was not outdated, like its ruins), a concept that covers most of the geographical South, but also encompasses places in the North (like Detroit) or the Middle East (Weizman 2007), to use conventional geopolitical terms. The ruins of the South are cruder and more menacing than those of the North. They are simply too big and too abject to be appropriated semiotically or in practice: leftover places, waste products (Bauman 2000: 103). They are not apt for urban explorers or artists. Consider the Heidelberg Project in Detroit: as of August 2014 its art installations have suffered eleven separate arson attacks, nine of them in only one year.[1] One can reclaim the ruins and empty spaces of Berlin and use art to transform the city (see White and Seidenberg, Chapter 1), but there is a limit to what art can do in cities with extensive material collapse, where social inequalities are rampant and economy as ruinous as the buildings themselves. Initiatives of afforestation and urban gardening in Detroit can be considered an implicit recognition that ruination has won the upper hand and that the city, as such, is beyond recovery.

In the South, it is less easy to distinguish between the picturesque ruin and the living environment, the industrial ruin and the slum. Thus, they all can

---

[1] http://www.thedailybeast.com/articles/2014/03/14/who-is-burning-down-detroit-s-world-famous-street-art.html (accessed 28 April 2015).

become the object of the voyeuristic gaze of the tourist or the photographer. This is what happens in Detroit, but also in Rio de Janeiro, where the favelas have become a tourist attraction. Ruins are not a specific spot in the city that can be fenced off and transformed into a theme park, they cannot be easily tamed: ruins are the city. Detroit again is a good case in point: how do you fence off 100,000 buildings? How do you reclaim 90,000 empty lots? How do you display them? The ruins of the South are not spaces for thinking through alternative ways of living the urban—in all events, they give lessons on how to survive the post-urban. They are not even an arena for subversion—although perhaps they are for revolution. They cannot be transformed into parks and art galleries. They can be painted over in bright colours, as slums are from time to time, but superficial manicuring will not change their substance. They are not spaces of resistance to the dominant regimented order of modernity and its master narratives (Edensor 2005; Hudson 2014). If anything, the inhabitants of the city as ruin would appreciate some order, orthodox planning and aestheticization of their environments. They would hardly consider that their ruinous streets with empty buildings are 'replete with affordances and stimulations' or that their decaying city represents 'an order of a different kind' (Hudson 2014: 213). What we nostalgically long for in the North (a bit of chaos and spontaneity) is a nuisance in the South.

If there is a master narrative in the South, it is one of perpetual failure, of sudden growth followed by immediate decadence. And to this master narrative the ruins of the South do not oppose, they attest to it faithfully. My stressing the negativity of the ruins of the South does not have to be regarded as paralysing pessimism. I intended it as a critique in Theodor Adorno's wake: a refusal of the fallacious ideology of positivity, because it naturalizes reality by erasing its contradictions and failures (Gordillo 2014: 187; also González-Ruibal 2008: 262). In fact, as Gordillo (2014: 265) has noted, by turning our attention from ruins—with all its aesthetic burden—to rubble (the ruin beyond ruination), we can stress the disruptive potential of places. Gordillo (2014: 265) argues that rubble, unlike ruins, is 'matter that belongs to no one and to everyone': it often turns what used to be private 'into a de facto part of the commons'. This might be so in some cases—and Detroit, again, offers wonderful examples of the collective reappropriation of urban space. However, the ruin beyond ruination holds a promise of another kind. Hannah Arendt (1995: 88–9) noted the relationship in classical Greece between the concept of the political and the concept of freedom. Not any kind of freedom, though: freedom to begin (*archein*). This is very different from the neoliberal concept of freedom as choice. Places turned to rubble are places where *archein* is still possible. My impression in visiting Detroit was that this was a city where there was room for *archein*, for starting something radically new. Something that is not related to conventional concepts of revival, gentrification, art, or even the city.

The problem with *archein* is that it is always at risk of being neutralized by economic and political interests, which strive to transform freedom of creation into a mere choice between things that are already given. In the case of Brazil's early post-industrial ruins this can happen in two ways: they might follow the cycle of destruction and construction that has characterized the history of the Americas. Their decay may end up in total erasure and their stories swell the layers of oblivion that make up the faulty historical sequence of the nation. Other buildings that celebrate the triumph of yet another capitalist boom and of another predatory social class will replace them—they are succumbing to that already.

But the beautiful art nouveau neighbourhoods can also be restored and gentrified (Figure 7.3). This might seem to go against what I have just said: that the ruins of the South are irrecoverable waste. What I understand by ruins of the South, however, is the city as ruin and the land as ruin. As spaces where waste is a structural part of its nature. I am not referring to specific buildings. These can, and indeed have been in some cases, reclaimed as heritage: this is what has happened with some early twentieth-century mansions in Pelotas. Mansions can be brought back from their ruinous state and preserved. Not just the buildings themselves, but also their stories—the nice ones. It is well known that human memory is tricky: we remember what we want to remember (consciously or not); we conceal what does not fit the image of ourselves. The same happens with things. It has been argued that things are the holders of their own memory, which is independent from humans (Olivier 2008; Pétursdóttir and Olsen 2014: 8–10), but this memory is not less biased than its human counterpart. It is not always a humble recollection that we, archaeologists, should care for as we should care for any human subaltern. Péturdóttir and Olsen (2014: 18) ask us to release ruins from our urge to domesticate them. The problem is that art nouveau buildings were erected with very specific purposes: to give shelter, for sure, but also to construct a master narrative of social success. They are so faithful to their semiotic mission that they still fulfil today, abandoned as they are. Left to their own devices or restored to their former grandeur, the delicate ruins of Belém, Pelotas, or Rio Grande continue to tell only half the story, the same story that their owners would have told. If we take care of the houses, they will remember, but they will still be a vehicle of oblivion: of the other ruins they helped to create. Ruins of the forest, invisible ruins of slave houses, the forgotten ruins of Canudos. The only way of appraising critically the post-industrial city is by looking beyond the city, tracking down the path of ruins that it leaves around.

Hardman (2004) contends that there are three modes of production of collective illusion in Brazil: the monumental, the elegiac, and the destructive. The elegiac mode has at its central motif the praise of ruins, the representation of a lost heroic past. It is difficult not to praise the art nouveau ruins of the South, to fall into their trap. 'Today we see the city with the perspective of the flâneur', writes Gorelik (2003, 14), 'we construct meanings released from any

Figure 7.3. The library of Pelotas (1878–81) with the ruins of an unfinished tower block in the background. Photo by Alfredo González-Ruibal, 2013.

mark of the city itself, finding in its projects the signs of a modernity that can be visited as the ruins of a historic city'. We have forgotten what cities were for. In our wanderings à la de Certeau through the fragmented city 'we reproduce and celebrate the fragmentation and dispersion, the mixture of times that are the product of conservative modernization' (Gorelik 2003: 27). Ruins, transformed into the memory of a bright past, become yet another ally of the authoritarian project of modernity.

7.5 CONCLUSION

In this chapter I have proposed the concept of 'ruins of the South' to make sense of particular forms of post-industrial ruination that cannot be appraised with the perspectives commonly developed for the North. The concept of the South does not refer to a geographical space only, but to a political-economic spatiality, which is more prevalent in Latin America or Africa, but is not restricted to them. Thus, cities like Detroit fit well the model of 'ruins of the South', that is, places that are beyond rehabilitation due to intrinsic material, social, political, and economic problems, themselves related to structural inequalities often global in character and therefore with no easy local solution. The negative nature of southern ruination has a positive side: they are uniquely positioned for imagining radically new beginnings.

Here I have illustrated the ruins of the South with the example of Brazil. The case of this country challenges assumptions regarding the nature of modern ruins and deindustrialization. It reminds us that, far from being a phenomenon inaugurated in the global North during the late twentieth century, post-industrial cities existed in South America well before they became the norm in the United States or Europe. The post-industrial cities of South America are a typical product of the boom and bust processes of global capitalism, which outside the North took a typically predatory character. The ruins of Brazil are illustrative of the role of predatory capitalism in producing fast material wealth and fast ruination. They also show eloquently the indissoluble link between the post-industrial metropolis and wider phenomena of ruination—of nature in the first place. Whereas in the North both growth and ruination are spatially dissociated and thus forgotten (Connerton 2009), in the South they cohabit.

The Argentinian poet Edgar Bayley wrote a poem called *Es infinita esta riqueza abandonada* ('they are infinite these abandoned riches'). The poem is punctuated by this recurring verse: *nunca terminará es infinita esta riqueza abandonada* ('they will never end, they are infinite these abandoned riches'). The verses capture well the sense of vastness and waste, of the awe before the enormity of wasted riches that produce the ruins of the South, the never-ending, always growing ruination of a continent under the light of darkness.

ACKNOWLEDGEMENTS

I would like to thank my colleagues at the workshop for the inspiring debates in and around Detroit. My warmest thanks to Beatriz V. Thiesen and Lúcio Menezes Ferreira for being my guides in Rio Grande and Pelotas. I am also grateful to the Universidade Federal de Rio Grande do Sul (FURG) for funding my trip to Rio Grande as part of the 5a Semana Acadêmica da Arqueologia in 2013. My visits to Belém and Maranhão were part of a research project directed by Almudena Hernando and funded by the Spanish Ministry of Science.

REFERENCES

Arendt, Hannah. 1995. *Qu'est-ce que la politique?* Paris: Seuil.

Augé, Marc. 2003. *El tiempo en ruinas*. Barcelona: Gedisa.

Barkemeyer, Ralf and Frank Figger. 2011. 'Fordlândia: Corporate citizenship or corporate colonialism', *Corporate Social Responsibility and Environmental Management*, 19: 69–78.

Bauman, Zygmunt. 2000. *Liquid Modernity*. Cambridge: Polity.

Chakrabarty, Dipesh. 2000. *Provincializing Europe: Postcolonial thought and historical difference*. Princeton, NJ: Princeton University Press.

Coelho, Geraldo Martires. 2005. *O violino de Ingres*. Leituras de História Cultural. Belém: Paka-Tatu.

Connerton, Paul. 2009. *How modernity forgets*. Cambridge: Cambridge University Press.

Coomes, Oliver T. and Bradford L. Barham. 1994. 'The Amazon rubber boom: labor control, resistance, and failed plantation development revisited', *Hispanic American Historical Review*, 74(2): 231–57.

Cury, Maria Zilda Ferreira. 2003. 'Fronteiras da memória na ficção de Milton Hatoum', *Letras*, 26: 11–18.

da Rosa, Estefânia Jaékel. 2011. 'Às margens do esquecimento: O percurso histórico da Charqueada de Santa Barbara', In *Seminário Internacional de Memória e Patrimônio* 5, 2011, Pelotas, Pelotas: UFPel, pp. 370–80.

de Figueiredo, Ana Maria. 2001. 'Review of E. M. Dias: A ilusão do fausto: Manaus, 1890–1920', *Revista Brasileira de História*, 21(40): 273–6.

de Sousa, Francisco Carlos Oliveira. 2009. 'Resíduos do progresso: urbanização, modernidade e limpeza pública em Natal na Primeira República'. In *ANPUH— XXV Simpósio Nacional de História. Fortaleza, 2009.* Fortaleza.

Dias, Edinea Mascarenhas. 1999. *A ilusão do fausto: Manaus, 1890–1920*. Manaus: Valer.

Dillon, Brian. 2011. *Ruins*. Cambridge, MA/London: MIT Press/Whitechapel Gallery.

Duarte, Durango. 2009. *Manaus: entre o passado e o presente*. Manaus: Mídia Ponto.

Eckert, C. and A. L. C. da Rocha. 2005. *O tempo e a cidade*. Porto Alegre: UFRGS.

Edensor, Tim. 2005. *Industrial ruins: Space, aesthetics and materiality*. Oxford: Berg.

Elmir, Cláudio P. 2004. 'Porto Alegre: a perdida cidade una (Fragmentos de modernidade e exclusão social no Sul do Brasil)', *Estudos Ibero-Americanos*, 30(2): 105–19.

Ferreira, Lúcio Menezes. 2009. 'Arqueologia da escravidão e arqueologia pública: algumas interfaces', *Vestígios: Revista Latino-Americana de Arqueologia Histórica*, 3(1): 7–23.

Funari, Pedro aulo Abreu. 2002. 'Desaparecimento e emergência dos grupos subordinados na arqueologia brasileira', *Horizontes Antropológicos*, 8(18): 131–53.

Garrett, Bradley L. 2013. *Explore Everything: Place-Hacking the City*. London: Verso.

Gitahy, Maria Lucia C. and Francisco Foot Hardman. 1997. 'Brazil in the global world: Five centuries of lost memories', *Macalester International*, 5: 75–95.

González-Ruibal, Alfredo. 2008. 'Time to Destroy: An Archaeology of Supermodernity', *Current Anthropology*, 49(2): 247–79.

Gordillo, Gastón. 2009. 'Places that frighten: residues of wealth and violence on the Argentine Chaco frontier', *Anthropologica*, 51(2): 343–51.

Gordillo, Gastón. 2014. *Rubble: The Afterlife of Destruction*. Durham, NC: Duke University Press.

Gorelik, Alejandro. 2003. 'Ciudad, modernidad, modernización', *Universitas Humanística*, 56: 11–17.

Grandin, Greg. 2009. *Fordlandia: the rise and fall of Henry Ford's forgotten jungle city*. London: Macmillan.

Gutiérrez, Ester. 2001. *Negros, charqueadas e olarias*. Pelotas: UFPel.

Guillén, Mauro F. 2004. 'Modernism without modernity: The rise of modernist architecture in Mexico, Brazil, and Argentina, 1890–1940', *Latin American Research Review*, 39(2): 5–34.

Hardman, Francisco Foot. 1988. *Trem fantasma: a modernidade na selva*. São Paulo: Companhia das Letras.

Hardman, Francisco Foot. 1993. 'Memórias, ruinas e imaginação utópica: sobre algumas raízes românticas da modernidade no Brasil', *Anos 90*, 1(1): 145–59.

Hardman, Francisco Foot. 1996. 'Brutalidade antiga: sobre história e ruína em Euclides', *Estudos Avançados*, 10(26): 293–310.

Hardman, Francisco Foot. 2004. 'Pontos extremos: ruínas invisíveis nas fronteiras de um país'. http://repositories.lib.utexas.edu/handle/2152/4073 (accessed 28 April 2015).

Heckenberger, Michael and Eduardo Góes Neves. 2009. 'Amazonian archaeology', *Annual Review of Anthropology*, 38: 251–66.

Hell, Julia, and Andrea Schönle (eds). 2010. *Ruins of modernity*. Durham, NC: Duke University Press.

Hernando, Almudena and Elizabetha M. Beserra Coelho (eds). 2013. *Estudos sobre os Awá. Caçadores-coletores em transição*. São Luis de Maranhão: EDUFMA/IWGIA.

Herzog, Werner. 1982. *Fitzcarraldo*. Werner Herzog Filmproduktion.

Hudson, Joanne. 2014. 'The affordances and potentialities of derelict urban spaces'. In *Ruin memories. Materialities, aesthetics and the archaeology of the recent past*, edited by B. Olsen and Þ. Pétursdóttir, London: Routledge, pp. 193–214.

Jaguaribe, Beatriz. 1999. 'Modernist ruins: National narratives and architectural forms', *Public Culture*, 11(1): 295–312.

Jorgensen, Anna and Richard Keenan (eds). 2012. *Urban wildscapes*. London: Routledge.

Koepnick, Lutz P. 1993. 'Colonial Forestry: Sylvan Politics in Werner Herzog's Aguirre and Fitzcarraldo', *New German Critique*, 60(3): 133–59.

Lévi-Strauss, Claude. 1955. *Tristes tropiques*. Paris : Plon.

Olivier, Laurent. 2008. *Le Sombre Abîme du temps Mémoire et archéologie*. Paris: Seuil.

Pétursdóttir, Þora. 2013. 'Concrete matters: Ruins of modernity and the things called heritage', *Journal of Social Archaeology*, 13(1): 31–53.

Pétursdóttir, Þora and Bjørnar Olsen. 2014. 'An archaeology of ruins'. In *Ruin memories. Materialities, aesthetics and the archaeology of the recent past*, edited by B. Olsen and Þ. Pétursdóttir, London: Routledge, pp. 3–31.

Pflueger, Grete. 2007. 'Redes e ruínas', *Anais. Encontros nacionais da ANPUR*, 12: 1–14.

Pflueger, Grete. 2008. 'O papel das ruínas na contemporaneidade. Ruínas: Roma, Pompéia e Alcântara', *Anais: Seminário de História da Cidade e do Urbanismo*, 10(1): 1–13.

Pressler, Gunter Karl. 2012. 'Gurupá –das ruínas aos cemitérios', *Estudos Avançados*, 26(76): 351–72.

Rodríguez Torrent, Juan Carlos, Pablo Miranda Brown, and Patricio Medina Hernández. 2012. 'Culturas mineras y proyectos vitales en ciudades del carbón, del nitrato y del cobre en Chile', *Chungará*, 44(1): 145–62.

Rodríguez Torrent, Juan Carlos, and Patricio Medina Hernández. 2011. 'Reconversión, daño y abandono en la ciudad de Lota', *Atenea*, 504: 147–76.

Russell, Joseph A. 1942. 'Fordlandia and Belterra. Rubber plantations on the Tapajos river, Brazil', *Economic Geography*, 18(2): 125–45.

Santos Júnior, Paulo Marreiro. 2010. 'Vivências urbanas e conflitos culturais: inter-venções e ações na medicalização da sociedade manauara da Belle Époque', *Opsis*, 8(11): 299–317.

Scott, James C. 1998. *Seeing like a state: How certain schemes to improve the human condition have failed.* New Haven: Yale University Press.

Shanks, Michael. 2012. *The archaeological imagination.* Walnut Creek, CA: Left Coast Press.

Simmel, Georg. 1959. *Georg Simmel, 1858–1918. A collection of essays, with translations and a bibliography*, edited by K. H. Wolff. Columbus: The Ohio State University Press.

Stoler, Laura Ann (ed.). 2013. *Imperial debris: on ruins and ruination.* Durham, NC: Duke University Press.

Vargas, Jonas. 2011. 'O comércio de escravos envolvendo as charqueadas de Pelotas (RS) entre as décadas de 1850 e 1880'. In *V Encontro Escravidão e Liberdade no Brasil Meridional*, Rio Grande: UFRGS, pp. 1–19. Also available at http://www. escravidaoeliberdade.com.br/site/images/Textos5/vargas%20jonas.pdf (accessed 28 April 2015).

Vargas Llosa, Mario. 1966. *La Casa Verde.* Barcelona: Seix Barral.

Vergara, Camilo José. 1999. *American ruins.* New York: Monacelli Press.

Vilches, Flora. 2011. 'From nitrate town to internment camp: the cultural biography of Chacabuco, northern Chile', *Journal of Material Culture*, 16(3): 241–63.

Vilches, Flora, Charles Rees, and Claudia Silva. 2008. 'Arqueología de asentamientos salitreros en la Región de Antofagasta (1880–1930): síntesis y perspectivas', *Chungará (Arica)*, 40(1): 19–30.

Weinstein, Barbara. 1983. *The Amazon rubber boom, 1850–1920.* Stanford: Stanford University Press.

Weizman, Eyal. 2007. *Hollow land: Israel's architecture of occupation.* London: Verso.

Woodward, Christopher. 2002. *In ruins.* New York: Random House.

Yablon, Nick. 2010. *Untimely ruins: an archaeology of American urban modernity, 1819–1919.* Chicago: University of Chicago Press.

Zanettini, Paulo Eduardo. 2003. 'Arqueologia na caatinga: arqueologia de Canudos, em Canudos ou para Canudos?', *Com Ciência, Revista Eletrônica de Jornalismo Científico*, 47. Also available at http://www.comciencia.br/reportagens/arqueologia/ arq19.shtml (accessed 28 April 2015).

Section III

Political Action

8

Creative Destruction and Neoliberal Landscapes

Post-industrial Archaeologies Beyond Ruins

Sefryn Penrose

'[T]he problem that is usually being visualized is how capitalism administers existing structures, whereas the relevant problem is how it creates and destroys them', wrote the Austrian economist, Josef Schumpeter in *Capitalism, Socialism and Democracy*, in 1942 (84). He was describing his discipline's response to creative destruction; the process of continuous reinvention within capitalist markets.

Like Schumpeter's visualizing economists, are archaeologists in danger of bolstering a static view? Of pushing a preservation-of-decay agenda, appealing to a mass diagnosis of the rot of modernity? Ruin studies within contemporary and historical archaeology frequently present an overtly anti-capitalist critique, within an aesthetic conception of things and place, sometimes accompanied by an anti-heritage stance (cf. González-Ruibal, Chapter 7). In recent years archaeologists have recognized and at times moved away from, the problem of aestheticization, but continue to parade an underdog status for the stationary object that reverts to an uneasy stasis—an object from the ground—without an acknowledgement of the movement and change that both contemporary and historical archaeology have worked so hard to develop (e.g. Aldred 2014; Beaudry and Parno 2013; Holtorf and Piccini 2009). This can lead to a tendency to critique without fully situating ruin—site, place—in process, despite benchmark studies (e.g. Gosden 2004). Pictures capture a moment. A ruin illustrates an end. Memory mourns the past. What remains, decays.

In this chapter I address some of the landscapes considered epitomic of neoliberalism: the 'winners' in the landscape of capitalism, and consider whether current archaeological approaches to the contemporary have inadvertently, or indeed overtly, disqualified them from analysis. I present case studies that illustrate the 'creative' side of 'creative destruction'—the large-scale landscape transformation of deindustrialized areas. These sites were transformed through governmental interventions in policy—privatization, public–private investment frameworks, changes to the planning system—with the intention of transforming declined industrial areas into economic success stories in line with the push towards a service economy, away from industry.

There is of course another side to this story: as Arthur Marwick observed the reinvigoration of declined industrial areas is often characterized by 'a growing mismatch between the characteristics of those seeking work and the kind of jobs which [a]re available' (Marwick 2003: 153). *Creating* the service economy does of course entail selective destruction of the industrial economy and its workers (see McAtackney, Chapter 9, and Ryzewski, Chapter 3, for examples of this 'selective' destruction).

It is not my wish to be overly critical—indeed contemporary archaeology is not a large enough field to cover everything—however, without an attempt at balanced consideration of the landscapes that represent both the antithesis of ruin, but also in a sense another kind of ruin, we risk a thoroughly incomplete understanding of the systems we claim to critically dismantle.

8.1 BRITAIN'S DETROIT(S)

On 10 May 2014, *The Guardian* newspaper, a British broadsheet daily, considered the newspaper of the liberal left, published an article in its weekend supplement with the headline 'The north-east of England: Britain's Detroit?' (Beckett 2014). The article focused on the decline of industry in the North East of England, comparing its fate to Detroit's. Over the last two hundred years, the North East has been a heartland of industry, particularly coal mining and shipbuilding, but over the course of the later twentieth century, both have declined to vanishing.

The North East's decline follows, as does Detroit's, the changes in the cycles of capital which have led to the end of mining as an ongoing concern across most of Britain, and the various political and global shifts that have more or less ended shipbuilding in the region. We might see some shared issues—an over-reliance on a few core industries and companies and the ancillary works needed to support them; the shifting location of industrial manufacture due to cost; increasing technical innovation abroad; attempts to boost the economy through public–private initiatives and foreign investment—but also considerably different issues. Britain's industrial decline has been designed by successive governments. The overt destruction of the mining industry under Margaret Thatcher in the 1980s is well documented, and policy designed at Westminster or in Europe has also dictated the decline of shipbuilding. We can list inordinate interventions in policy and law that accelerated or brought about the failure of these industries.

These included European legislation which disqualified dockyards from involvement in defence *and* commercial manufacture; the short-termism of successive governments in influencing how dockyards worked; the clunky circumstances of nationalization and the asset-stripping of privatization; the desire to get British manufacturing off British books, and the deals done with German, Japanese, American, Indian,and Chinese companies to achieve this. These instances might have equivalents in Detroit—they are part of the same manufacturing universe after all—but all ruins have local context. Beckett's article ran with a photograph of Thatcher's 'walk in the wilderness' across the weed-cracked paving of an old iron works (Figure 8.1). It did not show, although it did mention, the Teesdale Business Park that now stands on the site. It did show Bruce and Freddy Shepherd, the businessmen who have bought up significant swathes of the rundown former docks of Tyneside at knockdown prices. They are part of the reinvention (for profit as well as regeneration) that is as much a part of the shift from the industrial to the post-industrial as ruin.

Figure 8.1. Margaret Thatcher takes 'A Walk in the Wilderness' at the former Head Wrightson Works, developed by the Teesside Development Corporation as the Teesdale Business Park. Photo by Ted Ditchburn/North News and Pictures.

8.2 KNOWING CAPITALISM

'Capitalism, then, is by nature a form or method of economic change and not only never is but never can be stationary', Schumpeter observed (1947: 82), and neither is it a total system, a unified field. It exists in a maelstrom of competing interests, 'lines of interference... opacity, division and wildness result' (Thrift 2005: 2).

Contemporary post-industrial ruins sit within capitalism representing human choice, deliberate process, and within that, *opacity, division*, and *wildness*. But they are not still: they are as momentary as the period in which they worked. They represent failure: the end of a path, but not necessarily forever. An end here is not an end everywhere. A technology can reinvent itself (or be reinvented, adapted, developed, transported).

In *Knowing Capitalism*, Nigel Thrift sets out the 'four methodological rules' for analysing capitalism. The first of these, the 'backward gaze', affords an approach to the present that involves looking back—'seeing vast numbers of unresolved issues, differences of interpretation, and general confusions, exactly as historians see the past now'. This is an approach similar to that I have described elsewhere as a 'future perfect' view; the way we have lived (Penrose 2010). Walter Benjamin's *Angelus Novus* takes a closer look and sees more than wreckage, travels forward into the past: more simply there is an understanding of the complexities of the present. Thrift argues that this approach will take us away from totalizing claims about 'modernity' 'which are meant to set the seal on history, to wrap everything up' (Thrift 2005: 2).

The second of Thrift's rules is the recognition of the accidental—the contingent—the accumulation of events. How instances that might have seemed insignificant play their extraordinary parts in shaping the way we have lived.

The playing of parts, the continuous rolling and shaping, the performativity of capitalism is Thrift's third rule: capitalism is never still, as Schumpeter observed (1947: 82; see also Ernsten, Chapter 10, for his discussion of capitalist incarnations in Cape Town). As worlds change, as systems change, as regimes and resources, requirements and resiliences change, so must capitalism. Mutations, innovations, brave and cowardly decisions (sometimes the same thing) shape capitalism. There is no plan. This is not entirely true: there are a million plans, but only the mutable survive. Economists put forward a number of narratives to explain for example, financialism, but they do not exclude the constant rolling need to change and innovate.

The fourth of Thrift's rules is the acknowledgement of the importance of the 'boring' and 'routine', not just the 'sexy'. Capitalism relies on the mundane, the daily task, the smooth running of infrastructure, operations, networks, relationships. Like Leder's 'absent body' (1990), capitalism can blend into the background when it is working: it is when it breaks down that we notice. This is Konvitz's 'myth of terrible vulnerability' referenced by Graham and Thrift (2007: 10). We see the problems, the breakdowns, and their problematic presence makes them unmissable. Meanwhile it is the working system that shapes us, makes us; and that we spend our lives shaping and making. It goes on, invisible, unnoticed, while it works.

In the years that have followed the publication of *Knowing Capitalism* the fundamental shake-up that followed the collapse in 2008 of the American subprime market has brought the broken body of capitalism into view. However, Thrift's maxims still hold, and if we are to avoid those easy damnations of 'modernity', and encourage a more sophisticated exploration of the capitalist world we would do well to, if not follow the rules, at least know they are there.

8.3 NEOLIBERAL LANDSCAPES

The landscape of the recent past might be seen, certainly across much of the UK and the USA to be a landscape of neoliberalism. Initially a term that reflected the 'third way', between the controlled state collectivism of the Soviet states and the classical liberalism of limited government intervention, it was coined in the 1930s, before being resurrected in the 1970s and 1980s with the theories of the Chicago school, especially Milton Friedman, who drew on the work of Friedrich Hayek. Following the relatively prosperous growth years of the post-war period, the 1970s saw a period of stagnation and decline in the liberal 'West' (Britain, the USA, Germany, France, and Italy in particular). Financial liberalization—the loosening of State regulation on the financial sector—influenced by the Chicago school, took hold. Britain became a pioneering driver in that liberalization, and before (but to a much greater degree, after) the election of Margaret Thatcher in 1979, financial deregulation put Britain, and in particular, London, in the top three global financial centres. Britain's drive to deregulate and privatize— to limit the size and power of the State against the possibilities of private growth—was unprecedented in speed and scale. Britain led the neoliberal way. Finding its way in the dark, the Thatcher government redefined the boundary between private and public. Issued with a reading list topped by Hayek—'this is what we believe', Thatcher apocryphally said to her cabinet as she slammed down a copy of *The Constitution of Liberty* (Ranelagh 1991)—it disassembled the Keynesian principles of the Welfare State and of nationalized industry. At the time, it purported to withdraw from what it claimed was a heavy-handed unworkable creaking framework that stifled innovation and drove away entrepreneurialism.

With that, and a nod towards Adam Smith's free trade and enterprise, Britain submitted to market rule.

Thatcherism and Reagonomics were informed by the tenets of neoclassical fundamentalism: market regulation in place of state guidance, economic redistribution in favour of capital—supply side economics—moral authoritarianism, international free trade, an intolerance of unionism. And with the aggressive swing to this theoretical baseline, combined with the concurrent release of so much land and so much capital, a significant physical alteration to Britain's industrial landscape was inevitable.

8.4 CREATIVE DESTRUCTION

The shift from a manufacturing to a service economy follows a business cycle much debated by economists. Schumpeter proposed one of the most enduring theories (Schumpeter 1947) based on his proposition that innovation is the basis of dynamic change in an economy. Schumpeter accepted the orthodox economic position that all economies tended to equilibrium—in which all markets clear. However, he argued that while much competition between firms was based on price, the true driving force was the process of innovation, in which a firm or an entrepreneur with the ability to bring an idea to market could undermine the existing status quo. Rival firms would be put out of business, industries would be revolutionized, or the foundations of national and regional economies, or even the global economy, would be shaken. Schumpeter used the term 'Creative Destruction' to refer to this process, capturing both the phenomenon of innovation and the potentially negative impacts on the economy and society (Schumpeter 1947). As firms or even whole industries die, communities that served them decline (see McAtackney, Chapter 9; White and Seidenberg, Chapter 1). There is no guarantee that new firms and new industries will grow in the same places as the old. They may require skills and assets found elsewhere. And in an increasingly networked world, information technology, for example, has allowed many firms to manage production across whole continents or even globally where once the end-to-end process took place within a few square miles.

These changes in business practice have created new landscapes, and in Britain in particular, the release of land and capital from nationalized industry into the private sector has led to the development of previously industrial sites, the reinvention of working landscapes, and the creation of a new era of land as balance-sheet asset.

In essence, what we have come to know as *creative destruction* relies on what Brenner and Theodore have described as:

...two dialectically intertwined but analytically distinct moments: the (partial) destruction of extant institutional arrangements and political compromises through market-oriented reform initiatives; and the (tendential) creation of a new infrastructure for market-oriented economic growth, commodification, and the rule of capital. (2002: 362)

8.5 ARCHAEOLOGIES OF CONTEMPORARY CAPITALISM

Brenner and Theodore made their case for neoliberalism's creative capacities (though not uncritically) against a prevalent view in the humanities that neoliberalism was overridingly destructive (Brenner and Theodore 2002; see also Larner 2000). Within archaeologies of the recent past, the emphasis has been on those destructive elements. Much contemporary archaeology has taken one of two paths: socially and politically engaged studies that privilege the subaltern, the dispossessed, the abject; and those that privilege matter. The former has been augmented in recent years by the added obligation that these stories must illustrate the failure of modernity or attempt to undermine it (e.g. González-Ruibal 2008; Harrison 2013). While the latter is characterized by, at one end, the acknowledgement of the co-constituting properties of people and things, to, at the other, attempts at non-narrativized understandings of the post-human (cf. Holbraad 2014; Witmore 2012).

Post-industrial ruin is the perfect setting for both kinds of study: desolate, abject, abandoned in both instances—sites that need an alternative (human) story to be told, and sites that have a (post-human) afterlife that is beyond human telling. Returning to Thrift's rules—the focus of this chapter is on capitalist ruins—I find those twin paths of contemporary archaeology break Thrift's rules. Many current archaeological approaches *do* result in totalizing assessments of 'modernity,' (González-Ruibal for example, advocates 'materially exposing the *inherent* destructivity of modernity' [2013: 15, my emphasis]; a statement that makes 'destructivity' an essential characteristic). They do indulge in the 'sexy,' (we might think of Webmoor's (after Woodward 2012: 18) term 'entropic chic' [2014: 470]. Webmoor's argument that ruins are 'counter cultural' effectively owns this understanding of the *sexy*. What could be sexier than entropic chic?). They do overlook the 'boring'. Critically perhaps, their commitment to the exposition of 'trauma', telling the story of the dispossessed terminally neglects the other parts of the framework. Ruin exists because of change and creation, creative destruction. No longer viable places within neoliberal economic frameworks have counterparts—those places where economic activity has shifted: new labour landscapes; new uses for old places; new technologies. This is not a new complaint. Johnson (1998) set out in his afterword to Leone and Potter's *Historical Archaeology of Capitalism* the tension between telling the 'local' story and analyses of the 'global' framework. As Johnson stated in 1998, '[e]ven as we stress the individual and the local, we can only do so against a backdrop of global structure; even as we look at the small scale and the particular, we fit these into large scale processes' (1998: 220).

But within approaches to the deindustrialized recent past, there has been a tendency to demonize those large-scale processes—a strangely anthropocentric urge, in a field sometimes attempting to move beyond that—that leads to a wholesale abandonment of both baby and bathwater.

8.6 EXPLORING THE BORING

The landscape of neoliberalism is 'polycentric and multi-scalar' (Brenner and Theodore 2002: 351). The landscapes of new commerce have absorbed or incorporated or replaced sites of industrial ruination (see Beisaw, Chapter 6, for discussion of submerged landscapes in the context of New York's water). These kinds of landscapes might have been absorbed, expanded, refurbished, redeveloped, but I argue, have by and large, become unquestioningly part of the worldview of anyone living and working in post-Thatcher's and post-Reagan's—post-industrial?—Britain or the USA. Indeed, they describe any landscape where neoliberalism has become the prevailing economic orthodoxy.

They are inherently speculative. Where the business of the firm once created landscape—whether manufacturing, or financial, or otherwise—these landscapes are increasingly defined by their status as assets. But without the guarantee of viable industry, speculative landscapes—by their essence—require some kind of 'hook', and in some senses, these landscapes are hooked on an idea of ruined industry. The decline of industries associated with a strong sense of national identity—in Britain, car and ship manufacturing, for example—are interlinked with speculation, precisely because it was (and continues to be) the release of previously state-owned land (in this case, state-owned following large-scale nationalization programmes in the post-war period) into the private sector that have allowed both the run-down of industrial sites and their development. Here, rather than industrial sites being left to rot, to ruin, the *tendential creation* (Brenner and Theodore 2002: 362) of sites of new commerce overlies old industry. Of course, there remain significant regional and local differences. In the highly developed South East of England, for example, large-scale abandonment is a rarity, while rosebay willowherb strewn former industrial complexes are commonplace in the Midlands, north and west of Britain.

There is a talismanic quality in the use of the past in speculative landscapes. The value of assets depends of course on their worth to investors. The owners place the value, which is determined by their rental prices, which require tenants to pay those prices. To some degree, the base land value is what drives their investment value.

They are landscapes of work—requiring a workforce—just as the industrial sites before them. They are often situated in areas set up for workers to live in. But their success is not guaranteed. How they are built plays a role—both general and specific—in the social reproduction of the working culture (Buchli 2013) and their endurance as sites of work on historic sites of work belies a truth. Elements of what preceded them are incorporated, determinedly to lend legitimacy, a talisman of industrial success, and a posturing: a positioning to show power and success. We might see parallels in the use in industrial architecture of elements of the classical form, as Ballantyne describes:

> ... the cotton mills around Manchester, which pounded out fine fabrics, were given towers and turrets, and dressed to look superficially like the palaces of a new aristocracy. The thunderous engines that drew into St Pancras Station in London were screened from the city by a cavalcade of pinnacles and pointed arches. (2008: 1–2)

But there is a difference. There is something tentative in the *tendential creation* that accompanied the *partial destruction* that characterized the landscapes of the rise of neoliberalism. Thatcher's government assumed that a solution would arise from the short, sharp shock—the sudden removal of the props that held up industry through privatization—worsened the already existing divide between those formerly industrial areas and those that benefited from the clustering of service industries that Thatcher explicitly supported. The government would not bear the cost and pain of supporting industry, but would receive a return on the economic success of the private sector, and in return, the private sector benefited from deep discount on formerly national assets, principally, it would transpire, land.

8.7 URBAN DEVELOPMENT CORPORATIONS

State owned assets that had been allowed to run down, or were considered no longer a priority to be held up, included vast swathes of industrial land. The 1980 Local Government Planning and Land Act enabled the formation of Urban Development Corporations (hereafter 'UDCs')—essentially quasi-autonomous non-governmental organizations (quangos)—equipped with their own statutory powers and annually funded by the British Treasury (Figure 8.2). They were directly responsible to the Secretary of the State for

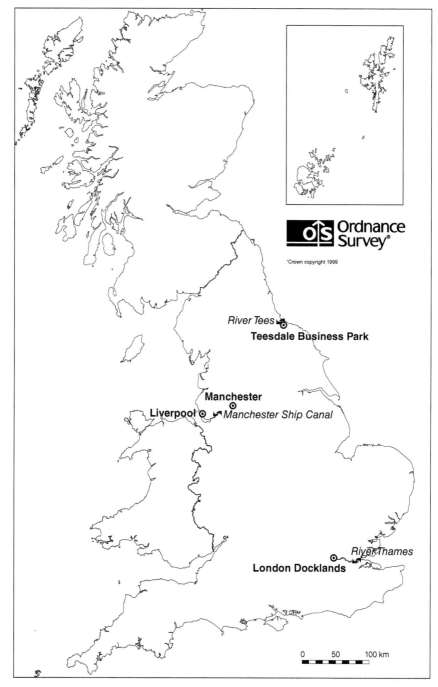

Figure 8.2. Map showing unitary development corporation locations. Reproduced from Ordnance Survey map data by permission of Ordnance Survey © Crown Copyright 2013.

the Department of the Environment. However, their boards comprised a majority of private-sector members and their essential remit was to replace local government as the primary promoters of urban regeneration. Aside from reduced bureaucratic constraints, what made the development powers of the UDCs different from those of local authorities, from whom they sequestered those powers, was their undisguised tilt towards private sector capital economics:

> [The UDCs] epitomised the subordination of redistributional to economic growth concerns in urban policy; they embodied the preoccupation with responding to ostensible private sector needs, and embracing the outlook of business in public policy; and they exemplified the pursuit of 'physical' intervention in local land and property markets at the expense of socially-focused regeneration.
>
> (Deas et al. 2000: 1)

In essence, UDCs existed to transform derelict and problematic areas of state-held land, and in doing so, take the problem away from the state. In 1981 the first two UDCs were formed: the London Docklands Development Corporation (hereafter 'LDDC') and the Merseyside Development Corporation (hereafter 'MDC'). The land belonging to the dock companies was vested under the control of the new corporations.

8.8 LONDON DOCKLANDS

The London Docks had been in steady decline in the postwar period. Successive governments had long considered what might now be seen as 'master-planning' strategies. These were conceived to deal with the perceived problem of urban industrial rundown in an area that had been reliant on the docks as a source of employment, concurrent with the steady diminishment of industry as a whole in the area.

The pursuit of different aims of course led to significant strife between stakeholders. The friction between the aims of the LDDC and the needs of local groups was apparent early on, as it became clear that what the Docklands development was offering was a new financial and business centre for London, rather than an employment base that suited its position. But the LDDC persisted in its manufacturing of a new concept for Docklands—'projecting a confident image of the future' (Oc and Tiesdell 1991: 311)—as much a core part of the LDDC's remit as actually facilitating development works. Imagineering became a key concept—and part of it was reimagining and emphasizing exactly how bad it had been before. The LDDC consistently traded on the myth that there had been no investment in the docks, which had effectively been mothballed:

> The docklands inherited by the LDDC in 1981 was isolated both physically and
> emotionally from the rest of London . . . Docklands was beset by overwhelming
> problems of social deprivation, poor housing and bleak prospects . . . in a phys-
> ical context of dereliction and decay. No one but a few visionary pioneers who,
> like the LDDC, saw the tremendous potential of docklands and moved here to
> commence the process of regeneration, saw the area as having any value.
>
> (LDDC 1998: 4)

The facilitation of private sector development therefore included both the
downgrading of the recent past and the lionization of a deeper industrial
past. Docklands today is a monumental blend of epic architectures. Its
backdrop is the relict landscape of the docks themselves. The achievements
of structural engineering that the construction of the London docks represents saw England's national heritage agency, English Heritage, play a
distinctive part in the creation of the Dockland's aesthetic. In 1983 a number
of buildings and structures associated with the old docks were Listed (placed
on England's National Inventory of Listed Buildings) or Scheduled (placed
on the inventory of Scheduled—at that time—Ancient Monuments), thereby
ensuring some element of statutory protection for them. Within the area of
the old docks, the monumental aesthetic of the docks provided a fitting
backdrop to the monumental aesthetic of some of the office buildings that
were being planned. But the offices, warehouses, and workshops of the old
docks had already been identified in the determining of the Docklands
development.

Arriving at Docklands along Narrow Street, for example, the cobbled
street along the River Thames lined with three-, four-, and five-storey
converted warehouses, the particularly 1980s aesthetic has become an attractive cityscape style in its own right. Here, old docks are given over to
marinas for leisure craft. This waterside living and working was heavily
influenced by the work of James Rouse in the US. His waterside developments of Boston and Baltimore are the obvious antecedents—new use of old
structures, an eye to tourism, commercialism (Rennie-Short 2013: 69; on
repurposing urban architecture in Chicago, see Graff, Chapter 4). It had a
successful London precursor in the conversion of the flower market in
Covent Garden into a cobbled tourist Victorian culture and shopping experience and the location of the Royal Opera House. The city as a stage. But
another influence, successful urban realm over massive hectarage, but not by
town planners, was Disneyland, where Main Street, USA was brought to
(larger than) life, sanitized, and reinterpreted (Ward 2012: 277). Dockland
living was riverside living, but not regenerated, instead, reinvented. The
years of decline were bypassed for the evocation of a bustling eighteenth-
and nineteenth-century docklands, with all of the mercantilism and derring-
do, but none of the squalor.

8.9 CANARY WHARF

Urbanist Peter Hall had proposed in the 1970s that for city areas that had become slums—considered impossible to turn around—the last ditch solution would be to create 'enterprise zones' where restrictions were lifted to encourage private innovation and investment without risk (Hall 1982; see Mullins, Chapter 12, for a case study in 'slum' clearance in Indianapolis). Michael Heseltine, Thatcher's Secretary of State for the Department of the Environment (1979–83) took the idea and adapted it. The Isle of Dogs Enterprise Zone was characterized by a lack of planning controls, rates, free business spaces, and the writing off of investments against tax liabilities for any company that chose to locate there. Thatcher personally wooed the few global developers she thought could pull it off. In a coup we could consider one of the biggest physical markers of her regime, she netted Olympia & York, a Canadian company that at the time was the biggest development firm in the world.

The development was regarded as highly controversial: the LDDC had sold the land at below half its market rate, and the local MP noted that it would be harder to get planning permission to open a fish and chip shop in Millwall (the tip of the Isle of Dogs). In the end, there was no doubt that the telling phrase in the LDDC's planning minutes 'political considerations favour the scheme' was the primary driver behind the development (Barnes, Colenutt, and Malone 2013: 18).

Canary Wharf, a business and commercial district of around 1,300,000 square metres, is now considered to be London's second 'City'—a financial district that essentially extends the work of the Square Mile into the east (Colour plate 10, top). One Canada Square was completed in 1991, and was at the time London's tallest building. Olympia & York filed for bankruptcy in 1992 and for some time, Canary Wharf was considered something of a failure— the folly of 1980s trading excesses—but it is hard now to imagine London without it. Even after the latest financial crash, London's embedding of the consistently repeated message that its success hangs on the financial sector—at home mostly in Canary Wharf—means Docklands thrives.

8.10 MERSEYSIDE TO MANCHESTER

To the River Mersey in the North West of England; the first of those UDCs where special planning measures enabled by Heseltine were instituted.

In many cities, the removal of city council mechanisms that were designed to prevent wholesale decline had left the Conservative government with dead

zones of total shutdown. In 2011 a number of classified documents newly
opened following the end of the then thirty-year embargo on their release
were published that detailed the Thatcher cabinet's discussions on the fate of
Merseyside. During the initial setting-up of the UDC, an area of Liverpool
long plagued by disharmony between residents and the authorities, particularly between the black community and the police, experienced serious
rioting. Heseltine found himself a lone voice arguing for considerable financial support to regenerate Merseyside: 'Isn't this pumping water uphill?
Should we go rather for "managed decline"? This is not a term for use,
even privately. It is much too negative, when it must imply a sustained effort
to absorb Liverpool manpower elsewhere – for example in nearby towns of
which some are developing quite promisingly', wrote Geoffrey Howe in a
personal note to Thatcher. Howe was Chancellor of the Exchequer at the
time, holding the nation's purse strings (Travis 2011). Heseltine argued that
the decline of Merseyside had been worsened by post-war policy: 'a tactical
retreat, a combination of economic erosion and encouraged evacuation'
(Travis 2011).

Merseyside's state of decline—due in no small part to similar issues afflict-
ing the London Docklands: the reduction in competitiveness in shipbuilding,
in suitability of the docks themselves, the growth of containerization and
associated need for larger seaports and better transport infrastructure, problems with local government, and conflicts with central government (sometimes ideological)—was unquestionably part of a broader narrative. Industrial
decline preceded the efforts of the Conservative government to crush unionism, although it was certainly not helped by it. The initial regeneration
package saw Merseyside woo Arrowcroft, a London-based development
group, who saw to the redevelopment of the Albert Dock—a Grade I Listed
Victorian dock—as a commercial and leisure area. The first warehouse conversion mezzanine flats were sold in 1986, and the Tate Gallery opened an
offshoot of its national collection in a converted warehouse in 1988. But the
project also saw land reclamation, environmental clean-up, housing, business
park development.

But the extent of the Merseyside dock system meant that, as in London, the
process of regeneration would take longer than the initial ten-year lifespan of
the UDCs. The decline in industry and the large scale of the land therefore
available for potential redevelopment/regeneration meant that the potential to
accumulate extensive areas as land assets became a growing possibility. Following the dissolution of the UDCs in 1998, the Mersey Docks and Harbour
Company, a company with origins and obligations not unlike those of the Port
of London Authority, regained control of Merseyside's docks. In 2005 it was
acquired by the Peel Group.

The Peel Group is a large (private) property development and investment
company still majority-owned by the entrepreneur John Whitaker who

founded the business in 1973. He acquired Peel Mills, a textile mill in Bury, and moved into the acquisition and development of large former industrial sites as business and warehousing sites. The company floated on the London Stock Market in 1981 and grew with the creation of an extensive asset portfolio that included the Manchester Ship Canal and the Port of Liverpool. It reprivatized in 2004, with the help of the Saudi investment conglomerate, Olayan Group, who hold approximately 25 per cent of Peel.

In a controversial development that raised the ire of Manchester City Council, Peel developed the Trafford Centre—one of Britain's first megamalls—which opened in 1998 on ship canal land. And more recently the Manchester docks—developed by Salford Council as 'Salford Quays'—have been augmented by Peel's investment in MediaCity, and a variety of other schemes that will form part of Ocean Gateway. Private consortia and companies such as Peel carry the investment and development abilities that local authorities no longer do. Ocean Gateway is Peel's 'vision' for the corridor of the Manchester Ship Canal—effectively a massive regeneration of the former industrial powerhouses of the North West, connecting Manchester to Liverpool via Salford, Warrington, Runcorn, and Birkenhead with a tagline of '50 projects, 50 years, 50 billion'. Ocean Gateway will be part of 'Atlantic Gateway', a board-led group of partnerships between local authorities (including Liverpool, Salford, and Manchester) and private business and consortia such as Peel—or rather some of Peel's enterprises/subsidiaries/assets such as MediaCity and Liverpool Airport. It is designed to drive growth and in its effort to do so will transform areas long known for their economic stagnation and industrial ruin. It is *tendential creation* on an epic scale. It is also a post-industrial asset portfolio, snugly entangled in the matted webs of tax accounting that investment groups specialize in.

8.11 CONCLUSION

In Detroit, a Chinese businessman who made his fortune building worker dorms in Shenzhen has acquired a few of the cities more iconic 'abandoned' early twentieth-century buildings—presumably because Detroit has infrastructure and a labour force and China's economy is slowing. It is a risky strategy, but a strong yuan and a weak dollar make risky strategies look reasonable in this mutable world and China is now the second biggest buyer of US real estate (Kaiman 2014). The 'Chinese takeaway' (as the buyout of British automotive firms by China was nicknamed in local pubs and tabloid newspapers) reshapes the mutable ruin. Of course, it does not reach those areas of Detroit where depopulation has become so bad that proposals to consolidate and return those areas to farmland (rather than leave them to ruin) are tabled. It recalls Cornwall, where the Devon and Cornwall Mining World Heritage Site—a tourist's mecca of picturesque harbour towns and scenic moorland—was once a mess of industry and now homes a population of less than a fifth that it did in its short-lived heyday in the late nineteenth century; a place where industrial talismans are clung to and converted despite the almost total loss of industry.

As part of General Motors' Chapter 11 bankruptcy, the car giant sloughed its unprofitability and debt, like the big British industries, accumulated from years of failures to modernize, bad investment decisions, too big and creaky a reach (as well of course of those well-rehearsed arguments about Japanese innovation and Chinese labour costs), into a new company, Motors Liquidation Company. The primary role of this company was to dispose of GM's dirty washing—from its accumulated debts, to its environmental pollution— taking with it a few old holdings. The terrible vulnerability of the end of American manufacturing—the ruins of Detroit—is not the end of the story, however. There is no end. GM's fortunes have picked up (although the recall of 6 million cars made between 2007 and 2014 has not been fortunate). Its English badge, Vauxhall, on the verge of being packaged off to a consortium in 2009, is thriving. Whereas, the Saab factory abandoned in Trollhättan, outbid by Vauxhall's superior production, finds itself starring in articles under headlines proclaiming 'Sweden's Detroit'. Saab's ruin is literally Vauxhall's increased capacity.

The post-industrial shift has occurred within a globalized network of capital ownership. Thatcher's revolution in government not only entailed the drawdown of industrial manufacturing in Britain that continued under the Conservative and Labour governments that succeeded her. It also actively pursued an agenda of private ownership that encouraged citizens to literally own their own assets.

The sweetheart deals and discount pricing that accompanied the sale of national assets to private companies have sometimes resulted in mega-rich companies that are markets in themselves. Companies are so large that their market share cannot be competed with and they can offer governments and councils opportunities too promising to refuse. We see Thatcher's successors as continuing the legacy of those governments, and we can see initiatives such as Ocean Gateway as successors to UDCs (and UDCs are making a comeback). This ensures the market, is as ever, forgiven with each new cycle of government support (including financial and tax incentives) for private initiatives.

In architecture, those illusory post-modern ruin-influenced forms say 'what came before is ours: we don't need to heed its structures', but they also use fragments of the past as architectural talismans. The Peel Group's timeline on its website begins at 1715 when the Liverpool docks opened, and includes the death of Robert Peel, prime minister and mill owner.

'Postmodern architecture is about providing the right ambience and affective state' (Svabo et al. 2013: 313), and indeed its bi-fold ambition in these case studies is to engender a belief in its longevity that will bring investors; and to create an affective state that will encourage productivity from those within it, whether they are buying or selling. It tries to do all this with a nod to a classical past that has been tried and tested in this manner since the eighteenth century, but also with an understanding of its industrial past. By doing so, it reinforces the strange belief that we appear to have in our industrial past; our love for the monumental, no matter how fleeting; our conflicted and often dishonest relationship with ruins; our resistance to change.

Perhaps because the contemporary is so close, and perhaps because seeing the living is so hard, archaeologists of the contemporary past run the risk of being myopic in their exploration of the theoretical embeddedness of economic, social, and natural processes within ruin. While the 'thingness' of ruins (Pétursdóttir and Olsen 2014), their inherent value, their own-ness, does indeed provide a fruitful avenue for material observation and the understanding of certain human conceptions and non-human growth cycles, it wilfully sidesteps both broad issues of economic change and detailed understandings of the complexity of place. In some ways this is comparable to the keen focus of industrial archaeology on specific technologies and the privileging of the machine: a neat paring of industrial and post-industrial archaeology in which things and places become isolated from all but the most obvious or immediate networks and systems, and a real critique of capitalism is missed, again. Neoliberalism's techniques are not limited to the ruin of heavy industry and the human cost that that entails. It is built on speculation and accumulation, the work of which is done from, and exhibited in a new landscape of commerce. If we look carefully, we can see neoliberalism's own uncertainty in these landscapes. An archaeological eye can track the gambles, pay-offs, big wins, and bigger losses in these forms. The deindustrialized is the post-industrial: the uncertain present grasping at a fleeting past to ensure a fantasy future. Sometimes, ruins can obscure the broader view.

ACKNOWLEDGEMENTS

My thanks are due to Laura McAtackney and Krysta Ryzewski for inviting me to Detroit, Michigan, in August 2014, for their editing, and their patience. Thanks are also due to the other participants of the Detroit workshop, and to the Wayne State students who took part in what was a wonderfully thoughtful, rigorous, and fun few days. I am also grateful to Sarah May for her comments on drafts of this chapter, and for her encouragement and friendship, to Angela Poulter for her support, and to Jago Penrose for his technical help.

REFERENCES

Aldred, Oscar. 2014. 'Past Movements, Tomorrow's Anchors: On the Relational Entanglements Between Archaeological Mobilities'. In *Past Mobilities: Archaeological Approaches to Movement and Mobility*, edited by Jim Leary, Farnham: Ashgate.

Ballantyne, Andrew. 2008. *Architectures: Modernism and After*. London: John Wiley & Sons.

Barnes, John, Bob Colenutt, and Patrick Malone. 2013. 'London: Docklands and the State'. In *Cities, Capital and Water*, edited by Patrick Malone, London: Routledge.

Beaudry, Mary and Travis Parno (eds). 2013. *Archaeologies of Mobility and Movement*. New York: Springer.

Beckett, Andy. 2014. 'The north-east of England: Britain's Detroit?,' *The Guardian*, 10 May 2014. Also available at: http://www.theguardian.com/uk-news/2014/may/10/north-east-avoid-becoming-britains-detroit (accessed 4 February 2017).

Brenner, Neil and Nik Theodore. 2002. 'Cities and the Geographies of "Actually Existing Neoliberalism"', *Antipodes*, 34(3): 349.

Buchli, Victor. 2013. *An Anthropology of Architecture*. Oxford: Berg.

Deas, Iain, Brian Robson, and Michael Bradford. 2000. 'Re-thinking the Urban Development Corporation"experiment": the case of Central Manchester, Leeds and Bristol'. *Progress in Planning*, 54: 1.

Gosden, Chris. 2004. *Archaeology and Colonialism*. Cambridge: Cambridge University Press.

González-Ruibal, Alfredo. 2008. 'Time to Destroy: an archaeology of supermodernity', *Current Anthropology*, 49(2): 247.

González-Ruibal, Alfredo (ed.). 2013. *Reclaiming Archaeology: beyond the tropes of modernity*. London: Routledge.

Graham, Stephen and Nigel Thrift. 2007. 'Out of Order Understanding Repair and Maintenance', *Theory, Culture & Society*, 24(3): 1.

Hall, Peter. 1982. 'Enterprise zones: a justification', *International Journal of Urban and Regional Research*, 6(3): 416.

Harrison, Rodney. 2013. 'Scratching the Surface'. In *Reclaiming Archaeology: Beyond the Tropes of Modernity*, edited by Alfredo González-Ruibal, London: Routledge.

Holbraad, Martin. 2014. 'How things can unsettle'. In *Objects & Materials: A Routledge Companion*, edited by Penny Harvey, Eleanor Conlin Casella, Gillian Evans, Hannah Knox, Christine McLean, Elizabeth B. Silva, Nicholas Thoburn, and Kath Woodward, London: Routledge.

Holtorf, Cornelius and Angela Piccini (eds). 2009. *Contemporary Archaeologies: Excavating Now*. Frankfurt: Peter Lang.

Johnson, Matthew. 1998. 'Historical, Archaeology, Capitalism'. In *Historical Archaeology of Capitalism*, edited by Mark P. Leone and Parker B. Potter, New York: Springer.

Kaiman, Jonathan. 2014. 'Does multimillion dollar Chinese investment signal Detroit's rebirth?', *The Guardian*, 22 July. Also available at: http://www.theguardian.com/cities/2014/jul/22/does-multimillion-dollar-chinese-investment-signal-detroits-rebirth (accessed 4 February 2017).

Larner, Wendy. 2000. 'Theorizing neoliberalism: policy, ideology, govermentality', *Studies in Political Economy*, 63: 5–26.

Leder, Drew. 1990. *The Absent Body*. Chicago: University of Chicago Press.

Marwick, Arthur. 2003. *British Society Since 1945*. London: Penguin.

Oc, Taner and Stephen Tiesdell. 1991. 'The London Docklands Development Corporation 1981–1991: a perspective on the management of urban regeneration', *Town and Country Planning Review*, 62(3): 311.

Penrose, Sefryn. 2010. 'Recording Transition in Post-Industrial England: A Future Perfect View of Oxford's Motopolis', *Archaeologies*, 6(1): 167.

Pétursdóttir, Þora and Bjørnar Olsen (eds). 2014. *Ruin Memories: Materialities, Aesthetics and the Archaeology of the Recent Past*. London: Routledge.

Ranelagh, John. 1991. *Thatcher's People: An Insider's Account of the Politics, the Power, and the Personalities*. London: HarperCollins.

Rennie-Short, John. 2013. *Global Metropolitan: Globalizing Cities in a Capitalist World*. London: Routledge.

Schumpeter, Joseph. 1942 [1975]. *Capitalism, Socialism & Democracy*. New York: Harper Perennial.

Svabo, Connie, Jonas Larson, Michael Haldrup, and Jørgen Ole Bærenholdt. 2013. 'Experiencing Spatial Design'. In *Handbook on the Experience Economy*, edited by Jon Sundbo and Fleming Sørensen, Cheltenham: Edward Elgar Publishing.

The London Docklands Development Corporation (LDDC). 1998. *A strategy for regeneration: the planning and development strategy of the London Docklands Development Corporation*. London: The Corporation.

Thrift, Nigel. 2005. *Knowing Capitalism*, London: Sage.

Travis, Alan. 2011. 'Thatcher government toyed with evacuating Liverpool after 1981 riots', *The Guardian*, 30 December. Also available at: http://www.theguardian.com/uk/2011/dec/30/thatcher-government-liverpool-riots-1981 (accessed 4 February 2017).

Ward, Stephen. 2012. '"Cities Are Fun!": Inventing and Spreading the Baltimore Model of Cultural Urbanism'. In *Culture, Urbanism & Planning*, edited by Javier Monclus and Manuel Guardia, Farnham: Ashgate.

Webmoor, Timothy. 2014. 'Object-oriented metrologies of care and the proximate ruin of building 500'. In *Ruin Memories: Materialities, Aesthetics and the Archaeology of the Recent Past*, edited by Þora Pétursdóttir and Bjørnar Olsen, London: Routledge.

Witmore, Christopher. 2012. 'The realities of the past: archaeology, object orientations, pragmatology'. In *Modern Materials: Proceedings from the Contemporary and Historical Archaeology in Theory Conference 2009*, edited by Brent Fortenberry and Laura McAtackney, Oxford: Archaeopress.

Woodward, Christopher. 2012. 'Learning from Detroit or "the wrong kind of ruins"'. In *Urban Wildscapes*, edited by Anna Jorgensen and Richard Keenan, New York: Routledge.

9

Repercussions of Differential Deindustrialization in the City

Memory and Identity in Contemporary East Belfast

Laura McAtackney

Contemporary archaeology has often combined the study of material culture with a strong social justice imperative, including examining the causes of abandonment of social housing (Buchli and Lucas 2001) and constructing lived experiences of homelessness (Zimmerman et al. 2010). Within this burgeoning field, archaeologies of cities have a significant role to play in interpreting the social implications of transition and change in the city by engaging with the spatial and temporal dimensions of material realities. By explicitly materializing the forgotten or hidden aspects of the post-industrial city, contemporary archaeology allows us to view global processes through the lens of local material expressions. Hilary Orange's edited volume *Reanimating Industrial Spaces* (2014) is indicative of the current fascination in contemporary archaeology with the meaning of abandoned places of industry, the link between people and places and the often difficult transition from functional industrial places to post-industrial heritage spaces. Such volumes use a variety of methodological approaches to show how people, place and materials constitute the contemporary, post-industrial city. In doing so they reveal how contemporary archaeology has the potential to critique official narratives that frequently highlight resurgence and development while ignoring inconvenient truths of degradation, unemployment and poverty (see also Ernsten, Chapter 10). The latter experiences speak to this case study of East Belfast in Northern Ireland.

For a society of its size Northern Ireland has been the subject of intense political and academic scrutiny, indeed often being accused of over-analysis to the point of exceptionalism (including Whyte 1990). Much of the research has centred on social relationships in urban areas impacted by internecine violence, however, in recent years this focus has shifted to the persisting problems of segregation and sectarianism as a remnant from the Troubles (*c*.1968–*c*.98) into the peace process. With the fifteen-year anniversary of the Belfast Agreement of 1998 (hereafter 'the Agreement') in 2013—a peace accord that at the time was positively greeted as the end of violence and initiating a move toward 'normalisation' (Irish News 2005)—there has been much debate as to the ongoing lack of substantive societal change. At the level of civic politics progress has been made, even if it has been non-linear and at times in danger of derailment. This has not been mirrored universally at the community level. Instead, recent media attention has focused on an unwanted, and unforeseen, repercussion of enduring divisions: the rise of racist, homophobic, and misogynistic attacks, most notably during the annual cycle of commemorative events (including Mercer 2014).

Political commentators have been swift to blame enduring and emerging conflict as both a repercussion of the Troubles—specifically linked to long-term segregation and enduring 'acceptable levels' of sectarianism and intolerance—as well as evidence of ongoing paramilitary power. These perceived links received official recognition in early 2014 when the Chief Constable of the Police Service of Northern Ireland (PSNI) claimed that 70 per cent of the attacks in East Belfast (where a sizeable number of anti-migrant hate crimes have been recorded) were connected to the loyalist paramilitary organization Ulster Volunteer Force (UVF) (Stewart 2014). Despite a variety of interpretations as to why this is occurring—including new migrants having predominantly moved into depopulated, working-class, loyalist areas in Belfast due to the comparatively cheap rental costs—it is clear that a synergy exists between loyalist paramilitaries active in working-class, urban areas and racist attacks (Stewart 2013).

From an early stage, politico-historical analyses of the evolving nature of loyalist identity during the peace process has placed an emphasis on the loyalist community retreating to a 'siege mentality' that frequently manifests in the rejection and exclusion of others (Finlay 2001: 3–20). Increasingly, aggressive defensiveness in loyalism has been interpreted as reacting to societal change as a perceived 'challenge to their culture and identity' (McAuley 2003: 60). However, it has also been more sympathetically viewed as a repercussion of trauma, at both the personal and collective level (Tomlinson 2007). In the context of facilitating the transition of Belfast from a city of conflict to a more normalized place the focus on healing inter and intra community discord and recognizing the needs of traumatized communities (including Gallagher et al. 2012) creates the space to question the roots of its problems. How might Northern Ireland transition to a more normative future while also 'dealing with the past'? Should we include a past that is not simply 'the Troubles'? The issue of the politics of the past has, until now, been deliberately bypassed at an official, societal level as too difficult to confront without reigniting conflict and reinforcing divisions (McGrattan 2009: 164). However, it has become clear that Northern Ireland, as a society, cannot move on while leaving these legacy issues unresolved. In this context, and through the following case study of East Belfast, I argue there is a need to more broadly consider other legacies of the past, their spatiality and how they materially 'trouble' the present rather than simply consign all societal ills to 'the Troubles'. In particular, in an attempt to move beyond the unquestioning acceptance of sectarian conflict as the root cause of all problems, the negative impact of urban deindustrialization will be emphasized. Such a broadening conception of the contemporary and historical city of Belfast aims to expand our understandings of differential experiences of the recent past, how global processes have interacted with local contexts to create these conditions and how they impact on the construction of 'self' and 'other' in the contemporary.

This chapter traces how industry and industrialization have been intrinsic to historical loyalist identity, its articulation of supremacy and difference from the rest of the island and how this persists with a negative emphasis in the contemporary. By exploring materializations of memory and identity in East Belfast, this reconception of the city as both 'conflicting' and 'deindustrializing' provides an alternative reading. It combines the undoubted impact of the Troubles with the devastating, and differential, socioeconomic impact of deindustrialization in East Belfast. In doing so this chapter highlights how economic decline has most negatively impacted on those who originally benefited from the industrial boom. In exploring the place of industry in working-class, loyalist identity one can begin to understand how the extended decline of the city of Belfast as an industrial powerhouse throughout the twentieth century has combined with other factors to skew it from a progressive, modern ethos to an increasingly inward-looking, defensive, and even intolerant community. This chapter will move between the global and the local and in doing so critique the overfocus on the peculiarities of Northern Ireland that have been used to justify inexusable behaviour as a symptom of an atypical, broken, and seemingly unfixable society (see McAtackney 2015). Following Vaughan-Williams I suggest we move beyond an acceptance of an unavoidable clash between two irreconcilable communities as these narratives 'reproduces rather than unravels sinews of conflict' (2006: 513–26). Instead the inclusion of the facet of deindustrialization allows a better understanding of how various localized problems in Northern Irish society have combined with global processes to result in differential impacts on community identity and how they materialize in contemporary society.

9.1 HISTORICAL BACKGROUND: SEGREGATION, SECTARIANISM, AND INDUSTRIALIZATION IN BELFAST

Belfast existed as a settlement—if not a nucleated, urban site—up to 2,000 years ago; however, it is from the date of the official foundation by Sir Arthur

Chichester in 1613 that the modern city took shape. Belfast was officially established in the same year as a number of other enduring settlements in the north of the island including (London)derry, Limavady, and Coleraine. Urbanization was a central policy of the English crown's plantation of the then largely rural province of Ulster with Belfast intended as a mercantile, rather than garrison, town from its initial conception (Horning 2013). The city had defended, if unwalled, boundaries that allowed a spatial distinction between the loyal, planted, Protestant Scottish and English Protestants residing 'inside', and the Gaelic-Irish Catholic populations who initially settled 'outside' while partaking in work within the town by day.

Archaeological evidence reveals that Belfast was successful in establishing industry, including ironworking, brewing, and hideworking, within the early years of its establishment (Horning 2013: 253). Indeed, its proto- and industrial establishments were so successful, especially after legislative changes from the mid-seventeenth century onwards, little survives of the city's medieval and early modern street plans due to the rapid expansion of the city. Horning has argued convincingly that this lack of material evidence has allowed a deliberately myopic understanding of Belfast's history, which reveals a distinct sectarian undertone. She suggests that the contemporary emphasis on the eighteenth- and nineteenth-century industrialization of the city as a cornerstone of its identity not only results from greater survivals of this period but also because it fits narratives of the city being essentially 'British' and 'industrial' rather than 'Irish' and 'agricultural' (Horning 2013: 255, footnote).

While there were distinctions made between the inhabitants of the newly established city based on ethnic identity they were not consistently nor strictly observed temporally and spatially until they became confirmed and re-emphasized with the movement of large numbers of lowland Scots in the eighteenth century to the North East of the island. From this time the native Irish were regarded with suspicion as 'the Irish in Belfast' (Boal 2002: 690), determining the development of Belfast into a form that is recognizable today, as a 'polarised city' (Boal 1994: 31). Clearly, the self-identification of Belfast as an 'industrial' city stems not from the creation of Belfast as an alien settlement of the seventeenth century but its later re-articulation as an industrial, Imperial powerhouse over a century later. During the Industrial Revolution Belfast was the centre of the industrialized zone on the island that increasingly differentiated and isolated itself from 'rural peripherialisation' of the more Catholic, 'Irish', and agricultural areas beyond its immediate hinterland (Cebulla and Smyth 1996: 40). This identity persisted despite there being an 'Irish' presence intimately involved in industry in the city throughout its history. Rather, the combination of rapid industrialization and lowland Scots' emphasis on commerce, industry, and Presbyterian values increasingly shaped wider loyalist identity and their understandings of themselves and 'industrial Belfast' as being entwined.

The interrelationship between industrialization and segregation was not unique to Belfast in the industrial world of the Global North. From the mid-nineteenth century onwards mass movement of migrant populations seeking work at a global level resulted in booming, segregated cities. It was common practice for new migrant groups to create ghettos and then integrate slowly into the pre-existing city structures (Boal 2002: 690). In this context, large numbers of Irish migrant workers practised a degree of self-imposed ghettoization in their new urban environments, where they were initially unwelcome, with the majority flocking to the cities of the UK or USA. However, unlike the Irish populations in Liverpool, Glasgow, Boston, Detroit, and Indianapolis (for the latter, see Singleton, Chapter 11) in Belfast this desire for physical security, safety, and support against the backdrop of a hostile environment showed little weakening over time. Belfast displayed some unique features for a migrant population: the colonial inhabitants who governed the city were a minority and remained insecure in their ability to control the larger 'Irish' populace. This insecurity was particularly significant as, unlike other cities that experienced an influx of Irish migrants during the mass industrialization of the nineteenth century, Belfast was in the unique position of being a 'British' city located within the island of Ireland. Thus the industrial city of Belfast was surrounded by both rurality and the new migrants' fellow countrymen. Intermixing undoubtedly did take place (as demonstrated in the artefactual assemblages analysed by Horning 2013), but the cyclical resurfacing of sectarian strife, which occurred from the time of the seventeenth-century plantations onwards, prevented complete rapprochement between the two self-perceived communities. The threat, as much as the actuality, of sectarian violence occurring at least once every generation from the late eighteenth century onwards resulted in an unwillingness by both Irish Catholic and British Protestants to fully integrate. In such a context A. C. Hepburn has shown that a long-term repercussion has been 'segregation increases more in bad times than it eases in good times' (Hepburn 2001: 93); and the formation of increasingly segregated workforces centring on particular areas of industrial Belfast acted to link the two phenomena.

The formation of the state of Northern Ireland, retained within the United Kingdom and constitutionally separate from the rest of Ireland, occurred with the Government of Ireland Act (1920). The partition of the island was a legal solution to increasing spatial delineation of the two majority ethnic communities on the island—Irish, nationalist, Catholic in the South; British, loyalist, Protestant in the North—legally enshrining the majorities in both parts of the island to maintain power and control. In Northern Ireland it facilitated the retention of political (and economic prosperity) for loyalists in a Unionist controlled economy focused on the industrial city of Belfast that continued for many decades (Cebulla and Smyth 1996: 45). The advent of the Troubles in the late 1960s accelerated and heightened pre-existing divisions that had been ever-present in the industrial city but at this time the solidification of religious segregation took place in a deindustrializing city. Pre-existing divisions increasingly materialized and solidified during the course of the conflict through the erection of so-called 'peace walls'; barriers created to stop interactions between the segregated communities. The most common form of peace walls are monumental walls that are placed at the interfaces between the two communities; however, they can take the form of landscaping, fencing, facilitated dereliction, urban planning, and road schemes that can be psychic as much as material divisions (see McAtackney 2011).

The relationship between industrialization, segregation, and communal identities that developed during the growth of Belfast as an industrial city, and exacerbated during its decline, have received little attention. However, it is clear that the differential effects of (de)industrialization have been deeply impacted by formalized, sectarian geographies. In particular, the areas associated with the loyalist, urban working classes (who primarily experienced the long-term benefits of industrialization) have experienced the most striking economic decline. The timeline of the transition of Belfast from the industrial to the post-industrial is particularly poignant in revealing its intertwining with sectarian conflict. Industrial Belfast was showing signs of decline from as early as the 1920s, but by the late 1960s most major industries had departed or were being drastically scaled down. Despite government intervention in the form of grants to attract investment, deindustrialization hit Northern Ireland simultaneous to areas associated with traditional industries across the UK. Where it differed from the rest of Britain was its differential impact on one community—working-class, Protestant, loyalist communities—and the intertwining with growing societal instability. No longer seen as efficient and cost-effective in comparison to the global shift to the industrial outputs of developing countries–a decisive factor in international companies looking elsewhere, not solely the threat of civic conflict (Frey et al. 2004: 17)—the shipbuilding, linen, manufacturing, and aeronautics industries in particular have dramatically scaled down and cease to be mass employers. Akin to other major industrial cities in the UK this steady decline was decades old before it became obvious from the late 1960s when it accelerated simultaneous to the eruption of sectarian civic conflict. In Belfast this was most evident in the locale of traditionally the biggest industrial employers, the shipyards of East Belfast.

Although divisions, usually based on socio-economic models, are common to many modern cities (Boal 1994: 30), factors that mark Belfast as distinct include heightened ethnic and sectarian identities, materialization of divisions and how that material form has evolved spatially and temporally. Clearly, the deindustrialization of Belfast has deeply impacted the communities located beside traditional industrial employers (see also González-Ruibal, Chapter 7; Penrose, Chapter 8; and Ryzewski, Chapter 3). However, differential experiences of deindustrialization within Belfast have been largely ignored outside of the realm of economic history in preference for an emphasis on ethnic conflict in explaining the transitioning nature of the post-conflict city. In the example of East Belfast, the interconnections between deindustrialization, the residual impacts of sectarian conflict, and the more recent emergence of anti-migrant racism in the contemporary demands examination. Indeed, the current interpretations of contemporary Belfast that emphasize the 'Troubles' legacy are unable to account for divergences in these responses across the city. Perhaps the contemporary malaise in loyalist East Belfast is not simply a legacy of 'the Troubles', it also connects to global experiences of the post-industrialized world?

9.2 CONTEMPORARY BELFAST: MEMORIALIZATION, COMMEMORATION, AND THE ISSUES OF 'DEALING WITH THE PAST'

Unofficial, community memorials commemorating the Troubles are a relatively recent but increasingly widespread phenomenon. These memorials are designed and implanted by members of the local community and are most frequently found in working-class, urban areas of Northern Ireland; the places most impacted by both deindustrialization and ethnic conflict. This phenomenon has been relatively under-researched in the context of the peace process (although, see Viggiani 2006), however, even a cursory examination reveals the proliferation of memorials follows global as well as local trends in materializing memory. Erika Doss, writing about the contemporary USA, has noted how memorialization is increasingly being used to remember a wide variety of people, events, and occasions (see also Shanahan and Shanahan, Chapter 5). She argues they are popular because of the potential for multiplicity of meanings and their ability to 'evoke memories, sustain thoughts, constitute political conditions and conjure states of being' (Doss 2010: 71). Community memorials to 'the Troubles' in the context of the Northern Irish peace process are especially significant in facilitating communities, or more precisely their self-appointed representatives, to materialize aspects of the past (almost exclusively related to the conflict) into the place where they are most meaningful. They act to fill the official vacuum that has arisen from politicians and civil society bypassing the difficult issues inherent in 'dealing with the past' (see McGrattan 2009).

Doss has argued that these memorials are particularly noteworthy because they do not simply materialize emotional responses to people, places, or events but they also claim states of being and therefore are inherently political in 'shaping and directing perceptions of social order, national identity and political transition' (Doss 2010: 10). Clearly their creation and placement in specific locations not only act to present locally accepted, and often one-sided, narratives of what happened in the past but also present hierarchies of who deserves to be remembered and how these memories should be articulated. Memorials are important because they tell us how the communities conceive local historical events, places, or people while simultaneously retaining the potential to reconfigure and direct memory in ways that are meaningful in the evolving contemporary.

How these memorial narratives are constructed, and interact, with aspects of deindustrialization is often overlooked due to the emphasis placed solely on remembering 'the Troubles'. This has ensured that academic analysis tends to focus on places most linked to sectarian conflict, especially nationalist West Belfast (see Viggiani 2006 and McAtackney 2015, 2011). In such instances memorials are read as articulating claims of victimhood and/or victories that are explicit in linking historic grievances resulting from sectarian conflict to contemporary conditions. However, I argue community memorialization in contemporary East Belfast reveals more complex and entangled narratives of place, identity, and conflict that rely on local understandings of the importance of deindustrialization as well as the recent conflict in the area. East Belfast is the only part of the city containing significant murals and public art related to the industrial past; reflecting the importance of industry to the area. Through exploring how community memorialization engages with recent deindustrialization, 'the Troubles', and other contemporary issues this chapter concludes by arguing for a need to connect global processes with local expression in understanding contemporary Belfast as a multifaceted and evolving city.

9.3 DEINDUSTRIALIZATION AND MEMORIALIZATION IN EAST BELFAST

Tensions between residents and new migrants groups have been a global experience of the industrial era often resulting from large-scale migrations to cities in short time scales accompanying economic booms. Historically, the majority of industrial migrants to Belfast originated from elsewhere in Ireland and the UK. They were a prominent group from the early nineteenth century until starting to slowly ebbing from the late 1920s. The impact of 'the Troubles' and declining industry resulted in only piecemeal migration from the 1960s until the signing of the Good Friday Agreement in 1998. Since that time Northern Ireland has seen an upturn in the number of migrants, often from emerging economies, including significant numbers of Eastern Europeans, South East Asians, and Africans. Many have chosen to settle in relatively inexpensive, centrally located, urban areas like East Belfast. In 2001 0.8 per cent of the population identified as being an ethnic minority; in 2011 this percentage rose to 1.8 per cent (Northern Ireland Statistics & Research Agency 2014). To break these numbers down further, in 1998 over 17,433 people moved to Northern Ireland (cf. 22,248 who left) and in 2012/13 this number rose to 23,100 (cf. 25,438 left). A highpoint of migration was reached before the recession in 2006/7 when 32,705 migrated (with only 21,755 leaving) (Northern Ireland Statistics & Research Agency 2015). Although these numbers are small they should be read against a backdrop of a total population of less than two million, Northern Ireland being historically an homogeneous society and the movement of migrants into largely working-class urban areas with highly developed senses of localized identity shaped by 'the Troubles'. The maintenance of sectarian geographies is an enduring remnant of 'the Troubles' with few Northern Ireland-born residents living in areas outside of their own ethnic group; this is especially true of urban, working-class areas. The contravening of these conventions by unwitting new migrants has been particularly noticeable and, at times, reacted to in aggressively negative ways. With this small rise in migrant numbers, particularly during a significant and long-term economic recession, there has been a rise in tensions and manifestations of racism often related to maintenance of housing areas as 'belonging' to traditional communities and accusations of migrants 'taking' local jobs. Racist graffiti—often daubed on the houses of migrants—have become a feature of recent years adding a new layer to the existing problems of positive placemaking that sectarian street art had previously dominated.

The Newtownards Road in East Belfast is a revealing case study to explore the interconnections of various facets of contemporary identity in the city that derive from long-ignored impacts of deindustrialization combining with emerging issues of increasing migrant populations as well as the omnipresent legacies of the Troubles. The Newtownards Road is an arterial road to/from the city centre that cuts through East Belfast and acts as a highly colourful focus of negotiation between unofficial claiming of space and official attempts at placemaking. The contest between these two types of sense of place is materialized in a significant number of high profile representations of local identity located in graffiti, murals, memorials, and officially sanctioned public art and murals in the area. Following Rodney Harrison, I argue that one must view such manifestations as a collective form of heritage rather than study them in isolation as they reveal where the power to materialize and direct memory lies. Together they materialize how the community they are located in can 'remake the past in a way that facilitates certain actions or viewpoints in the present' (2010: 154). Therefore, enduring proliferation of paramilitary and sectarian imagery, extensive numbers of national and paramilitary flags, and emerging daubing of racist graffiti must be considered alongside semi-permanent memorials and officially funded public art. Such a holistic approach to exploring East Belfast is necessary due to many memorializing forms coexisting, being accepted by the local community due to their temporo-spatial meaningfulness and being read by bypassers in various ways as reflecting the identity of the locale.

The difficulties inherent in freeing town centres and arterial roads, such as the Newtowards Road, from aggressive displays of sectionalism and racism while simultaneously retaining the rights of communities to materially articulate their identities is a tension that has been addressed in the recent government document *Shared Future* (2005). *Shared Future* has emphasized the importance of place and placemaking in transforming areas associated with conflict and tensions into neutral, welcoming places. However, the practicalities of achieving a significant change in meaning of place in a still divided society are evident in the limited aims of *Shared Future*. This document has focused on initiatives such as clearing arterial roads and town centres of paramilitary and offensive murals, graffiti, and flags while leaving the alleyways and minor roads of estates largely unchanged (OFMDFM 2005: 21). Even with these limited aims there is material evidence that official attempts at positive placemaking are being subverted when the Newtownards Road is examined as a single entity.

9.3.1 Public Art, Sponsored Murals, and the *Titanic*

Prominent public body-funded wall murals and public art depicting the *Titanic* on the Lower Newtownards Road reveals the importance of the historic shipbuilding industry to the area. Wall murals were created under the auspices of the Re-Imaging programme, a project initiated by Belfast City Council in 2005. The programme was funded for an initial three years with the aim of replacing the most sectarian and aggressive wall murals throughout the city, but due to its success it was funded for a further fifteen months (Crowley 2011: 27). Re-imaging murals have increasingly engaged with the importance of authenticity and location in placemaking by directly referencing spatio-temporally meaningful subjects. On the Newtownards Road the *Titanic* has been a dominant subject due to its role in representing the importance of the shipbuilding industry to the area. The *Titanic*, a ship built in East Belfast that infamously sank on its maiden voyage in 1912, may seem an unlikely identity-affirming symbol. However, for the local community it has become increasingly significant as a means of articulating a broader, superficially non-sectarian identity for Belfast and more specifically the proud tradition of shipbuilding of the loyalist working classes in East Belfast.

With the centenary of the sinking of the *Titanic* occurring in 2012, public and political interest in the ship reached a peak with a state-of-the-art, multi-million pound museum built in the vicinity of the historic shipyards to attract paying tourists in time for the centenary. The more negative aspects of the city's links with shipbuilding—including historic problems with cyclical anti-Catholic pogroms, insidious sectarianism, and the impact of deindustrialization on the working-class loyalists—have been largely ignored in the museum. These partial narratives have been extended to the public art situated on the Newtownards Road. Mirroring the shiny *Titanic* museum (Colour plate 10, bottom), murals and public art have concentrated on depicting a cautiously celebratory mixture of pride in superior workmanship and the opulence of first-class passage tempered by respect for the substantial loss of life associated with the ship's sinking.

Shipyards were traditionally, and continue to be, strongly connected with loyalist, working-class identity due to the segregated workforce in the city and the perception that industry 'belonged' to the loyalist working classes. Furthermore, Cebulla and Smyth have argued the shipyards played a significant role in creating the segregated city. The spatiality of industrialization was constituted to reinforce the realities of loyalist dominance and nationalist exclusion creating economic as well as segregated geographies (1996: 45). Conversely, this historical privilege has ensured that loyalist identity has been more deeply impacted by the loss and scaling down of these traditional workplaces resulting in the undermining of an identity based on productiveness and an employment monopoly. Despite the longevity of deindustrialization in the area this is an enduring issue due to the continuing lack of replacement employment. East Belfast now has significant problems with long-term, inter-generational unemployment with little perceived options for generations of young men, in particular.

As shipyards were almost entirely all-male environments, and segregation and sectarianism was more pronounced than in female-orientated workplaces (Byrne 1980), this has ensured a noticeably macho and aggressive response to the loss of industry. The almost exclusively male experiences of deindustrialization in the area was not a universal experience of industrial Belfast. It differs dramatically from the female dominant places of industrial employment in North Belfast's tobacco factories or West Belfast's linen mills. This highly gendered experience of industry in East Belfast is communicated in the forms of memorialization in the area, which are almost completely absent of female presence. The entanglement of memory of lost male industry alongside the current reality of significant deprivation and unemployment, also most notable amongst young men, may explain the aggressive and at times violent reaction to migrants settling in this area. For while the *Titanic* memorializes a proud, industrial heritage it also implicitly reinforces feelings of lost, male supremacy that loyalist working classes connect with the terminal decline of the nearby shipyards. Such a complicated reality is often ignored in preferences for myopic 'Troubles'-focused explanations for the ills of contemporary Belfast that are often also gender-blind (see Murphy 2015). They not only exclude the many narratives of women from these areas but implicitly allow

Figure 9.1. 'Ship of Dreams' re-imaged mural off the Newtownards Road, East Belfast. Photo by Laura McAtackney, 2013.

predominantly male issues of acceptable levels of violence and continuing loyalist paramilitary activity to be naturalized and normalized as universal and acceptable.

There are a number of *Titanic* murals of varying age, perspective, and levels of completion in East Belfast. Focusing on one of the re-imaged murals created around the centenary of the sinking of the *Titanic* in 2012 reveals it combines text and images to create a composite that has multiple layers of meaning (Figure 9.1). This includes a representation of the ship prior to the disaster, a number of images of those most associated with its building and sailing and the phrases *'Built in Belfast'* and *'Ship of Dreams'* as framing devices that connect to other re-imaged murals and public art initiatives in the area. To ensure there is no misinterpretation of the various elements of the mural the innovation of a plaque detailing the meanings of symbols and the names of those depicted, with a short biography, is embedded in the wall prominently alongside the mural. The presentation of the *Titanic* as sea-borne rather than sinking is a deliberate rhetorical device that avoids overconcentration on negative associations and thereby allows for flexibility of interpretation and the potential to conflate aspects of the *Titanic* with more positive and con-temporary meanings (see Renshaw 2011 for discussion of this use of photo-graphs in the context of remembering the Spanish Civil War). The materiality of this mural is significant in that it incorporates endurable 3-D plastic elements to create the main body of the design with only the background painted; an increasingly popular innovation employed in re-imaged murals that contrasts with wholly painted, community murals.

There are numerous reasons for this innovation. Aesthetically, the use of printed images is more true to the originals; using extant photographic images rather than relying on the inconsistencies of painted representations. Most importantly, they are also more enduring and therefore do not need frequent updating or invite easy eradication. Whereas a painted mural can easily be defaced, painted over or paint bombed, the 3-D plastic panels would need to be removed from the wall before effective repainting could take place and they also survive longer without requiring updating. This is especially import- ant given McCormick and Jarman's estimate that painted murals need some updating, or to have elements repainted, at six-monthly intervals (McCormick and Jarman 2005). The acceptance of a re-imaged mural at such a location— that is, it has not been vandalized or defaced, as happens when imposed murals have been 'rejected'—is significant as wall murals communicate the significance of their message and link to their wider context through place- ment as well as subject matter (McCormick and Jarman 2005: 51). Therefore, maintaining a re-imaged mural on a gable wall abutting a major thoroughfare in East Belfast over an extended time period is important. Clearly, the com- munity's proximity to the Harland & Woolf shipyards, where the *Titanic* was built, ensures the subject matter is still poignant and relevant; its enduring presence reveals the ongoing importance of the shipyard in local self-identity.

A local connection to the Titanic is further reaffirmed through a public art sculpture situated in close proximity. *Titanic Yardmen 401* was created by local artist Ross Wilson and was given a high profile unveiling by a cross-party group of politicians on 28 March 2012 (Figure 9.2). Again accompanied by an associated plaque it leaves no doubt as to the local and celebratory nature of its meaning with reference to '*East Belfast's shipbuilding force*' and its aim as '*a tribute to their culture, life and legacy. To the memory of men who built giants*'. The unveiling was widely reported in the media as marking the highpoint of the re-imaging project in the area that used the '*Ship of Dreams*' motif as a recurring theme in an attempt to emphasize placemaking initiatives to reframe the Newtownards Road as a historic industry powerhouse (*Belfast Telegraph* 2012). Like the wall mural, the bronze sculptures remain unsullied; empha- sizing the subject matter remains meaningful. It was also thoughtfully located. The Yardmen are adjacent to the side road where the majority of the Harland & Wolff workers would have journeyed home after working in the shipyards and the still-standing cranes of the shipyard act as an iconic backdrop. Despite the successful integration of this public art motif, it is still problematic as the representation of industrial East Belfast is unreflexively celebrating an andro- centric, industrial past rather than a diverse, post-industrial present. This is

(a)

(b)

TITANIC YARDMEN 401

The Yardmen is a Titanic centenary sculpture that celebrates the history and achievements of East Belfast's shipbuilding workforce. The people of Belfast are proud of their shipbuilding heritage. For over 150 years the names Harland and Wolff have been universally known for excellence in shipbuilding. Thousands of men worked and sustained their families through the yards order books. The shipyards years of production saw the creation of 1,700 large ships the most famous being the Titanic, a great ship now locked into worldwide history and romantic myth, fact and myth riveted together.

This sculpture honours all generations of Yardmen and is a tribute to their culture, life and legacy. To the memory of men who built giants.

4011541912

Figure 9.2. Top: (a) *Titanic Yardman 401* Bronze sculpture collective on Lower Newtownards Road; unveiled 2012; photograph taken by Laura McAtackney, 2013. Bottom: (b) associated plaque interpreting *Titanic Yardman 401*. Photo by Laura McAtackney, 2013.

problematic in moving away from reifying the past, acknowledging gender as a facet of identity and referencing the continuing problems of deindustrialization. However, one needs to explore the context of their wider setting, and how these official manifestations of public art fit into and conflate other, unofficial identifiers on the road, to appreciate their true place in local identity.

9.3.2 Unofficial Murals, Community Memorials, and Racist Graffiti

Jostling alongside official and re-imagined public art, the majority of murals and memorials are unofficial and reflect community manifestations of memory and identity that reference a wider range of meaningful contemporary subjects. The most common were commissioned by and celebrate paramilitary organizations, commemorate the dead from these groups, and/or attempt to claim their historical predecessors. There are varying degrees of explicit and implicit links and references to contemporary paramilitary activities in the many murals and memorials on the Lower Newtownards Road; few are completely free of paramilitary associations. The majority of memorials and murals are elaborate, colourful, and often utilize monumental forms; they are not dwarfed or overwhelmed by the neighbouring re-imaged *Titanic* murals and public art. By analysing these community murals and memorials we can begin to understand how meaning of place is directed in totality and how the multiple identities co-exist and interrelate in East Belfast (Bryan et al. 2010: 38–9).

One of the many explicit paramilitary murals in the vicinity appears on a gable end wall close to the *Titanic* re-imaged mural and public art sculpture. It commemorates '*Ulster's Present Day Defenders*' in a composition that directly references through replication of theme and form a nearby mural commemorating '*Ulster's Past Defenders*' (Colour plate 11). Both murals are triptychs with the centre encompassing an insignia (for 'Ulster's Present Day Defenders' this is the paramilitary group 'UDA' [Ulster Defence Association]) and either side depicting uniformed men. On the left is a full-length, frontal representation of a man wearing sunglasses—a common representation of a loyalist paramilitary from the 1970s—holding a book entitled 'members' and on the right a full-length, frontally orientated, camouflaged and balaclaved figure holds a semi-automatic gun pointing out of the image. The overt aggression of a gun pointing from a mural has been a relatively rare mural form in peace process Northern Ireland. However, alongside the re-emergence of explicitly paramilitary murals since 2010, such militaristic images are becoming more common as uncertainties grow about the real benefits, and beneficiaries, of the peace process (Bryan et al. 2010: 41). The text boxes placed below the images of the men likewise follow the trajectory of the images in displaying different degrees of menace. In the left text box the paramilitary reference is explicitly

Figure 9.3. Frontal representation of an unofficial memorial to RHC [Red Hand Commandos] dead located in an alley off the Lower Newtownards Road. Photo by Laura McAtackney, 2013.

contemporary rather than maintaining any pretence at being historical: 'The UDA was formed / in 1971 as an umbrella / for Loyalist Vigilante groups / which claimed to defend the / Protestant community from / IRA Violence. They Remain today.'

There are at least half a dozen community memorials either located on the Newtownards Road or visually accessible from it. They commemorate different aspects of the past, with some more explicitly related to sectarian conflict than others. Alongside memorials dedicated to Ulster's war dead from World War I—who are presented as direct ancestors of the contemporary community and by implication their contemporary 'defenders'—are memorials that commemorate loyalist paramilitary organizations and their members. Memorial gardens to both the UDA (Ulster Defence Association) and the Red Hand Commandos (Figure 9.3) are placed in separate side streets that are physically and visually accessible from the main road. These memorials display similarities—they both take the form of monumental structures with metal railings to allow visual, if not physical, access at all times. Inside the memorials there are plaques with paramilitary insignia and a list of members from the locale who died during the Troubles. In contrast to many of the nationalist memorials of the Troubles (see

McAtackney 2011) the memorials viewed during fieldwork in East Belfast in the summers of 2013/14 exclusively commemorated only male, active combatants from designated paramilitary organizations. Small plaques with lists of male names were displayed behind padlocked gates, ensuring the memorials were visually accessible but acted as exclusive, gendered spaces. This interpretation was affirmed when two local men, intrigued by my interest in the memorial, told me with a sinister laugh I would need to join the UVF (Ulster Volunteer Force) to gain access.

Alongside the more traditional memorials, murals, and flags the appearance of racist graffiti has become more prominent and commonplace alongside the Newtownards Road, corresponding with the perceived rise in the number of migrants living in the vicinity. Racist graffiti is not confined to East Belfast—or indeed to the very recent past—however, it has become increasingly prominent in the area and its placement and acceptance follows the argument made already in this chapter that such materializations are spacially specific identity markers. All materializations of memory and identity in such areas are meaningful therefore large-scale and site-specific racist graffiti must be included as a facet of placemaking due to its prominence and visibility in articulating an exclusionary place identity. Racist slogans in Belfast are usually daubed in highly public locations, such as along main roads, at intersections or interfaces, or, even more menacingly, on the front doors and living-room windows of recent migrants.

The appearance of racist graffiti have been especially prominent in the summer; traditionally a time of heightened sectarian tensions due to commemorative marches that coincide with long school holidays and bright summer nights when confrontation and rioting have historically occurred in Northern Ireland (Jarman and O'Halloran 2001). The temporality of racist graffiti acts to reaffirm and extend already exclusive local identities with the rejection of the contemporary other (new migrants) alongside the historical other (nationalists). As many of these attacks are not isolated incidents—it was claimed by the PSNI in July 2014 that some attacks in East Belfast were been 'orchestrated to spread fear' by attacking a number of homes on the same night (*Belfast Newsletter* 2014)—it is clear that racist graffiti is an organized attempt to reinforce the maintenance of a particular conception of East Belfast. Attempts to explain the appearance of racist graffiti often reference the loss of industry as much as perversions of social norms associated with 'the Troubles'. This includes the impact of lost official conduct codes associated with local employment in the shipyards (*Belfast Newsletter* 2014). Clearly, while the silent majority of the community do not participate in, or even support, such attacks, their appearance is perceived as being directly related to disaffection with the particularities of contemporary life in East Belfast; a life that includes the global impacts of deindustrialization as well as local experiences of sectarian conflict.

9.4 CONCLUSION

Bryan et al. have argued that the Newtownards Road in East Belfast is a place where the wider public read the relationship between murals, memorials, flags, and graffiti as explicitly acting as paramilitary territorial markers that are aggressive and exclusionary due to the layering and interconnection of meaning derived from their collective presence (2010: 38–9). There is a need to further extend this interpretation to include the flexibility and superfluity of meaning inherent in the interplay of traditional and emerging identity markers that are not simply related to 'the Troubles'. By including historical industrial images located in contemporary East Belfast one can see that not all contemporary facets of identity were formed by, or relate to, sectarian violence. One must include representations of (post-)industrialization—what it means and how it is being represented and interpreted—as well as racist graffiti as part of this exclusionary identity that directly feeds from the largely unarticulated but continuing impacts of deindustrialization in the city.

Exploring all manifestations of public and community art in East Belfast reveals that far from promoting a wholly positive place identity, officially sanctioned public art and murals celebrating historical industrial might without including gender, negative associations, and the devastating impact of deindustrialization is problematic. Whereas the *Titanic* is being used to promote past industrial greatness, it also implicitly references a sectarian economy that largely excluded minorities and women from their workplaces. These facets of industrialization, when considered alongside the wider context of sectarian, paramilitary, and exclusionary murals and memorials, reinforces the current aggressively, exclusionary place identity of the Newtownards Road. Together the public art and memorials act as a reminder of the community's past industry that excludes female experiences and roles and directly links to feelings of masculine lost supremacy that it is open to manipulation and re-articulation in increasingly intolerant ways when read in its wider landscape.

Taking a contemporary archaeological approach to examining East Belfast reveals it as a deprived, deindustrialized place (in contrast to Penrose's creative destructions in London, Liverpool, and Salford) that is increasingly, if unwillingly, housing new, transient populations. It is not just a working-class, inner city community afflicted by the traumas of 'the Troubles'. By analysing in totality the collection of memorials, murals, public art, and racist graffiti a local identity that holds unreflexive memories of past industrial glory; continues to suffer the impacts of deindustrialization; maintains a threatened identity; and actively wishes to exclude an evolving 'other' is revealed. In order to address these negative aspects of identity there is a need to move beyond a blinkered focus on 'dealing with the past' that implicitly means only 'the Troubles'. Instead, we must broadly conceive the negative associations—and impacts—of loyalist industrial and post-industrial experiences. In recognizing the differential impacts of (de)industrialization in Belfast we can enable places like East Belfast to remember and celebrate the past in ways that are nuanced but not exclusionary of others and allow a more positive loyalist identity to emerge by recognizing exactly what it is emerging from.

ACKNOWLEDGEMENTS

Many thanks to my colleagues and friends who presented and attended the Wenner Gren workshop in Detroit in August 2014. It was such a joy to have the opportunity to discuss these ideas with you all over the days of the workshop in a supportive but critically engaged environment. For the support of the research, Wenner Gren are primarily to be thanked for funding the workshop and the John Hume Institute for Global Irish Studies at University College Dublin for funding the research that this paper developed from originally (and my colleagues and friends—including the Director Brian Jackson and my fellow scholars including Aoibhín de Búrcá, Stefanie Lehner, Cillian McGrattan—for their support and questions).

REFERENCES

Belfast (Good Friday) Agreement. 1998. *Belfast Agreement*. Belfast: HMSO.
Belfast Newsletter. 2014. 'East Belfast racist attacks "orchestrated" to spread fear'. 29 July 2014. http://www.newsletter.co.uk/news/regional/east-belfast-racist-attacks-orchestrated-to-spread-fear-1-6206980 (accessed December 2014).
Belfast Telegraph. 2012. 'Titanic workers sculpture unveiled'. 28 March 2012. http://www.belfasttelegraph.co.uk/news/local-national/northern-ireland/titanic-workers-sculpture-unveiled-28731593.html (accessed 28 March 2012).
Boal, Frederick W. 1994. 'Encapsulation: Urban dimensions of national conflict'. In *Managing Divided Cities*, edited by Seamus Dunn, Keele: Keele University Press, pp. 30–41.
Boal. Frederick W. 2002. 'Belfast: Walls within', *Political Geography*, 21: 687–94.
Bryan, Dominic, Clifford Stevenson, Gordon Gillespie, and John Bell. 2010. *Public Display of Flags and Emblems in Northern Ireland 2006–2009*. Belfast: Institute of Irish Studies.
Buchli, Victor and Gavin Lucas. 2001. 'The archaeology of alienation. A late twentieth-century British council house'. In *Archaeologies of the Contemporary Past*, edited by Victor Buchli and Gavin Lucas, London: Routledge, pp. 158–67.
Byrne, David. 1980. 'The De-industrialisation of Northern Ireland', *Antipode*, 11(2): 87–96.
Cebulla, Andrea and Jim Smyth. 1996. 'Disadvantage and New Prosperity in Restructured Belfast', *Capital and Class*, 60: 39–59.
Crowley, Tony. 2011. 'The Art of Memory: the Murals of Northern Ireland and the Management of History', *Field Day Review* 7: 23–49.

Doss, Erika. 2010. *Memorial Mania: public feeling in America*. London: University of Chicago Press.

Gallagher, Elizabeth, Brandon Hamber, and Elaine Joy. 2012. 'Perspectives and Possibilities: Mental Health in post-Agreement Northern Ireland', *Shared Space*, 13(March): 63–78.

Finlay, Andrew. 2001. 'Defeatism and Northern Protestant Identity', *The Global Review of Ethnopolitics*, 1(2): 3–20.

Frey, Bruno S., Simon Leuchinger, and Alois Stutzer. 2004. 'Calculating Tragedy: Assessing the costs of Terrorism', *Working Paper Series: Institute for Empirical Research in Economics*, University of Zurich. Working Paper 205, pp. 1–32.

Harrison, Rodney. 2010. 'The politics of heritage'. In *Understanding the politics of heritage*, edited by Rodney Harrison, Manchester: University of Manchester Press, pp. 154–97.

Hepburn, A. C. 2001. 'Long division and ethnic conflict: The experience of Belfast'. In *Managing Divided Cities*, edited by Seamus Dunn, Keele: Keele University Press, pp. 88–105.

Horning, Audrey. 2013. *Ireland in the Virginian Sea: Colonialism in the British Atlantic*. Chapel Hill: University of North Caroline Press.

Irish News. 2005. 'The Road to Normalisation', 28 August 2005.

Jarman, Neil and Chris O'Halloran. 2001. 'Recreational rioting: Young people, interface areas and violence', *Childcare in Practice*, 7(1): 2–16.

McAtackney, Laura. 2011. 'Peace maintenance and political messages: the significance of walls during and after the "Troubles" in Northern Ireland', *Journal of Social Archaeology*, 11(1): 77–98.

McAtackney, Laura. 2015. 'Memorials and marching: archaeological insights into segregation in contemporary Northern Ireland', *Historical Archaeology*, 49(3): 110–25.

McAuley, James. 2003. 'Unionisms Last Stand? Contemporary Unionist Politics and Identity in Northern Ireland', *The Global Review of Ethnopolitics*, 30(1): 60–74.

McCormick, Jonathan and Neil Jarman. 2005. 'Death of a Mural', *Journal of Material Culture Studies*, 10(1): 49–71.

McGrattan, Cillian. 2009. '"Order Out of Chaos": the Politics of Transitional Justice', *Politics*, 29(3): 164–72.

Mercer, David. 2014. 'Hate crime against gay people is on the rise in Northern Ireland', *Belfast Telegraph*, 26 Nov 2014. http://www.belfasttelegraph.co.uk/news/local-national/northern-ireland/hate-crime-against-gay-people-is-on-the-rise-in-northern-ireland-30774921.html (accessed November 2014).

Murphy, Andrée. 2015. 'Why is the debate on dealing with the past in Northern Ireland gender blind?' http://eamonnmallie.com/2015/05/why-is-the-debate-on-dealing-with-the-past-in-northern-gender-blind-by-andree-murphy/ (accessed August 2016).

Northern Ireland Statistics & Research Agency. 2014. *Census 2011. Key Statistics Summary Report. September 2014*. Belfast: NIMA. Also available at: http://www.nisra.gov.uk/archive/census/2011/results/key-statistics/summary-report.pdf (accessed August 2016).

Northern Ireland Statistics & Research Agency. 2015. *The Population of Northern Ireland*. Belfast: NIMA. Also available at: http://www.nisra.gov.uk/demography/default.asp18.htm (accessed March 2015).

OFMDFM. 2005. *Shared Future—Policy and Strategic Framework for Good Relations in Northern Ireland*. Belfast: HMSO.

Orange, Hilary (ed.). 2014. *Reanimating Industrial Spaces: Conducting Memory Work in Post-industrial Societies*. Walnut Creek, California: Left Coast Press.

Renshaw, Layla. 2011. *Exhuming Loss: memory, materiality and the Mass Graves of the Spanish Civil War*. Walnut Creek, California: Left Coast Press.

Stewart, Gerard. 2013. 'An Assessment of Racial Violence in Northern Ireland: A comment. 12 December', Institute of Race Relations. http://www.irr.org.uk/news/an-assessment-of-racial-violence-in-northern-ireland/ (accessed December 2014).

Stewart, Gerard. 2014. 'An overview of racist attacks and convictions in Northern Ireland', Institute of Race Relations, 10 April. www.irr.org.uk/news/spotlight-on-racial-violence-northern-ireland (accessed July 2014).

Tomlinson, T. 2007. *The Trouble with suicide: mental health, suicide and the Northern Ireland conflict*. Belfast: Queens University.

Viggiani, Elizabeth. 2006. *Public forms of memorialisation to the 'Victims of the Northern Irish Troubles' in the City of Belfast*. MA Thesis. Queen's University of Belfast.

Whyte, James. 1990. *Interpreting Northern Ireland*. Oxford: Clarendon Press.

Zimmerman, Larry, Courtney Singleton, and Jessica Welch. 2010. 'Activism and creating a translational archaeology of homelessness', *World Archaeology*, 42(3): 443–54.

10

A Renaissance with Revenants

Images Gathered from the Ruins of Cape Town's Districts One and Six

Christian Ernsten

'How can I say what these fragments mean to me? The awkward truths of my life take shape in their negative spaces. In the lengthening shadows of the official histories, looming like triumphal arches over every small, messy life, these scraps saved from the onrush of the ordinary are the last signs I can bring myself to consult.'

Neville Lister (Vladislavić 2011: 174)

10.1 AFTERLIFE

In this chapter I explore District One and District Six, two inner-city areas in Cape Town, South Africa, by means of a series of images gathered from its ruins. As a point of departure I quote Neville Lister. Lister is the first-person narrator of Ivan Vladislavić's novel *Double Negative* (2011). He is a white middle-class young man from Johannesburg whose life overlaps with the city's post-apartheid transformation. Vladislavić's story, in which Lister becomes a photographer, was inspired by a volume of photographs of Johannesburg taken by renowned South African photographer David Goldblatt (Goldblatt 2010). As his protagonist finds himself in the post-apartheid city, Vladislavić highlights the complexities of attempts at representing a coherent visual narrative regarding South Africa's disjunctive urban history.

Over the course of the last decade or so I have visited Cape Town many times. My personal life converged with the city's transformation as a result of fortuitous encounters I had first as a student, then as a tourist, and finally as a researcher. The six photographs discussed as part of this chapter are the product of collaborations in 2013 and 2014. Recalling the epigraph of Bettina Malcomess and Dorothee Kreutzfeldt's book about Johannesburg, *Not No Place* (2013), I suggest the impressions conveyed by the images include, at best, 'fragments of spaces and times' representing post-apartheid Cape Town. Referring to Walter Benjamin and Thomas More, Malcomess and Kreutzfeldt describe the capture of the 'double negative' of the utopia (translated as 'no place'), the materialization of 'impossibility and always deferred potential' (Malcomess and Kreutzfeldt 2013: 12). Like these critics, I focus on the difficulty of capturing the complex transformation undergone by Cape Town's District One and District Six (see also Penrose, Chapter 8, for issues in capturing complex, capitalist transitions).

Cape Town appeared as number one on the *New York Times* list '52 places to go to in 2014'. Journalist Sarah Khan wrote, 'Cape Town is reinventing itself, and the world is invited to its renaissance' (Khan 2014). It is a story about boutique shops, property values, gentrification, self-stylization, and the self-conscious craft of hipster appeal. I am interested in the meaning of this renaissance, and of the image of the city as the ultimate holiday destination and African creative metropolis. I am interested in the images of Cape Town, which are othered as a consequence of this reinvention. Following Gayatri Spivak, I do not consider the qualities of District One and District Six to be mirror images, since they would then depict merely 'the self othering the other, indefinitely' (Spivak 2012: 16). Instead I attempt to reach beyond the hopeful rhetoric of reinvention. I intend to reach to the others who inhabit the negative spaces of modernity (see also González-Ruibal, Chapter 7). Reiterating theorist Jacques Derrida, Spivak proposes use of the empathetic power of imagination as way of 'touching of the distant other' (Spivak 2012: 68).

Against the backdrop of the work of other scholars on the visual discourse of southern Africa's history (Grendon et al. 2015; Hartmann et al. 2001; Judin and Vladislavić 1998; O'Connell 2013, 2015; Shepherd 2015a; Skotness 1996), this chapter attempts to understand how the materiality of the ruined landscape of the city of Cape Town offers ways of experiencing degraded personhoods of both the past and present. District One and District Six resonate with Cape Town's unresolved histories of slavery, colonialism, and apartheid. The stories of these places begin in the seventeenth century—specifically 1652—with the Dutch East India Company's arrival at the Cape. The afterlife thereof, including subsequent struggles of the Khoi, the indigenous people of the Cape, of individuals brought to the colony as slaves, and of those removed during apartheid, plays out in the contemporary city as a 'ruin memory' (Shepherd 2013). Following Grendon et al. (2015: 19) my aim in this chapter includes a 'fractured uncovering' and the construction of 'space for openings and prospects' of different experiences of the city.

As I consider the challenge at hand, a number of questions come to mind: how to construct a narrative in the present that consists of images concerning the ruins of a violent past? What is this empathic power of imagination? I am drawn to an analysis of W. G. Sebald's novel *Austerlitz* (2001); cultural-studies scholar Silke Arnold-de Simine argues that this story can be read as a project of 'secondary witnessing' with regards to the traumas of the Holocaust. Images are central to the narrative as they function 'to assist remembrance and to accrue remembrance' via contextual association. Arnold-de Simine suggests that instead of straightforward access to the past Sebald insists on 'the painful dissociation between past and present, experience and memory, seeing and knowing, self and other'. Following this, I compose a story about the ruined material afterlives of District One and District Six, relying solely upon found images and their 'associative and imaginative correspondences and analogies, on real and virtual connections' (Arnold-de Simine 2012: 27–30).

10.2 LAND

A linear timeline locates the two districts on the edges of the old colonial grid-city. Before the arrival of Jan van Riebeeck and the Dutch East India Company, these areas belonged to the Khoi. The nineteenth-century expansion of the city of Cape Town forced its way into the site of formal and informal burial grounds north-west of the city and east into the freehold slave-holding farm Zonnebloem ('sunflower'). The burial grounds and farmlands were subsequently subdivided and sold as real estate; in consequence, Districts One and Six were formed. George Thompson's plan of Cape Town (developed in 1827) gives an impression (Figure 10.1). It is actually a mirror image: the sea should be north of the city. District One's burial grounds are visible on the bottom right and District Six starts above the castle.

To continue the aggregated history: these areas would have been the neighbourhoods of the creolized working classes in the nineteenth-century colonial city, the slums of the garden city, and, at last, communities impacted by apartheid's Group Area Act during the twentieth century. The latter period had devastating impacts on the cityscape during the 1960s and 1970s, coloured and black residents were removed by force; most of their houses were destroyed as part of a programme of slum clearance. From the 1980s on, District Six became the site of community activism and of a counter-discourse regarding historical justice and land restitution. In the post-apartheid city, particularly in the context of preparations made for the 2010 FIFA World Cup and the 2014 World Design Capital, both districts became the dreamscapes of a global Cape Town. As such, they were transformed; rapid gentrification and new forms of spatial exclusion ensued (Ernsten 2014).

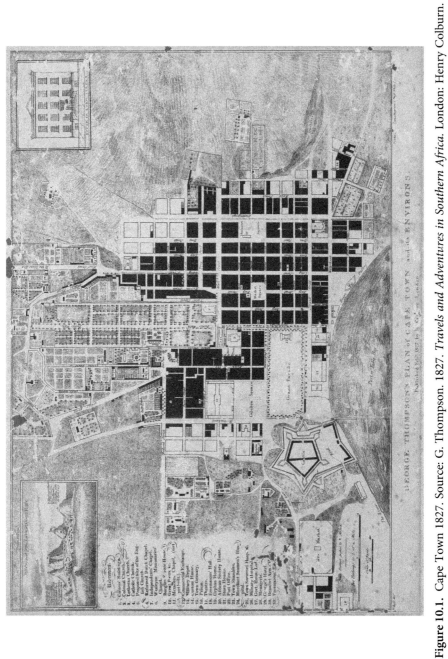

Figure 10.1. Cape Town 1827. Source: G. Thompson. 1827. *Travels and Adventures in Southern Africa*. London: Henry Colburn.

In 2013 I engaged with this particular history of the city in the framework of 'Land', a public event hosted by the Gordon Institute of Performing Arts ('GIPCA') in Cape Town. I worked as programme assistant to choreographer Jay Pather, director of the GIPCA. The year 2013 marked the centennial commemoration of the infamous South African Native Land Act of 1913. This piece of legislation formalized the material inscription of colonization, as it decreed that only 13 per cent of South African territory could be owned legally by 'natives' (Anonymous 2013b). GIPCA's 'Land' project—a response to this centennial—comprised a four-day event, including a programme of performance and visual art and a series of public lectures held in Cape Town. The programme was designed to address issues of ownership, historical trauma, restitution, and art in the city. The performances, lectures, and exhibitions took place in various city spaces that bore historical significance and embodied contemporary contestation. Two of these spaces were District One and District Six. I use 'Land' as a way of opening my story concerning these two areas.

10.3 HOMAGE

This night-time scene (Colour plate 12) is dated 21 November 2013 and was taken at the corner of District One's Somerset and Buitengracht Streets. It shows a woman and man dressed in white; their skins have been painted white; in the background, a car is passing. The frame captures a moment of expectation—the performance of two individuals seated on a wall in front of the Prestwich ossuary building. They stare off into the distance. The man and woman are dancers from the Jazzart Dance Theatre, performing a piece named 'Waiting for Rain'. Artistic director Jacqueline Manyaapelo describes it as 'a fusion of ritualistic calls to ancestors and spirit forms using indigenous instruments' (Anonymous 2013a). Just before this photo was taken, the GIPCA's 'Land' event officially began. Archaeologist Nick Shepherd was one of the keynote speakers, addressing the audience, including myself, at the ossuary he said:

> We meet in a haunted space ... We share this space with 1624 boxes of human remains. (GIPCA 2013a)

What is the meaning of ritualistic calls to the ancestors? And why is this ossuary a haunted space?

Shepherd refers to Derrida's term 'hauntology', meaning history's 'disavowed terms, absent presences and spectral remains' (Shepherd 2013: 241). The ancestors, in this case boxed and stored at the memorial, are the unidentified dead who were exhumed from District One in increments since 2003 (CoCT 2013).

Of all the exhumations at District One since work began in 1994, the 2003 disinterment of the dead of Prestwich Street, a mere block from the ossuary, was documented most widely (Jonker and Till 2009; Ralphs 2008; Shepherd 2007a: 14, 2007b; Shepherd and Ernsten 2007; Shepherd 2015b). The informal burial ground at Prestwich Street furnished the largest archaeological unearthing of human remains to have taken place in South Africa. The individuals buried here (of which there were more than a thousand) constituted the colonial underclasses: slaves, free blacks, artisans, fishermen, sailors, maids, washerwomen and their children, executed criminals, suicide deaths, paupers, and the unidentified victims of shipwrecks (Tim Hart, pers comm, 2003). Their discovery—as a by-product of the construction on a luxury development—spurred a public outcry.

The controversy that followed focused on the meanings of justice and restitution, specifically those that bear upon the urban transformation of District One generally, and Prestwich Street particularly. Indeed, some Capetonians—in particular, two who were removed forcibly from District One during apartheid—claimed they were descendants of these dead. Moreover, they argued that the burial site should remain where it was and be developed into a national heritage site (Malan 2003: 10).

History followed a different course, however. The discovery of the dead at Prestwich Street did not constitute a moment of seizure, of recognition of the process of witness-bearing when it came to the horrors of historical dehumanization of black bodies, and memories associated with slavery and apartheid's forced removals (Shepherd 2013). The fate of the resurfaced dead remained 'the death of the subject who is considered dead before actually dying', to quote Nelson Maldonado-Torres (2011: 17). The dead of District One would be exhumed only to be reinserted into a past already neat and organized. In fact, their new home, the Prestwich ossuary, is currently managed by a City Improvement District company, which provides services in terms of 'security, cleansing, and social intervention' (Truss 2014). The remains were transformed into a commodity, contributing ultimately to the 'regeneration' of the post-apartheid city.

Underlying the images featured in this chapter is an argument that the 2003 Prestwich Street exhumation constituted a decisive discursive shift with regards to Cape Town's urban transformation. I argue that this moment represents the key to interpreting contemporary urban conjunctions in Cape Town. With the interment of the human remains of Prestwich in the ossuary, a discourse of the city centred on reconciliation lost ground (but it also touched on issues of reparation, restitution, identity, and memory as well). It was replaced by discourses that framed heritage issues in terms of urban development and design—a discourse that in turn enabled the projection of Cape Town as a global city. As such, the human remains were eventually exhumed and the Prestwich ossuary ended up located on a 'fan walk' that led to Cape Town's football stadium (both the walk and stadium were constructed in preparation for the 2010 FIFA World Cup).

Shepherd labelled his keynote address for 'Land' an act of homage. He referred to the ways in which these dead, as well as their proximity during his speech, challenged us.

The archaeologist presented a photograph of his own. The picture he displayed seemed somewhat out of place: it was a historical image portraying two men seated at an archaeological site at Oakhurst Cave on the Southern Cape coast. On the left was noted South African archaeologist John Goodwin (1900–59). On the right was Goodwin's co-worker Adam Windwaai. Only after thorough investigation did Shepherd manage to identify Windwaai. In researching Goodwin's photographs, which in turn were documenting his exhumation of cave dwellers' remains, Windwaai's piercing presence permitted an alternative reading of the archive. The archaeologist posed questions regarding Windwaai's relationship with the archaeological work done on the bones. 'What has passed between the two men? Are they at ease in one and another's company?' (GIPCA 2013a).

Projected on one of the walls of the memorial, Windwaai's gaze was directed at us—the audience seated in the Prestwich ossuary. Shepherd questioned his expression. Of what does it consist? '[C]hallenge? Reproach? An unexpected candour?' (Shepherd 2015a: 4) How does the nature of the Goodwin/Windwaai collaboration reflect contemporary dealings with the dead of District One? How does the image of Goodwin and Windwaai redirect our gaze from the present to the spirits of Prestwich Street? I want to propose here that the interstices represented by the proximity of the bones in the ossuary, the Jazzart performance and the gaze of Adam Windwaai mark a space suited to empathic imagination in relation to the contemporary city of Cape Town.

Beginning with another image furnished by the 'Land' project, I discuss how these issues play out at District Six.

10.4 WITNESS

Once again, the image (Figure 10.2) is quite peculiar; this one appeared on Day 2 of the 'Land' event (22 November 2013). The photograph shows a porcelain kitten on a windowsill. The image contains little of reference: the wall is white, the view is blurred, and the cat is facing the other direction, away from us. The photograph was taken at 70 Chapel Street, in a newly constructed home that forms part of the second phase of the District Six redevelopment programme. The kitten in the image is part of a larger art installation, 'Witness', for which

Figure 10.2. WITNESS, a site-specific exhibition by Haroon Gunn-Salie. GIPCA's 'Land' project, 22 November 2013, Cape Town. Photo by Ashley Walters, © GIPCA.

artist Haroon Gunn-Sali collaborated with Mrs Fasia Adams, a former District-Six resident (Libsekal 2014). The caption reads: 'One day my kittens will return', a reference to the District's history of forced removal. By 1982 60,000 coloured and black residents were evicted and their homes demolished as a result of the Group Areas Act of 1950, instituted by the apartheid administration.

Besides the eerie green fields and an easy-to-miss plaque at St Mark's Anglican Church, which lies just off Keizersgracht Street, there are no reminders of these acts of urbicide at District Six. Gunn-Sali's project speaks to this void and tries to raise the ghosts of this past (Kelman 2014). He explained how he bore witness to the story of his parents' forced removal to Athlone, a township at the city's outskirts (GIPCA 2013b). The act of witnessing has been a central strategy for members who made up the 1988 community initiative, 'Hands Off District Six'. 'Hands Off District Six' aimed to prevent District Six land being emptied for the purposes of bigger development. The campaign's objectives are to keep the District Six land 'open and bare, a memorial scar within the cityscape' (Layne 2008: 56–7). Yet, poignantly, Gunn-Sali's kitten refers also to issues of return and, consequently, complexities attached to land restitution and redevelopment in neoliberal Cape Town.

In 2003 construction began on the first of the buildings that comprised the District Six redevelopment programme. In response, the District Six Museum, which emerged out of the 'Hands Off' campaign, changed its strategy: instead of 'hands off', it became 'hands on'. Its aims included becoming a partner to the government in the process of redevelopment (Bennett et al. 2007). Historian Ciraj Rassool understands this significant strategic change as having taken place 'in the shadow of Prestwich [Street]'. Rassool points to the lack of recognition of the Prestwich Street burial ground as a heritage site; he noted that 'the claims of memory [were] pitted against the demands of property development'. Rassool is of the opinion that the formal heritage policies proved inadequate regarding District One in the face of memory and in the midst of processes of urban regeneration (Rassool 2007: 36; see also Russell, Chapter 2, regarding the use of heritage as a tool of power). Unfortunately, the same happened at District Six. The Museum's hands-on strategy centred upon the endowment of a national heritage site status on District Six. This endowment failed. Moreover, in consequence, their ideal of the realisation the new District Six—a place of racial harmony and equity—was ruined (Ernsten 2015).

10.5 TRUTH

Over the street from the District Six Museum, and inside the Prestwich ossuary, lies a coffee shop named 'Truth'. Contrary to what you may think, this is not a government-supported initiative reminding visitors to the area of key heritage sites related to the Truth and Reconciliation Commission and the gains of national reconciliation. Truth is instead the crude trade of the neoliberal city.

Visitors to 'Truth' in its early years at the Prestwich ossuary will remember the image that the coffee grinders then sported: the iconic logo of a skull with a capital 'T' protruding from its eyes and mouth. Indeed, a café entitled 'Truth' opened their first store in the ossuary in 2010 (prior to the FIFA World Cup); then again in 2012 (in time for the 2014 World Design Capital), they opened a shop opposite the District Six Museum. 'Truth' was celebrated in 2016 by the British newspaper *The Telegraph* as No. 1 on its list of 'world's best coffee shops' (*The Telegraph* 2015). Previously, David Donde, owner of 'Truth' coffee roasters, was criticized for 'building on slavery'; as a result they took off the skull logo, leaving a conspicuous absence—especially poignant since their initial strategy had not changed (Donde 2014).

History and memories, it seems, became a marketing opportunity, as well as a location-focus for 'Truth'. Donde explained in an interview:

> We needed an area that was going through gentrification or was likely to go through gentrification in terms of property values. We wanted to secure good values for ourselves. We also wanted something which was cool, slightly grungy [and] on its way up. (Donde 2014)

A recent piece of Truth advertising consists of a series of illustrations of the roastery's three coffee blends—'1652', 'Resurrection', and 'Steampunk'. The retro design of these ads suggests a historical context in which coffee-blending takes place—namely the start of the Dutch occupation ('1652') and the 'resurrection' of the bones at Prestwich Street. Taking inspiration from colo-nialism, as well as from historical slavery, the Truth Café entrepreneur con-verted the discovery of human remains at District One into commercial messages. The steampunk blend riffed off the interior-design style of the café on Buitenkant Street—a style conceptualized by South African designer Haldane Martin (Anonymous 2012).

Steampunk is a science-fiction or fantasy genre based loosely upon the aesthetics of nineteenth-century industrial steam-powered machinery. I would argue that Donde created a themed environment by applying styles and objects associated with a historical dreamtime—objects and styles that over-write local histories and memories associated with Districts One and Six. Their playful reinterpretation of history contributes to a further disavowal of the wounds and suffering related to historical traumas that affected communities in these areas (Bogues 2010: 44). To those who experienced forced removals during apartheid, the message appears: 'Not only do you inhabit a different space, you also inhabit a different time.' In my understanding, and in the shadow of Prestwich Street, this constitutes colonial disavowal: while some discuss reconciliation and restitution others take off on an adventure in a fantasy time-space. Reiterating Johannes Fabian, this represents the denial of coevalness (Fabian 2014).

This problematic does not lie with Truth alone. The coffee roasters are exemplary of the larger urban-regeneration enterprises flourishing in and around old colonial Cape Town. This is the urban renaissance the *New York Times* refers to: Cape Town is becoming part of modern time-space, 'a universal story of human emancipation' (Shepherd 2016). In practical terms, such a reinvention encapsulates a series of utopian projects focused on property values and capitalist ventures that annihilate history and rename localities: District One first became part of Green Point; since the early 2000s it has been marketed as De Waterkant ('the waterside'); District Six became Zonnebloem during apartheid and, since 2004, has been called the East City (except prior to the 2014 World Design Capital, when it was temporarily renamed the Fringe) (Boraine 2013).

My analysis of Truth's marketing strategies resonates with the work of scholars such as Jennifer Robinson, Achille Mbembe, and Sarah Nuttall on how dreams, fears, and desires drive post-apartheid urban transformation (Mbembé 2004; Mbembé and Nuttall 2004; Robinson 1998). Truth also represents a particular (Capetonian) genealogy of urban design; in fact, it is a powerful reiteration of the violent nature, or, to use Walter Mignolo's terms, the 'deathly logic', that lay at the heart of colonial modernity (Mignolo 2011: 63; see also González-Ruibal, Chapter 7, on attempts to redevelop Belém). Coffee blends such as '1652'or 'Steampunk' and the renaming of city quarters highlight what Shepherd calls the 'conquest of time'; in neoliberal cities, this is the result of the globalisation of Western time-space (Shepherd 2016).

10.6 PERCOLATE

How might the proximity of the Prestwich dead inspire us to see District One and District Six differently? How might 2003 represent a moment at which to begin observing fractures—to begin making space for openings and prospects? How might it be read as a point of departure as we attempt to apprehend some other (that is, *not* universal) time. Spivak responds to photographs of Alice Attie of Harlem: '[i]nscriptions are lexicalized into the textuality of the viewer and it is the unexpected that instructs us' (Spivak 2012: 18). With Sebald in mind, I situate lexicalization of sites or places by imagining connections or recalling moments. As such, I looked for traces and spatial inscriptions at District One and Six.

Figure 10.3 is the first image I want to consider. We see the unused parking lot of the Salesian Institute on Somerset Road. Photographer Dirk-Jan Visser and I came here as part of a walking tour entitled, 'The landscape of early colonial burial in Cape Town' (Halkett et al. 2008); this tour was originally designed by the Cape Town-based Archaeological Contract Office (ACO) for participants of the 2008 Association of South African Professional Archaeologists conference. The block adjacent to this parking lot is a well-known Prestwich Street site. The block's name ('The Rockwell') is just visible on part of its façade. As Dirk-Jan and I arrived, a group of teenagers had just finished skating; they were resting in the shade of the trees. The ramps on which they had just recently occupied themselves were vacant, offering

Figure 10.3. Parking lot of the Salesian Institute on Somerset Road, Cape Town, 2014. Photo by Dirk-Jan Visser.

something of a reminder of what local histories lay underneath. As contract archaeologists Tim Hart and David Halket point out, the burial grounds continue beneath the parking area (Halkett et al. 2008). If you were to narrow your eyes and look at them, you might picture one of District One's burial grounds, the skate ramps as old tombstones.

Under the trees—visible in the right of Figure 10.3—lies some old brickwork. We also discovered an abandoned statue of sorts showing Mary with a young Jesus—probably the remains of a more formal burial site. The Malmesbury shale stone underneath the statue reminded us of the material used at the Prestwich ossuary. It was at this point that we are able to imagine the neighbourhood differently. We understood the 'deep map' of District One (Pearson and Shanks 2001: 158). We noticed how old walls were heightened. Were these the prescribed borders of some ancient graveyard? Was the unofficial burial ground beyond these walls? Did the communities that buried their loved ones here gaze up at Maria in search of solace?

We saw many old trees around the Prestwich Street site. We speculated about their nature: are they graveyard trees? Do their roots reach down to some deeper time? They quite literally connect us with ancestors buried deep within the earth; likewise, they reach the families that lived around them, the children that once attended Prestwich Primary School—until the day when all were removed.

Skate ramps, walls, old bricks, and trees become points at which one might enter other time-spaces. Referring to Michel Serres, performance artists Mike Pearson and archaeologist Michael Shanks write that time does not flow, 'it percolates' (Pearson and Shanks 2001: 178). It filters into the present, becomes a revenant—returning as a box that contains human remains or a dance to be performed in the street. The lexicalization of traces and inscriptions like that noted with respect to District One offers a point at which to begin writing and visualising the frame of another time-space.

After taking the tour, Dirk-Jan and I wandered into the parking garage underneath The Rockwell. The elevator took us back to De Waterkant—now a haven for our vehicles rather than a haven for our ancestors. This is the deathly logic of colonial modernity. In the next section I attempt to circumvent such logic using photographs of District Six.

10.7 SCAR

Figure 10.4 is one of the classic representations of the scar that the destruction of District Six left upon the fabric of urban Cape Town. The scar is the unearthed remains of Horstley Street. Horstley Street is a key location in the

Figure 10.4. Horstley Street, District Six, Cape Town, 2014. Photo by Dirk-Jan Visser.

District Six Museum's application for a national heritage site for the neighbourhood. The cobbled-stone road evokes the romantic and aesthetic qualities of some other period. The District Six Museum—called 'the face of the District Six story'—reminds us via its work on memory of the community life played out on this street and in the adjacent houses (Coombes 2003: 118). Modern ruins such as these have garnered attention recently from anthropologists and archaeologists. Some critics have argued for an understanding of ruins in relation to non-linear patterns social transformation or of ruins as a spectral presence. (Dawdy 2010; González-Ruibal 2008; Gordillo 2014; Pétursdóttir and Olsen 2014; Stoler 2008), while others have drew attention to the politics of ruin photography (Mullins 2014; Ryzewski 2014). Following anthropologist Ann Stoler, I am interested in understanding Horstley Street as 'an act perpetrated, a condition to which one is subject, and a cause of loss' (Stoler, 2008: 194–5). Moreover, I wonder what it takes for Horstley to avoid becoming another heritage commodity—in the same way as the Prestwich-Street dead.

Citing Roland Barthes, archaelogists Þóra Pétursdóttir and Bjørnar Olsen argue that the photograph taken of a ruin channels magic, as it enables the 'emancipation of a past reality' (Pétursdóttir and Olsen 2014: 23). The scar of Horstley Street reminds me of colonial modernity's deathly logic; that is, the denial of a 'transmodern' world—a world into which many worlds fit (Maldonado-Torres 2011: 18). The magic of the ruin of Horstley Street allows many connections to be made. For example, in the recently constructed homes that are part of the District Six redevelopment programme we can observe new residents' attempts at privatizing a public parking space with number plates beside the curb and 'residence parking only' signs upon the wall. I read this as the insertion of one individual's private life in an urban space—a space from which apartheid's social engineering wiped away all intimacy. I read this as the re-inscription of an individual's returned life following forced removals. I would argue, however, that the scar of removals offers other connections as well.

Let us consider Colour plate 13 (top), *A pair of shoes and a bottle*, an image shot by photographer Sara de Gouveia. Rubbish? I want to suggest, regarding these objects, that we see a different (yet intimate) form of relationship between persons and District Six. The ruins of District Six have been the hideout of many homeless Capetonians. Some call them 'bergies'—referring to the act of seeking shelter upon the slopes of mountains ('berg' means 'mountain' in Afrikaans). As the neighbourhood-improvement districts in the inner-city areas become more and more successful, homeless folks are driven out and find refuge at times in high grass, ruins, and tree trunks around District Six. This photograph might be of somebody's resting place. My point is that the magic of the scar of Horstley Street allows one to imagine connections between lives that perform vagrancy. Lives that are marginalized—or do not fit well beside concepts of citizenship in the contemporary city—allow us to conceive of meanings of degraded lives in other temporalities.

I argue also that the scar emancipates the messiness of past realities. Interestingly, the Cape Town Partnership, a private–public partnership that championed the East City Design programme and many city-improvement districts, hired ethnographer Evan Blake in 2014. Its aim was to map the 'social geography of marginalized groups' in the East City. As an unintended consequence of an exercise labelled 'Mapping Moments' Blake found a lexicalization of ruined spaces in District Six. In the Partnership's annual report, he presented the terms 'marginalized' individuals used to describe their spaces:

'A corner to watch drama unfold', 'A shady spot to be chased away from', 'Once a king's throne', 'A work zone', 'Opportunity to meet with skyways', 'A corner for Evelyn to throw a fit on', 'The gatherings corner—where world collide', 'A stop with a view to drink coffee', 'The urinal', 'Once a king's throne' and 'A spot to hide if harassed'. (CPT 2014)

Colour plate 13 (bottom) conveys my reading of how said terms might indicate what are likely to be sites that undergo constant change. My point is that these terms recapitulate time-space relations, allowing us to understand worlds within worlds, 'where worlds collide'. The scar points to these terms, allowing us to attain different understandings of the unofficial, the unknown and the marginalized in the city. They capture an instant of transformation, or, as Spivak refers to it—a moment 'congealing into a past'. (Spivak 2012: 18) As at District One, I want to propose that it is at the interstices of District Six, represented by the proximity of the scar of Horstley Street, Gunn-Sali's temporary art installation, and for example, the site that was once a king's throne, that we can reach out to deeper time and a distant other. It is here that we can find something of the vanishing traces of those who lived on the edge of the colonial and apartheid city.

10.8 DRAMA

By way of conclusion I refer to Derrida's use of the terms 'dramaturgy' and 'gospel'. These, I think, are useful when it comes to thinking about the meaning of Cape Town's renaissance and global experience. They provide the creative space needed for a light-hearted re-imagination of cities' pasts (Derrida 2006: 125).

In this chapter images gathered from scenes in of Districts One and Six offer us fragments of other imagined worlds, messy worlds with corners at which one talks with the revenants of different pasts. It is at these interstices that we bear witness to the traumas of the unresolved histories of racial slavery and apartheid's forced removals in contemporary Cape Town. In addition, it is here that we can begin a reading of these ruins as artefacts of loss and of violent pasts. 'We must investigate and imaginatively constitute our "own" history with the same teleopoietic delicacy that we strive for in the case of the apparently distant', writes Spivak. As such, a different urban text with regards to the ruins of District One and Six might 'sediment meaning' in the face of Cape Town's renaissance. (Spivak 2012: 17 and 33).

REFERENCES

Anonymous. 2012. 'Coffee in Steampunk', *Design Indaba* (updated 16 October 2012). http://www.designindaba.com/articles/creative-work/coffee-steampunk (accessed 26 January 2016).

Anonymous. 2013a. 'Jazzart Dance Theatre to present Waiting For Rain at Artscape Theatre'. http://www.mediaupdate.co.za/media/56137/jazzart-dance-theatre-to-present-waiting-for-rain-at-artscape-theatre (accessed 15 January 2016).

Anonymous. 2013b. *Plenary Panels. Land Divided: Land and South African Society in 2013, in Comparative Perspective*. A conference held at the University of Cape Town South Africa, 24–27 March 2013. http://www.landdivided2013.org.za/content/plenary-panels (accessed 6 January 2016).

Arnold-de Simine, Silke. 2012. 'Memory Museum and Museum Text Intermediality in Daniel Libeskind's Jewish Museum and W.G. Sebald's Austerlitz', *Theory, Culture & Society*, 29(1): 14–35.

Bennett, Bonita, C. Julius, V. Layne, et al. 2007. *Reflections on the Conference Hands on District Six. Landscapes of Post-colonial Memorialisation. Cape Town 25–28 May 2005*. Cape Town: District Six Museum.

Bogues, Anthony. 2010. *Empire of Liberty. Power, Desire, and Freedom*. Hanover: Darmouth College Press.

Boraine, Andrew. 2013. 'Interview with Andrew Boraine'. Conducted by Christian Ernsten.

CoCT. 2013. *Prestwich Ossuary Box Audit May 2013 by the Environment & Heritage Resource Management Branch of the City of Cape Town*, Environment & Heritage Resource Management Branch of the City of Cape Town, Cape Town.

Coombes, A. E. 2003. History after apartheid: visual culture and public memory in a democratic South Africa, Durham, NC, and London: Duke University Press.

CPT. 2014. *Mapping the Work of the Cape Town Partnership. Anual Report 2014*. Cape Town: Cape Town Partnership.

Dawdy, Shannon Lee. 2010. 'Clockpunk Anthropology and the Ruins of Modernity', *Current Anthropology*, 51(6): 761–93.

Derrida, Jacques. 2006. *Specters of Marx*. New York and London: Routledge.

Donde, David. 2014. 'Interview with David Donde'. Conducted by Christian Ernsten.

Ernsten, Christian. 2014. 'Following the Ancestors: Six Moments in a Genealogy of Urban Design and Heritage in the City of Cape Town', *Archaeologies: Journal of the World Archaeological Congress*, 10(2): 108–31.

Ernsten, Christian. 2015. 'The Ruins of Cape Town's District Six', *Archaeologies: Journal of the World Archaeological Congress*, 11(3): 342–71.

Fabian, Johannes. 2014. *Time and the Other. How Anthropology Makes its Object*. New York: Columbia University Press.

GIPCA. 2013a. 'Land 2013: Introduction and Keynote Address'. Gordon Institute for Performing and Creative Arts, 21 November 2013. Video Recordings. http://www.gipca.uct.ac.za/project/land/ (accessed 15 January 2016).

GIPCA. 2013b. 'LAND. Panel 4, Displacements: Joshua Williams, Ismail Farouk, Tebogo Munyai, Haroon Gunn-Sali, Elgin Rust, Katherine Spindler'. http://www.gipca.uct.ac.za/project/land/ (accessed 24 January 2016).

Goldblatt, David. 2010. *TJ Johannesburg Photographs, 1948–2010*. Rome: Contrasto.

González-Ruibal, Alfredo. 2008. 'Time to Destroy. An Archaeology of Supermodernity', *Current Anthropology*, 49(2): 247–79.

Gordillo, Gastón R. 2014. *Rubble: The Afterlife of Destruction*. Durham: Duke University Press.

Grendon, Paul, Giorgio Miescher, Lorena Rizzo, and Tina Smith. 2015. *Usakos. Photographs Beyond Ruins. The Old Location, 1920s–1960s*. Basel: Basler Afrika Bibliographien.

Halkett, David, Tim Hart, Liesbet Schietecatte, Erin Finnegan, and Katie Smuts. 2008. ASAPA Mid-conference Excursion. The Landscape of Early Colonial Burial in Cape Town: A Walking Tour of Excavation Sites and Buildings of Interest in Green Point. Unpublished Guidebook, Archaeological Contracts Office, Department of Archaeology: University of Cape Town.

Hartmann, Wolfram, Jeremy Silvester, and Patricia Hayes. 2001. *The Colonising Camera: Photographs in the Making of Namibian History.* Cape Town: University of Cape Town Press.

Jonker, Julian and Karen E. Till. 2009. 'Mapping and Excavating Spectral Traces in Post-apartheid Cape Town', *Memory Studies*, 2(3): 303–53.

Judin, Hilton and Ivan Vladislavić (eds). 1998. *Blank: Architecture, Apartheid and After.* Rotterdam and Cape Town: NAi.

Kelman B. 2014. *Haroon Gunn-Salie:History's vigilante.* http://www.designindaba.com/video/historys-vigilante (accessed 8 February 2017).

Khan, Sarah. 2014. '52 Places to Go in 2014', *New York Times.* http://www.nytimes.com/interactive/2014/01/10/travel/2014-places-to-go.html?_r=1 (accessed 27 January 2014).

Layne, V. 2008. 'The District Six Museum: An Ordinary People's Place', *The Public Historian*, 30: 53–62.

Libsekal, M. 2014. *Haroon Gunn-Salie*, 3 March. http://www.anotherafrica.net/art-culture/89plus-haroon-gunn-salie-2 (accessed 8 February 2017).

Malan, Antonia. 2003. 'Interim Draft Report Prestwich Place Exhumation Project, Public Participation Process 9 July to 1 August 2003'. Prepared by Antonia Malan with assistance of Emmylou Rabe. Report Submitted to the South African Heritage Agency and the Global Asset and Investment Network. Cape Town: Cultural Sites and Resources Forum.

Malcomess, Bettina and Dorothee Kreutzfeldt. 2013. *Not No Place. Johannesburg. Fragments of Spaces and Times.* Auckland Park: Fanele.

Maldonado-Torres, Nelson. 2011. 'Enrique Dussel's Liberation Thought in the Decolonial Turn', *Transmodernity: Journal of Peripheral Cultural Production of the Luso-Hispanic World*, 1(1): 1–30.

Mbembé, Achille. 2004. 'Aesthetics of Superfluity', *Public Culture*, 16(3): 373–405.

Mbembé, Achille and Sarah Nuttall. 2004. 'Writing the World from an African Metropolis', *Public Culture*, 16(3): 347–72.

Mignolo, Walter. 2011. 'Epistemic Disobedience and the Decolonial Option: A Manifesto', *Transmodernity: Journal of Peripheral Cultural Production of the Luso-Hispanic World*, 1(2): 44–66.

Mullins, Paul R. 2014. 'Imagining Ruin Images: The Aesthetics of Ruination', *Journal of Contemporary Archaeology*, 1(1): 27–9.

O'Connell, Siona. 2013. *Martyrs, Saints and Sell-outs: The Photographs of Benny Gool, Adil Bradlow and Zubeida Vallie.* Cape Town: Centre for Curating the Archive.

O'Connell, Siona. 2015. 'The Aftermath of Oppression: In Search of Resolution through Family Photographs of the Forcibly Removed of District Six, Cape Town', *Social Dynamics. A Journal of African Studies*, 40(3): 589–96.

Pearson, Mike and Michael Shanks. 2001. *Theatre/Archaeology.* London: Routledge.

Pétursdóttir, Þóra and Bjørnar Olsen. 2014. 'Imaging Modern Decay: The Aesthetics of Ruin Photography', *Journal of Contemporary Archaeology*, 1(1): 7–56.

Ralphs, Gerard. 2008. *'If it's not Black Gold, then it's Bone Gold': Contested Knowledges of the Prestwich Street Dead.* Cape Town: University of Cape Town.

Rassool, Ciraj. 2007. 'Key Debates in Memorialisation, Human Rights and Heritage Practice'. In *Reflections on the Conference Hands on District Six. Landscapes of*

Post-colonial Memorialisation. Cape Town, 25–28 May 2005, edited by Bonita Bennett et al., Cape Town: District Six Museum, pp. 34–7.

Robinson, Jennifer. 1998. '(Im)mobilizing—Dreaming of Change'. In *Blank_Architecture, Apartheid and After,* edited by Hilton Judin and Ivan Vladislavić, Rotterdam and Cape Town: NAi, pp. 163–71.

Ryzewski, Krysta. 2014. 'Ruin Photography as Archaeological Method: A Snapshot from Detroit', *Journal of Contemporary Archaeology,* 1(1): 36–41.

Shepherd, Nick. 2007a. 'Archaeology Dreaming Post-apartheid Urban Imaginaries and the Bones of the Prestwich Street Dead', *Journal of Social Archaeology,* 7(1): 3–28.

Shepherd, Nick. 2007b. 'What does it mean "to Give the Past back to the People"? Archaeology and Ethics in the Postcolony'. In *Archaeology and Capitalism: From Ethics to Politics,* edited by Yannis Hamilakis and Philip Duke, Walnut Creek: Left Coast Press, pp. 99–114.

Shepherd, Nick. 2013. 'Ruin Memory. A Hauntology of Cape Town'. In *Reclaiming Archaeology: Beyond the Tropes of Modernity,* edited by Alfredo González-Ruibal, New York: Routledge, pp. 233–43.

Shepherd, Nick. 2015a. *The Mirror in the Ground. Archaeology, Photography and the making of a Disciplinary Archive.* Johannesburg: Jonathan Ball Publishers.

Shepherd, Nick. 2015b. 'Undisciplining Archaeological Ethics'. In *After Ethics: Ancestral Voices and Post-Disciplinary Worlds in Archaeology,* edited by Nick Shepherd and Alejandro Haber, New York: Springer, pp. 11–26.

Shepherd, Nick. 2016. 'La Arqueologia y la Conquista del Tiempo'. In *Arqueologia y Decolonialidad,* edited by Nick Shepherd, Cristobal Gnecco, and Alejandro Haber, Buenos Aires: Ediciones del Signo.

Shepherd, Nick and Christian Ernsten. 2007. 'The World Below: Post-apartheid Urban Imaginaries and the Bones of the Prestwich Street Dead'. In *Desire Lines. Space, Memory and Identity in the Post-apartheid City,* edited by Noeleën Murray, Nick Shepherd, and Martin Hall, London and New York: Routledge, pp. 215–32.

Skotness, Pippa. 1996. *Miscast: Negotiating the Presence of the Bushmen.* Cape Town: Cape Town University Press.

Spivak, Gayatri. 2012. *Harlem.* London: Seagull Books.

Stoler, Ann Laura. 2008. 'Imperial Debris: Reflection on Ruins and Ruination', *Cultural Anthropology,* 23(2): 191–219.

The Telegraph. 2015. 'The World's Best Coffee Shops'. http://www.telegraph.co.uk/food-and-drink/drinks/the-worlds-best-coffee-shops/ (accessed 26 January 2016).

Truss, Mark. 2014. 'Interview with Mark Truss'. Conducted by Christian Ernsten.

Vladislavić, Ivan. 2011. *Double Negative. A Novel.* Cape Town: Umuzi.

11

Encountering Home

A Contemporary Archaeology of Homelessness

Courtney Singleton

11.1 UNRECOGNIZED DWELLING: A PUBLIC–HOMELESS ENCOUNTER

On 17 September 2011 people flooded Zuccotti Park in Manhattan's Downtown Financial District to protest multinational corporations and major banking institutions. Protestors left their houses and established encampments in public parks in over a hundred cities across America to live in solidarity as the '99%'. The 99% were ready for conflict between citizen and state, public and private institutions, but they did not expect the conflict that erupted within the encampments between protestors and local homeless populations. Despite the fact that protestors were living 'homeless' for symbolic and political purposes, they had not anticipated how to handle the homeless communities who they actively displaced and engaged in the service of their politics. As they pitched their tents, strung up tarpaulins, established communal kitchens, and inflated blow-up mattresses the 99% encountered the already-present local homeless population: people who were both known and unfamiliar, but who were meant to remain hidden and invisible.

Cities where the Occupy Wall Street Movement (OWS) had a strong and quick start had more problems regarding homelessness than cities where the movement started later, but all Occupy protesters realized homelessness was an issue that had to be confronted (Ehrenreich 2011). Austin and Tampa, for example, used homelessness as the central organizing issue, one that could be easily grasped as a human circumstance with universal appeal. This was primarily because these cities were able to anticipate incidents that had arisen in New York, Denver, and Portland (see AP 2011; Nagourney 2011). Conflicts that first occurred in these cities allowed for later responses to be more proactive, and they subsequently positioned homelessness as a universalizing issue that everyone could rally behind (Ehrenreich 2011). In Denver, Portland, Boston, and New York City protestors expressed fear and apprehension towards the homeless, calling them 'protest imposters', 'freeloaders', and 'rapists and gropers of females' (Algar 2011; *Huffington Post* 2011a, 2011b; Occupy Wall Street 2011). One New York protestor stated that the homeless were 'mentally ill and out-of-control' (Algar 2011). The responses of the Occupy protesters at Zuccotti Park were rooted in a belief that there was a fundamental distinction between themselves and the homeless with whom they lived side-by-side and shared the same materials and spaces. This perceived distinction resulted in fear among the protesters because the objects mediating the immediacy of (mis)recognition during those encounters remained unknown and unquestioned.

In Zuccotti Park many of the 99% came to look upon the homeless with fear, terror, suspicion, and anger, leading to the creation of a homeless zone in the south-west corner of the park and a special security force to protect protestors against those inhabiting the designated area. The *New York Times* reported, 'A team of 10 security volunteers moved in to the trouble-prone southwest section of Zuccotti Park in a show of force to confront them [the homeless]' (Algar 2011). OWS volunteers in the Zuccotti Park's camp kitchen closed the facility and refused to serve gourmet food to the 'professional homeless' who were 'masquerading as protesters' (Algar 2011). When the kitchen reopened, they did so with a rule that anyone who was homeless could be denied food and referred to local soup kitchens. To detour 'freeloaders' the menu was also changed from gourmet and organic food to peanut butter and jelly sandwiches and brown rice (Algar 2011; *Huffington Post* 2011a, 2011b; Occupy Wall Street 2011). Zuccotti's Occupy camp claimed that the police department and the Mayor's office were purposely sending homeless individuals into the park to disrupt the protest (Occupy Wall Street 2011; Siegel 2011). The fact that these accusations were made is more important for understanding the relationship of homelessness within the Occupy movement than the truth of the accusations, as they position the homeless as being present within the state and yet not part of the public represented by the 99%.

The events at Zuccotti Park illustrate a perceived fundamental difference between the homeless and a 'homed' society that extended beyond the simple presence or absence of 'proper' shelter, one that is argued here to be rooted in an immediate object of home. As protestors occupied the park, they were forced to recognize the homeless and consequently excluded them from public and civic space. However, the material grounds upon which the homeless were recognized remained unarticulated. What was it, if not the absence of a 'proper' shelter that distinguished between the 99% and the homeless?

Another homeless encounter considered here asks similar questions from an archaeological perspective, through the results of a 2009–14 study of the

Davidson Street Bridge Encampment in Indianapolis, Indiana. As with the Zuccotti Park example, the forms present at the Davidson Street Bridge homeless encampment are not completely alien to dominant definitions of home, and yet they seem to be understood as irreconcilably different. In order to understand this relationship between a recognizable and unrecognizable concept of home, I examine the tension between two distinct objects (signs) of home within this encampment: a static, boundary-focused object of home and a fluid, centre-focused object of home. Through an archaeological inquiry of homeless homemaking within this general theoretical frame, an object of home and habit of homelessness might be articulated.

In his book *Fluid Signs: Being a Person the Tamil Way*, Valentine Daniel (1984) presents a framework to address the conflated meanings of home via the terms *kiramam* and *ur*. According to Daniel, *kiramam* is a boundary-focused referential equivalent to 'village' and 'nation' that operates as a political unit, while *ur* is a centre-focused unit that references a place of belonging and being in the world (Daniel 1984: 63–104). *Ur* is a specific place defined as an ontic unit, while *kiramam* is an epistemic unit of space as understood by the 'revenue officer, the archaeologist, the museologist, or the historian' (Daniel 1996: 57). Daniel argues that while these two terms have been used interchangeably and sometimes do indeed overlap, they are radically different signs: the *kiramam* is a fixed sign and the *ur* is 'not so much a discrete entity with fixed coordinates as a fluid sign with fluid thresholds' (Daniel 1984: 104). Likewise, home in relation to homelessness can also be viewed as an object that can be both discrete and fluid, boundary-focused and centre-focused signs. This work is relevant beyond its immediate context, and for the purposes of the case study considered here, in that it illuminates the dynamic actualizations and potentialities of home for those who are defined by the state as lacking a home or who are denied certain recognitions due to their relationship with an object of home embedded in political discourse. An individual may be living on the street, but still have a home. Our job as archaeologists is to try to recognize alternative material actualities of these different types of objects.

11.2 HOUSEHOLD ARCHAEOLOGY: THE ROOTS OF A DISCRETE HOME

Archaeologically, one of the first studies of the house can be traced back to folklorist Henry Glassie's research on eighteenth-century folk housing in Middle Virginia (Glassie 1975). As a folklorist Glassie incorporated methods of ethnography, oral history, participant observation, and material culture studies to understand transformations in vernacular architectural forms. In many ways this work was before its time, as Glassie was 'pressing vernacular architecture study past buildings into the life that buildings contain and beyond buildings into their settings' (Glassie 1984: 53). In his later study of eighteenth-century Virginia houses, Glassie (1984) documented a transition in form that included movements from asymmetrical houses to symmetrical dwellings, from houses that were environmentally adaptive to those that were less so, and from those representing mechanical solidarity versus organic solidarity. Glassie approached the house as a nexus of mental and social relationships that reflected changing worldviews, economic systems, and political ideologies.

Aside from the archaeological aspects of Glassie's Virginia case study, the house or household as an analytical unit emerged within North American archaeology in the 1970s among processual archaeologists who approached the household as a scale and unit of analysis ideal for identifying and explaining adaptive cultural systems. Wilk and Rathje were the first archaeologists to focus on households as the most obvious way to 'bridge the existing 'mid-level theory gap' (1982: 617). Referencing Binford's Middle-Range Theory, households were seen as a crucial scale that connected the archaeological data of potsherds, plant remains, and architectural features with grand theories of economic and ecological systems. Since these beginnings, archaeologists have interrogated the household from various theoretical positions highlighting the construction of domestic space, the position of the household within an expanded landscape, the relationships between household-level activities to social structures, and the household as a form of social practice (see Hendon 2010; Joyce and Gillespie 2000).

However, as some archaeologists have pointed out, when examining nomadic or semi-nomadic societies within this framework material traces and forms of 'households' have been seemingly non-existent or classified as 'ephemeral sites' (see Barnard and Wendrich 2008). This is largely due to the absence of specific materials that have come to signify 'home' or 'dwelling' structures, most notably a 'roof', 'sleeping' areas, and evidence of spaces for cooking or food preparation. Within this conventional framework archaeologists tend to recognize sedentary forms of dwelling in the material record, but the sedentary perspective that renders certain forms of dwelling visible is also responsible for rendering 'mobile' peoples invisible. This paper builds upon Glassie's call for architectural studies to focus on 'other' architectural traditions, and his argument that by doing so 'we will become unwilling to disturb them and will decide to protect them against members of our society who do not understand them and so are willing, even anxious, to sweep them away. This attitude of protection will extend to dead as well as live cultures' (Glassie 1984: 60–1). The architectural traditions that Glassie spoke of were those structures not readily recognized as house forms within dominant academic discourse, one could say the traditions of the home-less.

The approach I am proposing adds to household archaeological research by exploring the tension between two different objects of home, signs that could be categorized as either ontic or epistemic units. This initial work uses an ethnoarchaeological approach to propose future theoretical and methodological frames within which work on issues of contemporary and historical homelessness can proceed. Is the homeless encampment at Davidson Street a form of home that is denied recognition in contemporary urban space? If so, on what grounds can we come to understand and recognize this alternative form of dwelling as such?

11.3 THE DAVIDSON STREET BRIDGE/IRISH HILL HOMELESS ENCAMPMENT

During the winter of 2010 the city of Indianapolis forcefully removed individuals from their homes located under a bridge on the city's south-east side, destroying personal property and forcing people to wander the streets in search of another space to call their own. It is the visibility of poverty and homelessness that results in the routine clearing or 'clean-ups' of homeless encampments in urban areas all over the United States, whereby an ongoing cycle of procurement and dispossession become a normal way of life within these communities. The Mayor of Indianapolis justified the clearing of the Davidson Street Encampment as a means to force the city's homeless into a local shelter 'for their own protection', a common rhetorical move that highlights the benevolence of the state and places blame on the homeless who refuse to use the services provided for them (AP 2010; Milz 2010; Tuohy 2010). The question of why so many people prefer life under the bridge to local shelters was never posed to the public or city officials; if it were, one would see that contested ideas, practices, and discourses surrounding home are at the heart of this issue.

The past reverberates in the form of a piece of grassy land called the 'jungle' directly adjacent to the Davidson Street Bridge, a railroad overpass in the city's south-east side (Colour plate 14, top). This neighbourhood, once called Irish Hill, had been the home to transient populations since industrialization in the mid-nineteenth century. Living beside the tracks was a way of life for migrant workers, and in the early 1870s 'hobo jungles' emerged along these railroads (Bodenhamer et al. 1994; Castle 2005a, 2005b, 2005c; Hensley 2002). Hobo jungles were typically just outside urban centres and contained temporary and semi-permanent shelters. As the term 'jungle' reflects, these spaces and the people who resided within them were seen as uncivilized and dangerous.

As time progressed, railroad workers began to settle and build houses around the Davidson Street Bridge, creating a stable, predominantly Irish

American neighbourhood. This neighbourhood remained physically aligned with the railroad, which created an angle and direction that did not conform to the city's Jeffersonian grid, creating an identifiable and disjointed space within the city. During the 1920s a new railroad bridge was constructed just 30 feet south of the Davidson Street Bridge, ripping through the Irish Hill community and displacing them further east (Baist 1927; Hensley 2002; IHS 2004; Sanborn1898). This displacement created conditions ideal for industrial development, which soon transformed the area into a small manufacturing pocket within the city. Then, with deindustrialization start-ing in the 1950s, many of the plants were shut down and demolished, leaving ruined factories in their wake. Just as the original bridge shaped the Irish working-class neighbourhood, the current railroad bridges, patches of original brick-lined streets, dead-ends, and vacant lots of rubble also afforded particular possibilities of inhabiting and dwelling within this space.

After the 2010 removal of the homeless at Davidson Street, a padlocked chain-link fence was erected around the public space, and 'no trespassing' signs were posted with the intent to make returning to the site impossible (Figure 11.1). The erection of a fence is always a conspicuous political act, symbolizing ownership, state authority, citizenship, or defence and warfare.

Figure 11.1. The chain-link fence and 'No Trespassing' signs the city of Indianapolis erected under the Davidson Street railroad bridge after the 2010 eviction of first homeless encampment. Photo by C. Singleton.

The fence at Davidson Street restricted access to public space and reproduced the homeless as subjects existing outside the bounds of civil society. A few weeks after the eviction, Davidson Street residents returned, relocating to another railroad bridge 30 feet south of the original, continuing the production of their material worlds within this neighbourhood.

The reoccupied 2010 Davidson Street Encampment was communal on a general level with individual spaces maintained between the more permanent residents and drifters who wandered in and out irregularly. Piece-plotted cigarette butts demonstrated the sharing of goods in communal spaces and activities that included card playing and gambling. Evidence of drug and alcohol use was only present in private spaces, located away from the main encampment area. Despite the sharing of goods and the centrality of communal space, there was a spatial hierarchy that formed within the camp, particularly in the main area located on the east side of the street. Long-time residents constructed more permanent structures composed of mattresses, tents, cots, blankets, and storage containers for clothes. Strategically placed area rugs, coffee tables, guest beds, and a 'back porch' with lounging chairs—icons of home—resembled the creation of a Victorian-era domestic space (Colour plate 14, bottom).

Long-term residents inhabited the position along the cement wall under the bridge, which provided protection from the elements, was a position of surveillance within the camp, and afforded individuals more privacy. Those occupying the middle ground typically slept on cardboard or blankets spread out on the exposed brick street. The middle area of the camp was clearly visible from the street and had to be well maintained. Nothing could be left out during the daytime, so items were stored high in the beams, cached, or carried with the person. The camp was empty during the day, save one or two people who decided to sleep in or 'stay home'. Around five o'clock in the evening the camp exploded with activity and in a ritualistic manner everyone laid out cardboard and blankets, set up tents, took down bags, socialized, played games, drank, and traded stories. There were approximately twenty-five to thirty people who lived at the encampment when it was resettled after the 2010 eviction. The Davidson Street Encampment and the individual spaces within it were frequently referred to as 'home' by residents.

During the summer, one resident, Richard, slept on cardboard laid out on the ground. Richard had been homeless most of his adult life and sometime between 2006 and 2008 made his way to Indianapolis from Florida after being released from prison. Richard came to Davidson Street after spending approximately a year sleeping rough in the downtown district, occasioning Wheeler Shelter, and sleeping in abandoned houses. Despite his scant bedding, Richard had an elaborate home within his grocery cart, which neatly contained all of his possessions and occupied its own particular space within the camp. Richard's shopping cart held clothing, pictures, tools, bedding, buckets, personal journals, books, and anything he felt he might need in the future (Colour plate 15). When he was not present the cart was placed in one spot and covered with a blanket. No one at the camp touched anything in Richard's cart, respecting it as his personal space. The cart did have to be hidden from the police, who frequently confiscated carts from the homeless as stolen property. If they had taken Richard's cart they would have been taking away his security, his resources, and his history, violating his privacy.

Upon my winter visits Richard had moved up the hill and into a tent, as did most people when it turned cold. It was during this time that a mental health organization providing free medicine for his schizophrenia decided to change his prescription, a normal experience for those living with mental illness on the streets. As a result of this change in medication, Richard had become delusional. His stories became violent, scary, or simply incoherent. After a trip to the library he asked me if I saw the man get murdered in the bathroom. One morning he told me the police found his lost driver's licence on a man who had been using it to rape women. He said they had arrested him before I arrived and kept him in jail until they finally found the real rapist, who had been an ex-police officer following Richard from Florida. One evening he took an axe to Ashley and Damien's tent, then to Terry's tent, and also slashed a large hole in his own, which was filled to capacity with random stuff he found on the street. It was clear between my summer and winter visits that Richard's entire worldview had dramatically changed, and his material world reflected and supported what existed in his mind. At night he would climb in through the slashed hole of his tent and bury himself amongst his things.

After the summer of 2011 the Davidson Street Encampment grew to approximately sixty individuals with a maintained communal structure. In 2012 residents legally acquired a water tank that was filled by the fire department every week, as well as a dumpster and port-o-lets. They designated a 'Mayor', Maurice, who worked with city officials on problems that arose between the encampment and neighbouring businesses. Referencing the site's past, Maurice renamed the encampment Irish Hill. Unfortunately, the Irish Hill Encampment was short lived and the state gave notice for eviction during the spring of 2013. Five residents refused to leave and were subsequently arrested.

The changing nature of life for residents of the Davidson Street Encampment is reflected and affected by these places they call home. Encampments like Davidson Street exist in deindustrialized urban spaces throughout the United States. Although they all have their own unique structure, reputation, and different individuals who are drawn to them at particular moments in time, together they form relationships that extend and operate beyond city limits and state lines. These camps shift seasonally and individuals cycle through, but there is still permanence within this motion. A distinctive homeless material landscape is constructed and reflected within these spaces and practices over time. Though movement and change on an individual level may not be synchronized temporally or spatially with that of the camp or city, an individual leaves identifiable material traces through the process of constructing personal spaces of dwelling. For the individual, a home changes due to environmental conditions, political and social shifts, and mentality, but the possessions and spaces are meaningfully constructed and reproduced in particular forms. Although the function of home as shelter is important, the homes of the homeless also reflect the way people organize their worlds and their positioning within them. A shopping cart does not fit society's definition of home, ownership, or private property, even though to Richard it is all of those things.

11.4 CONCLUSION: THE POSSIBILITIES FOR AN ARCHAEOLOGY OF HOMELESSNESS

Current public policy surrounding homelessness emerged in the United States in the 1980s largely through the efforts of homeless advocacy organizations attempting to change the terms through which homelessness had been previously understood (Gowan 2010; Levinson 2004). During this time advocacy organizations strategically adopted the term 'homelessness' in an effort to 'humanize' the poor by creating a sympathetic connection between housed and unhoused peoples by way of an 'object' of home. According to the *Encyclopedia of Homelessness*:

> This 'politics of compassion' required convincing housed people that homeless people were neither slackers nor villains but victims caught in massive social processes such as deindustrialization and the collapse of affordable housing. Some organizations tried to present the view that unhoused people were 'just like you and me' except for an unlucky break that took them away from a mainstream life. (Rosenthal 2004: 221)

As a result of this shift in public discourse, contemporary homelessness has since come to be understood within various processes of deindustrialization and is a condition most recognizable within the context of deindustrialized urban spaces. However, this 'politics of compassion' and the public policy that has emerged as a result of it, is predicated on a notion of home, a form of dwelling, which remains largely uninterrogated. Within this language, homeless people are seen as lacking, somehow failing to maintain an ambiguously defined social norm. By focusing on the object or form of home that was articulated by the Zuccotti Park and Davidson Street Encampment examples here, this research adopts a household archaeological approach to argue that archaeological research of homelessness could lead to a deeper understanding this larger social issue.

Research on homelessness has tended to focus on systemic causal factors that result in the loss of shelter and the singling out of particular issues such as drug abuse, mental illness, domestic violence, or unemployment. Studies conducted by state organizations, non-profits, and social scientists result in the constitution (or reconstitution) of 'homelessness' as a static condition with little attention given to the dynamic processes involved in actually *being* homeless (HUD 2015, 2013, 2012a, 2012b, 2011; HEARTH Act 2008 S.896; United States Code 2016). This is most clearly seen during the nationwide annual headcount of the homeless that takes place every January in the United States, producing the primary data upon which most public policy is based (HUD 2015; Rice and Littlepage 2013).

The result of research focused on locating the fundamental causes of homelessness and head counts is a fractured homeless industry whereby any understanding of what it means to be homeless is overly simplistic, if not superficial. For example, following 42 US Code 11302, the Department of Housing and Urban Development defines homelessness as the lack of permanent shelter, characterized primarily by the absence of 'proper' sleeping quarters (United States Code 2016). It is important to note that ambiguous terms like 'adequate' or 'proper' distinguish the rules and regulations relating to homelessness, with no clear guidelines as to what specific material conditions these policies are referring. According to some policies these descriptors could or could not reference sleeping in a shelter, a friend's house, a hotel, or tent (HUD 2012a, 2012b, 2011). Institutions focused on domestic violence or drug abuse may consider sleeping in a group home adequate shelter, while others would deem it emergency housing, in which case an individual is still considered legally homeless even though they have adequate shelter. Furthermore, if one chooses not to seek out a particular form of housing they may be deemed homeless and will not qualify for some support services.

Many advocacy organizations have attempted to expand upon this basic concept of homelessness by creating subcategories based on duration of time spent in homeless shelters without taking into consideration time limits and entry restrictions enacted by individual shelters. One of the largest homeless advocacy groups in the United States, the National Coalition for the Homeless, has three categories of homelessness based on time spent in shelters; the chronically homeless, transitionally homeless, and episodic homeless (NCH 2009, 2014). Such categories define homelessness in relation to how a network of state-funded homeless shelters service homeless people, which ignores the majority of homeless individuals who prefer not to enter shelters or are ineligible to do so. State and ideological definitions rooted in the notion of 'proper' home stand despite the fact that homelessness is something that predominantly operates outside of the state institutions that have historically developed around it. Within the legal and public discourse surrounding homelessness the term 'home' is actually referencing an object that is quite specific and discrete, but the actualizations of this object needs to be better articulated. The current language and discourse surrounding homelessness is based on an unquestioned concept of home that remains largely undefined.

What does it mean to be home-less? This simple question opens up a field of relationships that allows one to redraw boundaries and identify relationships (material, social, and spatial) that constitute an object of home outside social service institutions and spaces designated for homeless use. The archaeological investigation that took place at the Davidson Street Bridge Encampment shows that an object of home can manifest in a myriad of material and personal relationships that do not conform with legal boundary-focused definitions of home. By interrogating the concept of home from an archaeological perspective we begin to see how specific forms of home emerge in the everyday lives of those living homeless and also begin to articulate the manner by which those living homeless create an object of home that opposes dominant discourse.

It is through the objects of home that homelessness has come to be simultaneously recognizable and unintelligible, familiar and unknown. Unfortunately, reactionary attempts by homeless advocacy organizations to counter dominant discourse just reaffirm the idea that there is a marked absence of home, which is used to interpret homeless bodies and homeless space as that which is lacking or as being 'less than'. I argue that homelessness cannot be reduced to a marked absence of immediate referents of home. Instead we need to understand how homeless communities produce, reproduce, and inhabit space through a habit of homemaking, through a relationship of signs as it relates to a dynamic object of home. In order to make this shift, the concept of home itself needs to be reconceived and articulated as that which operates within and through public and legal structures, as well as that which is more fluid, local, and operates outside these rigid structures. This is where archaeology, as a study of social, material, and spatial relationships, emerges.

Due to the conflation between these two forms of home and the current political climate surrounding homelessness, dispossession manifests regularly as violent acts that rupture a habit of homemaking. The state has not only enacted a pattern of physical displacement and the destruction of personal property through the routine clearing out of encampments, but they go so far as to disqualify the basic civic rights of the homeless to occupy public spaces through the placement of fences, spikes, bars, and other deterrents. When the homeless population grows and local, small-scale displacement is rendered ineffective, city officials in the United States have historically resorted to bussing the homeless out of the city. What this creates is a constant need for the homeless to procure objects of home, a never-ending process of homemaking. This habit of homemaking results in homeless sites like the Davidson

Street Bridge Encampment, but also involves a larger network of relationships that extend beyond city and state boundaries.

Future archaeological research can contribute to a better understanding of homelessness in the United States in the following ways: 1) archaeology may articulate different forms of dwelling, in line with Henry Glassie's call for vernacular architecture studies and the 'unrecognizable' structures of home. This can involve radical historic preservation politics (see Kiddey 2014, forthcoming; Zimmerman et al. 2010), but also simply articulating other forms of dwelling that exist in these urban spaces is important with regards to broader politics of recognition; 2) by focusing on the material landscape, archaeology allows us to move outside constricting and limiting public policy discourse that surrounds homelessness and to challenge that discourse more effectively; and 3) the production of 'raw data' related to subsistence strategies may improve the flow of resources and the efficiency of service providers and public policy makers.

ACKNOWLEDGEMENTS

I would like to thank Dr Larry Zimmerman, Professor of Anthropology and Museum Studies at Indiana University-Purdue University of Indianapolis, for his continued mentorship on this project and for allowing me access and the use of data published in this chapter. This research occurred under his guidance, for which I am incredibly grateful.

REFERENCES

Algar, Selim. 2011. 'Occupy Wall Street Kitchen Staff Protesting Fixing Food for Freeloaders'. *New York Post*, 27 October. http://nypost.com/2011/10/27/occupy-wall-street-kitchen-staff-protesting-fixing-food-for-freeloaders (accessed 7 February 2016).

[AP] Associated Press. 2010. 'Indy Homeless Camp Raises Concern' [online video]. WISH-TV, LIN Television. http://www.wishtv.com/news/local/marion-county/indy-homeless-camp-raises-concerns (accessed 14 November 2013; no longer available).

[AP] Associated Press. 2011. '"Occupy" Camps Provide Food, Shelter for Homeless'. *USA Today*, 22 October. http://usatoday30.usatoday.com/news/nation/story/2011-10-22/occupy-wall-street-homeless/50868444/1 (accessed 7 February 2016).

Baist, William. 1927. 'Indianapolis Baist Atlas Plan #4', *Indianapolis Sanborn Map & Baist Atlas Collection*. http://indiamond6.ulib.iupui.edu/cdm/ref/collection/SanbornJP2/id/1848 (accessed 5 February 2017).

Barnard, Hans and Willeke Wendrich (eds). 2008. *The Archaeology of Mobility: Old World and New World Nomadism.* Los Angeles: Cotsen Institute of Archaeology Press.

Bodenhamer, David J., Robert G. Barrows, and David G. Vanderstel. 1994. *The Encyclopedia of Indianapolis.* Bloomington: Indiana University Press.

Castle, Emily. 2005a. *Madison, Indianapolis and Lafayette Railroad Company Papers, 1822–1924.* Manuscript on file in the William Henry Smith Memorial Library. Indianapolis: Indiana Historical Society.

Castle, Emily. 2005b. *Lafayette, Muncie, and Bloomington Railroad Company Reports, 1877.* Manuscript on file at the William Henry Smith Memorial Library. Indianapolis: Indiana Historical Society.

Castle, Emily. 2005c. *Victor M. Bogle Indiana Railroad History Papers, 1826–1999.* Manuscript on file in the William Henry Smith Memorial Library. Indianapolis: Indiana Historical Society.

Daniel, E. Valentine. 1984. *Fluid Signs: Being a Person the Tamil Way.* Berkeley: University of California Press.

Daniel, E. Valentine. 1996. *Charred Lullabies: Chapters in an Anthropography of Violence.* Princeton: Princeton University Press.

Ehrenreich, Barbara. 2011. 'Why Homelessness Is Becoming an Occupy Wall Street Issue'. *Mother Jones.* 24 October. http://www.motherjones.com/politics/2011/10/homelessness-occupy-wall-street (accessed 19 January 2017).

Glassie, Henry. 1975. *Folk Housing in Middle Virginia: A Structural Analysis of Historic Artifacts.* Knoxville: University of Tennessee Press.

Glassie, Henry. 1984. 'Vernacular Architecture and Society'. In *Material Culture and Folklife: A Prologue and Dialogue*, edited by Simon Bronner, Ann Arbor: U.M.I. Research Press, pp. 47–62.

Gowan, Teresa. 2010. *Hobos, Hustlers, and Backsliders: Homeless in San Francisco.* Minneapolis: University of Minnesota Press.

HEARTH Act. 2008. S.896. Homeless Emergency Assistance and Rapid Transition to Housing Act.

Hendon, Julia. 2010. *Houses in a Landscape: Memory and Everyday Life in Mesoamerica.* Durham: Duke University Press.

Hensley, Roger P. 2002. *History of the Cleveland Cincinnati Chicago and St. Louis Railway Company.* http://madisonrails.railfan.net/bigfour.html (accessed 10 October 2011).

[HUD] Department of Housing and Urban Development. 2011. *Homeless Emergency Assistance and Rapid Transition to Housing (HEARTH): Defining 'Homeless' Final Rule.* https://www.hudexchange.info/resource/1928/hearth-defining-homeless-final-rule (accessed 7 February 2016).

[HUD] Department of Housing and Urban Development. 2012a. *Homeless Emergency Assistance and Rapid Transition to Housing: Continuum of Care Program: Interim Final Rule.* https://www.hudexchange.info/resource/2033/hearth-coc-program-interim-rule (accessed 7 February 2016).

[HUD] Department of Housing and Urban Development. 2012b. *Continuum of Care (CoC) Program.* https://www.onecpd.info/coc (accessed 14 November 2013).

[HUD] Department of Housing and Urban Development. 2013. *Homelessness Resource Exchange.* https://www.hudexchange.info/homelessness-assistance/ (accessed 23 January 2017).

[HUD] Department of Housing and Urban Development. 2015. *Homeless Data Exchange Website*. http://www.hudhdx.info (accessed 7 February 2016).

Huffington Post. 2011a. '"Occupy Wall Street" Takes a Stand Against Pretend Protesters', *Huffington Post*. 28 December. http://www.huffingtonpost.com/2011/10/28/occupy-wall-street-banish_n_1044548.html (accessed 7 February 2016).

Huffington Post. 2011b. 'Occupy Wall Street and Homelessness: Millions Spent to Evict Camps, While Cutting Shelter Funds'. *Huffington Post*. 27 November. http://www.huffingtonpost.com/2011/11/27/occupy-wall-street-and-homeless-evictions-cities_n_1111094.html (accessed 7 February 2016).

[IHS] Indiana Historical Society. 2004. 'Guide to Railroad History Materials in Manuscript and Visual Collections at the Indiana Historical Society'. Report on file with at the Indiana Historic Society, Indianapolis, IN.

Joyce, Rosemary and Susan Gillespie (eds). 2000. *Beyond Kinship: Social and Material Reproductions in House Societies*. Philadelphia: University of Pennsylvania Press.

Kiddey, Rachael. 2014. *Homeless Heritage: Collaborative Social Archaeology as Therapeutic Practice*. PhD Thesis, Department of Archaeology, University of York.

Kiddey, Rachael. Forthcoming. *Homeless Heritage: Collaborative Social Archaeology as Therapeutic Practice*. Oxford: Oxford University Press.

Levinson, David (ed.). 2004. *Encyclopedia of Homelessness, Vols. 1 and 2*. London: SAGE Publications.

Milz, Mary. 2010. 'Indianapolis Installs Fence to Keep out Homeless'. *WTHR Channel 13 Eyewitness News*. http://www.wthr.com/Global/story.asp?S=12069463 (accessed 12 October 2011).

Nagourney, Adam. 2011. 'Dissenting, or Seeking Shelter? Homeless Stake a Claim at Protests'. *The New York Times*. 31 October. http://www.nytimes.com/2011/11/01/us/dissenting-or-seeking-shelter-homeless-stake-a-claim-at-protests.html?_r=0 (accessed 7 February 2016).

[NCH] National Coalition for the Homeless. 2009. *Who is Homeless?* http://www.nationalhomeless.org/factsheets/Whois.pdf (accessed 7 February 2016).

[NCH] National Coalition for the Homeless. 2014. *Building a Movement to End Homelessness: Publications*. http://nationalhomeless.org/references/publications (accessed 7 February 2016).

Occupy Wall Street. 2011. 'WTF is Going on with OWS Blacklisting Homeless People from Meals?' *Occupy Wall Street Forum*. http://occupywallst.org/forum/wtf-is-going-on-with-ows-blacklisting-homeless-peo/ (accessed 5 February 2017).

Rice, Jennifer N. and Laura Littlepage. 2013. *Point-in-Time Count: Identifying the Most Vulnerable Homeless in Indianapolis*. Indianapolis and Bloomington: Indiana University Public Policy Institute and Coalition for Homelessness Intervention and Prevention.

Rosenthal, Rob. 2004. 'Homeless Organizing'. In *Encyclopedia of Homelessness. Vol. 1*, edited by David Levinson, London: SAGE Publications, pp. 220–3.

[Sanborn] Sanborn Map Company. 1898. '1898 Indianapolis Sanborn Map #310', *Indianapolis Sanborn Map & Baist Atlas Collection*. http://indiamond6.ulib.iupui.edu/cdm/ref/collection/SanbornJP2/id/521 (accessed 5 February 2017).

Siegel, Harry. 2011. 'A civil war in Zucotti Park?', *New York Daily News*, 30 October. http://www.nydailynews.com/opinion/occupy-wall-street-central-rift-growing-east-west-sides-plaza-article-1.969320 (accessed 5 February 2017).

Tuohy, John. 2010. 'Homeless Forced to Abandon Overpass Encampment'. *Indianapolis Star Media*. http://www.indy.com/posts/homeless-forced-to-abandon-overpass-encampment (accessed 10 October 2011; no longer available).

United States Code, Title 42, Chapter 119, Subchapter I. 2016. 'General Definition of Homeless Individual'. Washington, DC: Government Printing Office.

Wilk, Richard and William Rathje. 1982. 'Household Archaeology', *American Behavioral Scientist*, 25(6): 617–39.

Zimmerman, Larry, Courtney Singleton, and Jessica Welch. 2010. 'Activism and Creating a Translational Archaeology of Homelessness', *World Archaeology*, 42(3): 443–54.

12

The Optimism of Absence

An Archaeology of Displacement, Effacement, and Modernity

Paul R. Mullins

In the 1960s Edward J. Zebrowski turned the razing of Indianapolis, Indiana into a compelling show of forward-looking community optimism illuminating the power of displacement. When Zebrowski's company toppled the Knights of Pythias Hall in 1967, for instance, he installed bleachers and hired an organist to play from the back of a truck as the twelve-storey Romanesque Revival structure was reduced to rubble. Two years later, the 'Big Z' hosted a party in the Claypool Hotel and ushered guests outside at midnight to watch as the floodlit building met its end at the wrecking ball (Figure 12.1).

Zebrowski's theatricality perhaps distinguished him from the scores of wrecking balls dismantling American cities, but his celebration of the city's material transformation mirrored the sentiments of many urbanites in the wake of World War II. The post-war period was punctuated by a flurry of destruction and idealistic redevelopment in American cities like Indianapolis just as the international landscape was being rebuilt from the ruins of the war. In 1959 the *New York Times*' Austin Wehrwein (1959: 61) assessed the University of Chicago's massive displacement in Hyde Park and drew a prescient parallel to post-war Europe when he indicated that 'wrecking crews have cleared large tracts, so that areas near the university resemble German cities just after World War II'. Indeed, much of Europe was distinguished less by ruins and redevelopment than demolition and emptied landscapes removing the traces of warfare that states wished to reclaim or efface; in the United States, urban renewal likewise took aim on impractical, unappealing, or otherwise unpleasant urban fabric and the people who called such places home (see also Ernsten, Chapter 10, for this process associated with the policies of apartheid in Cape Town).

Figure 12.1. Edward Zebrowski's demolition firm razed much of Indianapolis, Indiana's historic landscape to make way for post-war construction. In 1962 Zebrowski tore down the 1876 Marion County Courthouse while the new City-County Building rose in the background. Indiana Historical Society, W. H. Bass Photo Company Collection.

These global projects removed wartime debris and razed deteriorating pre-war landscapes, extending interwar urban renewal projects that embraced the fantasy of a 'blank slate' as they built various unevenly executed imaginations of modernity. However, many optimistic development plans in Europe and the United States alike were abandoned or disintegrated into ruins themselves, simply leaving blank spaces on the landscape. Consequently, the legacy of urban renewal and post-war reconstruction is not simply modernist architecture; instead, post-war landscape transformation is signalled by distinctive absences dispersed amidst post-war architectural space and traces of earlier built environments.

Few architectural forms provide more compelling testimony to urban renewal ambitions than the fate of public housing communities like Detroit's Brewster-Douglass (see also Ryzewski, Chapter 3). Eleanor Roosevelt hosted a demolition ceremony for the Brewster Homes slum clearance project in September 1935 at which she celebrated the razing of the neighbourhood's existing homes (*New York Times* 1935: 23; Kinney 2011: 41; Martelle 2012: 133; Figure 12.2). In an optimistic moment of theater Edward Zebrowski would appreciate, the First Lady ceremoniously waved a handkerchief, and a truck attached to a derelict house by a cable lumbered forward, pulling down the house with 'a roar of splintering timbers and falling bricks. Mortar dust was showered over speakers and 20,000 spectators' (*New York Times* 1935: 23; Martelle 2012: 133). In 1938, 701 African-American families moved into the first Brewster Homes (Kinney 2011: 41; Thomas 2013: 21), and expansion included six 14-storey Frederick Douglass Apartment towers completed in 1952. Brewster-Douglass was astounding for its ambitious scale, housing between 8,000 and 10,000 residents at its peak, and the prominent high-rises were impossible to ignore, covering five-by-three city blocks looming over the heart of the city.

Brewster-Douglass is among the modernist redevelopments that are now going under the wrecking ball in contemporary moments of optimistic destruction that are ironically much like those once orchestrated by Eleanor Roosevelt, Edward Zebrowski, and many more community planners and residents. Brewster-Douglass's decline was driven by familiar issues that dogged nearly all American public housing projects: racist housing policies by the Detroit Housing Commission perpetuated broader material marginalization (Kinney 2011); indifferent maintenance hastened physical erosion; and a new interstate sliced alongside Brewster-Douglass in 1963–8, displacing much of the African-American community in the heart of Detroit. The last Brewster-Douglass residents moved out in 2008, and in 2014 Mayor Mike Duggan convened a news conference as the towers were theatrically demolished behind him. Near the spot where Eleanor Roosevelt had once proclaimed that 'you must all rejoice today that this great work has begun', Duggan delivered Brewster-Douglass's death rites and pronounced that 'We are not demolishing for the sake of demolishing. We are demolishing for the

Figure 12.2. In 1935 Eleanor Roosevelt opened a Detroit clearance project with a ceremonial demolition at 651 Benton Street, where the Brewster-Douglass homes would be built. Virtual Motor City, Wayne State University.

purpose of rebuilding' (Guillen 2014). As Detroit contemplates how to use the newly created expanse, Brewster-Douglass is at least temporarily another empty lot dotting the reimagined post-war landscape, testimony to the cycles of destruction, absence, and reconstruction that characterize twentieth-century space (cf. Millington 2010).

Alfredo González-Ruibal (2008) argues that transformation involving material destruction if not human displacement may be among the most distinctive characteristics of post-war society. Marc Augé (1995) coined the notion of 'supermodernity' to describe what he saw as the intensification and exaggeration of twentieth-century modernity, and González-Ruibal champions an archaeology of supermodernity that examines the extraordinary scale of landscape transformation leading up to and following World War II. Landscape absences like the footprint of Brewster-Douglass are key if somewhat overlooked evidence of extraordinarily widespread destructive processes that González-Ruibal paints as the landscape of supermodernity (see González-Ruibal, Chapter 7, on the Ruins of the South; see Graff, Chapter 4, for discussion of contemporary Chicago).

Much of the archaeological ambition of a study of contemporary absences is to illuminate apparently banal spaces that pass without reflection in everyday life (cf. Bille et al. 2010; Buchli and Lucas 2001; Hetherington 2003, 2004; Lucas 2010). Such a scholarship should confront why specific landscapes are now voids; illuminate how such absences lurk near the surface or just below awareness; and spark a material imagination that reveals contextually specific processes of destruction and reconstruction that have shaped much of the world since World War II. That mission borrows from González-Ruibal's picture of a consciously politicized contemporary archaeology that focuses on spaces that are 'beyond social remembrance, where memory is erased'.

This paper focuses on twentieth-century absences in two communities and examines the ways local heritage has been shaped by post-war landscape transformation. In northern Finland, much of the World War II landscape has been uprooted, decayed, or replaced by post-war architecture. Between 1941 and 1944 the Finns and Germans were co-belligerents at war with the Soviets, and the German military transformed much of the landscape in northern Finland. Finns have an exceptionally rich public memory of the war (Kivimäki 2012a, 2012b), and traces of the German presence can be found in ruins or razed spaces scattered throughout northern Finland. Nevertheless, the contemporary Finnish landscape provides few preserved or commemorative spaces to materially illuminate the Finnish wartime experience. In Indianapolis, Indiana much of the city was transformed by urban renewal projects like those that produced Brewster-Douglass. Many of the Indianapolis projects expressly targeted and displaced historically African-American neighbourhoods. Much of that community space is today occupied by the campus of Indiana University-Purdue University, Indianapolis (IUPUI), and there are very few traces of that African-American neighbourhood visible on the contemporary landscape.

Landscape absences and the material traces such spaces harbour provide potentially compelling places to illuminate, interrogate, and acknowledge contested dimensions of the very recent past. The absences and crumbling remains left by warfare, urban engineering, and economic and industrial collapse provide telling evidence of global destructive processes and many optimistic imaginations of a reconstructed post-war world that has itself eroded into ruins (see McAtackney, Chapter 9, for discussion of this process in Belfast). A fixation on narrowly defined material culture and built landscapes hazards ignoring the consequence of these voids that narrate myriad failed efforts to rebuild the post-war world. Absences may demand somewhat distinctive interpretive gaze and material imagination, but they can provide especially compelling spaces to interpret the fascinating and often-unsettling international mission to reconstruct the post-war world.

12.1 COLLECTIVE MEMORY AND MATERIALITY
IN POST-WAR FINLAND

On 10 June 1941 the first German Operation Barbarossa troops arrived in a series of communities along Finland's Bothnian Gulf, and the town of Oulu became home to the largest Waffen-SS encampments in northern Finland. Military bases, hospitals, and training areas for troops (as well as prison camps) were located in and around Oulu between June 1941 and September 1944, the period that Finns refer to as the Continuation War. As the Nazis' 'co-belligerents' the Finns and Germans shared a common Soviet enemy, a complicated military coalition that Finns argue was neither a formal political alliance nor an occupation (Silvennoinen 2013). Finland remained a parliamentary democracy throughout the war, and Finns often view the Continuation War and the German partnership as logical extensions of the November 1939–March 1940 'Winter War', the Soviet invasion of Finland that left Finland wary despite a 1940 treaty (Kivimäki 2012a: 492). During the Continuation War the roughly 220,000 Germans based in northern Finland built garrison and supply bases on the outskirts of northern towns like Oulu, Tornio, and Kemi and in the city centre of Rovaniemi (Ylimaunu et al. 2013). Such bases were sometimes referred to as 'Little Berlins': roughly 10,000 Finns worked on Nazi construction projects, Soviet prisoners expanded community and regional infrastructure, Germans paid rent to Finnish residents, and the Germans and Finns often built close personal relationships. Finland was perhaps pro-German in terms of common military interests, but it was cool to Nazi ideology, and Finns sometimes uneasily distinguish between Germans in Finland and Nazis linked to genocide elsewhere (Holmila 2009, 2012; Vehviläinen 1987). That Finnish memory of the Germans runs directly counter to the predominant historical picture of the Nazis; Finnish public memory of German soldiers is often neutral and in many cases quite positive and personally warm (Kivimäki 2012a: 492).

In September 1944 the Moscow Armistice between the Soviet Union and Finland ended the Continuation War. The Finns turned against the Germans in the final phase of World War II, which is referred to in Finland as the Lapland War. During the Lapland War the retreating Germans destroyed many camps and bases, leaving relatively little standing architecture from roughly one hundred small prison camps and a network of military posts. Rovaniemi was almost entirely laid waste by fires in the wake of the German retreat, and images of Rovaniemi reduced to a scatter of standing chimneys and ash have often been used to symbolize the destructiveness of the Germans' scorched earth withdrawal. During their bitter retreat to Norway the Germans burnt about 16,000 buildings, killed tens of thousands of heads of livestock, and placed over 130,000 land mines in their wake (Seitsonen and Herva 2011: 177; Figure 12.3).

Figure 12.3. Chimney stacks and a sole tree were all that remained in Rovaniemi on 16 October 1944 after the German withdrawal from the Northern Finnish city. Photo SA-kuva, Finnish Armed Forces.

Much of the wartime landscape of military support structures was used at least temporarily after the war, but most of it is now gone. Where new housing and development did not remove the German landscape, the thick forest reclaimed the more ephemeral features like trenches, firing ranges, and foundations. The gradual removal of wartime material features in Oulu was not an especially strategic effort to expunge the war from collective memory, and in fact the war is perhaps the most widely commemorated national event in Finnish heritage (Aunesluoma 2013). Much of Oulu's German military architecture was modest buildings that fell into disuse and were eventually razed without any contemplation of commemorating the prosaic material evidence of the wartime experience. Despite the loss of wartime German architecture, Oulu's modest population density and the Finnish favour for spatially dispersed settlement has ensured that much of the city's wartime fabric survives as modest traces and ruins in the community's open and wooded space, even though it is not clearly commemorated on the landscape.

Unlike well-studied monumental Third Reich architecture, the Finnish support centres planted an idiosyncratic range of material designs on the Nordic landscape. These landscapes were shaped by a complex confluence of functional provisioning needs (German support materials were imported), military regimentation, and concrete environmental conditions that required the Germans to adapt to places like Oulu and Lapland. A few pieces of distinctive National Socialist architecture were erected in northern Finland, and much of the German installation outside Oulu was a systematically planned military landscape. Nevertheless, the majority of the German land-scape was informally planned, and it was dominated by relatively insubstantial spaces and structures designed for specific functional purposes (e.g. barracks, harbors, prison camps, garages, etc.). Oula Seitsonin and Vesa-Pekka Herva's (2011) archaeological fieldwork at the Peltojoki camp in Lapland has likewise revealed that the roughly 30,000 Soviet prisoners building roads and supplying bases were housed in a series of very small camps like Peltojoki composed of very modest frame or sod structures in hastily erected spaces.

Well-preserved wartime debris remains scattered throughout much of Lapland, but many of the prison camps and posts were insubstantial turf or frame structures that have long ago eroded from visibility. The absence of much disturbance has left material like vehicles, cans, and ceramics still relatively well-preserved on the surface since 1944. However, metal salvaging and efforts to provide a pristine environment for ecotourism threaten to remove much of that refuse from the contemporary surface (e.g. one prom-inent programme calls itself 'Keep Lapland Tidy').

In the aftermath of the war Finland quite assertively turned to rebuilding its national landscape and redeveloping spaces like the German military tracts in Oulu. Finland has an exceptionally rich history of twentieth-century munici-pal planning responding to a series of crises in the country's first decades of Independence. The Finnish planning tradition was born after a brutal four-month Civil War in 1918 in which 37,000 Finns died just months after the nation declared independence in December 1917 (Kivimäki 2012a: 483). In the wake of the war, Finnish architects and municipal planners secured significant sway over the shape of Finnish communities. Architects invoked rural values reflected in predominately low-density, single-family settlements assertively placed in the midst of green spaces (Salmela 2007). Many of these ideals were not especially cost-effective or practical in Finland's urban centres after World War II, though, when over 400,000 wartime immigrants and veterans settled in Finnish towns. Much of the nation's post-war attention focused on planning suburbs, including designed landscapes in places like Helsinki and Oulu as well as more rapidly constructed veteran's housing (Lahti 2008: 152; Soikkeli et al. 2008).

The Finnish architects Otto-Iivari Meurman and Aarne Ervi collaborated on the post-war master plan and reconstruction of Oulu. The heart of their reconstruction plan was completed in 1952, but much of the German installation in Alppila, the port of Toppila, and the northern Linnanmaa suburb remained largely undeveloped until the 1960s and later. After the war the Alppila neighbourhood's German structures were used by the Finnish Army for storage; some barracks housed soldiers and their families until the deteriorating structures were vacated in 1954 (Ylimaunu et al. 2013: 253). Across from the Toppila harbor in Hietasaari 18 of the German barracks continued in use as housing into the 1970s. Over roughly 25 years most of the structures erected by the Germans deteriorated and were razed without any particularly clear strategy to remove the material traces of the German period, and there is no evidence that removing this home front wartime landscape was viewed as an effacement of an admittedly conflicted heritage. The removal of wartime structures coincided with the development of suburban Oulu, and those communities generally followed the Finnish favour for dispersed, architecturally homogenous neighbour-hoods with green space. Much of that green space was occupied or rapidly reclaimed by Finnish forest, so the archaeological footprint for many German features (e.g. training trenches) is still visible in the woods around the former base, though there is no systematic survey of those features or a preservation plan.

Two particularly distinctive material remains of the Continuation War depart from the apparent absence of wartime material features. Perhaps the most distinctive German building that remains on the landscape is the Waffen SS officers club, a gable-roofed structure that loosely evokes timbered Alpine architecture (cf. Taylor 1974: 12). National Socialist landscapes have been routinely examined as mechanisms of nationalist ideology in Germany itself, but the German architecture in northern Finland reflects no concerted effort to incorporate their Finnish hosts. Built in 1942, the officer's club was one of the few distinctive structures in the German military complex, a neighbour-hood now known as Alppila in reference to the Alpine style lodge. The officer's club reproduced the alpine chalet folk styles that were used in the construction of Hitler Youth hostels, with one hostel very similar to the Oulu officer's club constructed in 1936 in southern Bavaria (Lane 1968: 198). A series of such countryside hostels invoking various rural traditions were constructed throughout Germany in a host of folk styles, including 'Bavarian farm houses, Black Forest chalets, Frankish half-timbered houses, lower Saxon homes, or Prussian country seats' (Taylor 1974: 241).

After the war the Oulu officer's club was used first by the Finnish army before successively becoming home to the Society of Karelians (composed of Finns who were displaced when Finnish Karelia was ceded to the Soviet Union after the Winter War), a youth hostel, and until 2013 a fire station. Today, its future remains undetermined as Oulu contemplates how to use the former officers club. Placed on one of the few high points on the flat suburban Oulu terrain, the officers club overlooked a host of German military support structures that no longer survive. In the wooded areas to the north of the Alppila club the German military practised on a firing range and trained in trench construction under the supervision of their Finnish hosts, but only a streetscape dotted with a variety of small industrial enterprises survives today.

No markers identify the origins of the officer's club or commemorate the German military base.

Much of post-war Europe was subject to a rapid wave of commemoration of battlefields and Holocaust landscapes, but Finland erected a more modest host of material monuments to the war. Home fronts like Oulu enjoyed a relatively settled life in comparison to the terror of the battlefront; of about 96,000 Finns who died between 1939 and 1945, less than 2,500 were civilian casualties (Kivimäki 2012a: 484; Kivimäki and Tepora 2012). With such a clear distinction between battlefield and home front, the everyday material impression of the German landscape in places like Oulu passed without much commemoration after the war (Junilla 2012). Finland's post-war commemoration instead focused on 'Heroes Cemeteries', a memorial landscape that originated during the 1918 Civil War when 'White' soldiers who had fallen to Soviet-based 'Reds' were repatriated to their homes for burial (Kivimäki 2012a: 485). After 1939 roughly 600 such cemeteries were expanded or founded, including every town or parish in Finland, and they continue to be the focus of memorial ceremonies into the present (Tepora 2014: 177–8).

A small stone marker in Alppila is one of the most distinctive material traces of the war on the contemporary Oulu landscape (Colour plate 16). In July 1942 a German soldier likely erected a memorial to the 6th SS Mountain Division Nord that now sits in a traffic circle in suburban Linnanmaa. The little monument tenaciously illuminates the area's German experience and reveals how the war remains a part of contemporary landscapes, even if such material culture passes largely without comment (see Shanahan and Shanahan, Chapter 5, for a comparative of long-lasting monuments in Melbourne). Many places like Oulu have the rather mundane material reminders of war, often left to abandonment, removed without any thought to their significance, or simply preserved without any especially coordinated heritage strategy. The Waffen marker sits amongst post-war architecture and contrived green spaces that largely efface the wartime landscape, but it was moved to its present position from an adjoining corner several years ago by the city. Preservation of the monument confirms the consequence of the German partnership, but it does so rather implicitly, entrusting Finns' public memory to contextualize wartime heritage in the incongruous placement in a commonplace post-war suburb.

12.2 THE AESTHETICS OF URBAN RENEWAL

In 1953 the *Indianapolis Star* ran a series on the Indiana capital's slum clearance programme that sounded a commonplace lament over the impact of slum life on community morality and public health. The newspaper despaired that their evocative narrative and images could not capture the experience, frustrated that the 'disease and rat-infested sties and rookeries are more vile than even our reproduced photographs will reveal...Some scenes from the slums are so revolting as to offend even the most hardened viewer' (*Indianapolis Star* 1953: 12). Such rhetoric signalled a shift in sentiments about the aesthetics of decline and an increasingly common belief that the city's fate rested on the eradication of the slum. In 1899, in contrast, traveller William Archer (1899: 27) painted a comparatively enchanting picture of the aesthetics of New York's slums, indicating that they had 'a variety of contour and colour—in some aspects one might almost say a gaiety'. The slum loomed in such turn-of-the-century literature as an aesthetic and sensory abstraction, but as the twentieth century progressed the urban imagination became increasingly unsettled by material decline and took a progressively resolute aim on the city's failures. Rather than rehabilitate the slums or allow the city to erode, ideologues and the state championed wholesale displacement to revive the urban core.

In 1943 economist Alvin Hansen (1943: 69) advocated the production of forward-thinking master plans for all American cities, arguing that 'the large scale replanning and rebuilding of our towns and cities is one of the most urgent tasks of the post-war future'. Such municipal plans were often transparent booster statements if not ideological broadsides, evading various threads of xenophobia and lobbying for expanded municipal planning power in the service of fantasy landscapes. In 1958, for instance, the Indianapolis Redevelopment Commission produced a master design for the near-Westside that included an undergraduate campus alongside the Indiana University Medical Center, which had sat in the predominately African-American neighbourhood since 1903. The 1958 plan imagined a fascinating future city, fantasizing the development of a riverside marina and massive park south of the Medical Center as well as a downtown heliport, all underscoring that 'those concerned with planning in Indianapolis should formulate a positive approach to civic beauty' (Metropolitan Planning Department 1958: 6). Such visions of the post-war city imagined that the removal of the impoverished and antiquated landscape would restore the city to a lost glory.

The neighbourhood surrounding the Medical Center was settled from the mid-nineteenth century onward, and by the turn of the twentieth century it and neighbouring Indiana Avenue were the heart of African-American life in Indianapolis. Migration waves at the turn of the century and once more for World War II employment swelled the population density, and strict residential segregation prevented significant African-American population movement from the predominately African-American neighbourhood. However, the university was increasingly covetous of these neighbourhoods as a blank canvas for the Medical Center's expansion, which eventually grew in the 1960s to include the establishment of the Indiana University-Purdue University, Indianapolis (IUPUI) campus.

In 1921 the Indiana University Medical Center took its first aim on its predominately African-American neighbours when it developed a plan for a convalescent park adjoining Riley Hospital, which was then under construction. African-American physician Sumner Furniss complained that the segregated hospital would not equitably serve any of the African-American residents it was removing, adding that he 'did not think it wise to throw from 1500 to 2000 persons out of their homes' (*Indianapolis Star* 1921: 5).

The most extensive transformations of the neighbourhood came after World War II. Between 1945 and 1962 the Indianapolis Redevelopment Commission (1962: 4) conducted twelve projects razing 576 acres in total, including two displacement projects conducted on campus. Both took years to complete: beginning in 1956, Project F adjoined the Dental School, and in 1963 it was still removing the last of 372 residents, when 90 per cent of the properties had been acquired and 80 per cent had been razed (Indianapolis Redevelopment Commission 1962: 6). The redevelopment commission was simultaneously razing eighteen acres beside the hospital (Project D; *Indianapolis Recorder* 1956: 1), with the city's costs reimbursed by the university.

In 1959 the Federal Housing Act made universities an especially active mechanism of such transformation and displacement when the law was amended to provide federal aid for 'urban renewal areas involving colleges and universities' (Hechinger 1961: E7). However, Indianapolis' city government was unwilling to turn over redevelopment to federal funding sources and external developers, so by the early 1960s the city refused nearly all federal urban renewal funding. Consequently, the landscape that became IUPUI in 1969 began to be purchased by the university as individual properties starting in about 1964. Like many post-war urban campuses ringed by existing neighbourhoods, IUPUI had no particularly consistent growth plan for their expansion into those neighbourhoods, despite developing at least eighteen master plans since the 1960s (Gray 2003: 54). Ground was broken for the first three IUPUI academic buildings in September 1968 (*Indianapolis Recorder* 1968: 1), but the university landscape took shape based on opportunistic property purchases. Through the late 1960s the university typically purchased between ten and twenty properties each month, acquiring just over 2,000 individual house lots as well as some commercial properties and churches (Gray 2003: 48).

Through the 1980s the piecemeal acquisition process gradually opened up space in modest patches rather than large tracts. When the university acquired most homes they tore the structure down immediately after the residents had been resettled (if the residents did not want to move they rented their home indefinitely from the university). The neighbourhood quickly became a chequerboard of standing structures alongside open lots in the place of former homes. Residents recognized that these vacant lots left in the wake of university and highway demolitions alike convinced successively more neighbours to move. In September 1966, for instance, the community group Homes Before

Highways met with the Governor about simultaneous highway and university displacement projects and complained that 'residents are forced to move out of the property and then the weeds take over—lowering the value of other neighbourhood properties' (*Indianapolis Recorder* 1966b: 1–2).

The university's expansion came at nearly the same moment that the state was acquiring vast swaths of African-American Indianapolis for interstate arteries slicing through the centre of Indianapolis. In 1958 an Indianapolis Chamber of Commerce official told the *Saturday Evening Post* that 'Our big job in Indiana today is to build enough roads to get employees from factories to their homes' (Martin 1958: 103). That position recognized Indianapolis' commitment to house its urban white labour force in postwar suburbs that were 'exploding outward in all directions'. Meanwhile in the urban core one droll 'city planner estimated that, at its present rate, slum clearance might be completed in 120 years' (Martin 1958: 104). As slum clearance inched forward, the suburbs remained inaccessible to nearly all African-Americans into the 1970s: the Federal Housing Administration (FHA) would not extend loans to suburban neighbourhoods that included even a single African-American homeowner, so there were few housing options for wealthy or impoverished African-Americans (Jackson 1985: 208).

The path of Interstate 65 through the predominately African-American community was aired at public hearings in 1959 and 1960, and it was largely settled in 1961 (Ripple 1975: 481). Right-of-way was being acquired by 1963, but the project continued to be bitterly contested over nearly a decade of displacement and construction (*Indianapolis Recorder* 1961: 1–2; Ripple 1975: 487). By one 1967 estimate, about 4,500 properties were required for the construction of Interstates 65 and 70 through the heart of Indianapolis (*Indianapolis Recorder* 1967: 1). *The Criterion* (1965: 4) characterized the highway's path as a 'serpentine coil of concrete around the inner city', calling the elevated interstate a 'Chinese wall' that 'would seal off the heart of the city, encourage the growth of slums along the outer edges, destroy needed recreation areas, and needlessly displace thousands of persons'.

In October 1966 Homes Before Highways accused 'the highway department and the university of browbeating homeowners in the path of the inter-loop portion of the inter-state highway system and the Westside residents whose homes occupy land wanted by the school for the expansion of its Indianapolis campus' (*Indianapolis Recorder* 1966c: 1). They threatened to bring Martin Luther King Jr to lead a rally, arguing that they were 'seeking to protect the rights of elderly and undereducated Negroes who are, it is charged, being exploited by shady real estate dealers and fly-by-night landlords and coerced by university and highway officials' (*Indianapolis Recorder* 1966b: 1). The community advocates singled out the University, charging 'that Negroes are also being coerced, especially by representatives of Indiana University, to sell their homes at prices far below what it would take to find similar dwellings at today's prices' (*Indianapolis Recorder* 1966a: 1).

The interstate's completion near the new IUPUI campus made the university especially convenient to suburban commuters, and it ensured that parking became one of the institution's most prominent engines of displacement. The initial 1958 plan of three buildings amidst the African-American neighbourhood quickly reached across hundreds of acres as a law school, administrative spaces, and a host of programmes gradually emerged, but it made nearly no concession for parking. Much of the open campus space became parking lots that were hastily gravelled or paved to accommodate cars. Planners were ambitious to fill the ever-expanding open spaces with a host of new university buildings, so many of the expanses cleared around the campus were theoretically being temporarily converted to parking lots before grand university buildings rose in their place. For instance, the plans to fill the Project F space with student housing languished as the acquisition and demolition dragged on for several years and university funding was persistently delayed. The tract was converted to parking lots in the early 1960s, and it remains surface parking and a parking deck today.

Unlike some urban universities that remained firmly situated within living communities, IUPUI covered roughly 500 contiguous acres with expanses of grass between buildings. Gradually much of the existing streetscape was itself removed from the campus as well, so the razing of existing structures and streets erased nearly all of the material traces of the neighbourhood that had still clung to the area after the war. Planners were eager to build many new structures as the campus holdings mushroomed in the 1970s, so the university invested little energy in landscaping the campus. With the exception of a few pieces of public art installed as early as 1975 and irregular plantings of modest greenery, much of the space between buildings remained starkly blank awaiting possible future construction that has rarely occurred anywhere on campus. By the 1980s the last historic structures were removed, leaving vast swaths of asphalt parking lots and patches of grass that optimistic master planners continue to eye for campus growth.

12.3 COMPELLING ABSENCE

To characterize the IUPUI campus or the Oulu suburbs as 'absences' rhetorically illuminates how both landscapes are the products of demolition and ambitious planning that submerged the landscapes' histories, and in many ways they are like many other post-war landscapes. Certainly neither history has been utterly effaced in either popular imagination or even material reality. Finns, for instance, tend to have exceptionally deep understandings of the war; they generally recognize the complex heritage of co-belligerency and the legacy of the harsh post-war treaty with the Soviets; scatters of wartime landscape features and

structures remain in varying conditions; and there are some conventional memorial landscapes in Finland. However, the contemporary northern Finnish
landscape provides few commemorated traces of war. The Finnish experience
of the war perhaps situates heritage primarily in collective imagination, rather
than on everyday landscapes in communities like Oulu. Places like Oulu were
home fronts, so in Finnish memory they are not always linked to the war because
they were not really battlefields. Finnish wartime heritage is clearly registered in
Finnish consciousness, but the everyday wartime experience is reduced to an
abstract event rather than a genuine place in their midst.

IUPUI actually has erected modest historical commemorative markers
around campus, new dormitories are named after community historical figures, and inevitably a phone app is being developed that will provide a walking
tour of the otherwise invisible landscape. Yet that relatively conventional
commemoration circumspectly negotiates the relationship between racism
and the contemporary landscape. Much of the IUPUI community has an
ambiguous awareness that the campus was once an African-American neighbourhood, and that recognition of an absent and displaced community elicits a
persistent uneasiness that occasionally disrupts the spaces' representation as
functional if not ahistorical expanses. Yet there is not an especially concrete
recognition that the open lots and deteriorating buildings in the city today are
the legacy of post-war transformation.

There is not particularly clear evidence that the IUPUI campus is perceived
as an absence at all; rather, it is simply experienced as an asocial and ahistorical gulf in the movement between 'real' places. Like many more fragments of
the subterranean and destroyed twentieth-century landscape, the eroding
trenches in the Finnish woods and stark gulfs of the IUPUI parking lots
belie compelling histories that are submerged in everyday consciousness. Yet
perhaps especially compelling histories deeply embedded in our experience of
everyday life might be told with counter-intuitively banal things: parking lots,
eroded wartime ruins, and landscape voids may provide distinctively arresting
points of historical imagination, just as the seemingly blank starting points of
newly created post-war absences were often considered symbols for optimism.
There may well be many different concrete mechanisms to reimagine the
histories of particular landscape absences, but archaeology may provide an
especially rich methodological and creative approach to invest a lost presence
and a concrete history in a place that is somehow perceived as emptied.

ACKNOWLEDGEMENTS

My travel to Oulu was funded by grants from the University of Oulu; the Indiana
University Office of the Vice-President for International Affairs (OVPIA); and the

Fulbright Scholar programme. The paper would not be possible without the help of Timo Ylimaunu, Vesa-Pekka Herva, Titta Kallio-Seppä, and Glenn White. Thanks to all the participants in the Wenner-Gren session for their firm and thoughtful comments on the earlier drafts. All of the weaknesses of the paper are my responsibility alone.

REFERENCES

Augé, Marc. 1995. *Non-Places: An Introduction to Supermodernity*. New York: Verso.
Aunesluoma, Juhanna. 2013. 'Two Shadows over Finland: Hitler, Stalin and the Finns Facing the Second World War as History 1944–2010'. In *Hitler's Scandinavian Legacy: The Consequences of the German Invasion, Then and Now*, edited by John Gilmour and Jill Stephenson, London: Bloomsbury, pp. 199–220.
Bille, Mikel, Frida Hastrup, and Tim Flohr Sorenson (eds). 2010. *An Anthropology of Absence: Materializations of Transcendence and Loss*. New York: Springer.
Buchli, Victor and Lucas, Gavin M. (eds). 2001. *Archaeologies of the Contemporary Past*. London: Routledge.
The Criterion. 1965. 'Why?', 7 May: p. 4.
González-Ruibal, Alfredo. 2008. 'Time to Destroy: An Archaeology of Supermodernity', *Current Anthropology*, 49(2): 247–79.
Gray, Ralph D. 2003. *IUPUI—The Making of an Urban University*. Bloomington: Indiana University Press.
Guillen, Joe. 2014. 'Brewster-Douglass projects' last 4 towers go under wrecking ball; development planned'. *Detroit Free Press*, 10 March.
Hansen, Alvin H. 1943. 'The City of the Future', *National Municipal Review*, 32: 68–72.
Hechinger, Fred M. 1961. 'Campus vs. Slums: Urban Universities Join Battle for Neighborhood Renewal', *The New York Times*, 1 October: E7.
Hetherington, Kevin. 2003. 'Spatial Textures: Place, Touch, and Praesentia', *Environment and Planning A*, 35: 1933–44.
Hetherington, Kevin. 2004. 'Secondhandedness: Consumption, Disposal, and Absent Presence', *Environment and Planning D: Society and Space*, 22: 157–73.
Holmila, Antero. 2009. 'Inland and the Holocaust: A Reassessment', *Holocaust and Genocide Studies*, 23(3): 413–40.
Holmila, Antero. 2012. 'Varieties of Silence: Collective Memory of the Holocaust in Finland'. In *Finland in World War II: History, Memory, Interpretations*, edited by Tiina Kinunnen and Ville Kivimäki, Leiden: Brill, pp. 519–60.
Indianapolis Recorder. 1956. 'Slum Area to Give Way to Medical Center', 13 October: 1.
Indianapolis Recorder. 1961. 'Northsiders Lose Battle to Reroute Interstate Highway', 20 May: 1–2.
Indianapolis Recorder. 1966a. 'Dr. King May Lead Housing March Here', 10 September: 1–2.
Indianapolis Recorder. 1966b. 'King Agrees to Lead Housing March', 17 September: 1.
Indianapolis Recorder. 1966c. 'March Decision Now Hinges on Governor: HBH Leaders', 1 October: 1.

Indianapolis Recorder. 1967. 'Houses Made Available to Dispossessed', 6 May: 1.

Indianapolis Recorder. 1968. 'Mayor Breaks Ground for IU Project', 7 September: 1.

Indianapolis Redevelopment Commission. 1962. *1962 Annual Report.* Indianapolis Redevelopment Commission, Indianapolis, Indiana. Unpublished document available at *Indiana Historical Society.*

Indianapolis Star. 1921. 'Urge Plan for Hospital Park: Riley Memorial Association and City Officials Discuss Proposal to Acquire Land', 1 September: 5.

Indianapolis Star. 1953. 'Now Let's Clean Up!', 19 August: 12.

Jackson, Kenneth T. 1985 *Crabgrass Frontier: The Suburbanization of the United States.* New York: Oxford University Press.

Junilla, Marianne. 2012. 'Wars on the Home Front: Mobilization, Economy, and Everyday Experiences'. In *Finland in World War II: History, Memory, Interpretations,* edited by Tiina Kinunnen and Ville Kivimäki, Leiden: Brill, pp. 191–232.

Kinney, Rebecca J. 2011. *The Mechanics of Race: The Discursive Production of Detroit's Landscape of Difference.* PhD dissertation, University of California, San Diego.

Kivimäki, Ville. 2012a. 'Between Defeat and Victory: Finnish Memory Culture of the Second World War', *Scandinavian Journal of History,* 37(4): 482–504.

Kivimäki, Ville. 2012b. 'Introduction, Three Wars and Their Epitaphs: The Finnish History and Scholarship of World War II'. In *Finland in World War II: History, Meaning, Interpretations,* edited by Tiina Kinnunen and Ville Kivimäki, Leiden: Brill, pp. 1–48.

Kivimäki, Ville and Tuomas Tepora. 2012. 'Meaningless Death or Regenerating Sacrifice?: Violence and Social Cohesion in Wartime Finland'. In *Finland in World War II: History, Memory, Interpretations,* edited by Tiina Kinnunen and Ville Kivimäki, Leiden: Brill, pp. 233–75.

Lahti, Juhana. 2008. 'The Helsinki suburbs of Tapiola and Vantaanpuisto: post-war planning by the architect Aarne Ervi', *Planning Perspectives,* 23(2): 147–69.

Lane, Barbara Miller. 1968. *Architecture and Politics in Germany, 1918–1945.* Cambridge, Massachusetts: Harvard University Press.

Lucas, Gavin. 2010. 'Triangulating Absence: Exploring the Fault Lines Between Archaeology and Anthropology'. In *Archaeology and Anthropology: Understanding Similarity, Exploring Difference,* edited by Duncan Garrow and Thomas Yarrow, New York: Oxford University Press, pp. 28–39.

Martelle, Scott. 2012. *Detroit: A Biography.* Chicago: Chicago Review Press.

Martin, John Bartlow. 1958. 'The Changing Midwest: The Old vs. the New', *Saturday Evening Post,* 230(30): 31, 103–5.

Metropolitan Planning Department. 1958. Central Business District Indianapolis Indiana Report. Metropolitan Planning Department, Marion County Indiana.

Millington, Nate. 2010. *Post-Industrial Imaginaries: Nature, Representation, and Ruin in Detroit, Michigan.* MA Thesis, University of Wisconsin, Madison.

New York Times. 1935. ' "First Lady" Starts a Housing Project: At a Signal From Her Workmen Pull Down First Detroit Structure', *New York Times,* 10 September: 23.

Ripple, David Alan. 1975. *History of the Interstate Highway System in Indiana, Volume 3: Route History.* Indianapolis: Indiana State Highway Commission.

Salmela, Ulla. 2011. 'Happy homes and stable society. Otto-Iivari Meurman and *omakoti* in interwar Finland Planning Perspectives', *Planning Perspectives,* 22: 443–66.

Seitsonen, Oula and Vesa-Pekka Herva. 2011. 'Forgotten in the Wilderness: WWII German PoW Camps in Finnish Lapland'. In *Archaeologies of Internment*, edited by Adrian Myers and Gabriel Moshenska, New York: Springer, pp. 171–90.

Silvennoinen, Oula. 2013. 'Janus of the North? Finland 1940–1944: Finland's Road into Alliance with Hitler'. In *Hitler's Scandinavian Legacy: The Consequences of the German Invasion, Then and Now*, edited by John Gilmour and Jill Stephenson, London: Bloomsbury, pp. 129–46.

Soikkeli, Anu, Risto Suikkari, and Kalle Reinikainen. 2008. Renovation as a Threat for the Identity and Integrity of Karjasilta Area. Paper presented at International Council on Monuments and Sites conference, Quebec.

Taylor, Robert R. 1974. *The Word in Stone: The Role of Architecture in the National Socialist Ideology*. Berkeley: University of California Press.

Tepora, Tuomas. 2014. 'The Mystified War: Regeneration and Sacrifice'. In *The Finnish Civil War 1918: History, Memory, Legacy*, edited by Tuomas Tepora and Aapo Roselius, Leiden: Koninklijke Press, pp. 159–200.

Thomas, June Manning. 2013. *Redevelopment and Race: Planning a Finer City in Postwar Detroit*. Detroit: Wayne State University Press.

Vehviläinen, Olli. 1987. 'German Armed Forces and the Finnish Civilian Population, 1941–44', *Scandinavian Journal of History*, 12(4): 345–58.

Wehrwein, Austin C. 1959. 'Chicago U. Spurs Renewal Project', *New York Times*, 1 November: 61.

Ylimaunu, Timo, Paul R. Mullins, James Symonds, Titta Kallio-Seppä, Hilkka Heikkilä, Markku Kuorilehto, and Siiri Tolonen. 2013. 'Memory of Barracks: World War II German "Little Berlins" and post-war urbanization in Northern Finnish towns', *Scandinavian Journal of History*, 38(4): 525–48.

13

Conclusion

A Future for Urban Contemporary Archaeology

Krysta Ryzewski and Laura McAtackney

Historical, contemporary, and future-oriented urban identities are presently being challenged worldwide at an unprecedented pace and scale by the continuous influx of people into cities and the accompanying effects of deindustrialization, conflict, and social differentiation. Archaeology is unique in its capacity to contribute a materialist perspective that views recent and present-day struggles of cities as part of longer term cycles of urban life that include processes of decay, revitalization, and reclamation.

The aim of this volume is to position contemporary archaeology in general, and studies of cities in particular, as central to the discipline of archaeology and as an inspiration for further interdisciplinary, materially engaged urban studies. In doing so the contributing authors collectively challenge prevailing approaches to cities. Whereas scholars have routinely conceptualized contemporary cities within the bounds of particular analytical categories, including cities as gendered, deindustrialized, global, or urban ecological units of study (see Low 1996 for an overview), the cities discussed in this volume do not fit neatly into these individual analytical units, nor do they exist outside the influence of capitalist policies or institutions (Harvey 2012: xvii). They are instead recognized by the authors as operating within increasingly globalized systems, but also, following Jane Jacobs' concept of open cities (2011), as places that are full of alternative possibilities.

Rather than adhering to particular classifications of cities, the volume's contributions are intentionally broad and attentive to the dynamics of the local and everyday in specific urban places—the politics, people, interventions, and materialities of specific urban places and the ways in which these dynamics operate across conceptual categories, temporal boundaries, and spatial terrain. *Contemporary Archaeology and the City* consciously employs a critical, materially engaged perspective that considers urban centres as both discrete and networked entities that are interrelated with places beyond geopolitical city limits. While many cities have characters formed from their vibrancy and centrality, their successful functioning often also relies upon the exploitation and even ruination of peripheral and rural hinterlands.

The preceding chapters are original contributions inspired by the fieldwork of archaeologists who work in Europe, North America, Africa, Australia, and Western Asia. They incorporate a diversity of perspectives from across contemporary archaeology and beyond in responding to very different national, social, institutional, and cultural contexts. The compilation provides a nuanced approach to contemporary cities that avoids reducing their present situations or reifying particular aesthetics (Millington 2013: 280). In its totality this volume echoes Herron's reflections on post-industrial Detroit by recognizing that contemporary cities are 'neither one thing nor the other, neither the empty dark places nor the shiny restored ones; [they] are both at once, back and forth: a land of a monumental gestalt puzzle' (Herron 1993: 27).

13.1 EMERGENT CHALLENGES

As evident in the preceding chapters, archaeologies of contemporary cities include the use of a multitude of methodologies and approaches, often involving (rather than objectifying) present-day communities, to examine and interrogate the material impacts of socio-political and spatio-economic urban transformations. These approaches to examining the contemporary city, specifically with regards to the volume's themes of creativity, ruination, and political action, connect with the role and real impact of effective place-making strategies (including McEvoy-Levy 2012), both at grassroots levels and in top-down, official interventions. One of the consistent arguments to emerge from the volume's authors is that studying contemporary cities must engage with how the past has constructed the present—memory, change, conflict, and divisions are central to examining the city as an evolving entity.

A number of emergent challenges for conducting urban contemporary archaeology are also raised by case studies in this volume and warrant further consideration. These challenges call attention to particular issues that were less prominent foci in the case studies, but, we argue, are critically important for future studies of contemporary cities. As scholarship continues to develop the topics of gender, trauma, and heritage management demand more conscious attention and reflection; we present brief concluding thoughts on each of these themes in an attempt to establish the momentum for future trajectories of urban contemporary archaeology.

13.1.1 Gender

Gender is an important theme that is implicitly connected to all of the papers in this volume. The preceding chapters succeed in making humans central to our understandings of contemporary archaeological studies of cities, but there is a general absence of differentiating between gendered experiences as a distinct facet of related human experiences. Whereas the dynamics of class, politics, and ethnicity, and how they configure with access and control in the city, are present in most of the chapters, the issues of gender are often implied or silent. The lack of explicit engagement with gender when con-ducting contemporary archaeologies begs the question: do we need to in-clude gender? Categorically, we argue for the need for greater consideration of gender in the contemporary archaeology of cities. Given the number of insightful and thought-provoking publications on gender in historical and contemporary archaeology in recent years (including edited volumes by Voss and Casella 2012 and Spencer-Wood 2013), it is evidently a perspective that can add greatly to the nuance of our interpretations. From the chapters in this volume that include gendered aspects, it is clear that by theorizing how gender can impact on our understandings and experiences of cities its potential to destabilize broader issues of power, access, and control may be recognized.

How can we locate and integrate the materiality of gendered experiences of the contemporary city? In Chapter 2 Russell highlights the importance of female artefacts in the *Museum of Innocence* in opening up the potential for broad conceptualizations of gender in the contemporary Turkish state. In particular, Russell details his project, *An Innocent City*, which saw a gendered object being conceptually relocated back into the city by a female student in a process that cyclically engaged with its original meaning, as well as its accessioning as museum artefact (all the exhibits currently on display were found by Pamuk in the locale and inspired various aspects of the novel before being curated into the resultant museum). Shanahan and Shanahan likewise highlight how gender is an appropriate vector to explore the creation and evolving nature of memory in Melbourne's parkscapes. In particular, they convincingly argue how hegemonic memorial practices of valorizing white, male, elite individuals can be contrasted with the more gender and class neutral Aboriginal commemorations. McAtackney highlights the highly gen-dered nature of public space in her case study of East Belfast and notes the almost complete material absence of women in both official and community memory, as materialized in murals, memorials, and public art. In this respect the absence of gender follows a notable trajectory in deindustrializing places; where the 'men' of industry are remembered and women are either forgotten or their roles are deliberated obfuscated. Following Mullins (Chapter 12), we agree that contemporary archaeologists should be conscious about including absences as much as presences in studies of gender in contemporary cities. We argue that gender is an issue that needs to be addressed in much greater detail as it promises to reveal differentiation of experience that contemporary archaeologies of the city can enhance.

13.1.2 Recognizing and Working with Trauma

As archaeology repositions to engage with contemporary society the discipline cannot shrink from exploring its dark underbelly; rather it should actively aim to expose what examining material culture can bring to our current understandings about trauma in people and places. Linked to issues inherent in studying 'conflicting cities' the aftermaths of death, disaster, and destruction are important facets of living in many cities and so archaeology is well-positioned to follow the lead of other arts and humanities disciplines in dealing with the consequences of natural and human disasters (see Dawdy 2006 on post-Katrina New Orleans), as well as the dark side of modernity (see González-Ruibal 2008). At its most superficial level contemporary archaeologies must engage with the concept of trauma, and its close relative victim/survivorhood, as destructive events often leave a material signature on things, structures, and landscapes. Taking inspiration from anthropology, archaeology needs to engage not only with how trauma materializes but how it impacts on meanings, relationships, and what Rebecca Lester calls 'the unmaking and remaking of worlds'; where people can turn to the safe and the material in order to anchor themselves after a traumatic rupture (2013).

While the majority of contemporary archaeologies are not focused on sites that are linked to mass death, destruction, or violent rupture (although Ernsten provides an important case-study of the enduring material traumas of apartheid in Cape Town, Chapter 10) it is important to remember that there is a broad spectrum of traumatized people and places that many of us may encounter (see Pantzou 2015). Relatively few archaeologists will actively work in 'traumascapes' of genocide or mass disasters: places of natural or human disaster where death continues to have resonance long after destructive acts have taken place (Tumarkin 2005). For those who do, Tumarkin (2005: 233) has argued how important the materiality of such landscapes are: '[they] are not poetic or metaphorical terrains, but, rather, concrete, material sites were visible and invisible, past and present, physical and metaphysical came to coexist and share a common space'. More commonplace, is the need to engage with issues of trauma and traumatic rupture in places of insidious but low level conflict or rapid and all-encompassing deindustrialization; places of mundane or piecemeal traumas. To contemporary Belfast where the young and vulnerable are increasingly being treated for post-traumatic stress disorder (see Gallagher et al. 2012) while the streets remain scarred with barricades and semi-permanent walls that materialize divisions supposedly remedied with the signing of peace agreements (see McAtackney 2011). Through to Cape Town, which continues to resonate with the obfuscated and continuing injustices of forced removals through entrepreneurial exploitations of both place and narrative that act to further distance the displaced (Ernsten, Chapter 10). Or the mass abandonment and ruination of vast swathes of Detroit, where desertion leads to dereliction and then often collapse or wilful destruction via arson, with only piecemeal attempts to remedy the encroachment of nature (see Ryzewski 2014, Chapter 3).

In the context of conducting contemporary archaeology of cities issues of trauma are not simply restricted to war zones nor experienced solely by the injured and/or dead. Historian François Hartog has been critical of the increasing emphasis on trauma, victims, and survivors, and how they reflect a seismic change in our studies of the past that has been brought about by 'intensification of the public use of the past' and their valorizing of both the victim and the witness as receptacles of authenticity and emotion (2014). Such a turn not only affects history but any discipline that focuses on the study of society. We argue that this refocusing should be welcomed, but cautiously so, as it changes not only how we examine society but who and what becomes our focus. Trauma, the traumatic experiences of those implicated in our studies, and the material traces of trauma are integral to conducting contemporary archaeologies that are timely, relevant, and ethical. This importance of considering the various forms of trauma in people, as well as in things and places, and of including material traumas alongside psychological ones, is evident in most of the chapters in this volume.

13.1.3 Heritage Management Practices

The methods and outcomes of contemporary archaeological practices are deeply embedded in issues of heritage creation, selection, and preservation. By choosing what we consider to be worthy of examination and interpretation in the contemporary city archaeologists extol value and partake in the process of heritage creation and its associated political implications. As the preceding case studies demonstrate, cultural heritage plays a crucial role within political discourses at the level of the city as it frames and structures power relationships that determine access to space, financial support, and material resources for expression and affective experience (see Russell, Chapter 2 and Shanahan and Shanahan, Chapter 5). In the context of cities both contemporary archaeology and heritage management face unrelenting challenges due to the intersection of heritage practice, urban planning, and hierarchies of power amongst communities. Christian Ernsten illustrates, in the case of Cape Town's Prestwich Street dead, that the recourse to heritage management is not always a successful turn when the economics of private enterprise trumps the emotional connection of community needs. The deindustrializing emphasis on the triumvirate of high unemployment, neglected infrastructure, and faith in the economic returns of development is not unique to Southern Africa (although see also Weiss 2014: 8; Keitumetse et al. 2010). Numerous papers in Hilary Orange's volume on reanimating industrial spaces (2014) examine the varying success rates of places that attempt to make the now familiar post-industrial journey from industrial mass employer to meaningful and profitable tourist attraction. Some places are more able to make this transition than others, but clearly the transformation of deindustrializing zones into heritage sites cannot be a panacea for all.

In practice, cultural heritage requires consideration of ownership and authenticity, as well as possibilities of participation. As contemporary archaeologists it is important, if difficult, to be continually mindful of our aspirations for deliberative and participatory models of heritage. Slight variations in structure can open up or close down opportunities for participation in the making of new platforms for inclusion and for community formulation of a heritage that is meaningful to them (Russell, Chapter 2; Ryzewski, Chapter 3; Ernsten, Chapter 10). Approaching heritage management as a creative practice, rather than an end result, allows what a community designates as their heritage to be opened up to a wider range of participants. This provides greater ability for public bodies to support and facilitate an evolving community-defined heritage that can widen participation in composing new and reconfigured heritages of an ever-changing entity. The volume's contributions wholly support this aim and thereby resist the tendency for heritage to be subsumed into an authoritized heritage discourse (Smith 2006) that is designated as a method of controlling political ecologies and determining whose history and identity is important and whose is not. Instead, in the preceding cases, heritage management practices are critiqued and models are advocated that manage through ongoing consultation and deliberation to ensure retention as a shared resource.

13.2 METHODOLOGICAL CONSIDERATIONS FOR URBAN CONTEMPORARY ARCHAEOLOGY

Archaeology as a discipline is based on a variety of methodological approaches used to engage with and interpret material culture. With an emphasis on, and often interchangeably defined as, 'excavation', the physical 'digging' of the past from a subterranean context has been central to archaeological approaches since the inception of the discipline. However, in the context of conducting urban contemporary archaeologies it is necessary to re-evaluate more closely the vast range of methodologies that can be employed, particularly in regard to recovery techniques and issues of scale and temporality. Indeed, it is only through explicitly considering the different types of understandings we expect to derive from studying particular forms and personal interactions that we can consciously begin to create methodologies that are appropriate to our places of study (see McAtackney 2014, on how overreliance on particular material forms can skew understandings of political imprisonment in Northern Ireland). Due to the sheer multitude of material remains, contemporary archaeologists have the opportunity to engage with a vast quantity of material forms and human actors, through various methodological approaches, in a multitude of combinations and outputs, to enable nuanced understandings of the city. The chapters in this volume reveal that the process of conducting contemporary archaeologies entails conscious selection, which necessarily excludes certain forms of materials. They also call attention to significant methodological challenges facing archaeologists of contemporary cities and contemporary archaeologists in general. Recovery techniques, scale, and temporality are the three of the most important methodological considerations in contemporary archaeology.

13.2.1 Recovery Techniques

Harrison (2011) has convincingly critiqued the idea that an archaeology 'of and in the present'—essentially the 'contemporary archaeology' that we discuss in this volume—needs to be based in excavation. However, there is an additional need to consider, when conducting archaeologies with an almost unquantifiable range of materials at hand, what particular material forms we focus on and how we conduct these archaeologies. The traditional toolkit of the archaeologist involves photography, mapping, systematic survey, as well as material culture analysis and examining documentary evidence. In contemporary settings, recovery methods can be even further widened to include ethnographic observation, participatory community involvement, engagements with public policy initiatives, and the use of remote sensing, mobile, and open-access technologies for documentation and dissemination.

The selection of recovery techniques and related scopes of analysis become of primary importance when conducting archaeologies of contemporary cities. Not only is the city defined and constituted by its range of material forms— from ephemera, artefacts, standing structures, to urban planning—but the archaeologist is challenged to determine their relationships, interconnections, and how they meaningfully constitute, speak to, and challenge each other. While Harrison (2011) positions archaeologies of and in the present to relate to 'surface assemblages', these ready-to-hand, often portable remains provide very different understandings of the city than a materially engaged approach to individual or collections of standing buildings (see White and Seidenberg, Chapter 1; Graff, Chapter 4), or expansive urban landscapes (see Ryzewski, Chapter 3; Shanahan and Shanahan, Chapter 5; Singleton, Chapter 11; Mullins, Chapter 12).

Furthermore, our ability to study an infinite range of materials does not mean that excavation becomes redundant. Excavation retains the potential to retrieve the hidden and subaltern pasts in contemporary archaeologies on at least two levels. Firstly, the contemporary city cannot be understood as an isolated moment in time. Cities are not self-generating entities that exist in the present with no tangible link to their past realities or future potentialities. The contemporary city can only be understood while simultaneously engaging with the past events that have shaped it—both positively and negatively—as they often retain psychic and physical, if partial and often hidden, presence (see Graff, Chapter 4). Secondly, the rate of change in contemporary cities means that what is considered functional and thriving can quickly be consigned to obsolescence and destruction. The subsurface remains of once important structures like Detroit's Brewster-Douglass public housing complex, which stood derelict and decaying for six years before its demolition in 2014, are no less important in providing compelling testimony as to urban renewal ambitions than when they were standing and occupied (see Mullins, Chapter 12). Indeed, those aspects of the city that are deliberately destroyed, hidden, or unarticulated, including Beisaw's exploration of the rural impact of the urban need for water in New York City (Chapter 6), are central to our explorations of meaning, identity, ownership, and power in contemporary cities. Contemporary archaeologies do not need to discard traditional archaeologies, rather they should consciously consider the most appropriate methodologies for retrieving material realities of cities that are not so easily recovered through other means and sources.

13.2.2 Scale

We argue that issues of scale are a fundamental reason why more contemporary archaeologies of cities have not been conducted. The scale of the city, the scale of post-industrial remains, the scale of deliberate erasures all present particular logistical and conceptual challenges to archaeologists who have the potential to move between contained artefactual remains (see Graff, Chapter 4) to vast, global comparatives (see Gonzalez-Ruibal, Chapter 7). Issues of scale do not predetermine that the large and unbounded must trump the minute and contained. By considering the challenges of the various scales of analysis present in our studies of the city we are forced to explicitly determine the most appropriate materials to focus on in order to reveal the significance of the city in understanding its inhabitants and the modern world. The overwhelming range of extant material culture that we can potentially harness to create our material narratives of the city ensure that we need to consciously engage with scale by acknowledging that not all materials present are equally important. In other words, not all substantial remains can tell us as much as small, ephemeral traces (on scale in contemporary archaeology, see Edgeworth 2013).

One particular challenge in working among an overwhelming range of remains is that absences—of artefacts, structures, and landscapes— deliberately eradicated, hidden, or subverted must not be forgotten. Absences should, when possible and/or relevant, be forefronted to create more complete understandings of contemporary urban societies. Mullins (Chapter 12) is particularly conscious of the need to historicize, contextualize, and include significant absences in our approaches to studying cities. In his discussion of racialized erasures in Indianapolis, as well as the disengagement with the realities of the World War II in Northern Finland, Mullins considers a variety of mechanisms to reimagine the histories of particular landscape voids. Following Buchli and Lucas's seminal introduction to *Archaeologies of the Contemporary Past* (2001), when they famously argued for the use of archaeological techniques to help us to presence absence, Mullins (Chapter 12) argues that archaeology may provide an especially rich methodological and creative approach to rematerialize presence and memory in a place that for various reasons is currently conceived of as empty.

13.2.3 Temporality

The issue of time, and its relationship with space, will always be a challenge in conducting contemporary archaeologies of cities. Temporality's association with the present and recent past has been an ongoing issue since the first 'archaeologies of us' were published in the US in the late 1970s and early 1980s (Gould and Schiffer 1981; Rathje 1979). This concern was mainly due to an initial assumption that archaeologists should be focused on excavated retrieval of material remains from an unspecified *distant* past. The first 'archaeologies of us' were received as useful in that they could help to resolve methodological questions (see González-Ruibal et al. 2014) due to a lack of receptiveness in the discipline that archaeology could have meaningful interpretations of the present. Increasingly, the perceived need to justify studying the recent past through the lens of a discipline originally focused solely on the distant past has been at the forefront of many studies exploring remains of and in the present. Temporality is a challenge that has also been addressed at some length by socio-cultural anthropologists in their debates about the concept of the 'contemporary' and how it affects the practice of anthropology in the present (Rabinow 2011; Rabinow and Marcus 2008).

The chapters in this volume reveal a variety of reasons why we use archaeological approaches to understand how society functions in the present. Penrose argues that the very proximity of the archaeologist to studies of the contemporary city ensures that our disciplinary lens adds material observations about non-human growth-cycles. However, she warns that there are limitations that archaeologists must be conscious of, including running the risk of being myopic in explorations of the theoretical embeddedness of economic, social, and natural processes within abandoned post-industrial remains. Referencing the recent, influential work on ruins by the 'Ruin Memories' collective (including Pétursdóttir and Olsen 2014), Penrose sees a wilful sidestepping of both broad issues of economic change and detailed understandings of the complexity of place in creating and maintaining ruins. González-Ruibal also emphasizes the need to explore deindustrializing processes through a joint vector of time and space, arguing that the Brazilian rainforest evidences the accelerated destruction of supermodernity in the 'Global South' in comparison to our usual focus on the slower, more sublime decay of the 'Global North'. White and Seidenberg and Singleton focus on capturing the ephemeral, and fleeting, existence of particular material forms in understanding the contemporary city; be they the temporary dwelling of artists in Berlin or the precarious 'home' of the designated homeless in Indianapolis and New York City.

More static memorials are discussed by McAtackney through a material collage of memory, identity, and meaning constructed to speak of, and to, the traditional inhabitants of deindustrializing East Belfast and by Shanahan and Shanahan in the contrasting meanings and reception to colonial and post-colonial memorials in Melbourne parks. Ryzewski and Penrose each take a broader perspective on the very different fates of long-term abandonment in both Detroit and post-industrial localities in the UK. Beisaw and Graff individually explore the long-term material remains of the past in the New York City hinterland and on the streets of Chicago. Ernsten contrasts a neoliberal Cape Town that celebrates commerce and progress at the expense of engaging with its enduring colonial scars, while Russell and Mullins discuss the potential for using everyday objects to tell alternative stories of the present-day cities of Istanbul and Oulu, respectively. In these instances the heritage process is democratized as an empowering tool for the city's citizens, arguing how everyday objects and other material remains have the potential to presence largely absent pasts that should not be forgotten. The variety of approaches to temporality, in its interconnections and fragmentations between the past, present, and future, and in relation to conducting contemporary archaeologies of the city, is central to *Contemporary Archaeology and the City*.

13.3 A FUTURE FOR CONTEMPORARY CITIES

Conducting contemporary archaeology in cities presents constant and unavoidable challenges in terms of scale, politics, and the sheer volume of material remains, all of which can be daunting to address. With limited opportunities for archaeologists to conduct extensive and long-term fieldwork in cities it can seem beyond the hopes and ambitions of many to be able to meaningfully engage with the city as a connected, material entity open to logical dissection and comprehension. While the challenges inherent in conducting these archaeologies are manifold, urban spaces offer tremendous potential to engage with a variety of issues and to better understand the flows and impacts of modernity in its most relevant manifestation. Cities present the opportunity to examine facets of our discipline unique to contemporary archaeologies—including the involvement of people as sources and how we link archaeology and heritage creation—as well as issues that confront all archaeologies—selecting the most appropriate methodological approaches and dealing with multiple temporal contexts.

Clearly these studies of the contemporary city prompt a wide range of themes and expressions that cannot be fully articulated in just one volume, but it is important to note areas of significance that this compilation does explicitly consider—including creative potentialities, industrial ruin, community heritage, nature-culture relationships, and impacts of public policy. Other points of intersection emerging from the volume's case studies, including gender, trauma, and the demarcation of space, will hopefully inspire further research agendas.

Contemporary Archaeology and the City makes no attempt to limit the range of interpretative approaches to the study of cities, and it does not define the city, its limits, or even list definitive characteristics. Instead, this volume embraces the variability and diversity inherent in contemporary archaeology and allows individual researchers to select the case studies they think are relevant to explore and to employ the approaches that best suit their investigations. In doing so all of the chapters retain their own unique methodologies, insightful interpretations and highlight various aspects of the cities they find of interest. None claim to be definitive in how they characterize or engage with the city; instead they aim to reveal a critical snapshot of the material city as it presented at the time of their engagement. The chapters all speak to present-day issues and consider how people are implicated in their material studies in ways that are unique to the temporal and spatial contexts of their case studies. The contributors engage with mundanity, as well as exceptionalism, the forgotten, and obfuscated, as well as high profile and conspicuously enduring material remains. They create 'archaeologies of us' that simultaneously reflect more broadly on the relevance of archaeology as a discipline and challenge it to incorporate human-centred approaches, considered methodologies, and diversity in interpretation. Overall, the volume chapters have strong synergies, but they leave any concluding discussion on how we conduct contemporary archaeologies of the city as open-ended, provocative, and even contradictory.

This volume has aimed to position contemporary archaeology as a mindset and the contemporary city as a scale, time, and place of analysis that is central to archaeology. Yet the very definition of what contemporary archaeology is, what subject matters it engages with, and how it should be conducted remain open; they are matters determined by the geopolitical and historical contexts of our studies, as well as by our intellectual interests. It has been the explicit aim of *Contemporary Archaeology and the City* to acknowledge these differences and in doing so to strengthen the potential of contemporary archaeology to be an engaged, socially-relevant specialization that straddles the fields of anthropology and archaeology.

REFERENCES

Buchli, Victor and Gavin Lucas. 2001. 'Introduction'. In *Archaeologies of the Contemporary Past*, edited by Victor Buchli and Gavin Lucas, London: Routledge, pp. 158–67.

Dawdy, Shannon. 2006. 'The Taphonomy of Disaster and the (Re)formation of New Orleans', *American Anthropologist*, 108(4): 719–30.

Edgeworth, Matt. 2013. 'Scale'. In *The Oxford Handbook of the Archaeology of the Contemporary World*, edited by Paul Graves-Brown, Rodney Harrison, and Angela Piccini, Oxford: Oxford University Press, pp. 379–91.

Gallagher, Elizabeth, Brandon Hamber, and Elaine Joy. 2012. 'Perspectives and Possibilities: Mental Health in post-Agreement Northern Ireland', *Shared Space*, 13 (March): 63–78.

González-Ruibal, Alfredo. 2008. 'A time to destroy: an archaeology of supermodernity', *Current Anthropology*, 49(2): 247–79.

González-Ruibal, Alfredo, Rodney Harrison, Cornelius Holtorf, and Laurie Wilkie. 2014. 'Archaeologies of the Contemporary Past: an interview with Victor Buchli and Gavin Lucas', *Journal of Contemporary Archaeology*, 1(2): 265–76.

Gould, Richard and Michael Schiffer (eds). 1981. *Modern material culture: the archaeology of us*. New York: Academic Press.

Harrison, Rodney. 2011. 'Surface assemblages, Towards an archaeology of and in the present', *Archaeological Dialogues*, 18(2): 141–61.

Hartog, François. 2014. 'The Historian's Present'. In *Materiality and Time: Historical Perspectives on Organisations, Artefacts and Practices*, edited by Francois-Xavier de Vaujany, Nathalie Mitev, Pierre Laniray, and Emmanuel Vaast, Basingstoke: Palgrave Macmillan, pp. 173–83.

Harvey, David. 2012. *Rebel Cities: From the Right to the City to the Urban Revolution*. London: Verso.

Herron, Jerry. 1993. *After Culture: Detroit and the humiliation of history*. Detroit: Wayne State University Press.

Jacobs, Jane. 2011. *The death and life of great American cities*. 50th anniversary edn, Modern Library edn. New York: Modern Library.

Keitumetse, Susan O., Laura McAtackney, and G. Senata. 2010. 'Memory and Identity as elements of heritage tourism in southern Africa'. In *Cultures and Globalization: Heritage, Memory and Identity, Series 4*, edited by Helmut K. Anheier and Yudhishthir Raj Isar, London: Sage, pp. 201–15.

Lester, Rebecca. 2013. 'Back from the edge of existence: a critical anthropology of trauma', *Transcultural Psychiatry*, 50(5): 753–62.

Low, Setha M. 1996. 'The Anthropology of Cities: Imagining and Theorizing the City', *Annual Review of Anthropology*, 25: 383–409.

McAtackney, Laura. 2011. 'Peace maintenance and political messages: the significance of walls during and after the "Troubles" in Northern Ireland', *Journal of Social Archaeology*, 11(1): 77–98.

McAtackney, Laura. 2014. *An Archaeology of the Troubles: the dark heritage of Long Kesh/Maze prison, Northern Ireland*. Oxford: Oxford University Press.

McEvoy-Levy, Siobhan. 2012. 'Youth Spaces in Haunted Places: Placemaking for Peacebuilding in Theory and Practice', *International Journal of Peace Studies*, 17(2): 1–32.

Millington, Nate. 2013. 'Post-industrial imaginaries: Nature, Representation and Ruin in Detroit, Michigan', *International Journal of Urban and Regional Research*, 37(1): 279–96.

Orange, Hilary. 2014. *Reanimating Industrial Spaces: Conducting Memory Work in Post-industrial Societies*. Walnut Creek: Left Coast Press.

Pantzou, Nota. 2015. 'War Remnants of the Greek Archipelago: Persistent Memories or Fragile Heritage?' In *Heritage and Memory of War: Responses from Small Islands*, edited by Gilly Carr and Keir Reeves, London: Routledge, pp. 234–54.

Pétursdóttir, Þóra and Bjørnar Olsen. 2014. 'Imaging Modern Decay: the Aesthetics of Ruin Photography', *Journal of Contemporary Archaeology*, 1(1): 7–23.

Rabinow, Paul. 2011. *The Accompaniment: Assembling the Contemporary*. Chicago: University of Chicago Press.

Rabinow, Paul and George E. Marcus. 2008. *Designs for an Anthropology of the Contemporary*. Durham: Duke University Press.

Rathje, William. 1979. 'Modern material culture studies', *Advances in archaeological method and theory*, 2: 1–37.

Ryzewski, Krysta. 2014. 'Ruin Photography as Archaeological Method: A Snapshot from Detroit', *Journal of Contemporary Archaeology*, 1(1): 36–41.

Smith, Laurajane. 2006. *The uses of heritage*. London: Routledge.

Spencer-Wood, Suzanne. 2013. *Historical and Archaeological Perspectives on Gender Transformations: From Private to Public*. New York: Springer.

Tumarkin, Maria M. 2005. *Traumascapes: the power and fate of places transformed by tragedy*. Melbourne: Melbourne University Press.

Voss, Barbara L. and Eleanor C. Casella (eds). 2012. *The Archaeology of Colonialism: Intimate Encounters and Sexual Effects.Cambridge*: Cambridge University Press.

Weiss, Lindsay. 2014. 'Informal settlements and urban heritage landscapes in South Africa', *Journal of Social Archaeology*, 14(1): 3–24.

Index

Figures are indicated by an italic *f* following the page number.